Leadership in pursuit of the vision

Leadership in pursuit of the vision

Integrated Business Leadership:

Brilliant performance from one team, one way, and one system based on one version of the truth.

Richard Watkins

You Caxton Publications
Oxford and Shrewsbury

The Author asserts the moral right to
be identified as the author of this work.

ISBN 978-1-913425-80-7
Published by YouCaxton Publications 2020
YCBN: 01

The Author asserts the moral right to
be identified as the author of this work.

Copyright © Richard Watkins 2021

All rights reserved. No part of this publication may be reproduced, stored in a retrieval system, or transmitted in any form or by any means, electronic, mechanical, photocopying, recording or otherwise, without the prior permission of the author.

This book is sold subject to the condition that it shall not, by way of trade or otherwise, be lent, resold, hired out or otherwise circulated without the author's prior consent in any form of binding or cover other than that in which it is published and without a similar condition including this condition being imposed on the subsequent purchaser.

YouCaxton Publications
www.youcaxton.co.uk

A catalogue for this book is available from the British Library

Contents

Table of Figures		vii
Preface		ix
1.	The Case For Change	1
2.	The Model For Change	33
3.	How Does It Work?	46
4.	The Underlying Process Steps	100
5.	Innovation	110
6.	Demand	133
7.	Demand Management	191
8.	Collaboration with customers	208
9.	Supply	215
10.	Lean	260
11.	Finance	274
12.	People	296
13.	Information Resources	311
14.	Priorities	314
15.	Vision and Mission	326
16.	Strategy	331
17.	Senior Team Review	342
18.	Making it Happen	354
Bibliography		382
Author biography		384

Table of Figures

Figure 1: Conflicting Objectives in Industry 4.0	3
Figure 2: Functional Organisation	6
Figure 3: Informal Company	14
Figure 4: Long-term planning	25
Figure 5: Integrated Business Model	34
Figure 6: Objectives for Integrated Business Leadership	35
Figure 7: Bottom-up and Top-Down planning	43
Figure 8: Wallace and Stahl 5-step process	47
Figure 9: Oliver Wight 5-step process	47
Figure 11: Pyramid of Families	59
Figure 12: Definition of Families	61
Figure 13: Where do you meet the customer?	65
Figure 14: Make to Stock v Make to Order	68
Figure 15: Distribution of height of men in the UK	73
Figure 16: Distribution of Demand for a product	74
Figure 17: Basic data table for volumes – Make to Stock	81
Figure 18: Basic data table for volumes – Make to Order	82
Figure 19: Meeting cycle for IBP	87
Figure 20: STP Format	90
Figure 21: Multi-site model for IBP	94
Figure 22: Process Map	104
Figure 23: Six Sigma DMAIC chart	105
Figure 24: Applying measures to process	105
Figure 25: IBP process development chart	108
Figure 26: Objective of Innovation step	115
Figure 27: Stage/Gate process	116
Figure 28: First cut analysis of projects	119
Figure 29: First cut project justification	123
Figure 30: NPD Performance report	128
Figure 31: Template for Innovation meeting	132
Figure 32: Demand Planning and management	136
Figure 33: Excuses for not forecasting	141
Figure 34: Definition of forecast	145
Figure 35: Forecasting process	147
Figure 36: CRM Pipeline	148
Figure 37: Pyramid structure for product hierarchy	150

Table of Figures

Figure 38: Bill of Material for Red Pen	151
Figure 39: Picture of Pen	152
Figure 40: Production Plan for Pens	152
Figure 41: Planning Bill structure	154
Figure 42: Fishbone analysis for Forecast Accuracy	165
Figure 43: Forecast Accuracy Target	167
Figure 44: Impact of Biased Forecasts	169
Figure 45: Forecast Waterfall chart	172
Figure 46: Product Segmentation	174
Figure 47: Assumptions are core to forecasting	179
Figure 48: Demand Manager job description	182
Figure 49: Demand Planning v Demand Management	183
Figure 50: Demand review chart by Family	188
Figure 51: Demand Review Meeting template	189
Figure 52: Forecast Consumption table	194
Figure 53: Customer order detail for consumption	196
Figure 54: Order for 10 accepted from Y	201
Figure 55: Example of Abnormal Demand	203
Figure 56: Collaboration progress	210
Figure 57: Graph of Required Capacity v Demonstrated Capacity	230
Figure 58: Detailed capacity plan	234
Figure 59: Pen Bill of Material	236
Figure 60: Time Fence Policy	239
Figure 61: Root Cause Analysis for Schedule Achievement	246
Figure 62: Responsibility for planning and execution	250
Figure 63: Master Scheduler is at the centre	254
Figure 64: Thinking and Doing	256
Figure 65: Supply Review meeting template	259
Figure 66: Flow diagram	268
Figure 67: A Lean process	269
Figure 68: Value Stream Map	271
Figure 69: Impact of Perfect Order on ROCE	291
Figure 70: Effect of core measures on Profit	292
Figure 71: Finance Review	295
Figure 72: Emergenetics Wheel of Behaviour and Thinking	301
Figure 73: People Values	303
Figure 74: Typical organisation structure	305
Figure 75: Human Resources Meeting	308

Figure 76: Stahl and Wallace 5-step diagram	315
Figure 77: Oliver Wight IBP model	316
Figure 78: STP document	320
Figure 79: Global IBP process	321
Figure 80: Multi business unit structure	322
Figure 81: Family summary information	324
Figure 82: Strategic Dimensions	334
Figure 83: Functional activities aligned with market discipline	339
Figure 84: One-page strategy	341
Figure 85: Link from leadership to execution	346
Figure 86: Senior Team Review template	352
Figure 87: Three-dimensional view of the IBL model	353
Figure 88: Who resists change and its impact	360
Figure 89: Project Structure	366
Figure 90: Education and training in conference rooms	376

Preface

All companies are forever seeking ways of achieving better business performance. They do so in an environment that is incredibly challenging. It almost goes without saying that change is constant. Customers buy three sizes of what they want over the internet and send two back. Getting products delivered to your back garden by drone is no longer a fantasy; it is a reality, care of Amazon Prime. Biological viruses cause worldwide disruption to demand and supply chains.

The internet age has everyone used to the idea of instant response. In the pursuit of lower costs, all companies, big or small, put manufacture of their products in low-cost countries – often the Far East – to serve a global community of customers and consumers. Longer lead times are the result.

Meanwhile, customers want products delivered to their door in less than thirty minutes, from a click on their phone, and are demanding it as the new normal.

Shareholders in Hong Kong, New York, London and Frankfurt get 24/7 updates of information on the performance of companies, and CEOs are under pressure to deliver consistent share price growth and dividend yield to satisfy their shareholders' requirements. CEOs have to meet their promises.

Back in 1988, there was a great book published called "Orchestrating Success" written by Richard C. Ling and Walter E. Goddard (Goddard & Ling, 1988). This book was a seminal work in developing the ideas that I have put together here. In fact, at the bottom of page 5, there is an interesting footnote: *"Sales and Operations Planning (S&OP) should not be confused with Standard Operating Procedure (SOP). But we believe that S&OP should become a routine part of SOP in all manufacturing companies."*

The interesting fact is that in many companies (even in some very, very big companies), "S&OP" is still not "a routine part of the way that the business is run". In fact, many companies still run themselves in the same way that they were run in the early part of the 20th century and do not run themselves in a way that is fit for purpose in the 21st century.

Back in around 1987, I was involved in a small project team of around five people in ICI's Agrochemical Division. We were implementing a new ERP system, which was a huge advance on the systems that we had in place before. We learnt the significance of S&OP from Dick Ling, George Palmatier, Mike Salmon and others from the Oliver Wight company. Over the next three years, we implemented a global S&OP process.

In summary, this meant that each month we produced a revised business plan, which had a horizon of 42 months, added up around 5,000 products into "families" in volume and value, and allowed our divisional executive board to keep the business on track and deliver the results. We had a strategic planning process updated every spring, which covered a ten-year horizon, and a budget which covered the following year. S&OP fitted in the middle and drove our budget.

The business suddenly had global visibility each month in a way that it had never had before. This clarity now drove local and global business, operational and financial planning. The improved control drove inventory down by 27% within 18 months, and service levels (which we had not measured properly before) to greater than 98% all the way around the world. The division saved around 1.5% of revenue to the bottom line. S&OP was a key enabler of all this, as it got the central and local leadership teams to buy-in and engage in an integrated way of working, based on one version of the truth. It was not just a new system. It was a completely new way of working that transformed people, processes and systems.

Since then, I have spent around thirty years working with companies big and small, helping them to implement integrated systems, and what has now become termed Integrated Business Planning (IBP). I have also seen other consultancies take the same concepts behind Sales and Operations Planning and call them all sorts of things like "Executive Sales and Operations Planning", "Sales, Inventory and Operations Planning", "Integrated Sales and Operations Planning" and so on.

There is no real difference between S&OP and IBP, in concept. The desire to "rebrand" it has come from an apparent inability of many companies to accept the process. I have seen people say, "We implemented SOP, and it did not work. We want to implement IBP now." Indeed SOP v IBP has taken on a life of its own with people being for and against it – as if it is some political or philosophical movement. I have seen people say that for a while a company "ran SOP" and then it fell out of favour, and then all the principles were lost; then sometime later it was revived and came into favour again. In this book, I address the impact of the "Leadership" on the development and management of IBP. The factor that determines the success of IBP lies in the hands of the leadership of the company. Does it embrace the need for SOP or IBP? Either they want to run it with the principles outlined in this book, or they prefer to stick to running the business in an "old-fashioned" way. I will explore the role of leadership in integrating business and its importance for the success of operating in a better way.

In ICI Agrochemicals, the CEO of the division, together with the finance director, saw and understood how it worked. Six of the board went to Stratford-upon-Avon to listen to a two-day workshop, and that switched them on to a different way of working. It became very difficult for managers not to want to implement it (and many resisted). The CEO was in favour of this way of working!

What is so different about this way of working? I will explain the key elements in this book. The traditional way of working in all companies is to manage and control the business by having an annual budget. Most companies go through a three- to six-month process – led by finance – to create the budget for the following year. Companies go through this process in a structured manner, and once signed off, it becomes the document and control mechanism determining how well the business is doing. Careers can depend on it. Ask many MDs/CEOs how the business is going, and they will talk of "doing well against the budget, or badly against the budget".

It is the core of the annual presentation to shareholders, and it is the benchmark by which the success of the business is measured. Indeed, as companies get to year-end, they will do everything to meet the budget and will even engage (perish the thought) in trying to make shipments happen in the current financial year, bringing business forward from next year. Personal rewards are related to success against the budget.

This leads to continual short-termism and fixation on the year-end. In turn, everyone ignores the visibility required beyond the end of the current year. It particularly affects Operations.

An effective IBP process requires that the leadership get rid of this "behaviour" and replace it instead with a monthly process which has a continual rolling horizon of 42 months (I will explain later the significance of 42, apart from the fact that Douglas Adams called the number the answer to the universe).

The other imperative for IBP is the fact that the annual budget, and all of the work striving to achieve the budget, is appropriate for a world in which there is not that much change – which was true in the 1950s and 1960s (and probably earlier).

Without a doubt, the pace of change has increased.

Justin Trudeau – Prime Minister of Canada – in 2018 observed: "The pace of change has never been this fast, and it will never be this slow again."

In this environment, running a company which is stuck with a single plan made once a year is irrelevant. I have seen companies review and revise their "budgets" once a quarter to recognise this.

The key problem that this raises from a leadership problem is one of accountability. If we do not achieve a plan, who is accountable for non-achievement?

Hence, when looking at the plan to decide whether we have achieved the plan, do we look at the "annual plan" or "budget" – or do we look at the revised quarterly plans?

Whenever I have asked this question, managers who operate the old-fashioned way will soon get into confusing statements like, "Oh! It's the annual plan that is the most important"; but then what is the point of re-forecasting each quarter? If you do not achieve the quarterly plan for two quarters, but then achieve the annual plan, have you done well or badly?

I will show how continuous monthly measurement encourages continuous improvement and how this process works much better psychologically as a means of motivation and control.

I will explore how the IBP process works, and how this aligns with the way leadership holds people accountable for the delivery of the plan. Ultimately, IBP is as much to do with accountability and responsibility as the quality of the process, systems or the measurement of forecast accuracy.

One of the key "mantras" I have picked up from clients recognises that the operational side should "plan the work, and work the plan". Equally, on the commercial side, sales and marketing should "plan the sale, and sell the plan". Measurement should be based on ability to meet the plan, and not beat the plan. The behaviour in many "old-fashioned" organisations is to drive the company to beat the plan/budget.

Thus, measurement is another key aspect of IBP that needs attention as part of the development of the complete process – it is about making realistic plans and achieving them.

I will also emphasise that IBL is not just a supply chain project. Many people have approached "SOP" or "IBP" as if it is a supply chain process. This sort of project often arises because the supply chain function gets blamed for too much inventory or poor customer service, and the supply chain director attempts to lead a project to implement SOP/IBP. They often fail, because there is no buy-in from the rest of the organisation.

The solution is not a supply chain-led process, but a business-led process with clear CEO leadership. IBP is a process that governs the whole organisation.

The key to the right understanding and operation of the IBP process is the fact that plans can and should change. How you manage, control and execute those changes will enable your company to achieve success for customers, shareholders, employees and suppliers.

This success requires effective leadership, and that will support the achievement of the vision and strategy laid out by the senior team through a formal process of communication.

It will also need education from the top on how the process will work. Oddly the word "education", which we use to cover teaching people how the world works, is derived from the original Latin word "dux" which means "leader".

Change does not happen unless the leader makes clear that this is the way the world of your organisation will work.

Chapter 1
The Case For Change

"Progress is impossible without change, and those who cannot change their minds cannot change anything"
– George Bernard Shaw

One summer day, I was happily sitting in a deck chair just outside the boundary of a cricket pitch, watching a game of cricket. The click of a ball on willow on a hot summer's day by a village green can be very pleasant. Sitting next to me was a retired chief financial officer, who had been in charge of the finances for a very large British company during the late 1990s and early 2000s. It was founded in the 1880s and by 2004 had a turnover of £10 billion, with 30,000 employees over six continents. He turned around to me and said: "What do you do?" I said I help companies change their planning processes and sometimes helped them get rid of their arcane budget processes.

It was with a snort and a harrumph that he said: "You cannot run a business without a budget" and with that, we both returned to watch the gentle to and fro of the cricket match – governed by the traditional rules that determine the game of cricket, which so many people claim they fail to understand. Cricket has adapted to the pressures of the modern-day to survive, I thought. Why not business?

All companies start from the principle that they should, and will, try and develop some unique concept and sell it to customers, and will succeed if they can fill a need in the market place, and can do so profitably.

If you look at most manufacturing companies, whether they make submarines or loaves of bread, then they all have the common issue that everyone recognises – namely that if you do not provide customers with what they want and when they want it, then in the modern world you are unlikely to retain them for very long.

If we take the traditional starting point of much modern manufacturing history – Henry Ford – then this company was established in the early 1900s. It was one of the first examples of mass manufacturing. Amazingly the line could convert from raw materials in the ground to the final assembled product in four days. Ford introduced the Model T Ford in 1908. The price was $825 and was viewed as cheap and simple to drive. It was new. In nineteen years, sales had reached 15 million units. Until the introduction of the assembly line to support lower costs per unit, the Model T was available in multiple colours. Ford made the famous comment: "Any customer can have a car painted any colour that he wants so long as it is black." He chose black because black had the quickest drying time in the paint shop. Now, of course, customers want cars in all sorts of different colours, with different engine sizes, different colours, different engine configurations, with multiple fuel types – petrol, diesel, electric, gas, etc. Many competitors have been attracted into the industry as they see it is profitable to do so, and companies make cars in many countries around the world.

Most industries have seen a similar story, and we can easily see that every manufacturing company now has to manage the following "conflict" as shown in Figure 1

People are talking about the "New World" with Industry 4.0. To respond to customers and give them what they want, companies need to operate "mass-customisation" to tailor products to customers' requirements. Thus, it does not matter whether you make cars, food or paint; you need to be able to provide multiple variants to customers. A company selling breakfast cereal adds honey, strawberries, raspberries, or chocolate to the product to satisfy customers' requirement for choice. A chemical company provides different grades. A mobile phone company has to provide updates every quarter. Pharmaceutical companies have to supply the same product in different formats to different countries around the world.

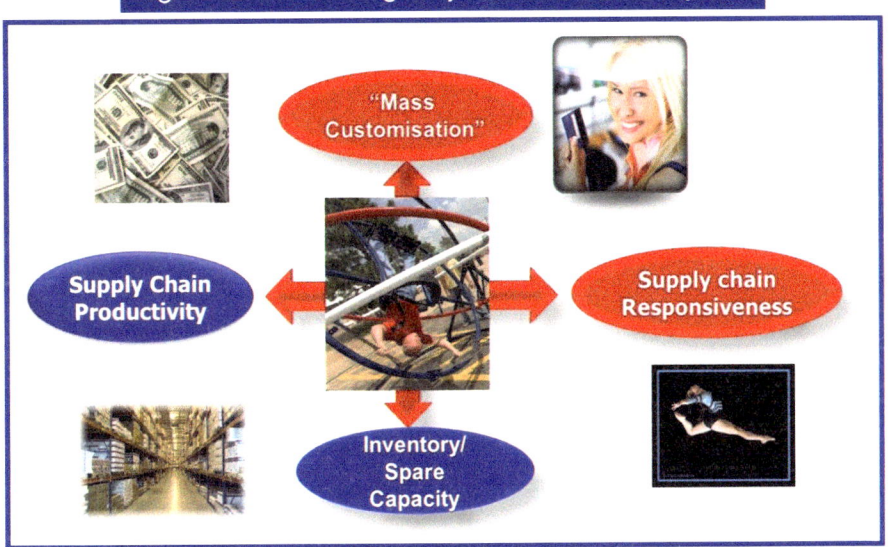

Figure 1: Conflicting Objectives in Industry 4.0

However, the pressure to compete means that we need to do so at a competitive price. Interestingly the price of a Ford car fell from $825 in 1906 to $360 by 1916. Reducing prices made the car affordable for more people, and hence contributed to the ability to reduce costs. Volume plays a strong part in contributing to supply chain productivity – through decreasing cost/unit, through reducing overheads per unit, and through general economies of scale.

There is, thus, a big desire to make a product for as long as possible in big batches, driving lower cost through improved productivity. That was the driver behind making just black Model T Fords. But in today's world, customers want flexibility.

If we can reduce the overhead cost per unit represented by changing over from one product to another, then we can be more flexible. This need for flexibility, though, is in principle, in conflict with the productivity obtained from making every car black.

The key conflict that was always at the heart of Sales and Operations Planning, and still exists today in Integrated Business Planning, is the balance between how quickly customers want a company to respond, compared with how long it takes to supply the parts and make our products – that conflict between flexibility and productivity. The main difference today is that customers want to make that time shorter and shorter, but the drive for lower cost forces the manufacture of products in central locations in cheap – often Far East – locations, which drives lead times in the opposite direction.

Hence, all companies have to have a clear strategic objective in this area, which can have a huge impact on cash flow because of the inventory and spare capacity that a company needs to manage. Hence flexibility and productivity is one axis of conflict. But the other is the flexibility which companies need to maintain in inventory or spare capacity versus the service level (speed and accuracy of response) which the company offers to the customer.

This critical policy has the "technical" term of "where do you meet the customer?"

Thus, if a customer wants to place an order today for delivery tomorrow, then we probably need to have the product in stock. In some cases, in the food industry, you even get customers wanting to place an order today for delivery on the same day (milk/yoghurt/orange juice).

At the other end of the spectrum, if you are making submarines, then you can operate on a Make-To-Order basis, and the government which buys them is prepared to wait eight to ten years or longer, in line with the full lead time for making the product.

You would not want to hold submarines in stock, would you? I once made one of those aside comments you sometimes make in workshops to a delegate who had come from a submarine company, along the lines of, "I bet you do not make to stock?" The delegate answered, "Actually, we have four submarines in stock today!" The UK Ministry of Defence had placed an order for diesel submarines, but the Cold War rendered them unnecessary. A diesel submarine salesperson had a great offer to make, along the lines of "Buy one get one free!" Promotions are not just for Fast Moving Consumer Goods (FMCG) companies!

But in making milk products for delivery today, you are still dependent on the lead time for getting the milk in from the factory, and ultimately on the lead time for cows. If you are making bread, you are still potentially constrained by the lead time for flour, nuts or fruits.

The need to be responsive to customers means that the demand on which we plan our supply may not be met by the actual demand we receive from our customers, and therefore we will have to hold inventory to balance supply and demand. If we cannot, or do not want to, hold inventory, then we may need to hold spare capacity. If there is not enough capacity, then this will lead to "waiting lists" for a product or service; the customer will have to wait their turn.

No company or organisation is immune from having to make choices between these four dimensions, and in particular where it should strike a balance between inventory/capacity and the speed/cost with which it serves its customers. The question every business needs to face is how do we manage the need to balance customer expectations, with the length of our supply chain, cost-effectively? Managing this decision is at the core of Integrated Business Planning. It is, however, not a supply chain decision. It is a business decision that impacts all aspects of the company.

It is made even more difficult by the organisational structure.

If you look at the traditional organisation structure for most companies, then we typically find different "functions". Skills normally form the basis by which companies organise functions. Skills are developed through school, university and working with a company. When you ask someone "who do you work for?" then the answer normally relates to some function, which operates around a skill.

The typical functional structure is illustrated in Figure 2.

"Sales" are out there each day with customers following up opportunities, setting up the contracts, and making sales happen. Without "sales" there is little revenue and little profit. They are key to the survival of the company. They are always well-dressed and great at socialising with other people. They have a great sense of humour. Marketing's function is to develop products and services which are as appealing as possible to consumers. If you sell clothes, then you need to develop a range of colours to match with the main seasons of the year – Spring/Summer: Autumn/Winter. If it is cars you sell, then you need to concentrate on all the gizmos that consumers will want. Each product has to be better than the last, and far superior to the competition. They want to develop a range of products to satisfy consumers' and customers' choices. They are great at concepts and ideas.

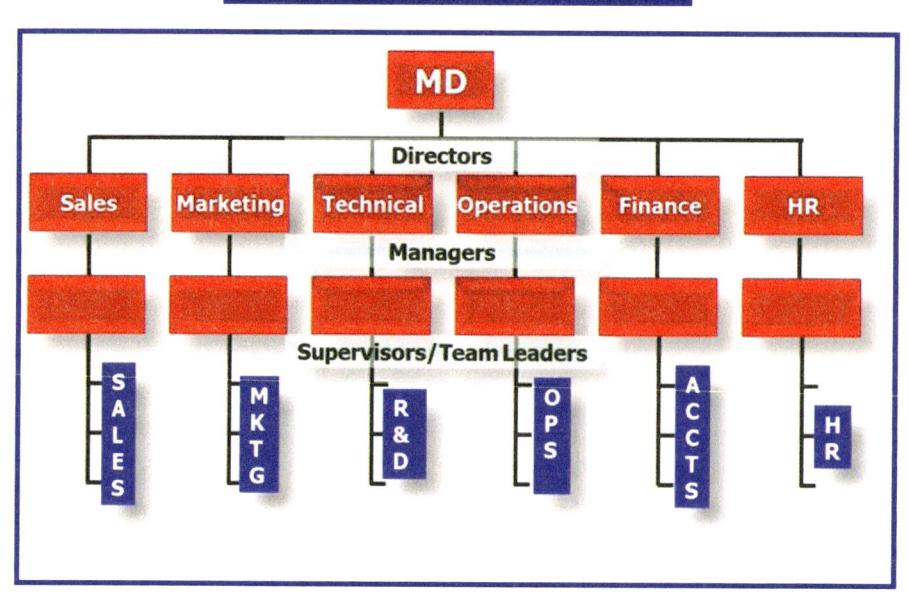

Figure 2: Functional Organisation

Operations are responsible for getting the product from the factory to the customer. They buy the raw materials and convert the products through the factory, and determine the cost of the product. Without Operations, customers would not receive the product they wanted to buy at the cost they want to buy it. They are pragmatic and make things happen.

The Technical function is responsible for product development and coming up with new ideas. They are the keeper of the way things work and coming up with new ideas. Without them, innovation would not be possible.

The Finance function adds up the numbers and provides the monthly reports. They monitor the performance of the organisation and make sure that funds are available from shareholders and banks to enable the business to trade profitability.

Human Resources look after the people and motivational side of the business, making sure that people are recruited, want to come to work, and receive training and development to enable them to contribute better to their function in the company.

All people have a different part to play and need to work together to achieve the aims of the company.

If you then were to ask all of these people in each of these functions in an off-site exercise, "Do you want a company that offers brilliant flexibility, at low cost, with low inventory, and phenomenal customer service?" then everyone would no doubt say "But of course we do. It is what we have to do."

But it is when you talk to each function separately that you begin to see the cracks appear between each function.

If you ask the operations director and the operations managers how many products they would like to make, usually they will say, "one – as long as it is black". If you ask them how much change would they like to see in what they are supposed to be making, they will say "none". If you ask them, "how much flexibility should we offer customers?", then they will say "none". If you follow through with a question as to "why is that?", then they will say that all flexibility comes at a cost. They are responsible for the cost of the product.

If you then ask a stereotypical marketing person how many products they would like to have, they would no doubt say "as many as possible". Customers want variety and choice. You cannot just have one size of the product; you have to have many. You cannot have just one colour of a product; you have to have several. You cannot have just one "formula"; you have to have several. "If you do not sell all of these variants, then our competitors will, and we will lose market share" is the response.

However, if you look at any product range in any company, you will typically find that 20% of the product range accounts for 80% of the revenue or profit of the company. There is always a huge tail. A Japanese company once observed that in most European companies, 20% of the products accounted for 200 % of the profit. It was the other 80% that accounted for minus 100% of the profit! Thus, most companies make a huge loss on the tail of their product range. But try and get the sales and marketing side of the business to cut back on the product range!

If you then ask the stereotypical salesperson how quickly the supply chain should respond to the customer, then they would want instant response. If you can't, you will lose the sale. You might then tell the salesperson that you would need to hold a mound of inventory to be able to respond to any order at any time. Does he or she care? Not really! Typically, they would want warehouses of inventory, as they never want to run out. They also want 100% customer service, however impossible that might seem. They are often accused of making ridiculous promises that no-one can keep!

If you then go to the finance director and ask how much inventory they think the business should hold, then you will quickly find that they think no inventory whatsoever. It costs money and becomes obsolete. "Why can't the salespeople sell what we make?" is a cry I have often heard. Not surprisingly, you quickly find a conflict between finance and sales.

The technical part of the company – responsible for development – is typically made up of boffins who are wrapped up in their world, inventing new products. They have to develop the concepts based on the latest technology and then help to get this to market. They are – typically – rarely worried about the supply chain or how the company makes the product. In one client company that makes loudspeakers, R&D was in a separate laboratory twenty miles from the factory – nearly another planet! They were developing speakers, which sold at around £50,000 per pair in the luxury export market. As part of that, they decided to include some sophisticated electronic kit, which only came from one specialist company, and it was on a fifty-two-week lead time.

It was not until they released the product to the factory and the market place that the business realised they could not launch it for another twelve months! R&D is often in conflict with sales and marketing, as they cannot get the product out quickly enough to the market place.

The HR department is sometimes labelled as the "Health and Happiness" department – or even worse, the "Human Remains" department! They view themselves as responsible for training, motivation and reward. But others do not view them in the same way. It works in its functional domain. Many companies also ignore this function in the overall scheme of things in the SOP process – which is often just restricted to just Sales and Operations functions. When you look at all companies, and the different functions in the business structured in this way, they are all typically in conflict with each other. Operations v Sales and Marketing. Finance v Sales. Manufacturing v Sales. Finance v Operations.

If you ask "why?", then you soon enough find that it is much to do with the way that people are measured. Companies frequently measure salespeople based on making as much sales revenue as possible. They measure operations on cost per unit. They measure R&D on developing technically superior products. These measures can drive contradictory behaviour.

Take, for instance, the question of who is responsible for inventory, which is a key balancing factor between service, cost and flexibility. If you ask this question – as I have done dozens of times – you will almost always get the response "operations" or "supply chain".

As a general point, surely responsibility should go to the person or function who causes or controls it, and who could operate differently to affect the thing for which they are held responsible?

If a speed camera catches a driver going too fast, then the person driving the car would go to court or have to pay the fine. If the driver tries to get the passenger to take the blame, then that is a serious criminal offence.

If you look at the reality of a company, inventory is not something which the supply chain or operations department typically causes.

A simple example should suffice: suppose that Operations asks Sales how many widgets they are going to sell. They say 100. Suppose, then, that the supply side gets 100 widgets made.

Suppose, then, that Sales then only sell 80 units. The resultant inventory will be 20 units. Who caused this? Surely it was Sales' failure to sell the 100 they said they were going to sell!

Let us take this further: suppose Sales says they are going to sell 100. Operations ensure that 100 widgets are made.

What happens when the customer says they want 120? Of course, Sales will say "yes" to the customer, and "sell" 120; they are responsible for the sales! Twenty units will then go on backorder, or they will not be supplied. Whose fault is it that customer service has failed? Sales, of course, as they said "yes" to the customer. But who gets the blame for the failure to deliver to the customer? Supply chain, of course. There is an inquisition, and the MD tells Supply Chain never to let a customer down again.

Let us suppose that next time Sales are going out to visit a customer they say they are going to sell 100.

Operations are still smarting from the inquisition over who let the customer down last time and make 150 to make sure the business does not run out. Sales then sell fifty to the customer; the customer does not want to buy from you because the company failed to deliver last time. The result is 100 in inventory.

Finance now spots the inventory and starts an inquisition on "why is there so much inventory of this product. Who caused the inventory?" Sales, of course. They failed to sell the product, and last time they sold too much and caused Supply Chain not to trust them. So surely Sales should be responsible for inventory? Of course they should. Sales had their feet on the accelerator! But Supply Chain is held responsible – they are held responsible for the inventory! But they are just the passenger in the driving seat. At the heart of the question is, who is responsible for what?

Here, then, is the first reason for changing the way the business operates through establishing IBP – responsibilities are functionally aligned, and each function does not care about their impact on other functions within the business. Worse than that, the way that people are measured drives the different functions into conflict with each other. The salesperson is rewarded by encouraging them to sell whatever the customer wants – not whether the business can fulfil the order. Sell 150 and bonus follows. Sell fifty all the time, and you get fired! Making a great sale is rewarded around the company, and even more so if it was unexpected.

We will explore all this in more detail later. But in summary, if customers want more and more "customisation", but the company measures supply chain/manufacturing on lowest cost per unit, (which means you can have whichever colour you like – as long it is black), then you are going to have a "dysfunctional" organisation. The conflict arises mainly because of the way each function is measured. Solving the conflict lies in changing the way that people are measured.

Changing the way that people are measured is at the heart of the development of the IBP process.

Changing the way that you measure people is not a trivial process. As someone once said, "If you measure me rationally, I will behave rationally. If you measure me irrationally, then I will behave irrationally.

If you change the way you measure me and do not explain the changes, then no-one will know how I will behave, least of all me!" Consistent measures will lead to consistent behaviour.

The second key area to address in the development of IBP is the extent to which the company operates in a formal and organised manner. There is much in management literature about different organisational styles – like autocracy, in which the CEO runs the business in a style of controlling everything that goes on. Alternatively, businesses can adopt a democratic style, which relies for its operation very much on the input of its people. A "co-operative" business is an example of this.

However, a lesser-known form is "adhocracy", described by Wikipedia as "a flexible, adaptable and informal form of organisation that is defined by a lack of formal structure. It operates in the opposite fashion to a bureaucracy."

Many CEOs/MDs and managers do not like bureaucracy. Indeed, bureaucracy can be very damaging to the way a business operates. There is a belief, for instance, in many organisations that the more you check expenses at different levels of the business, and the more that you have checks and balances in place, then the more control you have. But micro-management can be illusory. The cost of checking exceeds the cost of the potential saving.

In small companies, made up of a smaller number of people, there is a natural reliance on flexibility, and the ability to respond to customers flexibly and quickly. This way of working describes the "Entrepreneurial" model. This way of working is perfectly acceptable. I have worked with many small- to medium-size companies, but there comes a time in all their lives where managing everything in the head of the CEO becomes impossible – and it is a different point for every company.

The smallest company with which I worked had sales of around £5m per annum. At a meeting, the MD said he had been talking to the Finance Director about getting some money for a new project that the Head of Product Development was developing, and he was having difficulty getting the money.

After the meeting, I talked to the IBP project leader and asked: "Who is the head of finance and who is the head of product development that the MD was talking about?", "Oh!" said the project leader, "They are all the MD; it is just he likes to think that there are different people in charge!"

When that time comes to move from being small and entrepreneurial to becoming bigger and more organised, then businesses realise they can no longer work in an "adhocracy". Businesses start looking at themselves and recognise how much is happening informally, and how much they are dependent on ad-hoc meetings, ad-hoc spreadsheets, and ad-hoc decisions. Adhocracy is a menace and not a virtue. So, they start to look at how to implement Business Process Management. It is right they do so, and what I am going to describe as "Integrated Business Planning" is a potential solution.

However, what is much more worrying is when much larger companies work with adhocracy! Indeed, I have seen several very large companies work in an informal environment, but still manage to get products out to customers roughly when they wanted it. But the hidden costs of doing so rapidly justifies the implementation of IBP!

Indeed, "Business Process Management" is almost an industry in itself. The overall quality of a business is ultimately dependent on the quality of its business processes, which is why the International Standard ISO 9001:2015 determines a means to monitor and control business processes in a formal manner. It identifies the need to have "process owners" and performance measures which monitor the quality of the business processes. Many companies have used ISO 9001 as a way of putting a degree of control in place in the business. But it is still amazing to see that many companies big and large still operate in an overly informal environment – which risks being out of control.

The following figure illustrates the characteristics which I would see exhibited in these kinds of "informal" companies, where functions operate in silos.

Figure 3: Informal Company

- **Multiple sets of numbers**
- **Multiple spreadsheets**
- **Multiple ways of working**
- **Lack of clear roles/responsibilities**
- **Confusion over real objectives**
- **Defensive functional behaviour**
- **Rumours**
- **Ad hoc meetings**
- **Short-term focus**
- **Individual rather than team culture**
- **Heroes are favourites**

Silo Management

Multiple sets of numbers describes the observation that if you look at the details behind the numbers to which each department is working, then they are different. Sales are working to one set of targets. Operations are working on their production plans.

It is also often characterised by "second-guessing" or "sandbagging", which signals a lack of trust fundamentally. Thus, there is a sales forecast in place of 100. But Operations know that this number is understated because they think that Sales will inevitably sell more.

Finance does not trust the numbers that result, and so produce P&L forecasts, which either reduce the numbers because "they are responsible for producing conservative forecasts" or include "challenges" because they believe the forecasts are too pessimistic. Each function believes they have a right to come up with their numbers.

People then go to meetings and argue about who has the right numbers, and it takes 30 minutes in each meeting to come to some agreement – a rigmarole repeated at each meeting.

I found one company operating as described in Panel 1. SOP or IBP made a huge difference to them. That was not the first or the last time I found this situation to apply.

Panel 1: Multiple Numbers

I once visited a pharmaceutical company in Denmark, invited by the supply chain manager. All I wanted to do was understand how they planned and made their tablets, creams and liquids.

I started in the supply chain department, and was shown a number of spreadsheets, which had the usual format of product codes down the left, and numbers going from left to right with volumes in each cell for the next 12 months.

I then went to the sales manager, and asked him if they produced a forecast. He said "yes" and showed me his spreadsheet – but this was all in values, and at a product/brand level. I asked how they related to the supply chain numbers. He did not know.

I then asked the procurement manager how he knew how much to buy in the way of raw materials. He assured me he had been there 15 years and knew exactly how much to buy. He had reports which showed the average usage of components and raw materials, and bought enough to keep them with around two months' worth of stock.

Finally, I spoke to the finance director and asked him if he produced a forecast. He said "yes". But, of course when I asked if they were based on the Sales, Supply Chain or Purchasing forecast, he said "No! Why would I trust those? I know what we will do. Sales is always too optimistic."

Sometimes companies confuse themselves with the terminology they use, which also leads to multiple numbers – like "Targets" and "Budgets" and "Plans". Hence, I have heard people say their budget is 100 (the number that they will declare and be held accountable for). But in the next breath, they will say they have a target of 110 – the number they are aiming to sell, and the number they have told their salespeople to sell.

Manufacturing then set and determine the capacity and resources in line with the budget. Indeed, the manufacturing director is held accountable for the number of heads in the budget and the costs associated with the budget; but if the business is selling to the target, it is invalid, surely, to hold the manufacturing/operations director accountable for the costs associated with the Budget?

Even worse, though, when you want to determine if you have done well, then managers will get confused with anything other than a simple binary answer. We understand that things are either good or bad.

Suppose we sell 107. We have then failed against the target but succeeded against the budget. Have we performed well or badly? We do not know; we are confused, and performance then becomes fudged. As we always want to appear to have done well, then managers talk about "we have done well against the budget". What – then – was the point of the target? With which number was manufacturing/operations working? Which number drives the ERP system? It can only deal with one number to calculate the number of bits you need to buy, and the capacity you need!

So, when we come to evaluate performance, we cannot have the confusion of multiple sets of numbers as implied by having budgets and targets. It is a recipe for confusion.

IBP is the route to getting rid of multiple sets of numbers.

Multiple spreadsheets. Spreadsheets on their own are not bad things. They have their place for making ad-hoc reports. The problem comes with using them to make calculations (sometimes very complicated) which are entirely dependent for their maintenance on one individual. Formulae can be wrong; they often support multiple sets of numbers.

One client company discovered that their spreadsheet was overstating the required capacity, which meant that they were turning business away as they were capacity constrained. The consequences can be serious!

They are often also associated with a perception that the ERP systems do not work. Of course, the ERP systems, if they are standard systems, which have not been "doctored", do work. The problems normally result from inaccurate base data, or from the fact that people have been inadequately educated and trained in the use of the ERP systems, and hence they prefer to use things that they think they can control – spreadsheets. Spreadsheets are therefore masking the true problems.

The right solution is to put in place the right responsibilities and processes to get the data accurate, and train people effectively on how to use the systems. Correct data needs one database; duplicating data leads to errors.

Multiple ways of working relates to the fact that in many companies (sometimes in the same room, sometimes across different sites), people do the same job in different ways. Thus, a production planner in one factory will plan in one way with a given set of rules, and another in another factory will do things completely differently.

Each job description should describe each role in a consistent way, and each person who performs that role should do it in the same way.

Lack of clear roles and responsibilities relates to the fact that people can work in a job, but other people in the company do not understand the role, and hence there are constant "arguments" about what function the role should perform, or who should be responsible for the activity.

Let us take the question of customer service. It is a key requirement of any company, and yet when I ask the question, "Who is responsible in your company for customer service?", I have often found it is not clear. There is often a customer service department – but they only believe they take orders.

Is it Sales, who carry out the selling activity to the customer, that is responsible for "customer service"? But what if a salesperson makes a ridiculous promise to a customer, which subsequently the business fails to deliver? Is the failure to deliver an operational responsibility? If they failed to deliver because there was not enough stock with which to respond, and it was the finance director who had said you could not have too much inventory, is it the finance director's responsibility to provide proper levels of customer service? If you look at job descriptions, where do the responsibilities get assigned? In an informal company these are not clear.

Confusion over real objectives relates to the fact that often people in companies are told one thing, but are forced to behave differently. Indeed, objectives can change over the year.

Thus, a company could state that their prime objective is customer service – giving the customer what they want and when they want it. Indeed, often you see this on a sign in reception. However, because of cost constraints, people are often struggling to give the customer what they want and when they want it. Cost reduction is the real objective – it does not matter what the sign says in reception. People are frustrated in the company when told to do one thing when, in reality, they cannot do what they have been told they should do.

One of the examples I experienced gave me a positive example of how Customer Service should and did pervade a whole company. At the time, I had a great car, which Lexus offered on the basis that they provided remarkable customer service. I was living near Southampton airport and had to fly to Paris for a meeting. To save the car parking fee (!), I left my car at the local garage to have it serviced while I was away for a couple of days. They dropped me off at the airport (which was around ten miles away). But while I was in Paris, there was a massive snowfall in the Southampton area and as a result, I could not get back to Southampton. Instead, I took a train back to London. I realised I would not be able to get to Southampton until around 6.30pm following a meeting in London. I needed my car for the following day to go to a client and was worried that the garage would close before I got there.

So, I phoned the garage and explained the situation. The receptionist immediately said: "That will be no problem. Someone will come and pick you up from the station when you get there."

Sure enough, when I arrived at 6.30pm at the station, the general manager of the garage was there to pick me up and I got my car, leaving the garage at around 7.00pm I was naturally amazed, and asked the GM how did they manage to do this? Most other companies would not bother, and would say, "I am sorry, but we close at 6pm."

He said they were trying to establish a premium position in the marketplace, being a division of a Japanese car company more associated with volume, and "customer service" was their real focus, which would differentiate themselves from other major brands. Because of this, the company had trained everyone in what this meant (which was why the receptionist had said "no problem!"). That training had involved a course in which every delegate received £100 when they arrived, to go and buy something in the local town. The course leader then asked them to recount their experiences as customers trying to spend £100. The whole course had encouraged everyone to understand the true meaning of "customer" and "service". And that was why the general manager was happy to pick me up. A perfect example of walking the talk of a strategy built around customer service, and I bought another of their cars when I came to exchange that one!

Often, people have told me that there are other national cultures which are more aligned with the understanding of what it means to be a customer. I do not think this is entirely a cultural issue.

It is more to do with the values adopted by the leadership, and how those get communicated through to the "shop floor". It is about the consistency with which people adopt these values through the company, which has to do with the quality of the education process within the business. When companies fail to be clear about their strategy and deploy it through the company, then that is a failure of leadership.

I listened to a radio programme which was broadcasting an interview with the CEO of the same organisation. The interviewer asked him how he managed to control 200,000 employees in his business. His answer, which I paraphrase, was that he did not manage and control 200,000 employees. When asked what did he do, he explained that he spent most of his time at the sharp end of the business with the employees, asking them for improvements to ways they helped to run the business to deliver to the customer. That is a clear focus on the customer.

To me, this requires clarity about the objectives of the organisation and making sure that everyone is clear about them, and operates to the principles stated.

Defensive functional behaviour and blame culture are often rife in companies because they have deployed the wrong measures. A customer does not get what they ordered and when they ordered it; the immediate reaction in this kind of organisation is to blame operations for failing to deliver. Operations or Supply Chain are often on the thick end of this kind of exchange. They become rhinos with very thick skins, very capable of charging back when accused of failure. It normally includes words like, "If only you had provided me with a forecast of what you wanted, I might have been able to react." Sales then counter this by saying, "if I had forecast it, you still would not have taken any notice", and so it goes on.

Sometimes it is also due to lack of clear processes, or people not following them, which leads to a "breakdown" in communication.

I once worked with a major international pottery company in Stoke-on-Trent. I was doing a three-day course. On Tuesday we went through how long it would take to develop a range of new products. We listed all the complex steps that you need to go through, from agreeing on the design, getting the patterns and moulds made, and agreeing with suppliers the quality standards, arranging the production and then getting the product made and decorated. It all added up to around 16 weeks. As a group – we had all the functions in the room – we agreed that the company would introduce no new products within a 16-week time frame; that was company standard anyway.

On Wednesday, one of the delegates, who was an account manager, went off to a major customer to discuss the launch of the new product range. When they came back on Thursday, everyone asked him how he had got on. He said it was fantastic; they had got the contract for a completely new product range.

"When do we start?" went up the cry. "Straightaway," said the account manager, and, "we need to get the product into the stores in eight weeks!"

You can imagine the discussion as the air went blue. "I had to!" said the account manager. "We would not have got the business otherwise! Why can't Design and Manufacturing be more flexible?"

"But we agreed we would not do anything within 16 weeks; why did you make such a ridiculous commitment?" Ultimately, the account manager felt it was their job to get the business, and it was someone else's job to sort out the problems that they had created.

Sales were measured on getting sales; operations were measured on delivering the product.

Rumours and ad-hoc communication often abound in many organisations. There is no formal way of letting people know what is happening and the changes to what is going on. Corridors, smoking shelters and canteens become the way that people accidentally find out about things. It is a truism that any important information will find its way out through an organisation in one way or another, and people will get to hear about important issues like downsizing, restructure, reorganisation, etc. long before the company makes a formal announcement.

I was in a taxi going to a company, and the taxi driver asked me where I was going. I told him. "Oh! They are closing down the company and putting all the manufacturing in Poland." When I told the MD, he was amazed!

"How did you find that out? It's a company secret." The truth gets out somehow.

Short-termism is a constant problem. One of the biggest failures in many companies – particularly at the senior levels of organisations – is the focus on the short-term. The budget cycle drives this, which in turn forces executives to concentrate on achieving this year's result; hence, the focus is on this year, and in particular the end of this year.

I once went into a company and was talking to the operations director about long-termism etc. But it was the first week in December of an annual budget cycle that finished in two weeks. His mind was clearly on what he could do to get things out this year, and he was getting lots of phone calls as we were meeting to sort out this and that. He was clearly under a lot of pressure.

I said, "Why are you focused so much on what you can get out this year? Surely most of it is impossible, as your lead times are around three months?" He quickly answered back, "If I do not meet the sales target for this year, then next year is going to be academic."

One MD with whom I worked several times, who had implemented what I understood by SOP/IBP, once told me that by the time they had got the process in place, they could always be confident of what they were going to ship in three months, and hence three months before the year-end they knew exactly what the outcome was going to be. He then added, "We could then spend our time looking at the longer-term strategy, which we might get wrong, but at least we had thought about it!"

Heroes operate in these companies. In this environment, firefighting becomes the norm, and managers recognise individuals who are the heroes that "make things happen". Indeed, they are the people who get promoted, which then encourages "firefighting" to become the norm. Everyone lives off adrenaline, which is known to be exhausting. One client described all of their managers as dyed-in-the-wool pyromaniacs; it was so much fun to fix things all the time!

When potential clients view this list of typical issues, their normal reaction is to say, "That is us. How did you know we work like that? What is wrong with that?" Try ticking off the ones you think apply to your company!

What has this to do with IBP? The answer is that many people approach an IBP project largely because they are fouled up with adhocracy and do not feel in control on the day-to-day basis of the business. Tackling the above issues is very much at the core of an IBP project. It is about changing the way the company works, and in doing so, requires changes to systems, processes and people.

Changes happen, but managers in business feel that they are a victim of circumstance. They want to restructure the business and want the opposite of all that is listed above in place.

Thus, they want a single set of numbers, to use spreadsheets only as reporting tools, and an ERP system that works. They want clear roles and responsibilities, a "no-blame" culture, and to focus on the longer-term. They want a formal process for communication.

You could argue that this is simply just wanting to have a properly organised company. You would be right. And if you do not have one, then the likelihood is you should be putting in place "Integrated Business Planning". You could probably implement this without even calling it "Sales and Operations Planning" or "Integrated Business

Planning" and call it "Common-Sense Organisation." That would be fine.

But it is rarely easy to implement this.

I came across a great book called "Chimp Paradox" by Stephen Peters. (Peters, 2012). In summary, the human mind has three parts to it: a part that processes information very quickly and reacts all the time – the Chimp brain. It has a logical part, which operates to process things rationally and logically, and thinks things through. Then there is a "database" which stores how to react. Some people constantly operate in "Chimp" mode – and it is very difficult to persuade them to change. Changing behaviour requires changing minds.

The Problems with the "Annual Budget"

One of the issues that get in the way of the development of a common-sense organisation is the very nature of the annual Budgetary and Strategic Planning processes – where they exist. I have seen many of these processes over time. It appears that many companies have adopted from some textbook a standard way of operating, and continue to do this just because this is the way you do things. It explains the reaction from the CFO by a cricket pitch, stated above: "You have to have a budget."

Businesses that "do strategy" believe this is a once-a-year process carried out through an away day or two. Hotel groups must love strategising.

I had a very pleasant series of seven days in an expensive golf club just outside Dublin once, where the company reviewed and created its strategy.

It was winter, and the warm log fire helped to make it a very pleasant event. Indeed, it ended up creating a clear strategy for separating the company into two parts and then selling off one part, which was a logical result of looking at its products, where they fitted in the market place and the way the market was going.

The interesting part was that as we went through the process, we touched on projections of the business, profitability, etc. etc. and the CFO did all this on an instant spreadsheet. I could not help thinking that they would have approached it in a more structured way if they had IBP/SOP. Sadly, the CEO did not understand the need for it.

Many strategic processes are very unstructured, and deliver bald statements like: "We will double sales revenue over the next three years, and treble profits." There is little more detail than that.

Companies then create an annual budget, which is sort of consistent with the strategy.

Figure 4 describes the "linkage" between the various planning processes.

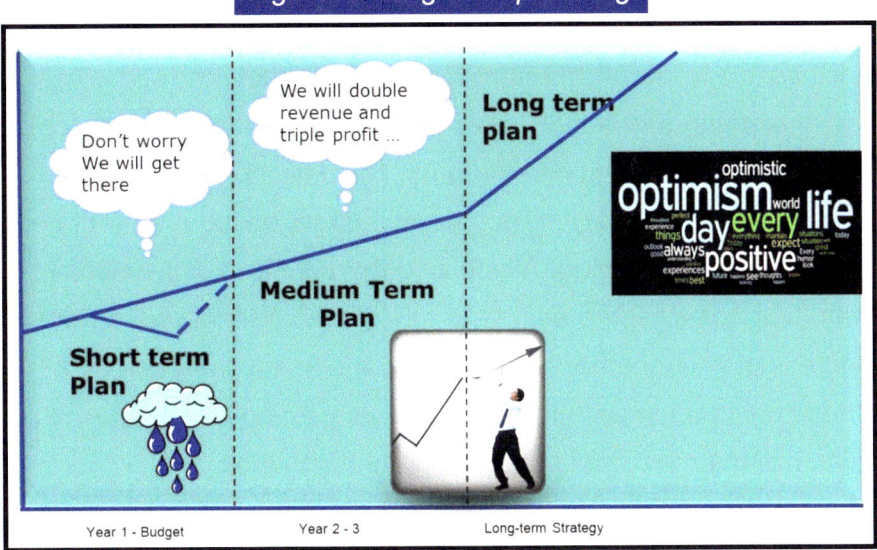

Figure 4: Long-term planning

The Year 1 process in this horizon is typically covered by what most companies call the Budget. A usual structure for this process is that approximately six months before the year-end, the budget process starts – and this lasts for the next three to six months, depending on the size of company and complexity. The bigger, the longer.

The steps in this process normally go through the following stages – all companies have a variation on this theme, and most companies recognise this approach.

First, the CEO expects the sales and marketing side to come up with their projections for the following year. They will look at the market place, product developments, assumptions on growth, market share, and will be very structured around coming up with their projections. Probably a large number of slides will be produced, and at the end, there will be a projection by Product Group/Brand and by Sales Region of Revenue and Gross Margin. Sales are often accountable for the revenue projections, and sometimes the Gross Margin. There is sometimes a product or marketing group who are responsible for Profit after Advertising and marketing expenses.

These numbers are then used by the operational side of the business to work out the number of people they need, the cost of raw materials, and factory overheads etc. to work out the cost of operations as an input into the profit calculations.

The CEO will ask R&D to prepare its budget based on the projects that they are managing. All other departments will then come up with their costs for the next year to form the budget and an overall figure is pulled together – normally by the finance director.

These numbers are around the same as the numbers achieved last year. It is the next stages that cause the problems.

The first step is that the sales and marketing director(s) do their presentation to the CEO. There are usually three outcomes that are possible:

- The CEO accepts the numbers
- The CEO says that they are too high
- The CEO says that they are too low.

Let us use a simplified example of a company, which looks as follows in Table 1:

Table 1: Budget Example

Item	Amount (£ m)	Amount (£ m)
Total Revenue		100
Materials	30	
Labour	15	
Factory Overhead	5	
Total Variable Costs		-50
Gross Margin		50
Sales and Marketing	15	
Admin	10	
Development	15	
Total Overheads		-40
Net Profit (EBIT)		10
Total Capital Employed		100

In around 95% of the occasions I have looked at this with companies, then I am told that the CEO tells the sales and marketing director that the numbers are too low!

The CEO explains that the strategic growth target for the business is to increase revenue by 20% for the next year (the output of the strategic planning away day team meeting over the weekend). Hence, they have to go away and work out a plan which will add up to £120 million revenue; they go away and do this, and then this becomes the budget for sales and marketing – for which they are accountable for delivery.

On this basis, the operations director comes up with a revised plan, which now works out as follows in Table 2:

Table 2: Initial Operations Estimate

Item	Amount (£ m)	Amount (£ m)
Total Revenue		120
Materials	36	
Labour	18	
Factory Overhead	6	
Total Variable Costs		-60
Gross Margin		60

Again, there are three possible outcomes to this discussion:
- The CEO says they are too low, and the operations director needs to spend more.
- The CEO says they are too high.
- The CEO accepts the numbers as they are.

Again, in most cases, I have found that operations directors say that CEOs then say they are too high, and they need to reduce the operational costs! The operations director has to go away and come up with a set of numbers which add up to £30 million materials and £20 million labour and overheads.

"We need to do more for less."

They do this. The operations director has to meet this budget.

Overheads are "capped" at £40 million – so all other departments are constrained in their expenditure. The finance director keeps the capital at £100 million (which means better debt collection, lengthening credit terms, better stock control and using the existing machinery for longer and more effectively).

Profit before Earnings, Interest and Tax is now budgeted at £30m, meaning a 30% Return on Capital Employed. Exactly what we want. Perhaps this is a little too abbreviated and a little too cynical, but it does seem to be what happens in most companies, small or very big!

We now have a budget (which is phased over the year and has a lot more detail behind it), which looks like the following in Table 3:

Table 3: Budget

Item	Amount (£ m)	Amount (£ m)
Total Revenue		120
Materials	30	
Labour	15	
Factory Overhead	5	
Total Variable Costs		-50
Gross Margin		70
Sales and Marketing	15	
Admin	10	
Development	15	
Total Overheads		-40
Net Profit (EBIT)		30
Total Capital Employed		100

However, this is sometimes not the end of the affair. The division takes these numbers to another "corporate" level in many companies. My experience is that 95% of companies find that they go through another process, whereby the £120 million revenue gets increased to a budget of £130 million. The operational budget then gets reduced from £50 million to £45 million, and the Gross Margin target then becomes £85 million. They cap the overheads at £40 million, and the net profit now works out at £45 million. That is what the chairman wants the local CEO to deliver – to give the shareholders what they want.

Now, this also may be an exaggeration of the "corporate effect" and a gross simplification of the budget process – but it is frightening how many companies I have seen over the last thirty years whose managers all nod with a giggle when they recognise that this is their process.

Asked whether they believe it is sensible, most managers believe it is complete nonsense. Asked why they do not change, their faces go blank and they say, "because that is just what we do".

Even worse is the fact that the CEO manages performance against these numbers. Thus, the standard report that the senior management team reviews is a comparison of the actual year-to-date versus the budget year-to-date. The report then looks at the Budget for the rest of the year, and the CEO still expects the business to achieve those numbers.

If we look at the Review process by quarter, it sometimes goes that at the end of the first quarter (based on the above numbers in Table 3, divided into four equal quarters of £30m, for the sake of explanation), the company has achieved only £25m revenue. That is £5m down against the budget. The senior leadership team discusses this, and the conclusion is that it has been a slow start to the year; the snow season was unusually long. The sales director, in answer to the question, "Will you still reach the year-end number?" says, "Of course we will; there is plenty of time to catch up."

At the end of the second quarter, the business has achieved £50m – now £10m short of budget. The discussion is a bit more robust. There have been quality problems in manufacturing, and failures to deliver. There has been a failure to deliver new products, which the business had expected to launch in the second quarter. The R&D director launches a stout defence and talks about technical issues related to changes customers wanted, which they could not have foreseen. Easter was not as good as it should have been, because of the weather.

When the CEO quizzes the sales/marketing director on whether they will meet the year-end figure, they bridle at the suggestion they will not be able to achieve the numbers, and categorically assure the CEO that they will meet the budget, although it will be a considerable challenge (looking forward to a pat on the back when they achieve it, and if they do not, they have the excuses from R&D to protect themselves).

It is not until the third quarter when there is panic when the Actual Sales only reach £75m, which is now £15m down against the Budget. The Board has an emergency meeting, and the CEO implements a strict cost reduction programme. HR terminate the contracts of all temporary employees. The board sends out the message that travel restrictions are now in place (use budget hotels). Switch off the lights if you do not need them. Reduce heating by two degrees. Get authorisation from your boss for all unnecessary expenditure. Quote for every enquiry going, in the hope that some more business can be won (and don't worry about the lead times for components!). Stop paying suppliers. Too little too late.

Of course, when we get to the end of the year, we achieve £105m sales, which is off-budget, but it is not so bad as it least shows 5% growth over the last year. We managed to get some sales out before the year-end by taking some sales due for delivery in January into December and running some extra promotions to make sure we got better sales than we thought possible in place.

I wonder just how many companies suffer from the mad year-end dash? All of this may be an exaggeration. But the real underlying problem of this process is that human beings learn from their experiences; if the sales director and operations director have been through this process one year, then the following year when they are putting together their budget, they will start low, knowing that their boss will bid them up higher or lower, etc. etc. It just lengthens the process and encourages second-guessing. It generates multiple sets of numbers.

Once, I made a presentation to a board along the above lines, and the sales director and the manufacturing director started to laugh. When I asked them why, they said: "We go through exactly the process that you have described."

But it was the CEO's response that was amazing. He suddenly said, "But I know that is what they do, and I tailor my behaviour exactly in line with what I expect them to do. If they ever changed what they did, it would destroy the whole exercise." The games that people play! No wonder companies want to grab hold of the idea of one set of numbers and telling the truth – which is what IBP establishes.

But for this to work, then the leadership process has to change. Leaders should not hold their subordinates accountable for beating the budget. They must be held accountable for meeting the agreed plan.

In case you think changing this budgetary process is some fanciful notion, then do pay a visit to the organisation which calls itself the "Beyond Budgeting Institute" at www.bbrt.org.

So, in summary, the case for change is based on three key issues which many companies find affect themselves:

1. A functionally organised business, which finds its functions in conflict with each other when it is trying to achieve the key goal of good customer service, at a lower cost. It is the measures which cause the conflict. IBP must tackle the way the business is measured.

2. Inadequate formal control of the business leads to adhocracy, which is driven by an infrastructure that is reliant on heroes who perpetrate firefighting. They, in turn, pour kerosene on the fires to make life at work more filled with adrenaline. IBP must help to create a formal way of working.

3. A business planning and control process built around an annual budget that drives people to take accountability for numbers which they do not believe, and forces short-termism, since the focus is permanently on the year-end. IBP will help create a formal process for revising the long-term rolling business plan monthly. Directors and managers will meet the plan and not beat the plan.

If all or some of these three issues are present in your organisation, then I hope you will read on!

If not, relax – your business has already probably implemented a common-sense process a bit like IBP!

Chapter 2
The Model For Change

"You can't do it unless you can imagine it"
– George Lucas.

Let's now turn to describe the key elements that contribute to "Integrated Business Leadership" and examine the Delos model that supports this for almost all organisations. While many of the examples relate to manufacturing companies, the principles can easily apply to other businesses. Every organisation is as unique as each human being. But there is a lot of commonality. I have had the privilege and pleasure to work across a large number of industry types – Agrochemicals, Pharmaceuticals, Automotive, Engineering, Defence, Hospital, Nuclear Processing, Scientific Development, Chemical, Food Processing, and Snack Manufacture. While the outputs might be different in terms of the products, the basic organisational elements for their business model are very similar.

I show the diagram that covers this on the next page. I describe the overall model as "Integrated Business Leadership"; this describes more particularly the activities that lie in the top half of the diagram – Vision, Strategy, People, Measures and Prioritisation. The processes that cover these elements are the responsibility of the senior leadership team, and leadership is about how you make people accountable for the delivery of the Vision and Strategy. The business will make decisions through the prioritisation process.

The name of the bottom half of the diagram is "Integrated Business Planning". This section describes the key activities or processes which the business has to carry out. There are two key "phases" to each business process, which covers the Planning and Execution of the business process. Thus, on the demand side, there is a Demand Plan (how are you going to make your product attractive and available to customers, and how many are you going to sell) and Demand Execution (how do you make the sale happen, get the order, and then invoice it to gain the planned revenue). The same is true on the supply side – how to make a Supply Plan for the materials and capacity, and then Supply Execution, which covers the making and delivering of the product/service to the customer.

Measurement of processes happens by comparing "actual" versus "plan". You improve performance through the use of continuous improvement tools such as Lean and Six Sigma – illustrated at the bottom.

Accurate data is a prerequisite!

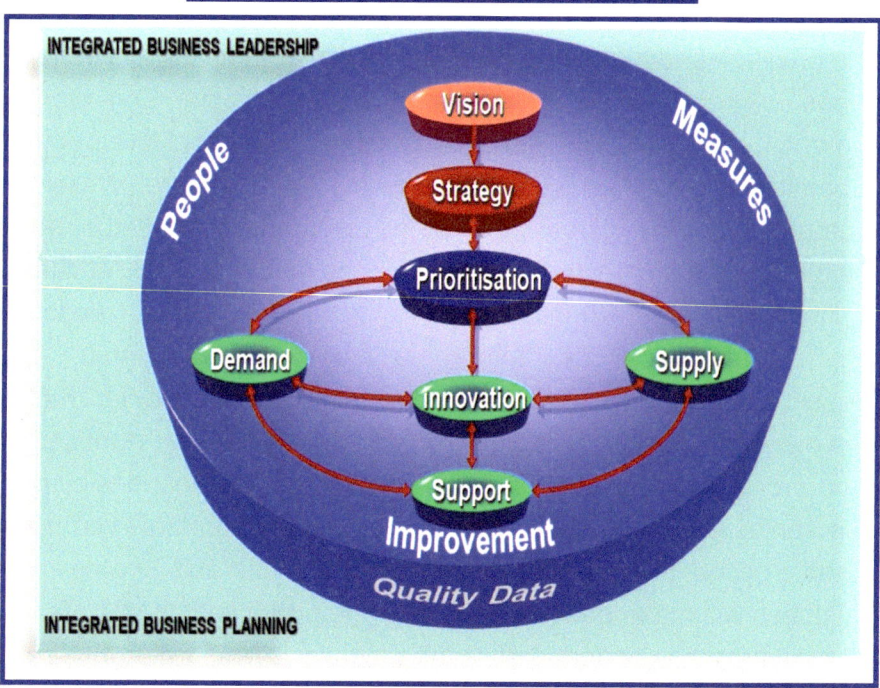

Figure 5: Integrated Business Model

Having looked at the typical problems that business faces in Chapter 1, we can outline the key objectives for operating the "Integrated Business Leadership model" as follows:

Figure 6: Objectives for Integrated Business Leadership

- Vision and Strategy supported by :
  - One set of numbers at all times
  - Integrated Plans
  - Realistic Plans
- Visibility and transparency [2-3 years]
- Clear roles and responsibilities
- Integrated robust processes
- Teamwork and cross-functional alignment
- More planning, less fire-fighting
- Consistent performance measures – driving right "behaviour"
- Decisions made in timely fashion
- Top Down guidance and bottom up communication on achievement
- Finding out truth as we know it
- Delivery of the strategy – do what you said you would do

I suspect few people would disagree with these objectives.

Vision and Strategy. Vision covers the long-term purpose of the business and where it is going, and the Strategy identifies the plan required to act on the Strengths, Weaknesses, Opportunities and Threats of the business in its position concerning competitors, customers, suppliers and shareholders.

We will explore the role of Vision and Strategy in Chapters 15 and 16. But the key principle is that there should be a long-term view of the purpose and direction of the company, supported by a set of numbers that describe future revenue and profitability. The business can update the numbers at any time, in the light of changing circumstances.

The other key part of this philosophy is that plans are realistic and not pure pie in the sky. Often strategies are based on generic statements like "double revenue in the next three years, and treble net profit". A proper strategy will state how this will be achieved, with the right resources to support this strategy.

It does not mean that the strategic objectives should not be challenging.

If you look at the famous Walmart objectives set up by Sam Walton in the USA, then they were certainly ambitious; but they were seen to be realistic, and they achieved them. His "Big Hairy Audacious Goals" were:

- 1945 "Make my little Newport store the best, most profitable in Arkansas within five years."
- 1977 to reach $1 billion.
- 1990 to double the number of stores by 2000 and to become a $125-billion company by the year 2000.

The strategy can be changed and updated over time, as this illustrates. The question we will address is how and when – and propose that this should not be just a once a year activity; it can happen at any time, and it should be executed all the time.

Visibility and transparency are cited as the most valuable part of the whole SOP/IBP process. Too often, companies suffer from "management myopia" – chronic short-sightedness. Myopia is a physical disease of the eyes that affects 25-30% of people, that makes distant objects appear to be blurred. Surgery will fix it with lenses and lasers. IBL corrects "management myopia" by setting out the right framework to support long-term thinking.

The horizon mentioned here of two to three years is also key. Change happens at any time and can be far-reaching. The coronavirus epidemic of 2020 was a case in point. If a company only has real visibility of volumes and values until the end of the current year, then it will not be able to make a decision based on consistent data that takes into account the long term. If a decision requires investment in capacity, then usually companies need to make a financial decision based on at least a three- if not five-year projection of cash flows to determine the pay-back of the investment.

The following couple of practical examples may help to illustrate this.

Back in the late 1990s, a famous chewing gum company was about to launch a new sugar-free variety, to enter the strategically important dental healthcare market. When they carried out their first test market in the Granada TV area in the UK, they found that the expected share of the market was going to be substantially higher than originally forecast. They ran their revised numbers through their SOP/IBP process, and using their 42-month horizon for the financial volumes and values that resulted, saw that they needed to invest £150,000 in new packaging equipment. They ran a few scenarios on upsides and downsides for the numbers, and the MD came to the conclusion that it was essential to invest, and so they bought the equipment and installed it. They completed all of this decision-making process within the one-month cycle for the IBP process. They did not have to check if they had the £150,000 in the budget to spend or get permission to exceed the budget. They "just did it".

They got to market more quickly with all the advantages that entailed, which was enabled by being able to make an "instantaneous" decision. At the cornerstone of their business process was that integrated rolling 42-month value (sales and profit) and volume plan, which was updated monthly.

The MD of that business understood what IBP was all about, and helped that business to grow at a phenomenal rate as a result.

In another case, a client supplied a major aircraft manufacturer with aluminium components that went into the wings of the aircraft. The manufacturer had realised that the aluminium components industry needed to invest substantially in machinery capacity to meet the growth in the market over the next ten to fifteen years. So, we worked with the component company on developing a five-year plan to support the visibility required. When we did the first cycle of the IBP process in February, it became clear that the business would need to invest £4m in November of that year to meet the long-term growth in their business – a figure which was not in their budget! They went to corporate HQ and quickly gained approval.

Many companies have operated to the mantra that IBP must cover just a two- to three-year horizon. Nonsense! The required horizon entirely depends on the industry and requirements of the company within that industry to support decisions that span the acquisition of material and capacity requirements in the long term.

Thus, in the submarine industry, where it takes 10+ years to build a submarine, then the horizon for IBP is/was 10-15 years. In the Nuclear Fuel re-processing industry, the horizon is/was 50 years when I developed the model there. That does not mean that the numbers keep changing for the longer term; it means that if you need to, then you can do so, within the framework of one database, quickly.

Clear roles and responsibilities are also needed within the framework of any business. We have illustrated how important customer service is for a company. On several occasions, I have asked who is responsible for customer service – and the answer has ranged from a vague "everybody", to supply chain, to the head of customer services.

I had an inspirational project leader in ICI Agrochemicals, who led their transformation project. He went to become the MD of a garden products company within ICI.

When he started, he had a small wooden sign built for his desk with the words "customer service is my job". Brilliant! That led him to bring about a transformation in the way that business ran, built around the IBP process. He made the sales and marketing director responsible for delivering an accurate forecast. He made the planning manager responsible for a realistic plan. He made the factory responsible for making the plan. He made procurement responsible for buying to the plan and getting suppliers to deliver. The head of NPD had to deliver new products to meet the new season. He got these accountabilities written into their job descriptions and reviewed their performance against the measures set.

The business grew, became more profitable and increased market share at a time when the business was very challenging in the market place – there was a recession, costs were increasing and so on.

He met his customers at Wimbledon every year. Before he started, they complained that the service was poor. After he implemented IBP, customer service was never an issue about which customers complained. He had done his job, and so had all his managers. They could enjoy tennis!

Integrated robust processes are essential to creating an effective Business Planning process. It also relates – as stated earlier – to the fact that efficient quality organisations should structure their business around the ISO 9001:2015 standard; this proposes clear responsibilities related to the business processes.

Teamwork is also a critical component of IBP. It is an overused word in management guru land. I have seen pictures emphasising teamwork in many companies' reception, or by the staircases, which show people rowing in boats. Phrases like "there is no 'I' in team" are everywhere. But in a functional world, where each department chases after its objectives, it is very difficult, if not impossible, for businesses to work as a real team. Where businesses measure functions in a way which drives them to compete against each other, then it is impossible. You will hear phrases like, "all I want is Manufacturing to deliver to my customers when I have sold the product" from the sales directors. Yes – but what if Sales made an unreasonable promise in the first place?

Consistent performance measures are at the core of IBP, which addresses the idea that teamwork requires creating a single plan to which everyone works, built around consistent measures.

Football is a team sport, and many authors have written reams about the subject. A couple of years ago the odds were 5000/1 against Leicester City winning the Premier League. They won with an inspirational leader. The most expensive set of players does not make the team and does not always win.

I was listening to football commentary on a game, and just as someone was heading towards the goal, the commentator said, "unselfishly he passed the ball to the right, and his teammate scored the goal". The key word is "unselfishly". Scoring a goal often gets the prizes and plaudits. As human beings, our parents bring us up to respond to the applause. Because of this, we will often behave in selfish ways. Twenty years ago, the hero would be the centre forward who got the goals. Now "assists" are measured as being just as important as scoring a goal. Teamwork is about getting rid of selfishness and in its place doing what is good for the team. Humans only do this if they see it is in their interests to do so. Hence it is essential to establish the right culture which encourages humans to collaborate.

In business, it is not just the salesperson who makes things happen (although I have heard some say "without me making the sales, then we would not survive"). Everyone in a company has a part to play in making it a success, and a successful leader encourages teamwork. The key is that the fundamentals of the organisation do not drive people apart.

As someone once said about a company that did not practise IBP: a "sales success is a manufacturing disaster". The salesperson may be delighted to hit their targets but if that leaves a trail of a disaster elsewhere, then that is not good for the whole organisation; it is not a team. Hence, I emphasise that we should measure sales on forecast accuracy, and not beating the budget.

Making decisions in a timely fashion is core to the IBP process. It supports decision making. I will describe the decision-making process later in the book. IBP is about how businesses can make decisions through the formal process to respond to significant changes in the external and internal environment. A decision about long-term and short-term issues can be made at any time; you do not have to wait for the next budget to decide on whether to invest in new equipment. It is when you make it that matters.

I recently got an enquiry from a company wanting to do a workshop on IBP, and they wanted a quote "for budgetary" purposes. It was about six months before the year-end. They could not decide on whether to do this for another six months! Suppose that the benefit of doing that workshop in advancing the implementation of IBP was around £50,000 per month. The delay in the decision will cost them £300,000! That is many multiples of the cost of the workshop. Companies often overlook the opportunity cost by deciding not to do something – just because "it is not in the budget".

Another client saw, through its IBP process, which had a horizon of 30 months, that they were going to run short of capacity next year. It was November, and the capacity problem was going to start in November/December next year. By making the decision now, they were able to tackle the issues far sooner, saving many millions of pounds.

Be honest and tell the truth sounds like an unusual moral statement to make in the context of IBP. Companies pay insufficient attention to the requirement for "truth in business". Much of the literature around IBP dwells on the process, or policies, and the need for a clear vision or strategy.

Truth is important throughout our lives. We are taught at school to tell the truth. Telling lies in court as part of a legal process is not accepted. In business, it is strange how the culture can force people into telling lies because of the way that they are managed, and indeed rewarded. It is almost as if at home we have one set of behaviours, but then we get in the car, or get on the train to work, we alter our moral compasses to point in the opposite direction!

In one client, which is a UK subsidiary of a European company, they had a budget of around £200m for the calendar year. The head of manufacturing told me he was constantly under pressure to meet the Sales plan. The planning manager was constantly under pressure not to increase inventory. Lead times were around six to eight weeks for the production of raw materials and capacity.

The European MD was insistent that the target of £200m would be met, and did not want to hear any other number. However, the managers that I met said that, when you looked at the numbers (it was around August), then they were heading for £170m, <u>realistically</u>. Nevertheless, the sales director refused to reveal that "truth" to the European MD, and insisted that the forecast, which was driving the planning and manufacturing processes, was kept at £200 million. He knew what would happen if he told the truth – the MD would find someone who still believed it was all possible!

It was not, therefore, surprising that inventory continued to rise as the year-end approached. The planning manager got the blame. But whose fault was it? The culture of the business did not support telling the truth. The leadership, which did not accept or allow people to tell the truth, and which created the fear that went with the telling of the truth, was ultimately responsible.

I once asked a senior team if they wanted to hear the truth. They all said "yes". My second question was, "Is it okay to tell the truth?" One director then said, "The last person who told the truth no longer works here." People quickly understand the culture of where they work, and fear of not finding another job forces them to behave in the way the culture demands. In this situation, IBP requires companies to change their culture. All should uphold the principle of "telling the truth to power".

Sometimes companies excuse themselves because they fear shareholder reaction. Certainly, directors have to make sure they hit the budgets which they report to their external shareholders, and we will look at this. But this is not a reason to conceal the truth. Shareholders do not like surprises. The right culture is that the planning process should allow managers to tell "truth as we know it". If there is a gap between the truth and what we would like to achieve, we should then work on how we close the gap between the truth and the business plan. If we do this early enough, then we have more time in which to close the gap and make our plans. The following chart describes the link between "the truth" and the Business Planning process:

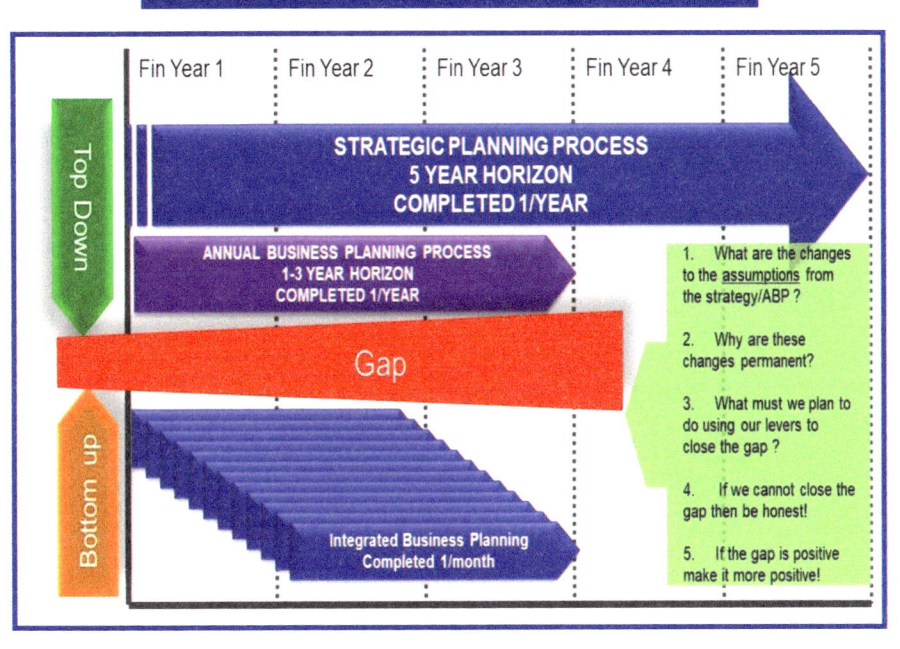

Figure 7: Bottom-up and Top-Down planning

```
                    Fin Year 1    Fin Year 2    Fin Year 3    Fin Year 4    Fin Year 5

Top Down            STRATEGIC PLANNING PROCESS
                    5 YEAR HORIZON
                    COMPLETED 1/YEAR

                    ANNUAL BUSINESS PLANNING PROCESS       1. What are the changes
                    1-3 YEAR HORIZON                          to the assumptions from
                    COMPLETED 1/YEAR                          the strategy/ABP?

                                                           2. Why are these
                              Gap                             changes permanent?

                                                           3. What must we plan to
                                                              do using our levers to
Bottom up                                                     close the gap?

                                                           4. If we cannot close the
                                                              gap then be honest!
                    Integrated Business Planning
                    Completed 1/month                      5. If the gap is positive
                                                              make it more positive!
```

The IBP process each month provides the bottom-up review to compare against the top-down "aspirations" of the Strategic and Annual Business Planning processes.

"Truth as we know it" might reveal a gap in the middle. If there is a gap we need to:
- Understand the changes that have made the gap appear
- Understand if these changes are permanent and what the impacts are
- Come up with plans to close the gap and the business/financial consequences of those plans
- If we can realistically close the gap, then we take the required action; but if we cannot close the gap, then we should be honest to ourselves and the relevant stakeholders. If they are shareholders, then

- shareholders hold a portfolio of shares, which – if properly diversified – will protect them against the ups and downs of the overall market place. The quicker they know, the better.

The Scope for Change

Having made a case for change, we should then see that the scope for change will be:

1. The processes for creating the Vision and Strategy <u>and</u> the processes for planning the business.
2. The culture of the business and the way that leadership is perceived to operate through the company; 'truth' and 'realism' are key watchwords.
3. Systems, and making sure these work effectively based on accurate data.

Integration should cover the whole business, and not just part of it – thus "Sales and Operations Planning" is the wrong term.

"Integrated Business Planning" is not a sufficient description of what is required to make this concept work. The right <u>leadership</u>, which drives the reward structure, the team-based behaviour, and the culture of truth and honesty, must also be in place.

There are many management books on "Leadership" but here are a few quotations, which I believe are relevant to this model:

"If you do not know where you are going, then any road will get you there." – Henry Kissinger.

"Inventories can be managed, but people must be led." – Ross Perot.

"A leader takes people where they want to go. A great leader takes people to where they do not necessarily want to go, but ought to be." – Rosalynn Carter.

Without the right leadership, it does not matter what type of business model any company tries to implement. I was lucky to have the right leader, which is why the process survived in ICI Agrochemicals and on into Syngenta.

Many companies that have failed to implement IBP have done so because of a lack of commitment to the ideas by the leadership. The old ways of working have fixated the leadership, and they believe the right way to manage accountabilities for performance is through conflict, rather than collaboration.

Sometimes it is a simple adherence to the principle of "divide and rule". In this case, it is this "mindset" which will need to change.

Chapter 3

How Does It Work?

"You never change things by fighting the existing reality. To change something, build a new model that makes the existing model obsolete." – Buckminster Fuller

One of the things that I have learnt from working with companies in helping them to design an IBP process, is that there is no single model which works for everyone. One of the big mistakes that I have seen is that companies see a model of how the process should work, then slavishly try to apply that to their existing organisation structure, but then find the process "does not work". However, there are some principles which can be applied to the structure of meetings that knit IBP together.

Figure 8 bases the model around a structure developed by Tom Wallace and Bob Stahl in the 1990s, which focusses on just Sales and Operations planning. It does not take into account all the other functions, explicitly.

Figure 9 describes the model developed in the late 1990s by Andy Coldrick of the Oliver Wight company.

Both are five-step processes, except they are a slightly different "five steps". The model in Figure 9 now explicitly recognises a step for "managing new activities" which covers new product development (which also brings in the important function of marketing), and also provides a step called "Integrated Reconciliation" which broadly replaces the Pre-SOP process. This step relates to identifying the gaps to the business plan and gap-closing activities which need to go on. As these inevitably require a Financial input, then the Financial function gets involved in this stage, but there is no explicit step for the Finance or Human Resources function to provide input. It is a very clear model, and I have seen those companies that have

How Does It Work

adopted this model talk of "Step 1" and "Step 2" meetings in support of their process.

Figure 8: Wallace and Stahl 5-step process

The 5-Step Executive S&OP Process

- Step 1: Data Gathering — End of Month — Actual Demand, Supply, Inventory, & Backlog + Statistical Forecasts and Worksheets
- Step 2: Demand Planning — Management Forecast 1st-pass spreadsheets
- Step 3: Supply Planning — Resource Requirements Plan Capacity Constraints 2nd-pass spreadsheets
- Step 4: Pre-Meeting — Decisions, Recommendations, Scenarios, & Agenda for Exec Meeting
- Step 5: Exec Meeting — Decisions & Updated Game Plan

Tom Wallace & Bob Stahl — www.tfwallace.com

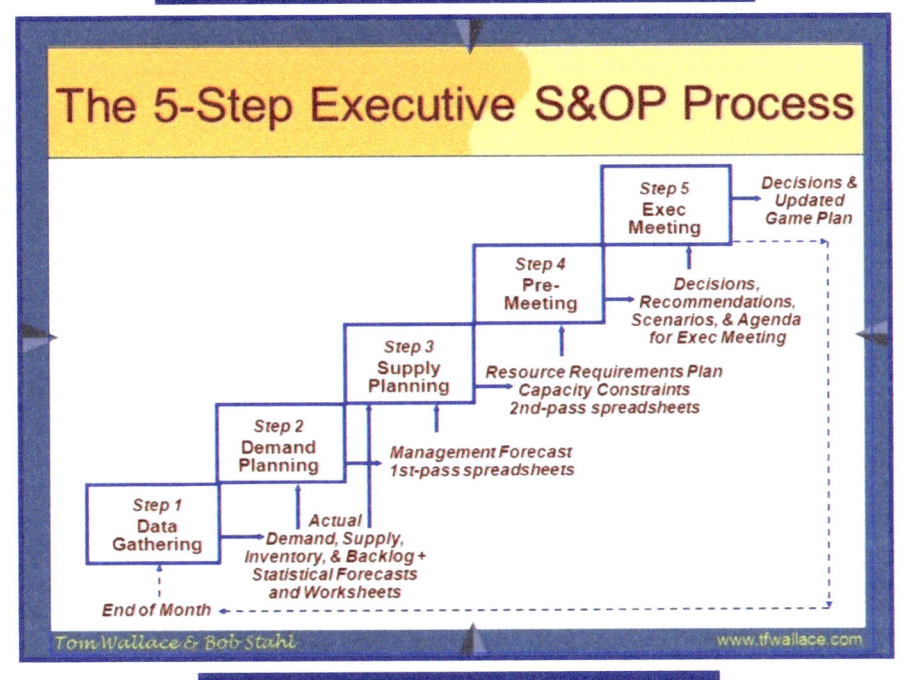

Figure 9: Oliver Wight 5-step process

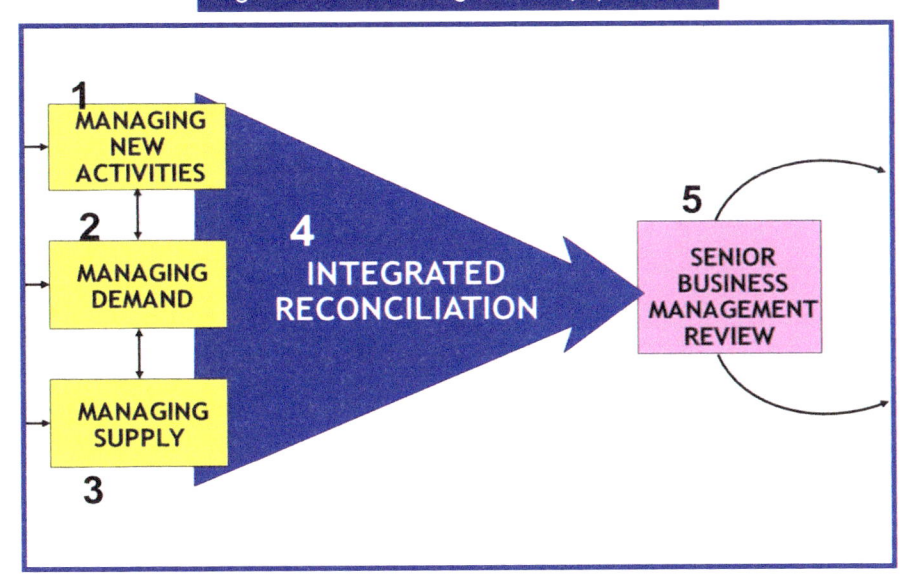

1. MANAGING NEW ACTIVITIES
2. MANAGING DEMAND
3. MANAGING SUPPLY
4. INTEGRATED RECONCILIATION
5. SENIOR BUSINESS MANAGEMENT REVIEW

47

However, I have seen companies take this model, put in place these meetings, which align with these models, and then try to get input and output from the meetings but find that people do not turn up. They then say that their SOP/IBP process is not working.

When I reviewed the details of how the process works in these companies, I found that the implementation had ignored the fact that the business was reasonably well developed. They had several meetings in place already, which filled many of the functions that these models suggest are required. They needed to have rearranged the structure and timing of what they were already doing.

In one company, they had established a Demand Review meeting. It "did not work" because the commercial director did not turn up. But this was because there was already an existing Commercial Board meeting, which the commercial director chaired. It did not cover all of the requirements of a Demand review. It would have been better to start by looking at the current meeting, rather than trying to shoehorn a new process and meeting into an existing structure. When they did this, the process worked.

In another company, they put in place a complete five-step process, believing this was what was needed. But looking at the total picture, this in effect created a parallel structure of meetings, and it was not surprising that there was no "buy-in" to the process. Again, it was a case of trying to "cut and paste" a model into an existing structure.

It is worth looking at the elements of the process, and understanding it first, before integrating IBP into your business. In this way, you will get a process that works for your business. Upfront education is crucial.

Let me now turn to the specific issues and questions, which I have seen companies need to address, when they set up the process.

- **A monthly cycle – why is this needed?**

Earlier on, we said that the traditional model of the Annual and Strategic Planning process failed because it happened once a year, and change can happen more frequently than that.

Change happens on an even more frequent basis than monthly – daily in fact. So, many ask the question as to why the IBP process should be based on a monthly cycle.

When SOP was invented, the term "Master Scheduling" was coined to cover the detailed, daily planning process. Master Scheduling is the mechanism for providing control to a plan, which in turn manages the planning and execution of the acquisition of raw materials (through Material Requirements Planning) and capacity (through Capacity Requirements Planning). This planning process happens through a daily and weekly cycle of activities.

The key feature of the software and process to support this is that you can and should "firm plan" the detailed Supply plan, and should do so out to the cumulative lead time for the products.

The Cumulative Lead Time (CLT) is a critical concept behind the whole process, and describes the term for the total longest time through a company's Manufacturing and Procurement supply chain, from placing an order for raw materials and components through to the point where the finished product is available for sale. This is different for different product types within a company and different industries.

The rule or convention then should be to "firm plan" planned works orders out to that horizon, which means that a planner (master scheduler) has to make controlled changes to the master schedule. They will only do so if the changes are feasible. Thus, a computer cannot make changes without a human being considering the consequences.

Beyond that horizon, the computer is free to alter the requirements for capacity and materials. The chart overleaf illustrates the principle: A company which uses an ERP system to calculate requirements for capacity and materials should update this every day. I realise that many operate their systems based on updating systems weekly. However, this fails to update the plans in light of the latest information.

Firm Planned Orders

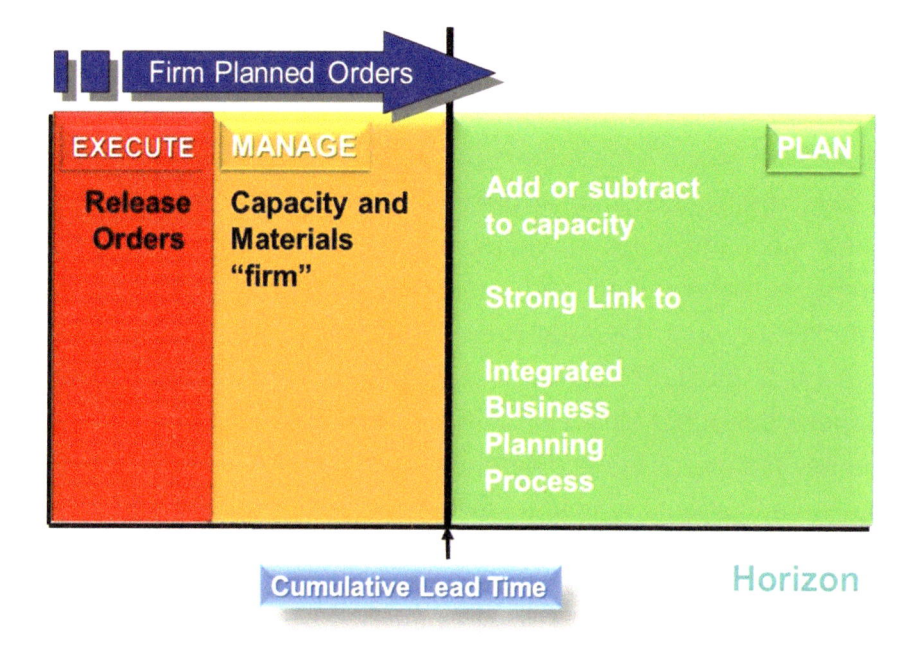

EXECUTE	MANAGE	PLAN
Release Orders	Capacity and Materials "firm"	Add or subtract to capacity Strong Link to Integrated Business Planning Process

Cumulative Lead Time — Horizon

So, this means that a master scheduler will manage all changes to plans, both short-term and long-term, on a daily basis, and there needs to be a daily and weekly process for updating plans. It covers the detailed changes that happen on a day-to-day basis.

SOP/IBP, therefore, focusses at the horizon beyond the CLT. If you do not look at the longer-term, then the short-term could be chaotic. Hence, companies can assume that for the longer-term it is valid to take a snapshot of the plans at a single point in time (beyond the CLT), and use that as a basis for discussion.

A company could take that snapshot weekly, if it believed that it needed to capture and review changes in a weekly cycle for the next two- to three-year horizon. That would require a lot more work in creating reports and so on.

Equally, a company could take a snapshot once a quarter to review the plans. The advantage would be less work. However, the downside of this is that you miss out changes, or – which is more likely – companies will set up an ad-hoc, unconnected process to cope with the significant changes that occur between meetings, and make decisions in a 'disintegrated' way. People will not wait until the next quarterly cycle to make decisions.

Monthly is, therefore, a compromise between too much change and too little capture of changes; pragmatically it is also a cycle which very many companies who have implemented IBP have made, whether they are multi-million or multi-billion-dollar sales revenue companies.

- **Horizon.**

One of the key benefits of IBP is the visibility it provides, as we outlined in Chapter 2. If you look around the literature, then you will find statements that SOP/IBP should cover a horizon of only 24 months. The literature is trying to make the point that SOP/IBP is a long-term planning process, as well as the fact that it should be a rolling planning horizon. We want to avoid the year-end being the end of the horizon. But it should not be limited to 24 months.

The key consideration for every business is the length of time they need to be able to make decisions, as outlined in Chapter 2. In making these business decisions for the long term, then typically companies need to be thinking about cash, capacity and any key long lead time raw materials.

We then need to answer the second question, which is: "When does the long-term start?" Thus, some companies have created an artificial barrier between the long-term and the short-term. This is built around the familiar distinction – coming from military planning – of Strategic, Operational and Tactical. Companies have broken this down into a simplistic statement that zero to three months is short-term and beyond that is long-term. But there is no universal point, which is "operational", and beyond that, "strategic".

As described in Chapter 2, I have seen and developed many models. Thus, in the aerospace market, typically the aeroplane manufacturers have an order book which can stretch out 18 months and beyond, to 10 years and more. Submarine manufacturers have an order book which stretches eight to 10 years and beyond. The planning process in the Nuclear Fuel plant construction and decommissioning business stretches out 50 years. On the other hand, fast moving food manufacturers will typically face a 24 to 48-hour order book.

Customer orders make a difference to companies as typically, once the customer places the order, then there is a commitment and demand should not change.

Additionally, when orders are accepted, much work has been done on working out the amount of capacity and materials required to support the order acceptance process, and we need commitment if we are going to buy the raw materials and capacity.

The first question to ask, in terms of the horizon, is how far out do we need to plan, given the constraints on the business from materials and capacity? Thus, this horizon is not going to be a standard for all companies. If a company makes cigarettes, they need tobacco, which can take several years to grow. If a company makes dried fruits, they need farmers to plant fields with fruit a year or more ahead of time. If a company makes milk products, they will need cows. If a company makes aeroplane parts, then it needs aluminium and titanium, which will be on long lead times. All these are key critical resources, and will contribute to the determination of the horizon.

Then there is the time associated with design and development. If a company makes one-of-a-kind satellite products, it may take three years to design the product. They need the engineers to design the products, who are a key resource requirement. The total design and build time will determine the horizon.

The issue is that each business needs to understand its key critical resources, both internally and externally within its supply chain. It then should determine the planning horizon for demand to align with the visibility required for acquisition of materials and capacity. It then needs to plan the supply of fruit or milk or aluminium or titanium, etc. out to that point in the future. Each business needs to work out where its degree of freedom exists and then make sure that the planning process aligns.

If it takes two years to plan the requirements for the fruit to drive a fruit processing business, then if someone changes the (forecast) demand within that period, someone will need to manage the impact of those changes on the supply side. Thus, the ultimate horizon for the IBP process should cover the total lead time for acquiring capacity and raw materials. As we move on in time to the present day, there will be decreasing degrees of freedom, depending on the lead times for materials and capacity. At some point, the company will commit to the number of farmers (and acreage). At another point, the company will potentially commit to the number of tonnes of fruit, and so on.

There will not be a standard zero-to-three-month lead time, as is sometimes suggested.

The other part of the planning process that impacts the rules is the horizon required to support the acquisition of cash – whether from shareholders or debtholders/banks. Thus, if the company needs to invest in capital equipment or make an acquisition or divestment, then typically this will require a Capital Expenditure Proposal complete with a Cash Flow Forecast. Many companies operate on the basis that all cash flow forecasts are supported by a Net Present Value (NPV) calculation which takes into account the cost and time value of money. To pay for the investment, a company may need several years before the investment becomes cash-positive. In the pharmaceutical business, for instance, this can be between seven and 10 years. Hence this can extend the horizon within which we need to operate.

Many companies will look for a standard number of years in which they recover the initial expenditure – thus a payback period of three years, for instance. This is not a good way of judging the financial viability of projects, but it does require that your planning process goes out at least three to four years, to demonstrate that the company will get a return on investment in three years.

It is not a good way for evaluating projects, as this implies a return of around 30% per annum, which is an exceptionally high return – and implies a high risk. Additionally, it might exclude projects which it could take on with lower rates of return, which are worthwhile investments (possibly low risk).

Since IBP will involve making financial decisions of this sort, the horizon must enable a decision-making process to decide on capital equipment expenditure. So, it is not just raw material and capacity acquisition that is the driver.

These considerations tend companies towards a standard horizon of three to five years, and possibly 10 (and even 50 years in the nuclear fuel processing industry as an extreme!)

The last consideration relates to the need to prepare an Annual Plan to report to shareholders (typically with revisions each quarter). Assuming a company has a financial year from January to December, then many companies will want to review the plan in July, for a final agreement in October.

Now clearly – as indicated in Chapter 2 – there are issues about creating budgets. We may still prepare a "budget" in the world in which we do IBP. The part that does not add value to the process is the behaviour which forces "sandbagging" and creating artificial targets, which in turn leads to short-termism. That behaviour has to change.

Then, if we prepare plans on a Financial Year basis, we need to add to our horizon an additional number of months to give us visibility that will align with our financial years.

Thus, if I were putting together a plan in July of the current year for the next three financial years, which start in January, then I would need six months' horizon to provide the outlook for the year I was in, plus 36 months to get the full horizon for which I need visibility. Hence the horizon would be 42 months. It is why some companies have selected 42 months as their horizon – and not just because the number 42 is – in *The Hitchhiker's Guide to the Galaxy* by Douglas Adams – the "answer to the ultimate question of life, the universe, and everything" (Adams, 1994).

There is thus no universal answer to all companies as to what the horizon should be; each company is different.

- **Strategy, Operations and Tactics.**

Sometimes people refer to the longer-term planning process as being "strategic". They then refer to the medium-term as "operational", and see the short-term as being "tactical". But we need to be careful as to how we treat these time-horizons.

So, let us be clear about what the difference is between "Strategic", "Operational" and "Tactical", and how companies should manage these different concepts.

Kaplan and Norton's "The Strategy Focused Organisation" (Kaplan & Norton, 2001), describes how a "balanced scorecard" helps companies create and execute their strategy. It is a great text for the performance management aspects for integrated business planning. In principle, they describe the strategy as being about aligning the activities within a business towards delivering a single "unique selling proposition". The book then concentrates on five key themes:

1. Translate the Strategy to Operational Terms – create a Strategy Map which describes the key activities/objectives that will support the delivery of your competitive advantage.

2. Align the organisation to the strategy. Broadly ensure each function knows their strategic priorities, and work on them.

3. Make the strategy everyone's everyday job. It is wrong to believe that strategy is something that only the senior leadership team are capable of thinking about and doing. Business must communicate the strategy throughout the organisation. Some fear communication will leak the strategy to the competition, but the counter-quote is the great statement from the CEO of Mobil, Brian Baker: "Knowing our strategy will do them (competitors) little good unless they can execute it. On the other hand, we have no chance of executing our strategy unless our people know it. It's a chance we will have to take."

4. Make the strategy a continual process. The book says that strategy is not a once-a-year process. Eighty-five per cent of management teams spend less than one hour per month discussing strategy – that was true then, and I suspect that is true now. You can practise this through the Integrated Business Planning process.

5. Mobilise Change through Executive Leadership. Transformational change – which is at the heart of the balanced scorecard – starts at the top. They cite the great change guru, John Cotter (Cotter, 1996), and his principles, which are that leaders should: (1) establish a sense of urgency; (2) create the guiding coalition; (3) develop a Vision and Strategy.

Strategy is indeed about the creation of the long-term plans for maximising the value from your unique selling proposition and the objectives required to achieve them, and a company should review this all the time.

Operations are the activities being carried out as part of everyone's everyday job, on a day-to-day and month-to-month basis (developing new products, marketing them, selling them, delivering them).

Tactical execution, or tactical delivery, is carrying out actions to bring the plan to a conclusion. Tactics typically cover the short-term. The key points, however, which align with the operation of IBP, are contained in points three and four above of Kaplan and Norton's book. A strategy is an everyday activity and is a continual process – not just a process to be carried out once a year. We need to be able to review this at any time.

Thus, we may build our strategy around Innovation, which is our unique proposition to the market place, and desire to get an increase in market share and market dominance through continually developing new products. It will lead to a strategic objective to develop 'XYZ' product(s) and service(s) in which we have a unique position (intellectual property, technical, cost, geography). It will lead to operational product development plans to develop those products, which will have milestones as part of the Project Plan.

Execution happens when we complete those activities and record milestones as complete.

But if a competitor suddenly enters the market, which we had not expected, then that may force a change in strategy. If a government somewhere suddenly puts up tariffs by 100%, in line with a policy of "put our country first", then this may cause us to re-evaluate our strategy and change our strategic activities. We cannot wait until next year's Strategic Review to alter direction.

So, Strategy, Operations and Tactics are different phases in our horizon that relate to the delivery of what we need to do to achieve our competitive advantage. But it does not make sense to do strategy just once a year or look at strategy as something that somehow happens "out there" somewhere, as if it belongs to a time-horizon in the 12-60-month time frame.

A company could develop a new strategy today if it wanted to – and needed to – in response to some change in the internal or external environment. Companies should carry out this activity as part of the Integrated Business Planning process; they do not have to wait until next year's Strategic Planning meeting.

There needs to be a discrete process by which you develop it within the framework of Integrated Business Planning, and companies that do this will be able to adapt quickly.

Charles Darwin is known for the phrase "survival of the fittest". He also made the point: "It is not the most intellectual of the species that survives; it is not the strongest that survives, but the species that survives is the one that can adapt to and adjust best to the changing environment in which it finds itself."

That applies to companies as well.

- **Level of Detail and "Families".**

When a company puts together any plan, there is a level of detail at which we need to operate. In a manufacturing company, people use the term "stock-keeping unit" (SKU) to define the lowest level of detail, and typically this will be uniquely defined by a product code and a product description. All companies need to have that level of detail to get something made and despatched to a customer. To get something made on the shop-floor or supplied by a supplier, then you will need an identification code. It is a way for the computer to be able to process that activity.

However, if we start to think about the IBP process as being about executives making decisions, then it is not going to make sense to look at every product, every month. That is "too much information!"

It makes sense to try and group products together so we can talk about broader activities – particularly when we are talking about capacity, which covers the manufacture of several products.

At this point, while the principle appears simple conceptually, it can become very difficult to work out the "families", or groupings, of products.

The difficulty stems in part from the fact that different functions will look at the same products, but will review them in different ways. Thus, marketing will be looking at the labels on the bottles and focussing on brands. Thus, we might have a brand which marketing has christened "Lemonfresh", or "Aquapure" or some name like that for a range of drinks. They understand that for a range of drinks there are several products which the company sells under that brand name, and they will refer to that group of products by its brand name. But it is often the case that the operational side finds that the name "Lemonfresh" as a brand name applies to products that are sold in several different production forms – for example, as fizzy and as plain.

If marketing talk about 100,000 units of Lemonfresh per month as a plan, this will be of no use to the supply side, as they will need to know the format and recipe of the products sold – will they be fizzy or plain?

Also, it is sometimes the case that all products come from some common source. "Lemonfresh" might need lemons as a core ingredient. Dried raspberries will need a supply of raspberries.

Tablets of aspirin will need aspirin as an active ingredient. Plates and cups and saucers all need clay. Crisps need potatoes. So, products could need to be grouped not only by the format in which the product is delivered, but also according to the basic raw material that goes to make the products.

One of the other considerations in grouping products together is so that we can have a fewer number of items to review. The ideal is around 10-20. Sometimes it is difficult to get down to this number. A company selling 20,000 SKUs is likely to struggle to get down to 10/20 items. I equally have seen a company with 30 SKUs end up with ten families. But 10-20 is a good target!

Hence, in setting up the "families", we will typically need to establish a hierarchical structure with which to group the products, and we may need multiple hierarchies with which to group the products.

In Figure 11, there is a "brand" structure on the left-hand side. On the right-hand side, there is a "production" structure. It creates a requirement to code each product with the correct "family code".

This, in turn, creates a need to ensure that this information is maintained properly in the ERP system – and indeed that the ERP system can cope with multiple hierarchies. Thus, a product can be part of the Lemonfresh brand, and the "Fizzy" product type.

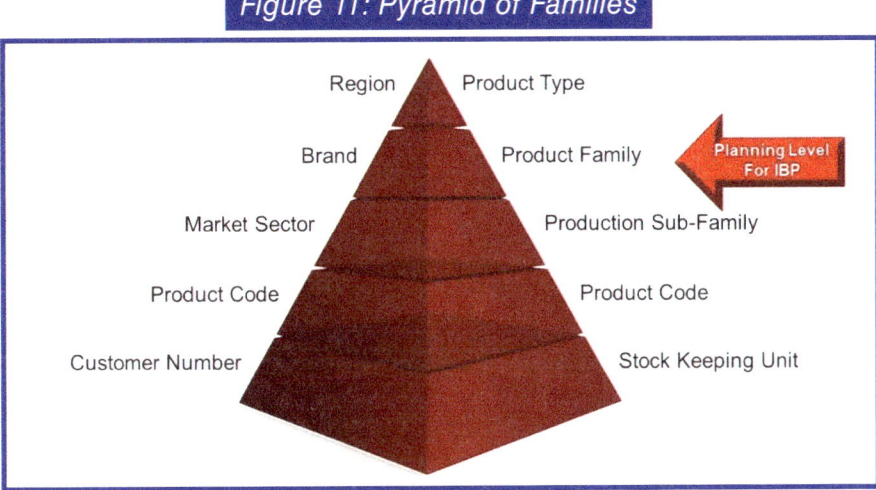

Figure 11: Pyramid of Families

Left side (top to bottom): Region, Brand, Market Sector, Product Code, Customer Number

Right side (top to bottom): Product Type, Product Family, Production Sub-Family, Product Code, Stock Keeping Unit

Planning Level For IBP (arrow pointing to Product Family / Production Sub-Family level)

It is also about creating a language which people understand, and it is about making sure that when we talk about 100,000 units of Lemonfresh, and we expect sales to increase by 10% as a result of an advertising campaign for Lemonfresh, that we can then translate that into, 60,000 fizzy and 40,000 plain bottles. It will allow operations to work out how many more to make to support the campaign.

If the advertising campaign could only relate to Lemonfresh fizzy products, then we may need to be able to operate at that level of detail [a sub-brand level of detail] on the marketing side, to create the right instructions as to what to make.

The system should support the ability to aggregate the detail to the right family level and then disaggregate the family information to the supporting detail. Hence, we might at the family level decide that the sales volume will increase from 100,000 units to 110,000 units. We then want to be able to increase all members of that family by 10%, without having to adjust each member of that family in turn.

Sometimes this also requires a "mindset change". I have come across the situation where the sales and marketing function is only interested in the brand "Lemonfresh". They do not understand how Operations makes the products, or even that the products even come from different factories.

They may not even be interested in volumes – they are just thinking sales revenue, profit, above-the-line expenditure, below-the-line expenditure, net profit, etc. The commercial side of the house does not understand the realities of the factory and operations. When the product is not delivered, they are quick to criticise the Operations side – even though the failure comes from the fact that they have not passed across the right information of what to make.

Companies need to address this "cultural issue" as part of the education of people through the company – which requires people to get away from just assuming that this level of detail is something about which "those Operational people" need to worry. Getting rid of the siloes involves mutual understanding of how others work.

I knew one CEO who dealt with this by saying that if two people from two different functions ever criticised each other, then he would swop over their jobs! It quickly silenced criticism.

So, we need a clear definition of the families and sub-families.

Companies build this structure around the fact that all products (SKUs) share some common characteristic, which typically is going to require the capacity of some type.

In turn, all of these will need to be turned into financial numbers to support financial decisions.

Figure 12 illustrates how a company should build its definition of families around the informational needs for all parts of the business – sales, marketing, development, operations and finance.

Thus 100,000 units of Lemonfresh as a brand cannot be the only family that the company uses for Integrated Business Planning. There will need to be a capability of looking at volumes in terms of fizzy and plain – which will be production "families".

Equally, if there is another brand called "Orangefresh", then these also may be sold as fizzy and plain. So, we need to group all fizzy and plain products – regardless of brand.

Figure 12: Definition of Families

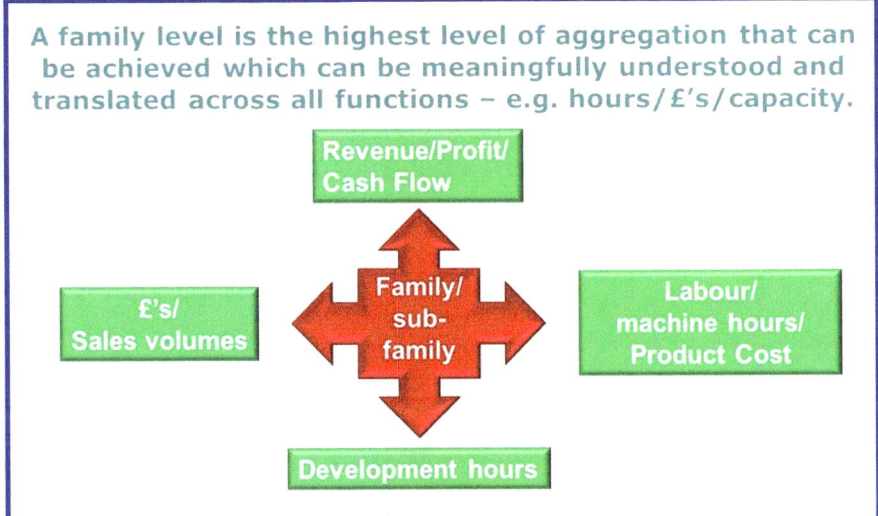

A family level is the highest level of aggregation that can be achieved which can be meaningfully understood and translated across all functions – e.g. hours/£'s/capacity.

- Revenue/Profit/Cash Flow
- £'s/Sales volumes
- Family/sub-family
- Labour/machine hours/Product Cost
- Development hours

Also, it could be the case that the company sells drinks products in a two-litre bottle category as well as a one-litre bottle category, which both happen to go down different lines. To know what capacity we want for one-litre products, then they will need to be able to group by bottle size – which may mean a further sub-family.

Capacity calculations drive the logic of how you establish families. The practical impact of this results in being able to correctly code each product so that you can aggregate and disaggregate correctly. For instance:

Table 4: Definition of families

		FAMILY GROUPING		
Product Code	Description	Brand	Product Type	Pack Type
123456	Lemonfresh 1L - Fizzy	LEM	Fizzy	1LT
123457	Lemonfresh 2L - Fizzy	LEM	Fizzy	2LT
123458	Lemonfresh 1L - Plain	LEM	Plain	1LT
123459	Lemonfresh 2L - Plain	LEM	Plain	2LT
123460	Orangefresh 1L - Fizzy	ORA	Fizzy	1LT
123461	Orangefresh 2L - Fizzy	ORA	Fizzy	2LT
123462	Orangefresh 1L - Plain	ORA	Plain	1LT
123463	Orangefresh 2L - Plain	ORA	Plain	2LT

Table 4 shows that a company can quickly end up with three dimensions for families (brand, product type and pack type). It will mean that there may need to be a conversion factor in place to convert products into "equivalent units". Thus, if you want to aggregate the volume into litres of liquid when the base unit is cases, then there will need to be a conversion factor in place to enable this.

Working out families is therefore not a trivial exercise. In case you think that somehow this issue is unique to drink type businesses, then just for information, ships can be commercial or defence, submarines can be nuclear, or diesel and nuclear submarines can belong to the Vanguard class or Astute class, and can be differentiated by missile type – Trident – and so on!

Indeed, companies can also often have very complicated naming conventions. In ICI we would have the original plant protection number, which was assigned when first discovered and which would then get a chemical name, which would then have a brand name – thus the same molecule would be called PP321, Cyhalothrin and Karate (and still is today!). Everything that had the name Karate would contain Cyhalothrin, but maybe not just that ingredient – it could be mixed. PP321 and Cyhalothrin were interchangeable.

It is also possible for the requirement for different family types to change over time. One client, which made kitchens, started by grouping together its production by base units. They added up the factory output into – for instance – 100,000 base units per annum. They designed the factory around making base units that went into the standard kitchen. When they looked at their capacity, then they realised they also made tall units, which used different amounts of labour to assemble compared with standard sized base units. It forced them to separate their families into standard base units and tall base units.

They started out assembling all kitchens by buying in all the doors. Then they decided that making some doors would improve quality, and save cost. So then they needed to split the families by those units which needed doors made in-house as opposed to those based on doors outsourced from a door manufacturer, to work out what capacity they needed for in-house door manufacture. Changing your manufacturing strategy can also impact how you structure your families.

The key to recognise is that we need a common agreed language and we need the ERP systems to enable us to be able to aggregate – or add up – from the base level (SKU) to the aggregate unit (family) to enable us to make operational capacity and financial decisions.

One of the small areas which this can affect is that if we want a horizon of 42 months for the IBP process, then we might need an SKU forecast going out the full horizon to enable us to be able to look at the different dimensions at any time – i.e. plain/fizzy or one litre/two litre and so on, to facilitate the aggregation and disaggregation of volumes needed to give the right capacity picture.

- **Where do you meet the customer?**

The last key bit of information that we need to put in place, which often causes a lot of debate, is the question of "Where do we meet the customer?" All businesses have choices on to how quickly they can respond to the customer. They have to be explicit on this to support the structure of IBP.

In today's supply chain landscape, we already have Amazon experimenting with delivery to consumers via drones, with a 30-minute delivery window with Amazon Prime. Wonderful for the consumer who does not want to get in the car, go to the local retail market, find the product in the shop, take it the counter to pay for it, and then go back home. Click on the screen, and it is with you at the same time it takes you to go shopping.

Similarly, when you go food shopping, you want to go to the shelf and get what you want there and then. The food manufacturer normally has a contract which specifies either day one for day one, day one for day two or day one for day three delivery – i.e. you get the order today and have to deliver it within three days. Equally, you can stay at home and get your food delivered at the click of a mouse.

But if you want to buy a BMW 7 series car, and walk into your local showroom, you will be able to specify lots of different options, but the salesperson will tell you that you will have to wait for 16 weeks before you can pick it up. Indeed, Morgan Cars have a typical lead time of six months – the waiting is part of the wanting!

A great illustration of this is the bicycle company which reduced the time between placing an order in its dealership and the manufacture of the product to 90 minutes. However, the lead time that it quoted to its consumers was two weeks. When someone challenged the CEO on this strategy, he said that they charged the consumer $2,000 per bike, and if they told the consumer that could have it in 90 minutes they would not think it was special and pay that price! It would become a commodity! The decision to be "make to order" is not necessarily anything to do with how long it takes to make the product.

Hence the decision of where to meet the customer is complex because it is a matter of managing customer expectations against the capability of the supply chain to deliver.

A company needs to tackle the balance between holding inventory and capacity vs instantaneous delivery, and the balance between being engineer or design to order vs delivery ex-stock. The following picture in Figure 13 shows the balance between the customer lead time (the time we allow customers between order placement and delivery) and the internal lead times for making and sourcing raw materials and capacity.

Thus, along the bottom, we can show the cumulative lead time – the total lead time it can take us from designing a product through to delivering the product to the customer, wherever they may be.

Up the steps, we go through the typical stages that a company will go through whether making bacon, cars or submarines to get to the final point of delivery.

Companies recognise that at some stage, we make a (general) commitment or contract with our customer on when they can place an order. At this point, we know what the customer wants.

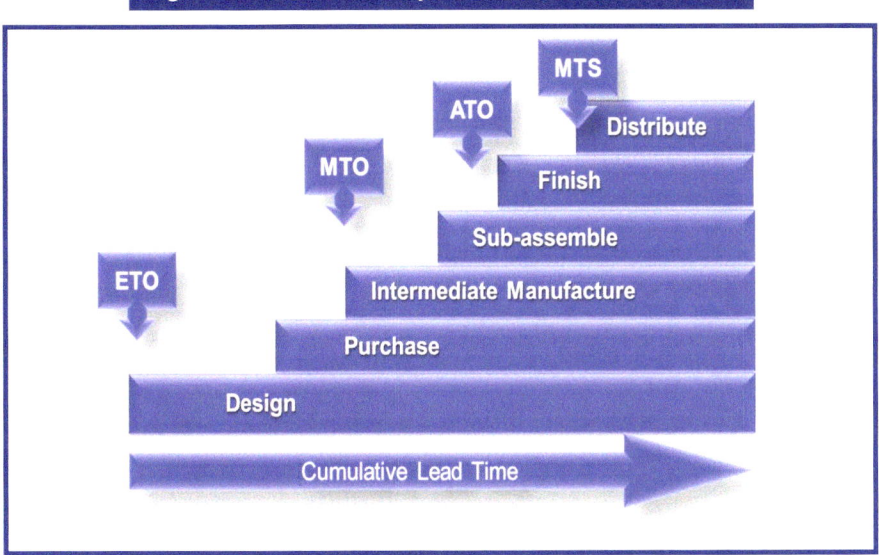

Figure 13: Where do you meet the customer?

Thus, we can tell customers generally that they can place orders four weeks from the date of receipt of order, and they can expect delivery four weeks later. In some cases, this might be one or two days from receipt of order. This "contract" will vary from company to company, and indeed market to market. This will depend on the expectations of customers, which will be conditioned by what competitors offer.

Companies within the Fast Moving Consumer Goods sector supplying supermarkets will find that customers expect delivery within one or two or three days. In the automotive components business, I have seen the time between receipt of a confirmed order and expected delivery to be as little as 20 minutes! It was a company that provided pressed steel parts to Nissan, and they were situated right next to the factory.

Setting these expectations for customers is key to the IBP process since if companies have cumulative lead times longer than the lead time that customers expect, the business will need to operate at risk. That means they will need to operate with a forecast of future requirements, and in turn, manage the risk.

We all know that forecasts will be wrong, and in turn could lead to too much inventory or too much spare capacity, driven by the forecast.

Hence a business needs to define for its products its supply chain strategy. This could be different for different products, markets or product groups. Thus, companies can offer a next-day lead time for domestic markets, but a four-week lead time for export markets. They can also offer next-day delivery for some fast-moving products, but offer a four-week lead time for rarely bought products.

I group these policies as follows, to provide clarity on where we meet the customer. The abbreviations relate to Figure 13.

MTS = Make to Stock. Here the commitment is that the customer can place an order today and get delivery today – the product has to be in stock. I have worked with lots of companies, from making radiator valves through to bacon, who operate on this basis – the type of product does not matter.

ATO = Assemble to Order. It means that the customer will place an order, and only after that point will the product get configured and made to the customer's requirements. A car is a good example of that, but then there are many different types of products which deploy this strategy. We need forecasts for items which are made or sourced in a time longer than the lead time quoted to the customer.

MTO = Make to Order. Here a product is only made once a company knows the precise requirements from the customer. Thus, special plates and cups and saucers with a specific design for the customer, or carpets and floorings with special designs that have the customer's name on them will qualify for being "Made to Order". We can forecast the total amount of clay we need to make plates, or wool to make the carpets, but we will not start the manufacturing process (execute the order and send it to the shop floor) until the signature is on the contract.

ETO = Engineer to Order. In this case, a product only starts its life when the customer signs on the dotted line for the design work to start. Hence a nuclear power station, submarine, satellite and similar are the types of product that generically fit into this category. They are usually very expensive, or bespoke to the customer – or both!

1. *Being clear about the manufacturing strategy is essential for three different reasons: The basic processes that support IBP vary for each type of strategy.*

2. *The way that companies manage the risk to the business from inventory and spare capacity vary for each strategy*

3. *The charts and diagrams and underlying calculations vary for each strategy.*

1. Basic Processes that support IBP

The question at the heart of IBP is: what are we going to produce in any given time period (month or week)? The forecast is an input to this, and these decisions will, in turn, drive our costs, cash flow and our profits.

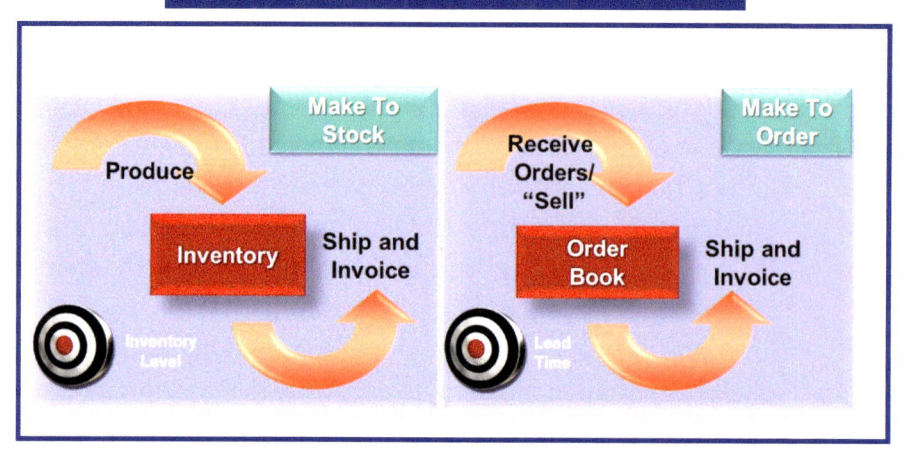

Figure 14: Make to Stock v Make to Order

On the left-hand side of Figure 14, we have Make to Stock. Production happens before order receipt, shipment and invoicing. The production goes into stock, and then sales are made from stock on the shelf – and if stock is not available then companies will register an order to follow or backorder or similar.

On the right-hand side we have Make to Order, which signals that we get the order from the customer, and then start production. In this case, orders get logged into an order book and when production of the order is complete, then and only then can the product get shipped. The customer order number and production order number are normally linked together.

In between these two strategies, Assemble to Order means that we could source and possibly assemble some of the components before receipt of the order, but we will not commit to final production of the customer's order until we have received the confirmed order. It means we will need to operate with a forecast for those items we need to put in place before the receipt of the customer order.

Definition of these processes also needs clarity about what "sell" means. There is often confusion in this area.

Sometimes I have seen companies define Sales as related to the point when a customer places the order. The salesman will say "I have made a sale" at this point.

Indeed, sometimes, companies incentivise salespeople on the volume and value of orders received.

Some define Sales as being made at the point at which the company delivers the product. That is the point at which they invoice the customer. This ties to the rules that companies have to follow around "revenue recognition."

Sometimes companies invoice the customer before they deliver the product (e.g. accept a deposit for a product).

In principle, there are three processes that occur when taking orders and delivering to the customer, which need to be clarified to get the picture right:

- Order acceptance and promising

- Delivering/shipping the order to the customer

- Invoicing the products to the customer (which is the point of revenue recognition).

Thus, the first step on receiving an order is to check availability of the product ordered and give the customer a promise on when the product ordered will be available. We should record the number and value of orders received so we can assess performance when we deliver them.

There are several issues here, which companies must address to ensure they get the right measure of performance.

Firstly, I have seen companies who are Make to Stock companies adopt a process in which they receive orders from customers, check if they have stock, and then only record the orders for which stock is available (crossing off the balance). This process is, of course, wrong, and leads to overstating the level of customer service, as it understates the actual orders received. We need to record all orders received to establish the total quantity received for when the customers required delivery. That is true demand.

Secondly, I have seen companies alter the date on which orders are due when there is a delay to the order. It overstates customer service delivery performance. Companies should measure delivery performance should against the first date given to the customer.

Finally, we should then deliver the product to the customer (either ex-stock or ex-production), at which point we can invoice the customer – which gives the financial sales revenue calculation.

2. Management of risk with inventory and spare capacity.

The next point is then to be clear about the activities that go on before order acceptance, and the risk that the business takes to anticipate customer requirements.

If you go to the (typically risk-averse) finance director, then they will want no inventory in place; thus they do not want to take risks by spending money on things that might go obsolete.

In principle, with a Make to Stock strategy, we make the product in its entirety before getting a customer order and it gets onto a shelf in the warehouse; from there, we pick it to send it to the customer. It is put on the shelf by part number, and we pick by part number.

However, as we have no orders for it before manufacture, we have to operate based on a forecast (which we will visit when we talk about forecasting in Chapter 6). We know one thing about forecasts – they are always going to be wrong. If only we could forecast the lottery or share prices; we could make a fortune! The issue is all about how we manage the risk.

Suppose we forecast 100 for a product three months from now (because our cumulative lead time is three months), and we buy the components for and make 100 items. Then if a customer or customers place orders three months from now for 101, we will run out of stock. Someone will be disappointed.

It would make sense for us to start with one extra – that is "safety stock".

Of course, it is not enough to look at just one month three months from now; it also depends on what happens between now and three months from now.

Let us look at the following example in Table 5 to help understand how safety stock would work. The question we need to answer is how much would we need to hold in stock at the beginning of the period to ensure we can ship what was demanded over the next three months, assuming we make just what is forecast?

Table 5: Calculation of amount needed for Safety Stock

	Month 1	Month 2	Month 3	Month 4	Month 5
Forecast	100	100	100	100	100
Make	100	100	100	100	100
Demand	120	120	120		
Shipped	120	120	120		
Cum Lead Time					

As we showed above, many companies do not record "true demand" (what customers order rather than what is shipped). But in this case, I define "demand" as what is ordered by customers.

The answer to the question is that we would need 60 units in stock at the beginning of the period to enable us to meet the demand of 120 per month – given that we make in line with the forecast. If we did not have this, we would only be able to ship 100 per month – potentially losing sales of 20 units per month. I call this "safety stock". One of the critical questions to ask is how much safety stock we should hold, and what is the optimum?

It leads us to the area of how to measure and manage safety stock, which is a critical decision.

I define forecast accuracy as the difference between actual demand and forecast demand. In this example, it is 20% each month – or 20 units.

With a lead time of three months, then we can see that the inventory buffer we should have is mathematically equal to (forecast accuracy x lead time).

The observation begins to answer the question of what our target inventory should be. Sadly, it is not as simple as that!

In the example, I used the illustration that forecast accuracy is always 20 per month, but in reality, it is not going to be like that. If only!

We need initially to understand what is the average level of accuracy we might expect. To get this, we need to look at the recorded accuracy for the product over the last 12 to 36 months.

Assuming that information is available, then we need to make another important assumption: that the forecast error is part of a statistically <u>normal</u> distribution. Thus 50% of the possible outcomes are above average, and 50% are below. Hence there is no institutional bias in the forecasting process.

What does this mean? Here, we need to understand something about statistics, and I am going to use a standard illustration of people's heights.

The average height of a man in the UK according to the Office of National Statistics in 2010 was 5ft 9 inches, or 175.3cm. The average height of a woman was 5ft 3ins, or 161.6cm. This average height defines the mid-point of the range of heights of all people in the UK – you would expect 50% of all people to be below that height, and 50% of people to be above that height.

We can also get information on the standard deviation of those heights, which is the "average error", which is 6.35cm for men.

Figure 15 illustrates the distribution of heights.

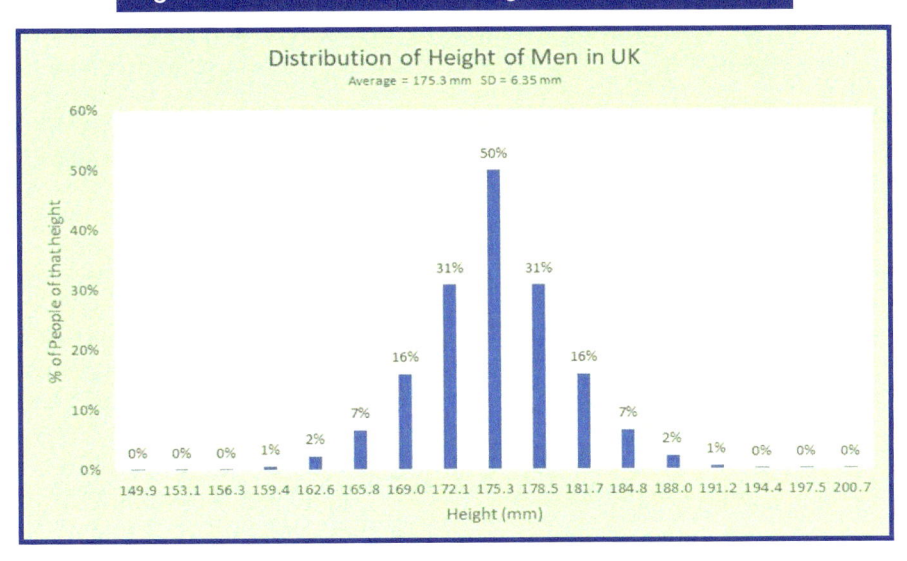

Figure 15: Distribution of height of men in the UK

Distribution of Height of Men in UK
Average = 175.3 mm SD = 6.35 mm

Height (mm)	%
149.9	0%
153.1	0%
156.3	0%
159.4	1%
162.6	2%
165.8	7%
169.0	16%
172.1	31%
175.3	50%
178.5	31%
181.7	16%
184.8	7%
188.0	2%
191.2	1%
194.4	0%
197.5	0%
200.7	0%

Y-axis: % of People of that height

Statisticians call this a normal distribution because the graph shows a standard bell-shaped curve, which we expect in a statistical sample or population. It also says that values further away from the average are less likely in terms of probability.

This figure shows the proportion of people you expect, up to and including that height on the left. Thus if you met someone who was 169cm tall, you would know that 16% of people were that height or less. If you met someone 175cm tall you would know that 50% of people were that height or less.

If you met someone who was 188cm tall, you would know they were taller than average, and that 2% are above that height. (To the right of the average the per cent means greater than that height.)

We can apply a similar concept in the world of demand planning, where we forecast, and where we can calculate a similar average error.

The risk or balance, which we need to judge, is between running out of stock against having too much stock. Let us use the example of a product which has an average demand of 100 and an average error (standard deviation) of 20. The question we need to address is that if we were to plan to manufacture based on the forecast (100), what would be the probability that the actual demand was 120, 130,140, and so on, such that we would be out of stock by 20,30,40 in the time before we could get some more? The impact of being out of stock by 20,30 or 40 will depend on whether customers cancel the order and we lose the business, or they have to wait for it, which may cause an inconvenience to the customers and for which we pay in the long term.

The graph for monthly demand is illustrated in Figure 16.

This graph shows the situation where the expected demand is 100 per month – and we would expect that 50% of the time the demand is more than that, and 50% of the time the demand will be less than that.

From this graph, we can see that 98% of the time, the demand will 140 units or less. The implication is that, given our forecast was 100 units, if we held safety stock of 40 units, then we would be in stock 98% of the time.

We can calculate from statistical tables the number needed to have a service level of 85%, 95%, or 99% (or any number) to work out the level of safety stock we need to hold. You calculate it with reference to the average error (standard deviation) related to the forecast. The figure 40 happens to be two standard deviations.

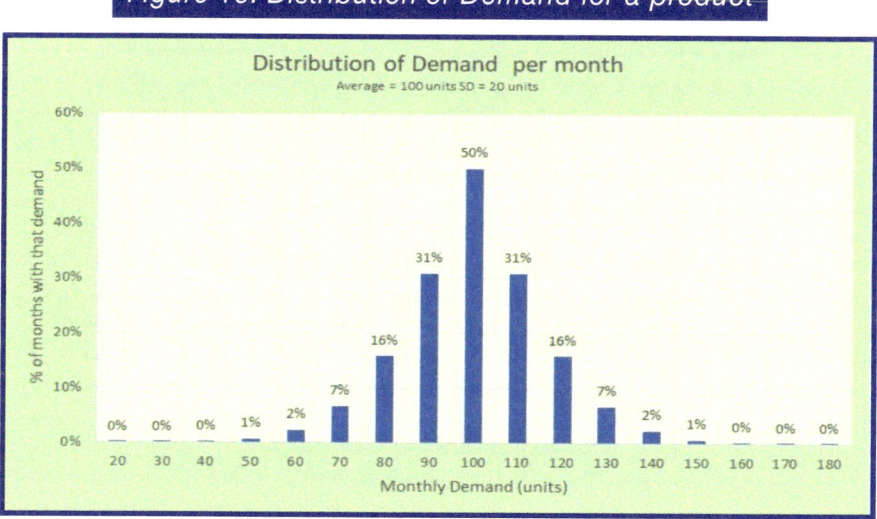

Figure 16: Distribution of Demand for a product

The statistical table will look something like the following, which will give us a factor (the number of standard deviations) that corresponds to the level of service we want to hold.

Table 6: Customer Service Factor Table

Factor	Level
1.00	84.13%
1.50	93.32%
2.00	97.72%
2.50	99.38%
3.00	99.87%
3.50	99.98%

You can read this in the following way: if you want to achieve 97.72% (approximately 98%) service level, then you multiply the average error – or to use its technical term "standard deviation" – by a factor of 2.00 as safety stock. So if the error is 20, then you will achieve 97.72% service level by setting a safety stock level of 40.

Notice from this table, therefore, that to go from 98% to 99.87%, the factor goes from two to three – this means you need to increase your inventory holding by 50% to get a small increase in service!

To optimise the level of inventory, you need to balance the cost of holding the inventory against the loss of revenue and profit by not holding it. Let us say the cost of the units in the example was £20 each. The cost of the inventory for 40 units would be £800. Let us say the cost would be 10% of that to warehouse it, and so on. The cost is £80 per annum.

If the profit per unit was £20, then the annual expected profit is £24,000. Two per cent of this is £480, and so it makes economic sense to invest in the safety stock. This example is a simple calculation to illustrate the principle. You need to take into account other issues around the likelihood of the stock becoming obsolete, frequency of replenishment, and so on.

Impact of Lead Time

In the above, we have just taken into account demand over one month. We also have just considered a lead time of months.

However, some companies deal in demand over days or weeks, and lead times could be in days or weeks. The same calculation applies – only we need to remember that we are either always working in weeks or months.

But if the lead time was three months (as in the case above at Table 5), then the calculation has to change because we will have to take into account the forecast error that might happen over the three months of the lead time – assuming that we cannot order any more in the three months. The lead time is a genuine fixed period.

We further need to take into account the fact that it is unlikely that each month the demand (as in Table 5) will be 20 above every month. If it were, then it is likely that the forecast is biased. The demand should be up one month and down the next two months, and so on. Instead of multiplying the error calculation by three months, we allow for this statistically by using the square root of the lead time. So the calculation becomes:

Equation 1

SS = Service Factor x Forecast Accuracy x sqrt (Lead Time).

Supply-side uncertainty

Also, lead times from suppliers can be variable, and we need to take account of this separately.

Similarly, we can work out the standard deviation of the lead time and adjust safety stocks accordingly for raw materials.

Application of science

The key message is that with a bit of "appliance of science," we can right-size our inventory and set proper targets. There is more complexity under the surface here. We need to take into account batch sizes, and hence frequency of purchase, the frequency with which we review our plans – all of which you can discover in a detailed book on Inventory Management, like Operations Management (Slack, Chambers, & Johnston, 2004).

The point behind all these statistics (and that is enough for now!) is that we <u>can</u> work out how much stock we should hold, and that we ought to make decisions on this – which then becomes a stock target against which we can monitor our performance.

I have often heard managers in companies make comments on stock which range from "we have too much stock" to "we just hold a standard seven weeks", and then when you ask why, I have found there is no appliance of science at all.

I appreciate all these calculations probably leave some people cold, as they left maths and statistics behind at school.

However, that should not stop companies from employing people who have a full understanding of this area and get them to apply the concepts. It also makes sense to employ software that enables these calculations, often available in forecasting packages.

Panel 2 illustrates a practical case of how one company saved money in this area and further, why the senior leadership team should understand these concepts, and how to manage the supply chain better. This company "right-sized" its stock levels through their Integrated Business Planning process, and as a result, saved a great deal of money.

Panel 2: Deciding Targets

One client found that it had around £40m in inventory. They made a range of products for the domestic and industrial heating and water markets, which included taps, valves and copper fittings.

The IBP team did an analysis of their inventory profile, classifying products as to whether they were Runners, Repeaters, Strangers and Aliens – how often they were bought. We also looked at how valuable they were within the total sales range (ABCD analysis, looking for which were the 20% of products which accounted for 80% of the sales, which were classified as "A-class" items, and so on).

This showed that around 30% of the inventory were D-class "aliens" – those products that were sold around once per year and contributed little to overall sales!

At a senior leadership team meeting I asked Commercial what level of service they wanted for all their products, and the commercial director was insistent on 99% for everything.

But the IBP project team went back to the board and demonstrated that a strategy of 98% for A and B class ("runners and repeaters") and 95% for all else, except for 80% for D class "strangers and aliens" would save £ 5m (around £ 0.5m per annum in stockholding costs). As it had little impact on sales, the CEO quickly made a decision to agree with the team.

A good reason to make the CEO responsible for inventory!

It required active involvement from the board in setting targets, and a compromise between the functions within the company – Sales and Marketing wanting 99% service levels, Finance wanting as little impact on cash flow as possible, and Operations wanting to make sure they had the right amount of stability.
The IBP process was crucial for facilitating discussion and decision making. It was also vital that all understood the concepts behind Inventory Management, to be able to participate in the process.
This illustrates the fundamental behind setting optimum stock targets in a Make-to-Stock environment.

Make to Order – capacity flexibility

With a Make to Order strategy, then the variable that we need to control is lead time. We do not want to hold stock at all, because it is too risky.

In this case, if we accept orders then typically we will make the customer wait a given amount of time. If we take too many orders, then customers will have to wait longer and our ability to be able to respond to un-forecast demand will be managed by having spare capacity.

The following table illustrates the key elements of Make to Order, and the relationship between lead time to customers and capacity.

Table 7: Illustration of Make to Order mechanics/maths

	Month 0	Month 1	Month 2	Month 3	Month 4	Month 5
Orders received		125	125	125		
Capacity		100	100	100	100	100
Production/Shipments		100	100	100		
Order Book	100	125	150	175		
Lead Time (weeks)	4	5	6	7		
CLT						

The table shows that if orders come in at the rate of 125 per month, where the business has a limited capacity of 100 per month, then the customer lead time (the time that the customer has to wait) will rise from four weeks to seven weeks over the three months, as the capacity available constrains output (production/shipments).

Sometimes I have heard people say that if you are "Make to Order", you do not need to forecast. This is not true. This example shows that this business would need to increase capacity to reduce lead times, and would need to forecast that need for extra capacity – i.e. that the orders will still come in at the rate of 125 per month.

But the key to this is that we should build the forecast around the capacity required – and we need to build our flexibility based on the amount of spare capacity which we require.

We can apply a similar approach to the calculation of safety stock above with respect to the calculation of the amount of spare capacity we need to have to manage variation in demand, and our ability to respond. The calculation will be based on the number of additional hours required to meet the error in forecast of demand.

Do we need to be Make-to-Stock?

Of course, the debate of whether companies want to be Make to Order or Make to Stock should also encourage us to understand how modern digital manufacture, which allows flexible manufacture and quick response in the pursuit of mass customisation, can support making any product any day, and cheaply. Printers used to make books in large batches because of the economics of manufacture. Now the chances are that you will be reading *this* book, which the printer printed on demand.

The pursuit of large-batch manufacture in Europe or the Far East only forces a risky approach to managing inventory that in turn forces increased transportation costs that are based on potentially illusory prospects of lower cost manufacture. Read the experience of a company called Lever Style, which is revolutionising clothes manufacture through small batch sizes and flexibility of supply (https://leverstyle.com/).

The impact of how all this works in practice, in terms of the reports that are required, etc. are excellently covered in Chris Gray's book Sales and Operations Planning – Standard System (Gray, 2007).

3. Charts and Data

To support the IBP process, you need charts and data based on a common schematic.

The schematic for **Make-to-Stock** is shown in Figure 17. It reflects on one page the need for previous and current forecasts, previous and current supply plans, and previous and current inventory plans – which we can use to compare against inventory targets.

Figure 17: Basic data table for volumes – Make to Stock

Family : Fizzy Drinks **Units :** '000s
Family Type : Make To Stock **Target Stock : 3 weeks**

Months	Oc	No	De	Months	Ja	Fe	Ma	Ap	Ma	Ju	Ju	Au	Se	O-D	J-M
Demand Plan	120	120	120	Last Demand Plan	120	120	120	120	120	120	120	120	120	360	360
Actual Demand	119	125	132	New Demand Plan											
Difference	-1	5	12	Difference											
Cum Diff	-1	4	16	Cum Diff											
Accuracy %	-1	+4	+10												
Supply Plan	125	125	125	Last Supply Plan	125	125	120	120	120	120	120	120	120	360	360
Actual Supply	119	118	121	New Supply Plan											
Difference	-6	-7	-4	Difference											
Cum Diff	-6	-13	-17	Cum Diff											
% Achieved	-4.8	-5.6	-3.2												
Stock Plan	71	76	81	Last Stock Plan	86	91	91	91	91	91	91	91	91	91	91
Actual Stock 66	66	59	48	New Stock Plan											
Difference	-5	-17	-33	Difference											
Stock cover - wks	2.1	1.8	1.6	Stock cover - wks											

Details of MTS Format

There should be history (not restricted to three months) comparing demand, supply and inventory, plus a comparison between this month's and last month's Demand, Supply and Inventory plans going out into the future for the required horizon.

As required, the reporting system should enable the user to add this up into monthly and quarterly and annual financial buckets. The basic building block should be the daily and weekly "Master Schedule" contained in the ERP system. It should be a direct extract. This shows a relatively simple format. But there should also be the ability/space to show different scenarios – upper-demand plan, lower-demand plan, depending on the possible outcomes.

There should also be the ability to see different supply outcomes depending on different supply plans – overtime/extra shift, etc.

The user should be able to see the impact on inventory levels of each plan – and indeed a combination of plans, such as a high-demand plan with a low-supply plan. The real advantage of the whole IBP process comes from looking at possible outcomes (what-ifs), and then making the right decisions for the business.

This table shows the basic numbers in a table; it is always going to be better to see the overall picture in a series of graphs as this is probably the way that most people can best see the outcome.

Of course, you also need a process for coming up with the numbers and scenarios – which we will look at later!

Details of MTO format

The principles concerning Make-to-Order are very similar. This is illustrated in Figure 18.

Figure 18: Basic data table for volumes – Make to Order

Family : Valves **Units : '000s**
Family Type : Make – To- Order **Target Lead Time : 3 weeks**

Months	Oc	No	De	Months	Ja	Fe	Ma	Ap	Ma	Ju	Ju	Au	Se	O-D	J-M
Demand Plan	70	70	70	Last Demand Plan	70	70	70	70	70	70	70	70	70	210	210
Actual Demand	71	75	80	New Demand Plan											
Difference	+1	+5	+10	Difference											
Cum Diff	+1	+6	+16	Cum Diff											
% Accuracy	1	7	23												
Supply Plan	75	75	75	Last Supply Plan	75	75	70	70	70	70	70	70	70	210	210
Actual Supply	60	62	67	New Supply Plan											
Difference	-15	-13	-8	Difference											
Cum Diff	-15	-28	-36	Cum Diff											
% Achieved	80	83	89												
Order Book Plan	61	56	51	Last Plan	46	41	41	41	41	41	41	41	41	41	41
Act Ord Book 66	77	90	103	New Plan											
Difference	-16	-34	-52	Difference											
Actual Lead Time	4	4.8	5.5												

We need a demand plan for the product group. It should be the expected orders by customer required date, out to the required horizon.

The history needs to be a comparison between the previous forecast demand, and actual demand based on orders received by customer request date.

The assumption behind the standard logic for Make-to-Order is that production or output is going to determine when you ship the product to the customer, which will be constrained by the capacity available.

This, in turn, drives your expected revenue or sales.

Here is the fundamental difference between Make-to-Order and Make-to-Stock. With Make-to-Stock, the Demand plan is the basis for calculating the revenue – we ship and invoice the customer the moment we get the order and ship it. It is relatively instantaneous. Hence, we can base this on the forecast sales. Production is disconnected from the actual shipment (until you run out!).

With a Make-to-Order environment, you have to calculate the revenue from the Production plan.

Thus, when you add up the revenue (and profit) for Make to Order products with Make to Stock products, you need to be careful that you take the production output for the MTO items and add that to the Demand plan for MTS items.

The last section with the Make-to-Order format looks at the "order book". The assumption is that as we take orders in, so they get logged into an order book. Then in due course, these orders get shipped and leave the order book.

Hence, the order book becomes a measure of how long customers have to wait. Many Make-to-Order companies feel that the larger the order book, the better; there is a sense of security. However, the danger is that the order book becomes so big that customers have to wait too long and will go to competitors who can offer a shorter lead time. So, the IBP challenge is to determine a target lead time that customers will accept, and work to maintain that.

In a Make-to-Order environment, the objective is to adjust capacity and the Production plan to bring the lead time in line with your target competitive lead time.

From a reporting point of view, these figures should also be capable of being turned simultaneously into a view of revenue, product cost and gross margin.

Hence, at a detailed level, it is clear why a business needs to have a single database, configured correctly to provide the users with the information they need to make the right decisions.

It is also essential that the people do not bias the numbers because of the behaviours illustrated earlier – e.g. sandbagging to make the numbers look good, and so on.

The Mixture of Make-To-Order and Make-to-Stock

It is possible that one product group can have a mixture of Make-to-Stock products and Make-to-Order products within the same family. In this case, you will need to have sub-sets of products, grouped by whether they are Make to Order or Make to Stock. That means there is a need to be able to separate these products by a code e.g. "O" = Make-to-Order, and "S" = Make-to-Stock, so you can add them up separately and view them separately. You could use "A" for Assemble-to-Order.

So, these are the basics of the set-up for the data for IBP.

- ## Create a New Plan Each Month

Each month, the executive leadership team should sign off a new plan which relates to the months beyond the cumulative lead time, which is then in effect handed over for execution by the management of the business – following a bottom-up review by the managers of the business.

Thus, suppose we have a horizon of 30 months. Let us suppose that the cumulative lead time is three months. In effect, then, each month we are signing off month four in the horizon, which will then become month three, and we expect that in months one to three we will now get parts purchased, made and shipped to customers. This does not mean that we will ignore changes that are required in months one to three, far from it. Change happens.

The hope is that the IBP process will minimise the changes in the short term. This is the essence of a rolling Business Plan that underpins the IBP philosophy.

Most companies also exist in an environment where they operate with financial years – because they report to shareholders and tax authorities in financial years.

Where a company operates in an environment where they use financial years, the business should review by family the current plan and its delta or difference from the previous plan in financial year buckets – which in the current year will have a mixture of year-to-date and forecasts.

I would also make a plea at this stage for making the information easy to read. Graphs are good!

Many people who produce charts and tables appear to take a positive delight in showing as many numbers before and after a decimal point as they can. A key mantra of the process is "roughly right, rather than precisely wrong". I learnt this from Andrew Ehrenburg, who produced a book called Data Reduction (Ehrenburg, 1975), which emphasises that data should be easy for readers to absorb. It is a great book and a great principle. Human interface engineering is a topic all in its own; too many people are excessively detail-obsessive!

The following is a suggested format that should be followed (for a 30-month horizon plan).

Family: XYZ
Plan Date: February 2020

Table 8: Summary Table for Integrated Business Planning (Finance)

	2020			2021		2022	
	Current Plan	Δ from Last Plan	Δ from Budget	Current Plan	Δ from Last Plan	Current Plan	Δ from Last Plan
Volume (Units)	20.0	- 0.5	0.3	22.0	0.5	24.0	0.2
Sales (£ m.)	40.0	- 1.0	0.6	44.0	1.0	48.0	- 2.0
Cost (£ m.)	20.0	- 0.5	0.3	22.0	0.5	24.0	1.0
Margin (£ m.)	20.0	- 0.5	0.3	22.0	0.5	24.0	- 1.0

The symbol Δ means "delta" or "difference from". This shows the difference from the last plan and budget for this year, and difference from the previous plan for the next two years.

- **Decision-Making Process**

The key to IBP is incrementalism. The senior leadership team requires <u>information</u>, and not data, with which to make the decisions they need to make. They need to understand what has changed and not all the numbers that can be published by anyone. They particularly need to know where these changes affect longer-term strategy.

Thus, in the process, we should be addressing:
- What has changed since last month?
- Is the change significant for the long term and strategy?
- What is the impact of the change(s)?
- What are the options around what we can do to deal with that change?
- What decision will we take?

To make those decisions – and the emphasis is on *decisions* – then we need to establish meetings which enable us to get the right people together.

Most companies and executives suffer from the weight of too many meetings. I have heard so many times people say, "We must discuss this. When are you next free?", "Let me have a look in my diary.", "Sorry, I can't see you for another ten days." There are many courses on making meetings more effective. These courses are great. But there can be a more fundamental issue: the company has not thought through the overall structure of meetings in the business. You can have more efficient meetings – but still just too many.

It almost goes without saying that for a meeting to be successful, it must have the following:
- A chairperson
- The right attendees for the meeting, who understand and can make decisions
- A clear agenda
- Information properly prepared to support the discussion
- Minutes and actions for the meeting
- A log of decisions, and who will complete by when.
- An organiser
- A timekeeper.

A kernel of the SOP/IBP process is to recognise that there needs to be a way in which the right people can get around the table to make the decisions required; but it is it not just about meetings. It is about how you structure those meetings to be able to make decisions based on one set of numbers.

It is essential that any company developing IBP looks at all the meetings that people regularly attend (and extend that to other meetings which happen ad hoc). They then need to understand what the IBP process requires and create an integrated approach as to how the business communicates up and down through the business to adjust and align business plans. This then needs to be linked to all other meetings in a formal way, which will create the right regular set of meetings, which will then enable the right people to be at each meeting to support the proper functioning of the business.

I want to focus now on the typical framework that I have worked with over the years, which forms the core of a structured IBP process. It represents a weekly cycle of meetings – or "process steps" – which will occur every month, as illustrated in Figure 19.

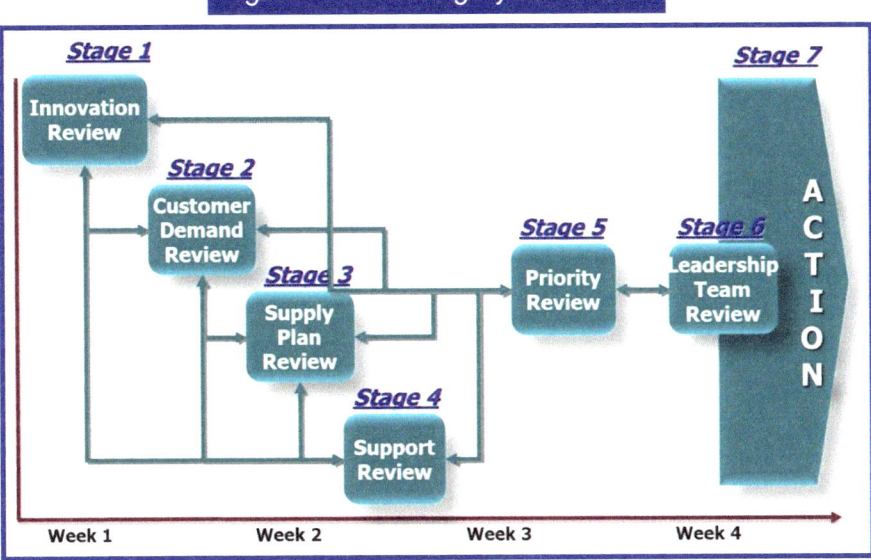

Figure 19: Meeting cycle for IBP

Stage 1 – Innovation Review (Week 1)
Stage 2 – Customer Demand Review (Week 2)
Stage 3 – Supply Plan Review (Week 2)
Stage 4 – Support Review (Week 3)
Stage 5 – Priority Review (Week 3)
Stage 6 – Leadership Team Review (Week 4)
Stage 7 – ACTION

Figure 19 illustrates the idea that in the first week of the month there will be a review of innovation (new product introduction and development). Then there will be a review of demand. That then enables a calculation of the supply plan, which then, in turn, feeds the financial plans, together with the HR and IT plans in the support step.

The Priority step is where we establish what decisions need to be taken forward to the senior leadership team meeting, and the last step in the process is to hold a senior leadership team meeting, at which the CEO or general manager facilitates the decisions required. This diagram also shows that the various business processes (innovation, demand, supply, etc.) are linked, and the arrows are illustrative of where the links go. It also shows some "feedback" loops – thus we might need to go back to the Supply plan when we find that demand exceeds supply, and we need to change the Supply plan (or Demand plan) to manage priorities.

I have run workshops several times which have simulated how companies make decisions and then shown how this process works to improve the way they make decisions. Nine times out of ten, the above model works well, and companies have accepted this model. Sometimes there are tweaks which people make – like the integration of the Demand plan and the Innovation plan. Thus, in one company the same people would turn up to both, the changes in demand were closely related to new products that were being ordered by customers, and it was logical to combine the two and save a meeting. One size does not fit all! It is simply a good starting framework.

This is, indeed, very similar to the models shown previously from Tom Wallace and Oliver Wight. However, there is a key difference in that it specifies a "Support Review".

This can be one step, which covers finance, human resources and business systems – particularly where one director manages all of these areas. Equally, this could be several meetings.

The basic concept is that in business, the senior leadership team meets once a month. That board meeting should be a decision-making meeting. The directors who attend that meeting should, therefore, chair the previous steps of the process, which prepares them to take the decisions at the senior leadership team meeting; hence the company should align the meeting structure with the organisational structure.

This structure is not absolute and sacrosanct, either, for each stage of the process. I have worked with many companies, and each has its organisation and structure. Some have been very small, and some have been very big.

For instance, I have seen companies which have several business units managing clear market sectors – big customers/little customers, animal/human, in-home/away from home, and so on. In these cases, there is a need for multiple Demand Review meetings.

On the Supply side, I worked with clients who have multiple factories in a country. Each factory needs to have a process for Demand and Supply planning, and potentially feeding into a central Supply Planning meeting to review total capacity and key issues by factory. Strategic decisions on where to site factories will require a more central approach, where companies have a choice as to where they can site capacity.

The other key difference is the box "priority review", which precedes the senior leadership team. This stage emphasises the point that many people need to resolve the priorities on which the business should focus, which require decisions from the senior leadership team and which require decision through delegation to the management team.

This is similar to the "integration and reconciliation" step of the Oliver Wight process. This, in turn, leads to an organisational issue of who should help facilitate this prioritisation step.

Each step of the process needs a facilitator – or captain – of that step (typically the manager of that step). Thus, there should be an innovation manager, demand manager, planning manager, financial controller, and so on.

The priority step of the process, then, should be a forum in which those "captains" can get together to sift out the key issues and make recommendations to the board on the options that need to form part of the decisions.

With one client, I developed an "STP" form to support this, which is illustrated in Figure 20.

Figure 20: STP Format

Situation: There is insufficient capacity to meet requirements in Jun-Dec 2019	Target To build temporary capacity from Jun-Dec 2019 in the xyz factory
Proposal Run a third shift from Jun-Dec 2019	
Risks Business may not materialise as expected	**Mitigation Actions required** Only confirm recruitment in May 2019 IBP cycle
Benefits	**Costs**
Decision made :	Date : _/_/_

They used this form to clarify the current issue – **S**ituation; then they described where they would like to get to – **T**arget; then they described the **P**roposal. It also summarised the risks associated with the decision, and then the cost-benefit analysis – with space to record what the decision was. (It is amazing how many times people forget this!)

They used this format as an input into each meeting, and in particular into the main senior leadership team meeting to focus the meeting on the decisions that are required. It is a great help in avoiding endless discussion and debate! Panel 3 describes a real-world example of how the Senior Leadership should be the forum for agreeing the single plan.

Thus, the eventual outcome of the leadership team review should be the decisions and actions required. It ought to go without saying that once the team takes a decision, then everyone should stick by those decisions.

But it is in the way of the "politics" in some companies that this does not happen! In one client, they had the meeting at which they decided that they needed to recruit another ten people to support the forecast growth. But the manufacturing director did not trust the forecasts and hence did not recruit the required people. Not surprisingly, they soon ran out of capacity. It's a team-based decision.

Equally, the meeting does not necessarily operate as a simple rubber-stamp. It can be a robust discussion on key issues. The difference in a good IBP process is the quality of the preparation for the meeting(s). It should bring forward the right topics for discussion, the right scenarios and hence facilitate the right debate.

I once went to a meeting and the CEO, in their frustration, said: "That was a wonderful discussion, but completely uncluttered by facts." IBP eliminated that. Panel 9 shows how vital it is to come to an agreed conclusion.

This, then, is the basic underlying structure.

- **Multi - Site Model**

The above model of meetings works very well for a single company with a single site. In my experience in the 1990s in ICI Agrochemicals, we had 35 different business units, which operated with inventory, and we sold to 100 other countries directly through distributors and a variety of arrangements.

We had many factories in-country and some large-scale factories in the UK and USA.

At the time, we created a model which I have seen adopted many times to integrate all these different demand and supply points. The models for different businesses tend to coalesce around industry types.

Panel 3 shows how it is important to come to an agreed conclusion

Panel 3: Decisions…

One client who is in the Defence and Technology industry during the period of the Afghanistan and Iraq war saw a considerable increase in business – taking them from a budget at the beginning of the year of around £60m to £100m.

They went through their IBP process and recognised that they needed to recruit a lot more people to support the growth.

They were part of a global organisation, and had to report to their divisional head what was their year-end Business Plan expectation – as usual.

The finance director wanted to "declare" £60m sales for the financial year. But of course, they also had to justify the recruitment to the divisional director, which was only justified by the figures relating to £100m.

Needless to say, there was a fairly robust discussion around coming to one set of numbers! Eventually all came to the £ 100m number.

Of course, one of the underlying issues was that they had not got the upward communication culture right! Too many companies fail to get everyone in the company to recognise that the IBP process allows changes to occur, and that everyone needs to work to the best set of numbers at the relevant time.

Fear of telling the truth, whichever way it goes, has to be eliminated.

Pharmaceutical companies tend to have several large-scale R&D sites, manufacturing sites and then several selling sites. Chemical companies are similar. Engineering companies tend to have very large central factories, with multiple demand points. Many companies have regional structures – based around groupings like Asia and Pacific, East Europe, Middle East and Africa, and so on.

The tendency is for companies to have a factory in Europe, a factory in China or the Far East somewhere, and then another in the Americas. The strategy of supply chain cost, economies of scale and service should underpin the structure of the supply chain from source to consumer. The economics of manufacture has normally driven centralisation of production.

Companies need to take real care to understand the value of being close to the customer vs the optimisation of cost. Optimisation of cost can force centralisation of manufacture far from the customer because they base unit costs on a false allocation of overheads. These companies also do not have mechanisms for recording how much business they (potentially) lose because they run out of stock, simply because they have long lead times to replenish products. For this reason, companies need to understand and record the value of lost sales and make a logical assessment of these losses compared with the artificial savings made from the centralisation of manufacturing.

The need for mass-customisation challenges the "old paradigm" of large-scale manufacture in large factories in the Far East, and in the future there will probably be smaller factories closer to customers/consumers, which focus on responsiveness and availability, rather than just simple £/unit cost. This requires a clear Manufacturing Strategy – developed through the detail of the Planning Process.

Because of this globalisation, then typically customers are located in several countries, with the selling and marketing activity localised because of language, taste and governmental differences that relate to regulatory control of chemical/electronics/pharmaceuticals, etc.

Where this applies, then the systems, process and people model need to be developed to cover the operating structure of the company. Thus, where there are local business units, they become responsible for sales and marketing, and managing the local requirements for their geographical unit.

The supply chain management organisation needs to get the product from the supply points to the business units. Responsibility for customer service, forecast accuracy and inventory need to be carefully defined and aligned with the geographical structure.

Broadly, local business units should be responsible for local inventory and forecast accuracy and bias, and the supply chain organisation responsible for delivery on time and in full to the local units and customers.

The model of Innovation, Demand, Supply, Support, Prioritisation and Senior Team review remains at the core of the process. This structure then needs to be expanded to be modelled across the geographic structure of the business. One size does not fit all.

Figure 21 illustrates an actual example drawn up for one client which had multiple markets (managed through global business units) and multiple factories, supported by global and local innovation.

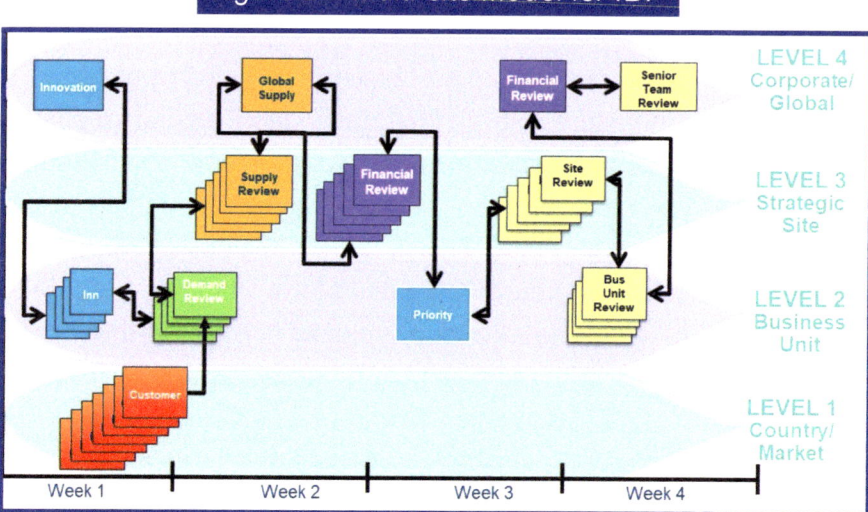

Figure 21: Multi-site model for IBP

Typically, this model of multiple sites/multiple market model over three or four layers – local/regional/global or local/business unit/regional/global. Each company needs to recognise the layers through which it operates, and the responsibilities within each layer. To work out the appropriate structure for your company, you need to trace through the activities that occur at the different levels of the organisation.

It is important to get this model right up front. I worked with one major international FMCG company across Europe. At first, they discovered SOP at their business unit level. Thus, each country across Europe had a business unit, and they introduced the standard model of product/demand/supply/integration/senior team review within each business unit. But as they rolled the process out across something like 25 different business units, they found that they had a central supply chain organisation which had regional control of each of their product groups.

In some large countries, they had complete control of the supply chain; but even those sourced some of their product from other countries. When they got to some of the medium-size business units, they found that these shared the capacity of common factories. Thus, a factory in Spain would supply, France, Germany and Italy. When these factories ran short of capacity, they had two problems. The first was that the central supply chain used the numbers that were provided by the annual budget process; they did not use the numbers produced through the brand new monthly SOP process running in the business units. They had not developed the "above-country" process to enable that kind of analysis.

Secondly, they did not have a formal Demand Management or Rationing process to manage the shortage of capacity. It very quickly became fraught. It is essential to work out the overall Process Structure first, and then implement IBP around this multi-level structure.

Coming up with this structure requires some really important decisions around global integration – which can lead to many hours of interesting discussion

1. There needs to be common ways of working across all business units and manufacturing sites so that when you are adding up the numbers, you are not adding up apples and pears.

2. There needs to be common definitions of how each site calculates capacity (it is amazing how these can differ!).

3. You need a common definition of what "truth" means across all markets when it comes to the provision of forecasts. You cannot have one market over-forecast because it wants to make sure it gets the product, and others working on what they need. Visibility through the whole supply chain becomes important to support this. Thus, I worked with a pharmaceutical company where they had real success with a cancer drug. Demand shot ahead at the rate of around a 10% increase each month. Meanwhile, the factory had problems meeting demand – it was a challenging product to make. As a result, all the markets regularly tried to overstate their demand for the factory. The head of supply chain regularly reviewed the in-market forecasts for the product to determine what was genuinely needed – and made sure that no patient missed out on the product.

4. Sometimes companies have to manage demand (i.e. cap the amount they supply within a constraint). There needs to be a clear process in place to manage demand, which is related to the forecasts that were made at the cumulative lead time (if you don't, then there will be no encouragement to forecast). There is often a need to change the culture and communication process in some businesses. The number of times I have heard people say, "but in our company, if we run short of product then the GM of XYZ country – usually one of the biggest or most profitable countries – just gets on the phone to the VP of production and demands they get their requirements, even if they never forecast them." Integrated Business Planning is not going to work in this environment as there is no incentive to adopt it if people do not follow the rules.

5. There needs to be common ways of defining performance measures, and those measures need to be in line with best practice – and not subject to local variations. If you are going to compare performance across countries, you need the same basis for measurement. People also need to adopt a "continuous improvement" culture to support performance improvement. Panel 4 illustrates a real world example of the need to have common correct measures.

Panel 4: Common Measures

A site manager arrived at a plant in Ireland, part of a major, well-known global brand.

He had been part of an SOP/IBP implementation elsewhere, and was used to "on time in full delivery" being properly defined, based on the first date of delivery agreed at the time of order acceptance. However, he found in this plant that they could change the promised date of delivery in response to their customers right up to the date of delivery. Naturally, the numbers looked very high, and they were regularly achieving 98% OTIF performance.

He felt this was wrong, and so changed it to first date of delivery given. He started to report numbers at around 60/70%.

One Sunday afternoon, his wife came out to the garden to say that the global VP of supply chain wanted him in Atlanta by Wednesday at the latest. When he got there, the VP demanded to know why his performance had plummeted since he had arrived.

The plant manager then explained what he had found in the way that the measure was calculated, and why it was wrong! The VP said, "Goodness. I had never realised the measure was being manipulated!"

It was soon changed. The plant manager was not very popular across all the other sites!

6. Companies need to have one integrated system to support quick and effective summing up of the numbers on a common platform across the globe.

7. There needs to be clear accountability for plans by country and factory site as circumstances change. Thus, in one client company, there was a shortage of product. They needed a decision on whether West Europe would get the production or the Far East. After some robust discussion, the Far East got the product. I then suggested that the plan for the current financial year should be reduced for West Europe and the plan for the Far East increased. The head of West Europe looked at me, thought for a bit, and then said: "I do not think we are that mature yet."

The IBP decision-making process often challenges the maturity of the thinking that lies at the base of how some companies operate.

Thus, a global business needs a global and local model, and needs clear-thinking through of the process and responsibilities involved – but the basic structure remains the same.

- **Rules of the Process**

  All of this should then lead to companies putting in place some basic rules which govern the discipline of the way the business is run. This should lead to a clear description of the key rules. The following suggests some:

- All meetings must run every month, with the right people attending. Naturally, on occasion people may have a good reason not to attend. But this should only happen occasionally.

  The head of a global car brand wrote to all his people saying, "I want this process to work. Everyone must attend their meetings. If anyone finds they have a problem with attending the meetings, then please contact my PA so I can be alerted to help you change your diary to attend." That sent out a clear message. Be there, or else!

- The captains of each of the meetings should prepare the meetings carefully. They must make sure the relevant information is circulated up to 48 hours before.

- Someone should be appointed to record minutes, actions and decisions.
- The horizon for the discussion should be the long term, and the discussion should be long term. There is nothing wrong with the short term, but the meeting should balance the right amount of time on each part of the horizon.

It, therefore, makes sense to have a Process Performance Checklist which can evaluate the quality of the process across the business, and this should look at:

- Did the right people attend?
- Was the meeting adequately prepared?
- Were actions completed?
- Were the right decisions made?
- Were performance measures reviewed?

The above model describes the building blocks of an IBP process for any business, and should enable you to create your own.

Many people have looked at this process and have said: "We do all that." Of course, they do; every business needs to do all of these things. But most times, potential clients then add: "But not quite in such a structured way."

That is the core point of the IBP process – it creates a structure to improve the decision-making process in the business, and hence lets it grow better by making it more capable of adapting to inevitable change. Organised common sense.

Chapter 4

The Underlying Process Steps

"CEOs hate variance. It's the enemy. Variance in customer service is bad. Variance in quality is bad. CEOs love processes that are standardised, routinised, predictable. Stamping out variance makes a complex job a bit less complex." – Marcus Buckingham, CEO and Coach.

The previous chapter might have made IBP look like it is all to do with meetings. It is not. It is as much about processes – or how you do things. There has been much talk about "process re-engineering" over the years, and I have found that – even so – "processes" are not necessarily well understood or defined. This work has come from the "quality" school of thinking. It examines the proposition that outputs that have poor quality come from the process, which converts inputs into output. As a result, the International Standards Organisation, which drives international quality standards, has developed ISO 9001:2015. Thus:

> ISO 9001:2015 specifies requirements for a quality management system when an organization:
> a) needs to demonstrate its ability to consistently provide products and services that meet customer and applicable statutory and regulatory requirements, and
> b) aims to enhance customer satisfaction through the effective application of the system, including processes for improvement of the system and the assurance of conformity to customer and applicable statutory and regulatory requirements.
> All the requirements of ISO 9001:2015 are generic and are intended to

> be applicable to any organization, regardless of its type or size, or the products and services it provides.

With one client, I spent a couple of days interviewing all the members of the senior team around what they understood by "processes" and the impact on the business. There was a very varied understanding of the idea. The key concept that they did not fully appreciate was how much all activities involved in converting raw materials into a finished product crossed several functions as they are bought, made, tested, delivered and invoiced and sold; this is the key fact behind processes – they tend to be cross-functional.

The SCOR model from the American Association for Supply Chain Management defines the basic processes that supply-chain companies use:

- Plan
- Source
- Make
- Deliver
- Return

It then goes on to define all of the more detailed sub-processes which go on beneath these high levels. Thus, under "Source" it creates a sub-definition of:

- S1 Source Make to Stock
- S2 Source Make to Order product
- S3 Source Engineer to Order Product

It acknowledges that it does not cover all of the business processes, including:

- Sales and Marketing (demand generation)
- Research and Technology Development
- Product Development.

It also does not cover Financial Management, Human Resources, Engineering Management.

It then goes on to break each sub-process down into a series of further levels, using standard "process decomposition", which means breaking each process down into the more detailed steps that occur in carrying out the activity. Thus, source will be made of: identify requirement – place purchase order – receive items – test items – put away item. The key value of this exercise is not only to understand how people carry out activities within a business, but also how a business should structure them to enable the measurement and improvement of the process.

Let us take the example of order fulfilment. We could have a process by which we take orders. It covers receives the order, checks stock, allocates stock, picks, packs and ship the product. We can then measure perfect order fulfilment as the percentage of orders fulfilled on time, in full, with the correct paperwork, by comparing the data for when the order is received for the original promised quantity and date with the actual quantity and actual delivery date. We can set a target of 100% delivery to promise date as a measure. Then if the result comes out at 75%, we need to analyse why this happened – was this the Delivery process (transportation), the Planning process (which created a failure to get materials and capacity), the Execution process (which took the materials and capacity, and converted them into product that was delivered) and so on?

Once we know that it was a delivery process (for instance), then we can look at the issues around whether it was to do with planning, booking the transport or the lorry itself.

On one occasion, a company that made radiators in south Wales for a UK car company in the north east was delivering several radiators using three lorries, which left the plant in the order A, B, C. The car company – being organised in a just-in-time way – had specified A, B, C.

However, they arrived in the order B, C, A. The car company complained that this destroyed their production line as they could not complete all the cars that needed the radiators that were on lorry A until that lorry arrived. They had scheduled the cars' assembly in the order that the radiators were sequenced; and this had held up the production line. They fined the radiator company for stopping the line.

The radiator company then carried out an investigation. They found that lorry A had suffered a puncture and that this happened on a stretch of the M5 where there were roadworks. Some debris left behind had caused the problem.

Since then, they check where there are roadworks before dispatching lorries!

In another company, which made breakfast products, they used to complain that failure to deliver, which happened occasionally, resulted from poor forecast accuracy and constant changing of plans – a familiar cry of many operational managers and directors. "It's not our fault; it's their (sales and marketing's) fault."

After they had implemented IBP, they started to measure schedule achievement (Did they make what they were supposed to make daily?). From this, they discovered that 40% of the failure was due to plant reliability. This led to a major investment in infrastructure, based on a five-year plan driven through the IBP process.

Hence IBP, structured around formal processes, should enable a company to get to the root cause of problems, and thereby improve its performance, through the control of the processes.

- **Process Map**

To enable this analysis, we need a map of business processes, along the lines of the SCOR model, which should define all the processes behind the business operating model, and then define all the sub-processes.

Every company is going to be slightly different, and each should identify the processes that apply to its business.

To help this exercise, Figure 22 creates a generic outline for this purpose, and also aligns with the basic operating structure to support IBP.

It is structured along the lines of the meeting structure in the previous chapter and expands the "Delos Model" in Figure 5.

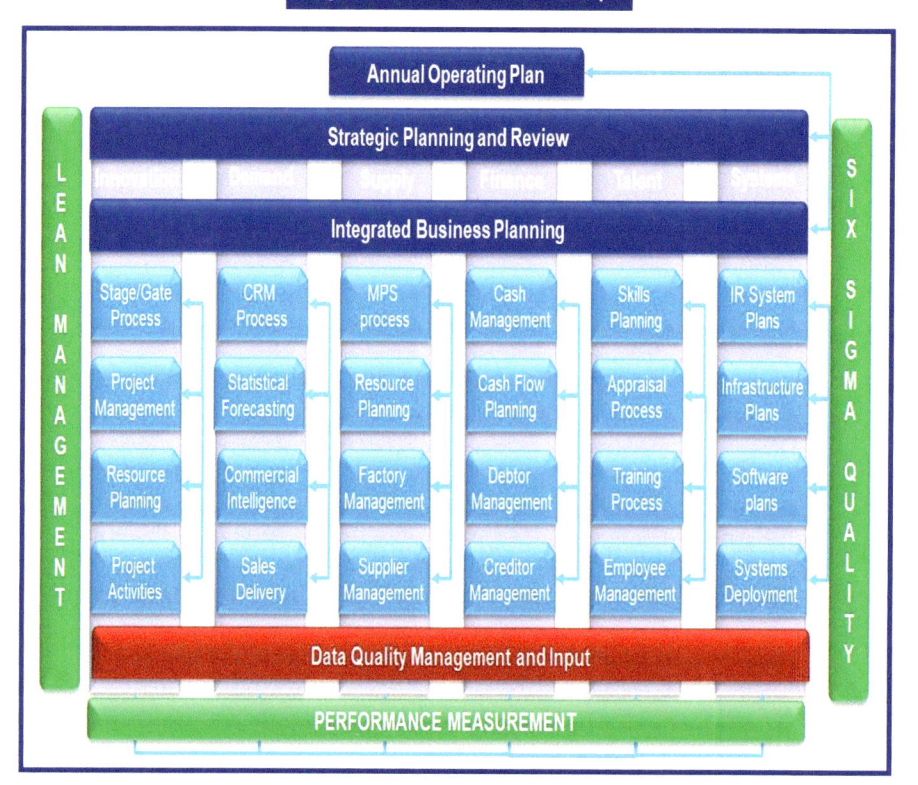

Figure 22: Process Map

Each of the vertical pillars describes the fundamental processes that are part of the IBP process and suggests some sub-processes, which go to support the overall process.

Down at the bottom is a box which covers performance measurement, and illustrates the idea that these performance measures should cover all processes.

On the right-hand side, there is a green box which relates to Six Sigma, or Quality Improvement. As part of this critical philosophy, there is a cycle of improvement designed to address all process issues – illustrated in Figure 23, which shows how the measurement process operates.

Thus, if we take the Order to Cash process, we need to define it, measure it, analyse if there are problems, and take action to improve – which leads to control, and so on.

The Underlying Process Steps

Figure 23: Six Sigma DMAIC chart

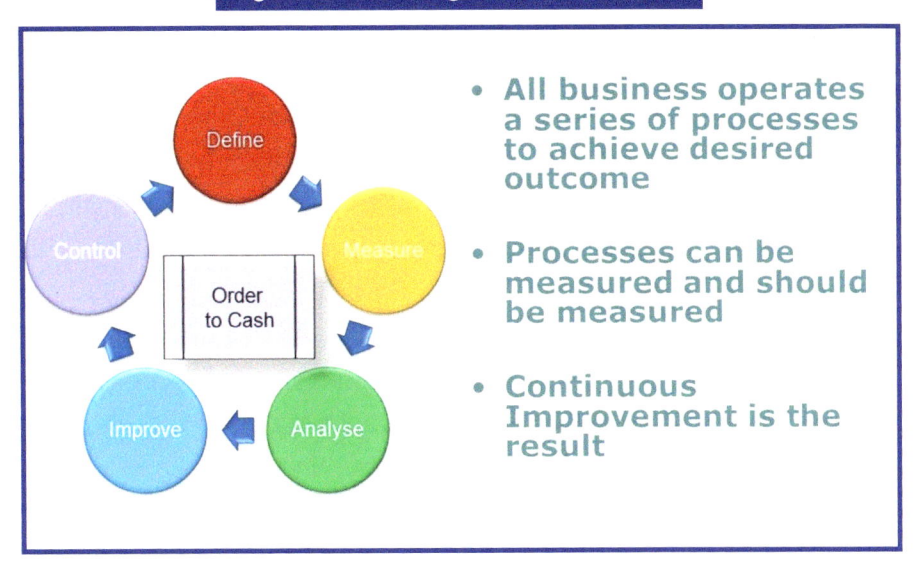

- **All business operates a series of processes to achieve desired outcome**
- **Processes can be measured and should be measured**
- **Continuous Improvement is the result**

(Define → Measure → Analyse → Improve → Control, centred on Order to Cash)

A common issue in many companies developing a Planning process is how to forecast. We also need to measure the accuracy of forecasts produced. Hence, Figure 24 suggests that we should apply the same principles to this process.

Figure 24: Applying measures to process

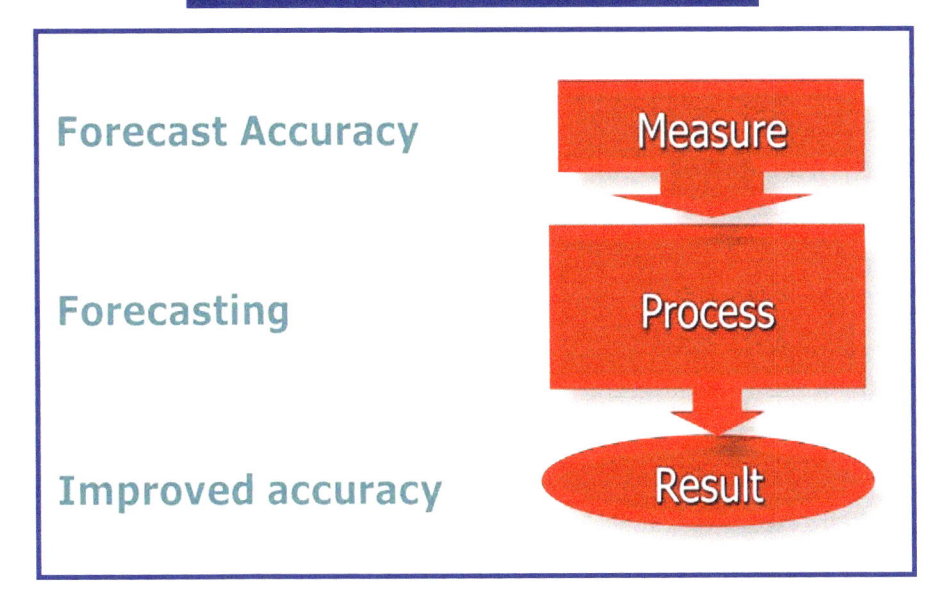

Forecast Accuracy — Measure

Forecasting — Process

Improved accuracy — Result

Thus, the process is "forecasting", the measure is "forecast accuracy", and the result will direct the company towards improved forecast accuracy. It seems to be an excellent approach to apply, but when I look at companies applying the Six Sigma/DMAIC approach, I find few apply these ideas to anywhere else, other than Manufacturing! A key organisational impact of this approach is that any business then needs to appoint a "process owner" to take accountability for each process. From Figure 22 – the Process Map Chart – you can see that there is a need for at least six process owners (innovation, demand, supply, etc.). If you take this chart further, you could add to that list, IBP, Strategic Planning, Annual Operating Plan, and Data Quality. Process owners should be director level.

In the company where we worked to find out whether they understood processes, we then went on to run a workshop to explain Process Mapping, etc. We then got to the part where we needed to identify process owners, and the CEO then asked for volunteers for each area. We started with the "make" process, and at this point, the HR Director volunteered. Naturally, there was an outburst from Manufacturing along the lines of, "what do they know?". But the HR director had a genuine interest in trying to understand what went on in manufacturing, and after some interesting discussion it was concluded that this was the right thing to do.

The HR director then went on and did an excellent job of analysing the processes with the manufacturing team, and facilitated some detailed discussions around how the process operated. For instance, it took 42 days to inspect a batch of one product. It always had done. But when the HR director challenged "why?", it was clear this was because once upon a time they had a problem and had to do further tests – but that problem never occurred now. Simple, but arguably identified because someone outside of the area had responsibility. Often those that have responsibility will not challenge so strongly.

In another company that was engaged in process improvement, the CEO gave the responsibility to the sales and marketing director for leading the development of the Supply Chain Planning Process. They made sure that the team designed the Supply Chain Planning Process to serve the needs of the customer rather than design one which had inflexibility at its core.

Hence, while it is perfectly reasonable to align process ownership with the "obvious" owners, I have seen instances where breaking this rule has produced spectacular results.

IBP should not just be about a series of meetings; it should determine how companies measure the effectiveness of the business in meeting their customer requirements to make a business fit for purpose.

- **IBP and Behaviour**

The other key aspect to recognise is that traditional process improvement models focus very much on analysis of the process and how people do things.

Many issues that occur within a business result from the culture embedded in the business. As I have illustrated above, measures drive behaviour. Thus "sandbagging" the forecast to make sure that the factory makes more than is required is human behaviour. It then leads to a lack of trust between Sales and Marketing and Operations.

This behaviour can be detected through measures of forecast accuracy and bias – which then must lead to a change in behaviour, which will improve a company's business performance.

Hence, we should be using the IBP process to identify "poor behaviour" and then address this.

When you develop IBP you, therefore, need to define the business processes, which requires the definition of inputs, outputs and purpose. It also requires you to identify the behaviours that people must adopt to support the process.

Figure 25 illustrates all the elements that go together to enable the operation of IBP and is a chart I have used many times with companies when putting together the initial working model.

The chart illustrates along the top what you need to define as the key elements of the process analysis. People use the acronym SIPOC for these, which stands for the following:
- Who are the **S**uppliers of information?
- What are the **I**nputs
- What is the **P**urpose of the process step?
- What are the **O**utputs?
- Who are the **C**ustomers of the process?

Figure 25: IBP process development chart

Process Name :			Process owner :		
Suppliers:	Inputs:	Purpose:	Outputs:		Customers:
People: Chair: Captain:	Behaviour Change :	Organisational requirements	Measures:		System
Link to other processes :					

Concerning the meetings that go to make up the IBP process, as described in the previous chapter, then Figure 25 also enables the definition of the people involved – who is the chair, captain, etc. of the steps(s) in the process?

It also identifies what behaviours need to change to make the process work, which in turn should force analysis of what measures are required to bring about the required behaviour.

Additionally, it raises the issues of what needs to change in terms of the organisation. As we go through this, we will see that there are often many organisational gaps identified as companies implement IBP.

It also requires the definition of the systems to be used in the process. Too often, companies try to implement IBP using spreadsheets. They make a certain amount of progress with spreadsheets – but they inevitably have their limits. Back in the 1980s, companies introduced SOP/IBP to help companies implementing business systems to put in place a proper structure to support them, and to link them formally to the decision-making process. Computers do not make all commercial decisions – yet!

You can play better golf with a better set of golf clubs, but the player of the game of golf will not improve their score unless they get their mind and body to work together, following effective education and training in how to swing a club and follow the rules of golf.

Hence, this table is critical to the development of the processes that support IBP – it is not just about a new system!

I have now described how the overall system works and emphasised that IBP is about changing processes – ways of working – which requires clear roles and responsibilities. I have also described the need for integrated systems. But IBP relies on the right behaviours, which drive functions to work together; this requires the right measures in place to drive the right behaviour.

I will now describe the details behind each step of the process, to enable you to put in place an effective IBP process.

Chapter 5
Innovation

"Innovation has nothing to do with how many R & D dollars you have. When Apple came up with the Mac, IBM was spending at least 100 times more on R & D. It's not about money. It's about the people you have, how you're led, and how much you get it." – Steve Jobs, founder of Apple.

Apple is probably one of the most iconic companies in the field of innovation in the last 50 years, and this has spawned many companies who have then gone on to follow their lead. Not every company is going to be iconic in this sense, but all companies need to develop their products and services. Those companies which have failed to innovate and evolve have died.

So, innovation in its widest sense has to be a key part of the Integrated Business Planning model, and there has to be a robust process in place to manage innovation. The key problem posed as part of the development of the IBP process is how companies integrate this process with all other parts of the company.

The difficulty lies in addressing the fact that the IBP process – for historical reasons – has focused on the marketing activities that are required to develop the product portfolio, rather than the full scope of innovation.

So, one of the first things to address is the exact scope of "Innovation". The word here describes the development of all new activities which have the potential of disrupting any other part of the business. So, a brand-new product – either under an existing brand name or new to the company – is innovation.

Where legislation changes – for example, the legal limit of the amount of sugar in products – which leads to a large number of existing products needing to have their formulation changed, represents an innovation.

Acquisition of another company is also a significant change to the company, as the new products and brand names will need to be absorbed, and the organisation will need to be changed. Often, the focus in an acquisition is too much about the reorganisation, rather than the integration of products, culture, and systems.

On the supply side, if a component of a product becomes obsolete, which results in the need to change the formulation or design of products, based on that component, then that is an innovation.

If a production line has reached the end of its useful life and the kit needs replacing, this is an innovation. The line will need taking out and production plans will need altering, and so on.

The key "universal" nature of all of these activities is that companies should manage them as discrete projects – thus, they have a series of activities that they need to coordinate with a specific timeline to achieve a specific objective. Some also need to be managed within the context that the activity contributes to the strategy.

They need to be delivered on time, in full, to the quality required.

In managing these activities, experience suggests that companies adopt a variable approach to project management. Some companies have a very detailed project management process, complete with appropriate systems to support this. Thus, I had a client which was responsible for supporting the railways with engineering resource to manage the information systems – displays and similar technology for platforms. It was very much built around the provision of people to sort out issues and install equipment, and they had a sophisticated project management system to manage resources. Equally, another company in the defence and systems business, which hired scientists to support technical development, also had sophisticated project management systems. These almost have to have sophisticated project management systems, and also need to put in place the right processes.

In many other companies, I have found that project management happens, but the process and systems aspect is weak – with not much more than a series of lines on an Excel spreadsheet which represents activities against a timeline drawn out along the bottom. There is no indication of resources required or any means of understanding the impact of capacity. They are often called "critical path" diagrams, with a nod towards project management theory. But they are incapable of working out the critical path through a project (the timeline, which is constrained by the sequence of activities and resources available). They are certainly not capable of managing the constraints across all of their projects.

One of the first steps is to identify all of the projects that are going on in the company. It is often scary to find out how many are going on – many below the radar!

The challenge then is to establish a way to manage the total resource requirements for all projects, to enable them to be completed on time and in full.

- **Managing Resources/Priorities**

The "Innovation" step within the IBP model is not about managing individual projects; it is about managing all the resources required for the development of new "things" for the business. These can split into those that are "demand" related and those that are "supply" related – but they can all potentially conflict with each other.

For instance, take a resource such as formulation or engineering development. Let us say there are 20 people in this area. Let us assume that there are around 40 hours available per working week for each of the people. Let us assume that in May, June and July of a year there are four, four and five weeks respectively, and then let us assume that on average the people are productive – i.e. work on projects – 70% of the time. Hence there are 560 hours per week available in a four-week month.

Let us also assume that there are three (to make it easy to illustrate!) projects that will be going through that department in that period. Then let us review the resources required and the availability in Table 9.

Table 9: Project resource requirements for the development department

	May	June	July
Project A	2,000		
Project B	100	2,000	1,000
Project C			1,500
Total required (hrs)	2,100	2,000	2,500
Total Available (hrs)	2,240	2,240	2,800
% Load	94%	89%	89%

So, at present, the load on the department is reasonable, based on these assumptions. Typically, all projects have an end date. Sometimes the end date is fixed in stone – we are going to be launching this new product at the Frankfurt exhibition which only happens every two years, which showcases all new products, and if we are not there, it will destroy interest in our new products! You can almost hear the fire-fighting! The threatened project this year happens to be Project A.

Let us now assume we are in February of the current year and we find out that there has been an issue on Project A, which will delay its development by three weeks, which will mean that the work in this department will be delayed by three weeks.

From the above table, we can see that 1,500 (3/4 of 2,000) hours will move from May to June. It has the impact of overloading June severely. So, this visibility will force us to address:

1. Can we bring forward the work on project B or C into May – what is the impact of this on prior or later steps in this project?

2. Can we get additional external resource in for June to help meet the resource requirement?

3. What will be the impact of the delay on project A for later steps in the process?

4. Can we delay project B and C by a month to enable project A to be developed in June – what are the impacts of this on resources required in August onwards?
5. Can we get more resources in from August onwards to support quicker development of projects B and C?

Several other options may be available, but it is clear from this simple analysis that we need to address the issues on these projects together, and this is the primary function of the "innovation" step within IBP.

This step, therefore, requires the project management systems in place to identify the activities, resources and costs to enable the analysis, and the processes to support the management of the individual projects involved.

- **Performance measures**

The other key aspect of managing projects in IBP is to know whether projects are on time and within cost. I have found that many companies in the Defence and Electronics sector (i.e. those who are typically engaged in major projects and hence have to develop good project management measurement processes) are very good in this area. The US and European Ministries of Defence, who are very conscious of the need for budget control, drive their suppliers to adopt good practice in project management. But for the most part, companies are very poor at knowing whether they are in control of projects.

Many develop a budget for a project. The question to address is that if you have a budget for a project of £1 million, and you are six months through the project and have spent £0.5 million, do you know if you are on track?

Clearly no! The questions that anyone needs to answer are:
- Have you done what you planned to do within those six months?
- Have you spent what you planned to spend on the activities which you planned to complete in those six months?

It leads to a need to derive a cost index and a schedule index for projects (ratio of actual to planned) to let you know if you are on track; and to do that you need to have a proper project management process and system.

The first place to start is always to create a plan for projects, which covers the activities, resources and costs for projects, and then add them up!

- **Portfolio Resource Management**

Figure 26 illustrates the concept of having multiple projects (which some call the portfolio), from which companies need to aggregate the resources of each project to give a total picture across all projects. Hence the purpose of Innovation becomes as stated in Figure 26.

Figure 26: Objective of Innovation step

1. To manage all "new activities" against strategic intent, and prioritise where needed

2. To review changes to plans and implications on resources and priorities

3. To review and improve overall performance in managing projects

Assumption : There is a process for managing projects

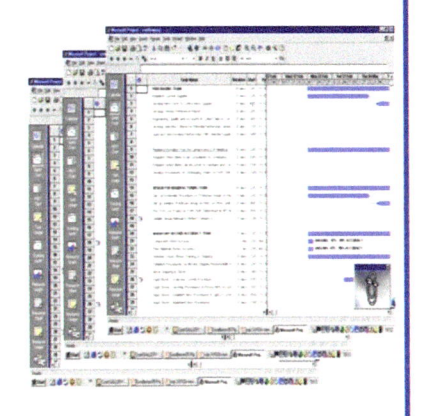

Hence this section of the book is not about managing projects. Thus, the assumption is that if there is an area of weakness, then you will get training in project management, which has its own body of knowledge. An excellent source for this training is Extraordinary Project Management Ltd. at https://extraordinarypm.com/.

- **Stage/Gate process**

So, if you do not have a Project Management process, then the first step will be to create a Stage and Gate process, which provides a framework within which to manage and control projects.

Within any project, it is usual to identify all of the activities, and in particular, milestones, which are Gateway activities, and decision points. We can then analyse the key phases of activity that a company goes through to get to these gateways, and hence we can develop an overarching "Stage/Gate" process designed to provide control of the project management process, which looks generically as follows:

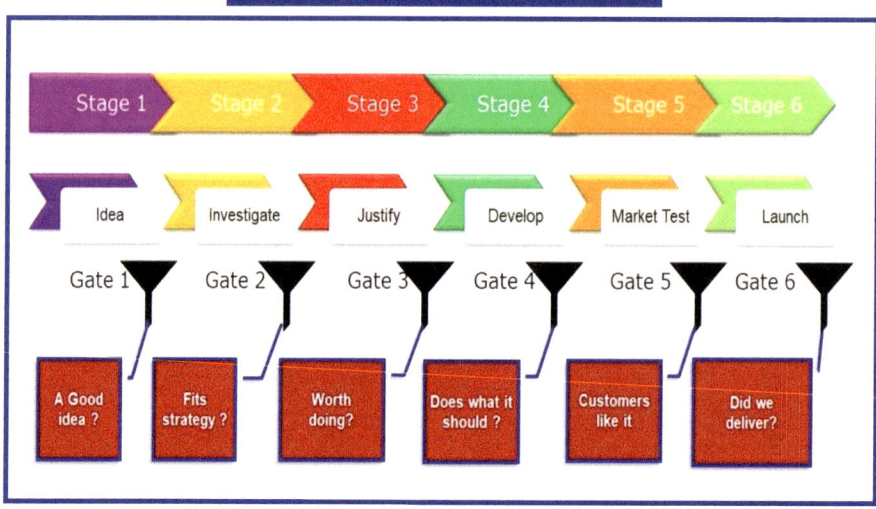

Figure 27: Stage/Gate process

Stage	Activity	Gate	Decision
Stage 1	Idea	Gate 1	A Good idea?
Stage 2	Investigate	Gate 2	Fits strategy?
Stage 3	Justify	Gate 3	Worth doing?
Stage 4	Develop	Gate 4	Does what it should?
Stage 5	Market Test	Gate 5	Customers like it
Stage 6	Launch	Gate 6	Did we deliver?

We should apply this generic Stage and Gate process to all projects. It is perfectly possible to modify this to suit different types of projects. There are several basic stages that each project must go through (idea, investigate, justify, develop, market test and launch) with decision points (gates) to control the progress of projects to their next stage.

That is the overall process. Companies can modify this process in several ways. Sometimes companies create an initial step to decide if it is a very big project, involving many millions, or a medium-size project, or a small project.

If it is a big project, then they will follow a complicated process which goes through all of these stages. If it is a smaller size project, then it will apply a light-touch to these projects, to avoid bureaucracy killing the golden nuggets.

Other companies add in other stages through the process and other gates, and so on. Again, one size does not fit all.

But the problem I have encountered many times is not so much the existence of a formal process; the real difficulty is getting people to follow the process! In their hurry to get the project to market, they try to bypass the process, which only leads to problems later on.

Stage 1/Idea

In any business, the first stage is often the critical step. The literature is full of examples of how new ideas have emerged and how they then happen and get through the first light of day from that "light-bulb" moment. Companies can spend fortunes on R&D and structured ways of developing new products. But equally, serendipity (the occurrence and development of events by chance in a beneficial way) can be just as influential in the field of Innovation.

Everyone, or almost everyone, now spends their working life close to or "attached" to a personal computer (PC). IBM launched the first PC in August 1981. Only 20 years before that, a computer cost around £3m, needed a quarter-acre air-conditioned room and 60 people to keep loading instructions. IBM launched the first PC at the cost of £1,200; it fitted on a desk, could link up to printers, displays and external memory devices, and it took only 12 months from concept to launch!

At the time, executives recognised that quick development in IBM would be difficult, and applications were not that much available. One analyst at IBM said at the time that "IBM bringing out a personal computer would be like teaching an elephant to tap dance." So they set up a small, dedicated project team focused on bringing the product to market within twelve months. They also went out to a little-known company called Microsoft to help develop applications! They quickly set up a team to develop the PC successfully, through dedication.

Yet in 1977 – only four years earlier – Ken Olsen, founder of Digital Equipment Corporation, had said: "There is no reason anyone would want a computer in their home!"

Darryl Zanuck, an executive at 20th Century Fox, made another one of those great predictions in 1946: "Television won't be able to hold on to any market it captures after six months. People will soon get tired of staring at a plywood box every night."

These comments were spectacularly wrong – but came from a lack of imagination of people, rather than any failure of systems or processes. If you look at the development of the PC, you will find that IBM did learn how to dance, but it is always a challenge for large companies to become flexible enough to bring new ideas to market. Many times, there are huge "vested" interests in place within companies, which will resist innovation.

Ideation

Ideation is one of those strange words that occasionally creep into the conversation, but represents a step that relates to "the formation of ideas or concepts". Within the IBP process, it is important to subject this step to taking all ideas and running them through an initial filter, to evaluate whether the ideas fit into the business from a strategic and technical point of view.

The typical structure that companies adopt, and if not available, will need to be initiated as part of the development of an IBP process, is illustrated in Figure 28.

Strategic fit

The first element is to evaluate how the idea fits into the overall strategy for the business – hence we need to refer back to the strategy for new product development, manufacturing, supply chain and so on.

Figure 28: First cut analysis of projects

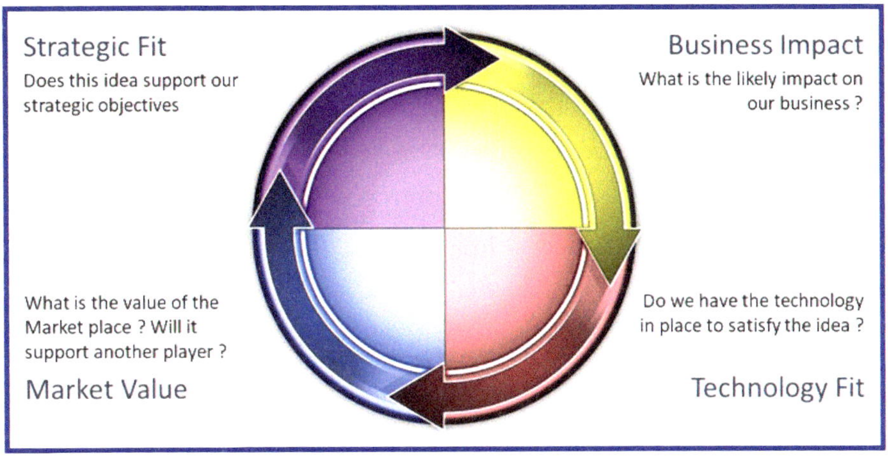

Strategic Fit
Does this idea support our strategic objectives

Business Impact
What is the likely impact on our business ?

What is the value of the Market place ? Will it support another player ?

Do we have the technology in place to satisfy the idea ?

Market Value

Technology Fit

It is helpful to create a product/process road-map for the next three to five years to provide a framework within which the company manages ideas.

It is essential to make sure that the strategy is broad enough in scope to enable real breakthrough development.

Nokia was well known for its development of mobile phones and was at the forefront of the development of small mobile phones. Before that, they had been a maker of paper. Their strategic view was along the lines that they were in the "communication" business. When their senior team saw that their market place was going to move from physical communication (paper products) to digital communication, they decided in favour of the development of digital products – mobile phones.

Business Impact

At this early stage, there are not going to be detailed forecasts for products. There should be an initial forecast at this stage, of the value of projects and whether they are worth pursuing. Ken Olsen's comment about TV unlikely to gain a hold in the market was wrong because his assumption was wrong. Your company needs to make sure that the business has carefully thought through the assumptions for the product, and rationally agreed to them through the business.

When Sony developed the first portable device for playing music – the Walkman, the CEO insisted on producing 70,000 units per week. However, others in the company did not believe it would sell that many, and as a result, they ran short of the product. Failure to agree assumptions can be a costly mistake.

As a member of the ICI Agrochemicals' Product Management department, I used to put together many analyses for new product development. When we did these, we normally put together a 10-year forecast, which resulted in a calculation of the NPV of the project, which in turn would go forward for approval. If we found that the NPV was not high enough, it would not get approved!

I was involved with one revolutionary new product for the domestic market; it tackled the issue of spraying garden plants with chemicals. Traditionally, this was done by mixing a liquid with a chemical to treat for pests, fungi and weeds, and then either selling it in a ready-to-use form or in concentrated form to be applied through a separately sold sprayer.

This completely new technology provided for the mixture sold in a special bottle, which would be attached to a handle which would contain batteries, and which would electrically charge the liquid to control the spray of the liquid. It was a revolutionary idea! It would reduce the amount of chemical required (the electronic droplets were attracted direct to the surfaces, and less was wasted).

An initial review suggested a huge potential for the product within Europe and globally, and a case was made for substantial investment in the equipment needed to make the products. The business case based its assumptions on the number of households that would buy the product, the number of times people would buy the special bottles, the number of applications for which it would be bought (roses, vegetables and pests, fungi and weeds).

With new products/technology, then products go through the stages of adoption, introduction, exploitation and saturation.

The original business case based its assumption on initial adoption of something like 10% of households buying the product within the first two to three years, and households buying four bottles of liquid three times a year.

But when we looked at more likely scenarios of slow adoption and less frequent use of the product, we concluded that the amount to be needed to be invested in the product was not worth it.

The business case was all down to the quality of the assumptions. It was clear that the business case was much higher than we could realistically accept, to get the project off the ground.

Since then, I have found that many companies end up suffering from the same issue – they have some hurdle rate or volume, or value which projects need to meet. Surprise, surprise: all projects seem to make it over the line!

It is essential to make sure that there is a realistic set of assumptions to understand the business impact.

It also makes sense to have a forecast accuracy measure for new products which measures how accurate are the eventual volumes and values when compared to the initial estimates, in timing and quantity.

Getting New Products into the Business Plan

We need to address the issue of how and when to include these projects into the long-term Business Plan. Thus, when you have put together your longer-term business plan, it is likely that there is an initial view of New Product Development as part of that strategic plan. At the stage that the Strategic Plan is put together, it may well not be clear which projects will fill that gap. It is a bit like a jigsaw with missing pieces; thus, we might have the following picture as part of the strategic plan, showing a split between existing and new products as illustrated in Table 10.

Table 10: Strategic plan for Product Development

£m	Year 1	Year 2	Year 3
Existing Products	100	110	120
New Products	5	10	20
Total	105	120	140

3 year Business Plan

Thus, today, we may not have identified all of the projects that will make up the £20 million in year 3. As we go through the monthly IBP process, we should select which projects we believe are most likely to succeed so that we can see how much cover we have in the pipeline for our longer-term business plan projections.

We should also measure how many projects do not pass through the initial stages of product development, to judge the health of the pipeline.

If we had £x million in the plan, and there were no projects, then we should be very concerned if our development timescales were >three years!

Technology Fit

Another key part of the initial gate should be the requirement for any new technology to support the idea. Some products may well fit on existing technology, and then it will be just a case of finding capacity for it.

However, often, a business may need to develop completely new technology, requiring new equipment, to support product development, and this will need to be made clear.

Market Value

The last dimension of this approach is to judge the market size and impact of our new product. Entering an existing or new market, and our success of entry, will depend very much on whether we are entering a large market, and hence whether a small share of a large market is sustainable, or whether we need to gain a large market share of a small market to make it viable.

So, at this initial stage, we can develop an analysis across all of our ideas, where we can categorise projects on a scale of 1 to 10 as illustrated in Figure 29.

Figure 29: First cut project justification

Project	Strategic	Market	Technology	Business Impact	Overall Average
1	10	10	10	10	10.0
2	10	8	7	10	8.8
3	9	8	5	8	7.5
4	7	6	7	7	6.8
5	4	7	8	7	6.5
6	3	8	9	5	6.2
7	7	4	4	5	5.0
8	6	5	4	5	5.0
9	2	3	2	3	2.5

Thus idea 1 fits all aspects well, and Project 9 is very low on the scale, and we can review this table in the IBP process to make sure resources are applied correctly to new ideas, and let them through to the next stages.

If the idea is a good one, we should then take it to the next stage, which is to investigate it thoroughly.

- **Stage 2: Investigation**

The next stage should be where the new ideas then go through a process of evaluation of the key elements of strategic fit, business impact, requirements for technology, and market impact.

A key output from this stage should be a high-level forecast for the potential sales of the project.

The business will go through all of the initial investigations of the usual commercial and technical impacts of the new idea on the business, and the endpoint will be for the idea to go to the next stage, which will be fully to justify the project.

- **Stage 3: Justification**

Once there is clarity about the scope of the project, then there will be a need to put together a business case for the project.

This business case should provide clarity about the scope, objectives, cost and timescale involved. I have often seen that Stage 1 and Stage 2 act to filter the ideas, and Stage 3 then becomes the key point at which good project management comes into play.

Hence at this stage, there should be a statement of work for each project, and a business case which defines the NPV of each project, so it is clear how big or little projects are. There should now be a clear linkage to the business plan and the requirements for capacity and materials. Through the project planning process, we will now get a clear idea of the resources required for the project.

Here, sales and marketing and supply chain functions should be fully engaged to make sure forecasts are supported. Accountability for the accuracy of forecasts for new products should be clear (typically marketing) with a formal review six months and 12 months after the launch of the project. I have heard so many times that warehouses are full of the ambitions of unrealistic projections!

Sometimes I have met companies who have said it is difficult to do the capacity planning etc. at this stage in the ERP system, because of a "trivial" issue that they cannot raise product codes until the full specification of the product is available. This can be overcome – and should be overcome – by using generic family level product codes with outline "design" Bills of Materials and Routings to enable capacity and raw material planning.

Innovation

A key part of this Innovation stage of the IBP process should be to prioritise projects within available resources. Hence, where there are finite resources, then there should be a formal review to determine which projects are a priority. Table 11 illustrates an approach to ranking projects.

Table 11: Ranking of the value of projects

Project Name	Value [£ m NPV]	Strategic Fit (5 = High)	Risk (1= High)	Rank
ABC	20	5	5	500
PQR	50	2	5	500
VWY	45	5	2	450
XYZ	20	5	4	400
DEF	33	4	3	396
RST	2	5	5	200
LMN	5	5	5	125
OPQ	100	1	1	100
FRG	40	2	1	80

The table shows the ranking of the projects according to their value (NPV of the project), multiplied by their strategic fit, and the risk of the project. The last two projects are – although potentially very valuable – ones that the business should abandon!

Sometimes, getting an agreement that a company should abandon projects is difficult to achieve, of course.

The key part of the IBP Innovation process should be to review all the projects and make sure you have the resource to be able to complete all the projects. If you do not have enough resource, then decide to drop some projects. Less is more!

One client was heavily involved in the development of new projects and had a large resource devoted to this activity. But they found that they were continually late on the delivery of projects. When they had visibility of the resources tied up in their projects through their IBP process, and could see that they were overloaded, they decided to cancel a project – which was a breakthrough moment for them. Their performance on delivery improved enormously. It is never a good idea to over-promise and under-deliver!

Sometimes companies and organisations do not have the "courage" of their convictions to abandon projects because of the politics of the project.

I saw one of these projects, and the company wasted many millions before they took the decision finally to abandon the project.

This problem is sometimes known as the "Abilene Paradox", outlined in Panel 5. The problem is how to get people to agree that they disagree!

Panel 5: Abilene Paradox

Often when projects are being managed, companies will need to take a decision on whether to continue or abandon a project.

There is a subtle problem in this respect, which is that often people will agree to proceed with a project because it is "politically right" to agree. It is not seen to be good to disagree. This is labelled as the Abilene Paradox syndrome – which comes from a story told by Jerry B. Harvey in his article The Abilene Paradox: the management of agreement. (Harvey, 1974: Volume 3, Issue 1. Pages 63-80).

> It was a hot afternoon, and the family were sitting on the verandah. The father proposes that they all go to Abilene, which is 50 miles away, for a dinner. In spite of protests the father insists and they all go. Wife and two children agree to "get along".
>
> The food was not good, the air-conditioning in the car was not working, and it was very dusty.
>
> When they got back, his wife and two children complained bitterly that they should not have gone. It was hot, etc.
>
> The father retorted, "Well, if you had felt that strongly, you should have said so before we went!"
>
> Everyone, of course, claimed that they had; the "boss" just failed to listen, and no-one really wanted to upset the "boss". It is a great story.

Once the company has justified a product, it goes through detailed development, test marketing, and final launch. With an effective process, the development of innovation will be more successful.
Often, companies miss out the step of post-product launch, to evaluate the success of projects; it should be an integral part of the performance review within IBP.

- **Performance Measures**

All of this says that we must have a clear approach to the measurement of performance of the management of projects, which in turn means companies need to have a proper project planning process.

Firstly, when projects get approval for the development, then at this stage we should have an agreed completion date for the project, plus milestones, which technically would be applied when the project is "baselined".

From this information, we can produce a report each month or quarter and establish whether we complete projects on time, and the report would look something like Figure 30.

Figure 30: NPD Performance report

Project reference	Planned Date	Actual Date	Hit/Miss	Comment
A1001	23/09/19	02/10/19	Miss	Scope change
A1096	23/09/19	15/12/19	Miss	Key components not available
B2304	24/09/19	17/09/19	Hit	
B2403	25/09/19	18/09/19	Hit	
D1237	26/09/19	27/09/19	Miss	Design issues
D1453	26/09/19	20/09/19	Hit	

NPD Performance
= 3/6
= 50 %

We can then do a further sub-analysis of this to see how we have performed against the milestones for the project.

Secondly, and more sophisticated, companies should adopt the "earned value" approach to creating indices of how successful companies are in meeting the cost and time of the projects. The US Defence department developed a regime of "Cost Schedule Control" a few years ago, which meant this became widely used as a methodology across the defence industry. If you look in Microsoft Project, you will also find the ability to track "earned value".

It is an approach which gets around the problem reviewed earlier of how to know if we are on track with a project. "Earned Value" allows companies to track both cost and activity, to see if it has spent what it planned to have spent, to complete what it should have completed on a project.

First, create a project plan with the activities and costs planned as part of the project at the point when the project is initially baselined. At this point, you will create a "budget" or "planned" value of work scheduled. We can then track actual time and cost against the projects, allowing you to compare actual work completed, and its cost, to get a schedule and cost index. The following Table 12 illustrates a project in its first six months.

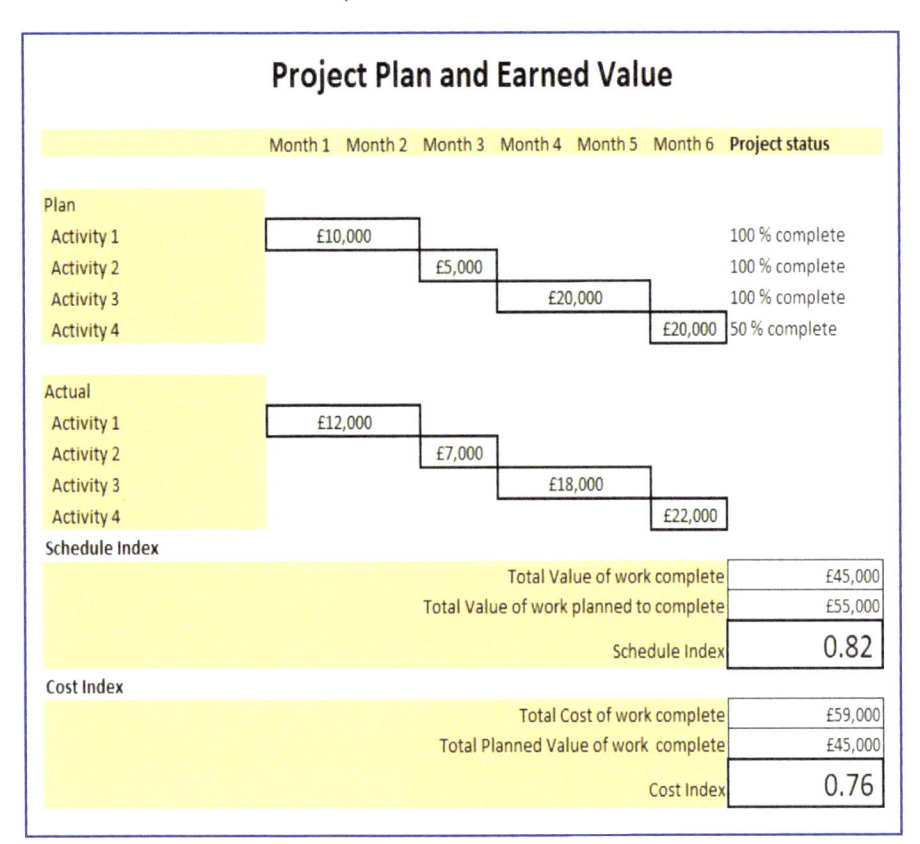

Table 12: Example of calculation of Earned Value

Project Plan and Earned Value

	Month 1	Month 2	Month 3	Month 4	Month 5	Month 6	Project status
Plan							
Activity 1	£10,000						100 % complete
Activity 2		£5,000					100 % complete
Activity 3			£20,000				100 % complete
Activity 4						£20,000	50 % complete
Actual							
Activity 1	£12,000						
Activity 2		£7,000					
Activity 3			£18,000				
Activity 4						£22,000	

Schedule Index

Total Value of work complete	£45,000
Total Value of work planned to complete	£55,000
Schedule Index	0.82

Cost Index

Total Cost of work complete	£59,000
Total Planned Value of work complete	£45,000
Cost Index	0.76

At the top are four activities, with the planned cost for each of these activities. By month six, all activities have been completed, except for activity 4, which is 50% complete. Hence the total "earned value" of work completed is £45,000 (value of activities 1,2,3 + 50% of activity 4).

If we compare this with the total value of work that was planned to be completed by the end of month six, then that adds up to £55,000. Creating a ratio of the value of work completed to value of work that the company planned to complete gives a figure of 0.82. A figure of less than 1 tells you that the project is behind schedule.

In the middle is the record of actual costs of work completed. Here, the sum of all the costs to date is £59,000. If we compare this with the value of the planned work completed (£45,000), we can see that we have an index of 0.76. A figure of <1, again, is showing that the project is overspent by £14,000. A total £22,000 has been spent on activity 4 when it is only 50% (£10,000) complete, which is a £12,000 overspend.

The clear advantage of this approach is that if one were comparing actual spent to date (£59,000) vs what was budgeted to be spent by this date (£55,000), we would wrongly conclude that we were only £4,000 overspent against the budget, and this gives an early warning that the project is overspending.

- **Organisation**

Organisationally, the implementation of IBP leads people to recognise that they do not have proper management of all projects (which can cover new products/marketing activities, supply projects/supply chain activities – or indeed ERP system-type projects), which often leads to the complaint: "We are doing too much as a business; there is so much going on, I do not know whether I am coming or going."

Several clients have, therefore, recognised that they need to have someone as an "innovation manager", who is responsible for reviewing and managing the total portfolio of projects.

They then become a "program office" manager or something similar. In terms of the IBP process, they would then become the captain of this step of the process, and are responsible for managing and coordinating the monthly cycle of Innovation meetings.

- **Structure of Innovation meeting**

Once you have established the Innovation process, then you need to establish the Innovation meeting or meetings to support the IBP process.

We also need to establish the link to other parts of a company's Innovation process, which will include the detailed Project Management processes, Project Management Reviews, and so on. As stated above, the need at this stage is to identify who will chair the meetings, who is the captain of the process, and who should attend. The chair should be the member of the senior team responsible for innovation within the business (e.g. technical director). The captain of the process should be the innovation manager. Those who should attend will typically be the product managers or project managers. It may well be useful to have someone from Finance to attend, to support thinking around the financial aspect of projects.

The inputs to the process will be the Strategy for Innovation, the individual project plans, the resource plans for all projects compared with the capacity available for all projects. The measures will also be a key input.

The output from the process will be issues identified, decisions that need to be made – which will go to the Senior Team review – and a review of the performance of managing products, based on the earned value analysis.

The key behaviours we need to address are realism in providing forecasts, the ability to work cross-functionally, and meeting deadlines. Throughout this book, I will describe a template for each step of the process to enable you to put in place your process, based on that shown in Figure 25.

The Figure 31 is a draft outline of the meeting that you might put in place to support this step.

Figure 31: Template for Innovation meeting

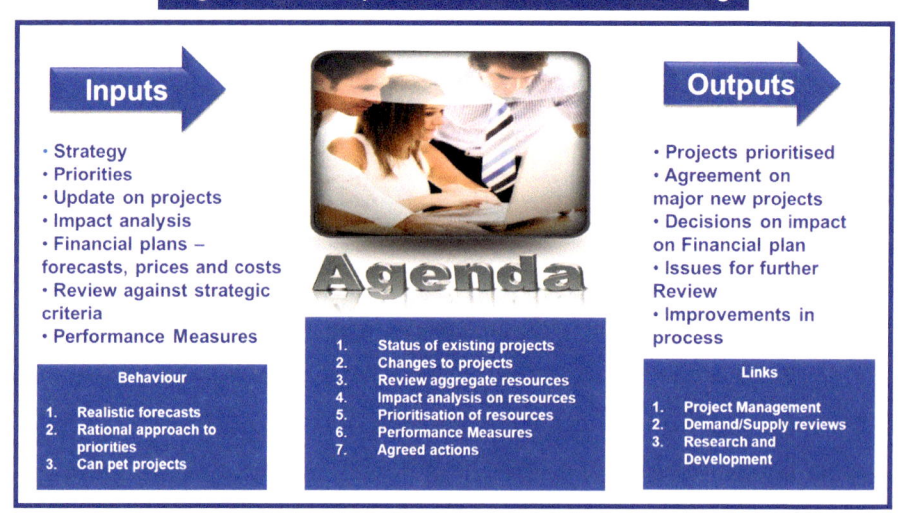

Inputs
- Strategy
- Priorities
- Update on projects
- Impact analysis
- Financial plans – forecasts, prices and costs
- Review against strategic criteria
- Performance Measures

Behaviour
1. Realistic forecasts
2. Rational approach to priorities
3. Can pet projects

Agenda
1. Status of existing projects
2. Changes to projects
3. Review aggregate resources
4. Impact analysis on resources
5. Prioritisation of resources
6. Performance Measures
7. Agreed actions

Outputs
- Projects prioritised
- Agreement on major new projects
- Decisions on impact on Financial plan
- Issues for further Review
- Improvements in process

Links
1. Project Management
2. Demand/Supply reviews
3. Research and Development

While this suggests one meeting, the actual number of meetings will depend on the organisation. It could be that there is one for new products (i.e. marketing projects) and one for Supply (i.e. Operations projects).

Then you need to review how and where you might share and prioritise resources for NPD and supply-side projects (like moving machinery around).

If you are a multi-site organisation, then there may be global and regional processes/meetings, and local business unit-level processes and meetings, which need integration. One size does not fit all, again! Innovation is a crucial activity for any company. Good companies have a well-developed stage/gate process. Integrated Business Planning should focus on ensuring the completion of projects on time, in full, by ensuring adequate resource across all projects, and an effective rationing process where there are insufficient resources. Effective performance measures will provide proper feedback on where you need to improve the process.

Getting projects delivered on time, in full, will enhance the profitability of the company enormously. It is not about bureaucracy – it is about learning to dance, as IBM found. Dancers need good choreography!

Chapter 6
Demand

"Prediction is very difficult, especially if it is about the future." – Nils Bohr

The history of the development of Sales and Operations Planning has brought this area into sharp relief.

Before the development of a forecasting process, companies used to rely on traditional re-order point; thus, they would work out when to get more components based on the average usage of parts – the so-called "two-bin system". Therefore, you ordered more parts when the stock fell below the demand over the lead time for that component. If the average weekly demand was 100 units per week, and the lead time four weeks, then you would order when the stock went below 400 units.

However, demand is rarely equal to the average, there are no fixed lead times, and the future is very rarely like the past! The critical event that changed how companies managed operations was the invention of Bills of Materials and the recognition that you could calculate the demand for components by creating a demand for the parent part. If you wanted to work out how many wheels and handlebars you needed to buy in making a bicycle, you did not need to work out the average consumption of wheels and handlebars separately. Companies were only required to work out how many bikes were going to sell. Now you can work out how many bicycles have been bought in the past, and then project that forward. That is a forecast.

The critical concept is that the bike is "independent demand" – thus it is the item that the company sells, which is at the interface between the company and the customer. The wheels, handlebars, chains and so on are "dependent demand", which a system can calculate.

More recently, some people have started to adopt a philosophy called Demand Driven MRP, which some advocates state eliminates the need to forecast. Forecasts are very uncertain, and why would you decide what to buy or make based on a forecast, goes the cry? "Just use orders!" This relies on a sophisticated form of reorder point and suffers many of the same issues. You still need to work out what you are going to sell and make. Some systems based on the DDMRP concept have developed a "projected daily usage" – which is still a forecast. The future is rarely like the past.

The reason for the need for a forecast is related to the question addressed earlier – "Where do you meet your customer?" If the cumulative lead time for your product is greater than the lead time that your customer demands, then you have to create a forecast.

The scope of Demand within "Integrated Business Planning" covers all activities which relate to the interaction with the customer. It covers the relationship with the customer, and how you manage that interface in terms of understanding potential requirements (forecasts), receiving orders, and then satisfying them.

It is vital to work out whether a business is going to operate a business strategy of being Purchase/Make to Order or Purchase/Make to Stock. If you are Purchase or Make to Order, then the company waits for the security of a customer order before buying or making to order. If your company is Purchase or Make to Stock, then your company is taking a (calculated) risk on ownership of materials.

In the Make-To-Order world, you might think that there is no need for forecasts. But this is wrong. In these companies, there is a vital requirement to manage enquiries and bids, and the uncertainties around winning new business; the delivery of existing business is ordinarily subject to delivery contracts and monthly schedules. The companies win new business, usually through a process which starts with an enquiry, leads to a proposal, can involve design, and then may end up with an order. However, the business may well need to invest in capacity before getting the order, and so forecasts will drive getting capacity. Sometimes Make-to-Order companies will need to invest in long lead time raw materials, and if they do this, they will need to operate with a forecast.

In the Make-to-Stock world of Fast-Moving Consumer Goods, pharmaceuticals and food, the issue is around how to deal with short customer lead times, and the impact of significant changes in demand which comes from seasonality, advertising and promotions. Everyone has to deal with the unpredictability of demand; none of us yet has access to the future. As Edgar Fiedler said, "He who lives by the crystal ball soon learns to eat ground glass."

Orders as they come in, rarely come in directly in line with the forecast timing and quantity of demand. Therefore, companies need to consider how they manage orders through the customer service department, and how they align orders with the forecasts. Typically, this function is responsible for accepting orders, but they usually do so without reference to the forecast. But, if orders are received which are un-forecast in terms of quantity or timing, then they will disrupt the supply chain. Companies need to manage demand when it exceeds the forecast – a point not lost on those managing demands which resulted from the COVID-19 virus!

So, part of developing an IBP process is to make sure there is an active and effective process for managing demand – significantly where demand exceeds supply. In this situation, lack of materials and capacity may require rationing of the demand.

Therefore, there needs to be a clear distinction between "Demand Planning" and "Demand Management".

Demand Planning is related to the longer-term, where there are few, if any, supply constraints. Demand Management is where there are constraints to the availability of materials and capacity, and where we need to take action to constrain demand. This decision must align with the limitations imposed within the cumulative lead time. Indeed, the whole of this area should focus on how the business will establish itself to meet customer requirements, and then how to manage customer demand if the forecast is (seriously) wrong. Figure 32 illustrates the critical points in the horizon, looking out from to-day.

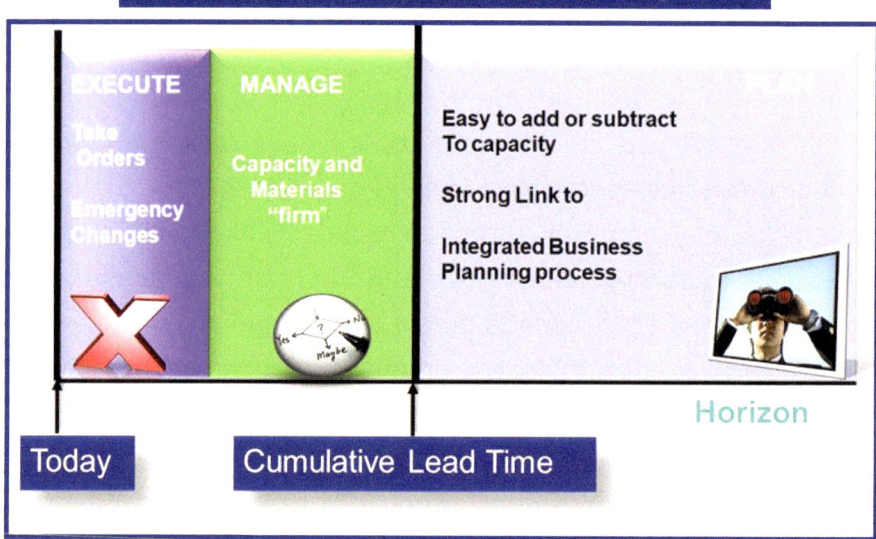

Figure 32: Demand Planning and management

Demand Planning v Demand Management

Thus, on the right side of this diagram, we should engage in Demand Planning as part of the IBP process, which is an area that we will cover in detail in this chapter. To the left of the line, which we call the Cumulative Lead Time (defined by material and capacity availability), lies the area where capacity or materials should be firm.

If you are making potato-based products, then companies might usually create a long-term contract for the year, and if total demand exceeds the amount agreed with farmers, you will need to restrict demand. If you buy precious materials – for instance, titanium –

and there is a shortage of titanium, then you will need to ration customers and consumers. Thus, in this area, companies typically need to constrain demand, and we need to build into our IBP process a <u>formal</u> process for restricting demand.

All companies manage this daily. The issue is how we handle this situation without damaging our reputation with customers.

See what happens next time you walk into a restaurant, and they tell you that they have run out of steak! They will tell you that they have some great alternatives, and try and sell you something else.

- **Demand Planning v Sales Forecasting**

Often people use the words "Demand Planning" and "forecasting" interchangeably. People say it is impossible to forecast. In some senses, they can be the same thing.

However, I find it useful to distinguish between the two. When people are saying it is impossible to forecast, they recognise that there are many things over which we do not have control. Weather is an often-quoted example. We cannot accurately forecast the weather. But this does not prevent various meteorological agencies providing short-term and long-term weather forecasts, using complicated algorithms and computer systems. They will take into account wind, weather patterns, temperatures, and so on to come up with predictions. It depends on a whole host of assumptions, built up over time.

However, if we use the word "plan", then this has a slightly different meaning, which is more appropriate in the context of a company looking to the future.

If someone says to you on Friday this week, "What are you doing next Thursday?" and you know that you are going to the theatre, it would be right for you to say, "I am planning to go to the theatre." That carries with it the notion that you have bought tickets, reserved time in your diary, and are fully intending to go to the theatre. If you change your mind or have to do something else, then you may suffer a penalty (you cannot exchange the tickets and would take pot-luck on selling your tickets, or give them to someone else) and will have to change your diary. If you had a cold, then you might still go; but if you had a severe case of pneumonia, then you probably would not go.

But if you said you were forecasting to go to the theatre, then it would perhaps signify that you had not yet bought tickets or reserved time in your diary, or even arranged for someone else to go with you! There is a lack of definite commitment.

Within the IBP process, we should consider that we are focussing on "Demand Planning", and not some vague "forecast". When it comes to dealing with customers, there are indeed many things we cannot control.

However, we have activities which we can undertake and control – around pricing, promotion, distribution and so on – which will have an impact on demand. We can also gather information about our market place, like history and trends, which we can use to build up our "Demand Plan".

The key objective, therefore, of the Demand Planning process is to provide a projection of "unconstrained demand"; it is to make sure that there are sufficient capacity and materials to meet customer requirements. You should base the demand plan on all your information, and your view of the impact of pricing, promotion and distribution on your products. Someone must take accountability for the Demand Plan, which I discuss below.

- **Demand Plan Error**

The one thing that we know about forecasts is that they will always be wrong. It does not mean we should give up. Some mistakenly believe that IBP only works with accurate forecasts. This is not true. The fundamental premise is that a business must agree on the level of uncertainty for which it wants to cater and get that agreement across all the functions.

Hence, we need an estimate of how wrong our forecasts will be so we can enable the supply chain (both our own and our suppliers' suppliers) to respond within agreed limits. It relates directly to the safety stock and safety capacity targets established (as described above).

In many clients, mainly where the Supply Chain function is the driver of the project to implement SOP/IBP, I have seen an illusory belief that the whole process is about getting a more accurate forecast. There is a false notion that, somehow, a good IBP process will yield a best-in-class result for forecast accuracy. It is mistaken because my experience is that different industries, different countries and different markets can show very different levels of accuracy. I have also tried benchmarking various sectors and countries, and while it is complicated to get comparative metrics, it is clear there is no universal standard of accuracy.

It is a sensible objective to reduce the inaccuracy of forecasts that result from defective practices, which are in the control of the company. This should get the company to the point where it has to deal only with the external variations, which they cannot control.

The two key issues to address in this area are:

1. To understand the accuracy of the Demand plans, and then enable the supply chain to be able to respond – dependent on the strategic decisions made by the senior leadership team on the level of flexibility that they believe they can afford to adopt.

2. To make sure that the measurement process does not adversely affect sales and marketing's behaviour. The process of forecasting/demand planning, and working out safety stocks and safety capacity works on the assumption that the errors are not in any way biased. In many companies, the measurement process encourages bias in the forecasts – whether through constantly over-forecasting to make sure product is available, or under-forecasting to make oneself look good because those who sell more than the forecast become legendary heroes.

It is worthwhile reiterating why we need to have a forecast, and where this fits in – even if we think that Make to Order implies that we do not have to forecast.

- The function of a customer order is to give the supplier a sense of certainty, because it is a contract. It is a contract to deliver a certain quantity of a particular product at an agreed price, on an agreed date, to an agreed location. If the customer does not take it, then contractually they are (all things being equal) capable of being forced to take the product.
- If we need to undertake <u>any</u> activity to make/buy materials and capacity (people and machines) before getting a customer signature for the contract, then a company has to make those decisions to acquire materials and capacity at risk against a forecast. The critical commercial point is that, in doing business with customers, there is always competition for the business; sometimes competitors can win business by offering a faster delivery lead time. Amazon, with their 30-minute delivery response time, believes they can!
- If someone decides to commit resources without gaining commitment from the customer, then they have to make a <u>forecast</u>. The question that companies must address as part of establishing the IBP process is how, when and who is responsible for making that commitment.

• The Importance of Forecasting/Demand Planning

When I have addressed this issue with many companies over the years, I have found a considerable reluctance to undertake this process. I have collected a series of excuses, summarised in Figure 33.

I remember once running a workshop with a group of sales and marketing people in Switzerland. They had all been there the day before, going through their regular Sales and Marketing review on opportunities. They had spent a lot of the day also looking at the fact that they wanted to introduce an IBP process and the fact that they were going to have a workshop the following day to explore the forecasting process.

When I put up this slide, someone immediately said, "I wish we had seen this slide yesterday. Every one of those excuses came up yesterday to defend why our guys do not want to get engaged in forecasting. If we had dealt with that yesterday, we would have saved a lot of time!"

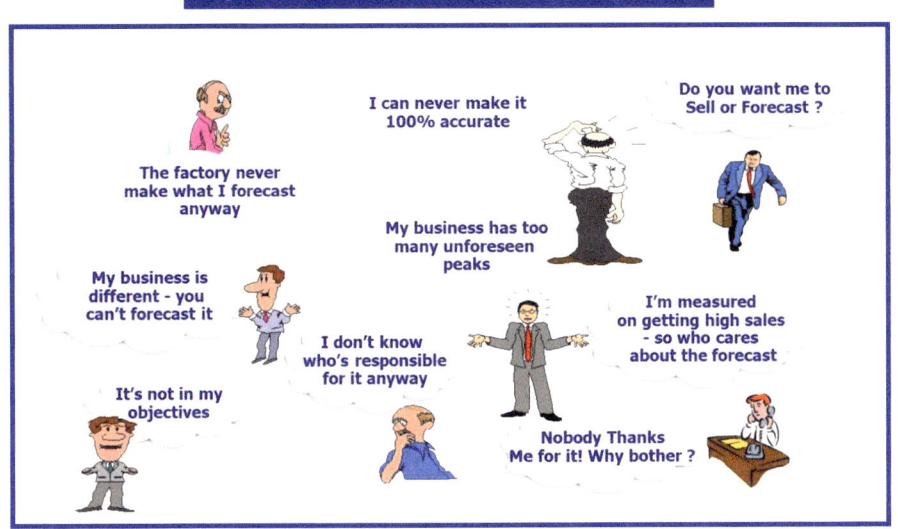

Figure 33: Excuses for not forecasting

- I can never make it 100% accurate
- Do you want me to Sell or Forecast?
- The factory never make what I forecast anyway
- My business has too many unforeseen peaks
- My business is different - you can't forecast it
- I don't know who's responsible for it anyway
- I'm measured on getting high sales - so who cares about the forecast
- It's not in my objectives
- Nobody Thanks Me for it! Why bother?

Key are the comments around, "I don't know who is responsible for it anyway", and "It's not in my objectives", as well as, "I am measured on getting high sales – so who cares about the forecast?"

• Responsibility and Accountability for Demand Planning

To answer the question of who is accountable for providing a forecast, we should start with the fact that the demand for a company's products comes from the customer. The functions that have direct contact with the customer are Sales and Marketing.

The usual definition of the role of the sales director and their team is to develop a direct relationship with the customer and manage the contract with the customer. Therefore, they are responsible for prices, customer-based promotions, and terms and conditions of sale. They influence demand by their decisions on the contract with the customer.

Where a company sells its products under its unique brand, then it is likely to have a function that carries out marketing – i.e. they determine the pricing, promotions, packaging and positioning of the products in their range.

Where the company is dealing with consumers, using methods of persuasion and influence like promotions and advertising (TV, social media, pack-marked pricing), then there will be a strong marketing emphasis on the types of promotional "persuasion" that the company uses. There will be a complicated financial relationship around managing the profitability and timing of the promotion – all of which will lead to influencing the demand for the company's products.

Both of these functions have robust control over the influencing of consumer and customer demand.

We can, of course, start with a statistical forecast. This will allow us to see the base, trend and seasonality of those products. We will examine this later in the chapter. But companies must review this information in the light of attempts to influence the demand. We call this "marketing intelligence", which Sales and Marketing should incorporate into the Demand Plan.

No-one else has a better knowledge of the market place than Sales and Marketing.

Hence, I believe it is essential that the responsibility for Forecasting/Demand Planning must belong to Sales and Marketing, and process ownership should belong to the marketing director, or if there is no one in place, the sales director. Where there are separate functions, then in effect, marketing is creating the demand and hence the plan; sales is then selling the plan.

I have heard many times the counter-argument to this, which runs along the lines of, "You cannot let sales and marketing make the forecast; what do they know? The only time you can tell if a marketing person is lying is when they move their lips."

This argument usually then leads to the Supply Chain function wanting to take responsibility for the forecast, and so they establish a demand planning organisation with ultimate responsibility to the supply chain director. That leads to continuing frustration with the Sales and Marketing function, and a failure to tackle the underlying problem. The problem usually is the measurement process.

If this is the case, it is up to the CEO to show leadership and make sure that Sales and Marketing take responsibility for the quality of the Demand Plan!

It is useful to explore in support of developing this argument the situation where demand is constrained: in this situation, there is often a need to decide which customers will get how much of what product. If Sales and Marketing are not accountable for the forecast, then they will be in the situation where they are supposed to achieve the numbers, but will not be in control of the decision.

The decision will be difficult. It will depend on the size and importance of the customers to the business, the extent to which they are strategic customers, their profitability and overall value to the business.

It would fundamentally be wrong for the Supply Chain/Operations function to be responsible for these decisions; if they were responsible for the planning of the demand, they could make the wrong decisions. Who would take responsibility for the numbers then? This leads to the conclusion that Sales/Marketing should always be accountable for the Demand Plan.

After all, if you are driving a car and press the accelerator too hard, and get caught speeding, then the person driving the vehicle is responsible, not the person sitting in the passenger seat!

The IBP process often leads to companies needing to document RACI, determining who is Responsible, Accountable, Consulted and Informed, for the Demand Planning process.

I base this framework (which you should use throughout the development of IBP and IBL) on the following principles:

Responsible: Person who performs the work or activity.

Accountable: Person at director level who can be fired if the process fails. Only one person is accountable.

Consulted: Person that needs feedback and who should contribute to the activity/process.

Informed: Role, function or person that needs to know about the activity or work completed.

A suggested format for the **Demand Planning** process is, therefore:
- The demand manager is **R**esponsible for the process
- Sales/Marketing director **A**ccountable
- Several functions (like Finance, Research and Development, Customer Service, Regulatory) are **C**onsulted
- The supply chain/operations and Finance (at least) are **I**nformed.

• Definition of a Forecast/Demand Plan

This then leads to the need to have a clear definition of a "forecast". When I have asked the question of people, then the response usually is for people to talk in terms of a "guess", "statement of future requirements", or "a random number".

None of these adequately deal with the seriousness with which people should treat sales forecasts.

A customer order is a contractual commitment. It has to contain various elements, such as part number, description, quantity, price, date required for delivery to a requested location, terms and conditions of payment, and most importantly, a signature of some sort, which means that it is a contract. A failure to deliver to the quality required typically has some penalty associated with it (whether direct financial or implied long-term penalty of no longer wanting your service). Equally, if a customer cancels an order, there usually are some penalties which can be applied. Indeed, in some cases, customers make the payment on order, or they give a deposit. Forecasts have consequences! Amusingly, I ran a promotional seminar once, and a local firm of solicitors turned up. I was excited at the prospect of a whole new line of work, thinking they had come to find out how solicitors should forecast their business. I am sure they do; however, in this case, they were there because several clients were entering into contracts with customers, which they built based on forecasts. They were creating contractual commitments on delivery performance in return for the customer providing a forecast/schedule. You do not need an order to create a legal liability!

The critical issue to address here is to communicate through the business the extent to which people must see that the forecast is not a trivial issue. It is and should be used to acquire materials and capacity. It can also lead to a massive amount of waste in the business, and frustration and loss of business from customers.

The challenge is to get everyone to understand that a forecast must be seen and respected as a critical piece of business information, which can be trusted and used in the management of the business. Many companies fail to have this understanding in place. It needs a proper definition.

The best definition of a forecast, which captures the essence of this area, is illustrated in Figure 34.

Figure 34: Definition of forecast

> **A forecast is a formal request to the Supply Management function from Sales and Marketing to have the product, materials and capacity available according to the quantity and at the time that they anticipate the demand will occur from the customer to ship the product to their premises**

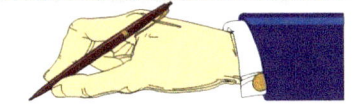

It is excellent at getting across the key elements of Accountability and Responsibility.

This means that a forecast is a commitment to win the business to ship to the customer on the customer's request date. This leads to the need to record the customer's <u>requested</u> date and quantity, to be clear on whether the order meets forecast or not. The actual shipment date and volume could be different.

One person from a client came on a forecasting course and stated she had real problems getting accurate forecasts from the product managers (responsible for marketing the products). They were domestic heating products.

When she went back from the course, she had a meeting with their product managers. At the end of the session, she passed the document containing the forecasts across to them, and said: "Can you sign this, please?"

"Why?" they chorused back.

"Because I would like to use them and if you do not sign this, I will not."

They got the message; they still followed the process ten years later! We can now turn to the mechanics of the process.

- **Forecasting Process**

Once the definition is clear, we then need a formal process by which the business prepares the forecast on a daily/weekly or monthly basis, turning it into a Demand Plan.

I have found some businesses – like milk, bread and yoghurt – require daily forecasts. Some, like food and drink and FMCG businesses, need weekly projections, and most others need monthly forecasts. The decision very much depends on the shelf-life of products, speed of consumption and degree of change in the numbers.

Many companies use spreadsheets for the maintenance of forecasts. They require people to fill in all the cells on the sheet to provide each of the numbers. I once asked a company how many products they were forecasting, and their horizon. They told me that they forecasted around 1,200 products out over 15 months. I observed that meant they were producing 18,000 wrong numbers manually each month! Crazy! There are plenty of forecasting systems out there, and you should have one if you have more than about 20 products.

In developing a forecasting process, it is useful to document the steps that the business should go through, turning it into a demand. Figure 35 represents a process flow, which represents a typical staged process for forecasting that companies can adopt, to support a formal process:

Figure 35: Forecasting process

- Capture Actual
- Filter Demand
- Compute forecast
- Review Accuracy
- Agree commercial plans
- Agree Exceptional demand
- Hold Demand Review
- CONSENSUS FORECAST

Assumptions written down and agreed

- **Statistical/Computer-Based Forecast**

The top blue box covers the process of creating a statistical forecast, and I assume that you have, or will have, a statistical forecasting package if you have a fair number of products which you regularly sell.

The first decision on the technicalities of a forecast will depend on the decision the business makes around "where you meet your customer", as discussed earlier in the book.

This decision will guide how and at what level you carry out a statistical forecast.

Make-to-order strategy

Some companies, which are typically make-to-order type companies are selling more "one of a kind" or "configured" products. In this case, a statistical forecasting package may not be appropriate, and they would typically have a "Customer Relationship Management" system. They use the CRM system to record interactions with customers, and to forecast "opportunities". CRM systems are still at a point where they are remarkably poor at providing the functionality to be able to provide forecasts. In this situation, companies may need to build some kind of database system. Thus, I worked with a company who needed a five-year forecast. Their CRM system only allowed the recording of the value of opportunities. So they created a system to record expected volumes and values by month for the next two years, and by years for the following three years to support this. Figure 36 illustrates the point at which you will at minimum have to create a forecast.

Figure 36: CRM Pipeline

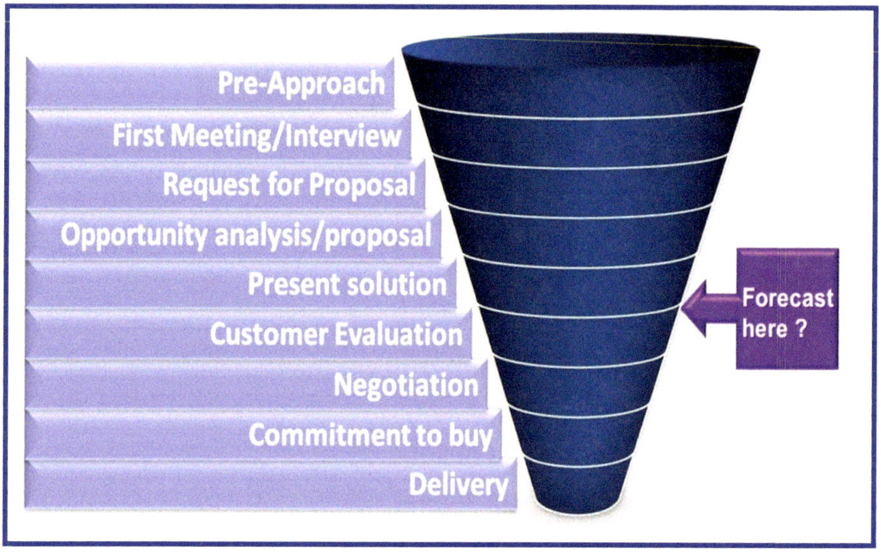

In this situation – where companies are Make to Order – then they usually would use a sales pipeline approach to manage their sales process. The only question is at what point they need to provide a forecast, taking into account the cumulative lead time for materials and capacity, and the point at which the customer will commit, by actually placing a purchase order. Figure 36 illustrates the point at which you will at minimum have to create a forecast.

Thus, because of the lead time for the components, it may be necessary to forecast at the point where the customer is evaluating the proposal when there is no commitment to buying the actual product. The company will need to purchase long lead-time materials. The issue then becomes getting ownership for the forecast. Companies often fudge the issue by using probabilities. Thus, in this situation (helped by the CRM system), people want to state that they have a 60% chance of getting the business, which is for 100 widgets at £10 each = £1,000.

So, they enter in a forecast of 60 widgets, with a value of £10 each = £600. But if they get the contract, they will get an order for 100 widgets – and it is no good telling the supply side that you forecasted 60 units when you knew it would be 100! You will still be 40 units short. Hence, the right way is to operate on a binary system – a simple "yes" or "no" will do. Either the salesperson thinks they are going to get the business or not!

In the Make to Order environment, it is entirely possible to aggregate the demands for products to a high-level (e.g. common raw material or common capacity), to apply a statistical forecast. Thus, one client – who provided floor covering products – knew that many of their products were customer-specific based on specific flooring design. So, they made customers specify what they wanted six to eight weeks out, against which they would order the exact print of the tile that the customer wanted. But they needed to establish capacity for a critical piece of machinery, as well as printing capacity at the supplier for the printed designs. When you added up the total number of floor tiles bought each month, you could see that there was a reasonably regular demand pattern for their products, around which they could plan capacity, and which they could predict statistically. So plan longer-term demand statistically, and in the medium term, get a commitment for the forecast where you require it.

Assemble to Order

Companies that operate in an Assemble to Order environment are typically offering lots of combinations of products around options they offer. They often can be grouped into "families" in line with the pyramid structure shown in Figure 37.

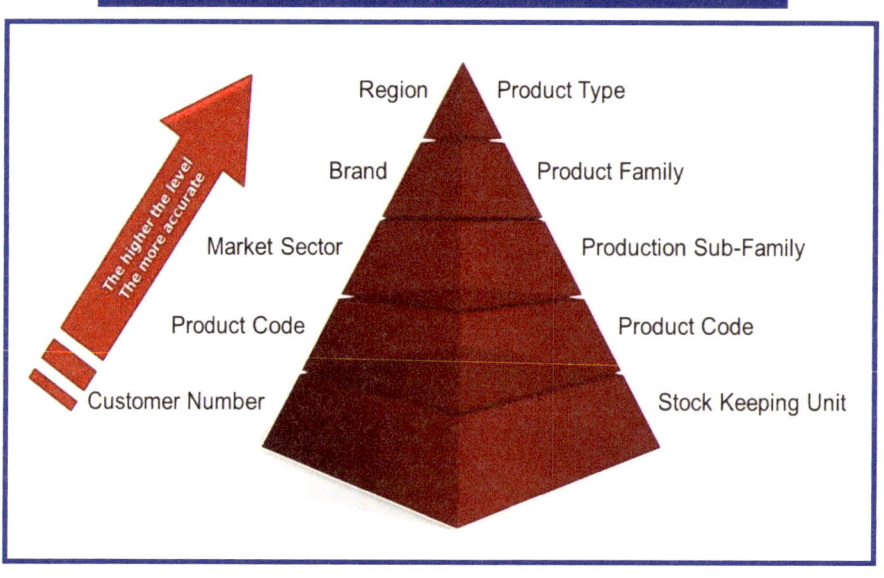

Figure 37: Pyramid structure for product hierarchy

Thus, on the right-hand side, we would be grouping products together into a production sub-family and creating the unique product code for the specific combination of options ordered, when we accept the order.

Let us take a "simple" example of felt-tip pens used in presentations. Let us assume we sell these in packs of four, in the four colours of red, black, blue and green. Then if we turn to the specific red pen,

Demand

we might see that the individual Bill of Material for a pack of four red pens might be made up as shown in Figure 38, which illustrates the makeup of the end item and the components that go into them. It shows the description of the part number, and "4 per" means four of each item to make the parent item.

LT is the lead time of the item to procure or make. Thus, you need four red caps, and the lead time to get them is 20 days.

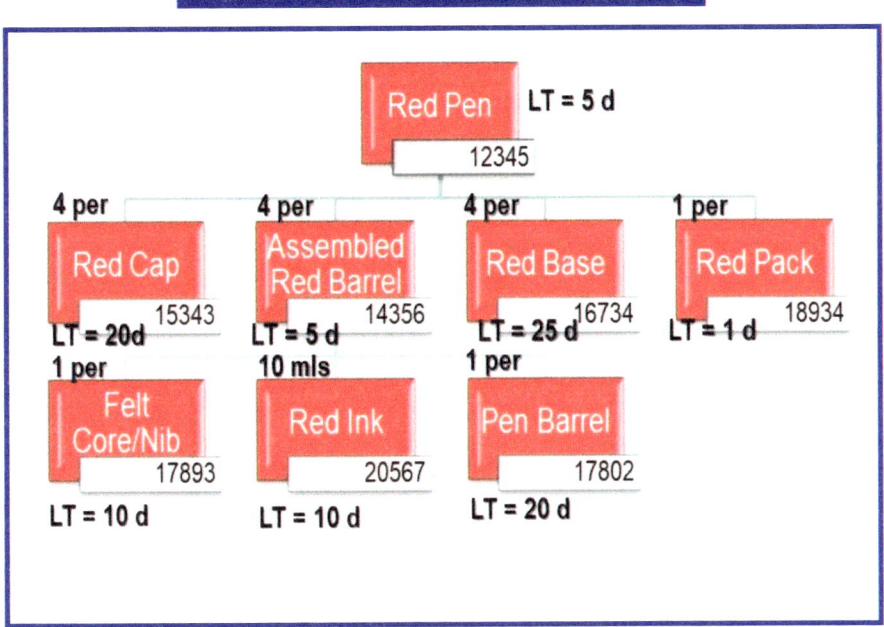

Figure 38: Bill of Material for Red Pen

```
                    Red Pen   LT = 5 d
                    12345

  4 per          4 per              4 per             1 per
  Red Cap        Assembled          Red Base          Red Pack
         15343   Red Barrel                16734              18934
  LT = 20d              14356     LT = 25 d         LT = 1 d
                 LT = 5 d
  1 per          10 mls             1 per
  Felt           Red Ink            Pen Barrel
  Core/Nib
        17893          20567                17802
  LT = 10 d      LT = 10 d          LT = 20 d
```

Now, if we determine that the competitive lead time is ten days (thus customers are prepared to place an order and get delivery within ten days), then we have time to assemble the part number 14356 "Assembled Red Barrel" from the component parts of the felt core/nib (178983), red ink (20567) and pen barrel (17802) when we get the order.

We also have time to order the red packing material and carry out the final assembly of the red pen pack.

So, in this case, we need to forecast the requirements for red caps (15343), red base unit (16734) and the components for the assembled red barrel.

Figure 39 shows the actual pen

Figure 39: Picture of Pen

The barrel (labelled with the makers' name and the words "flipchart marker") is black. This barrel is common across the pen family range – which consists of blue, red, black and green pens.

The unique requirement for each colour/pack is the coloured cap, and the coloured base, as well as the coloured ink, which goes into the felt tip.

Figure 40 illustrates a possible forecast and production plan (Master Production Schedule - MPS) for a week of the different pen types.

Figure 40: Production Plan for Pens

| Blue Pen | Red Pen | Black Pen | Green Pen |
| Part Number 12346 | Part Number 12345 | Part Number 12347 | Part Number 12348 |

Variant	Forecast	MPS	Actual Orders	Actual Shipped
Blue	40	40	50	
Red	60	60	70	
Black	30	30	20	
Green	70	70	60	
Total	200	200	200	

Thus, if we were to make exactly in line with the forecast, we would make 40 Blue Pens, 60 Red Pens etc.

If we then look at the actual orders we receive during the period (50 blue, 70 red etc.) then in principle we will only be able to ship 180 pens in total. We can only ship 40 blue ones and 60 red ones because that is all we had planned to make against the forecast. Then we can only supply 20 black ones and only 60 green ones because that is all for which we had orders.

However, in total, we had orders for 200 pens. So, the forecast was right at the aggregate level (pen family) but wrong at the mix level (each pen type) – which is a familiar problem. The result was that we failed on customer service (did not deliver the products which customers required in the period).

What causes the problem is the shortage of the "unique" items – i.e. red cap, and red base, and not the availability of common items – the pen barrel.

The solution to this problem is to break up the Bill of Material into common and unique parts so we can manage the unique parts on their own.

We achieve this by forecasting at a family level to drive requirements for common items, like the barrel.

For the items that make the product unique, then we can use percentages to drive the requirements for the unique items, based on the forecast for the family. Companies will use this approach in an environment where a company is "Configure to Order".

A client made kitchen furniture. The base units, for instance, were made of a core set of components (white panels). But the doors were made of different colours, and the backs could be of different colours. Customers could choose base units configured for left-hand or right-hand usage. The handles fitted could be from a range of 10. There were around 15 different "families" of types of kitchen or base unit. When you worked out the number of different stock-keeping units that you might need to forecast or manage, it went into several million. This situation is a classic example of where this approach is appropriate.

Hence, companies that operate in a Configure to Order/Assemble to Order environment will need a <u>Planning Bill</u> structure within their software to be able to forecast the configurations they may require. The Planning Bill of Material is the term given to the approach of creating a family forecast that creates a demand for common and unique parts.

In this environment, customers select a combination of options so that the factory can configure the required product against a predetermined "menu" of options. A car is a familiar example – but this is true for engineering companies who make valves, furniture companies that make kitchens, and many others besides.

Figure 41 illustrates a simple Planning Bill example structure for the felt tip pens above.

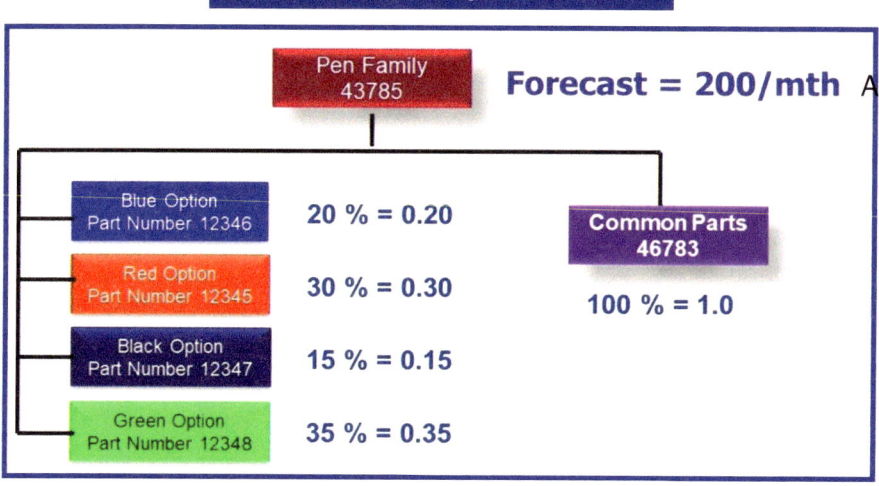

Figure 41: Planning Bill structure

Pen Family
43785

Forecast = 200/mth

Blue Option
Part Number 12346 — 20 % = 0.20

Red Option
Part Number 12345 — 30 % = 0.30

Black Option
Part Number 12347 — 15 % = 0.15

Green Option
Part Number 12348 — 35 % = 0.35

Common Parts
46783
100 % = 1.0

Planning Bill is thus a specific feature of an ERP planning system, and is essential for any company which is or wants to be "Assemble to Order".

In this model, you can forecast at the family level and then enter a percentage for each of the unique options (blue, red, etc.) Thus, when you forecast 200 per month for the pen family, and you put in 20% for the blue option, it will then calculate a forecast of 40 per month for the blue option.

In this system, you want the ability to group together all items that go to make the blue option.

You achieve this by creating a "Pseudo" Bill of Material, which groups together the cap, the base and the assembled barrel (12346 for blue in this case). This is a crucial feature of this kind of system.

In this way, the system makes sure that you have matched parts together.

In this system, you can apply the statistical forecast to the family level (in the example, the pen family).

This is a brief description of how planning bills of material work – and there is a lot more to cover! See Tom Wallace and Bob Stahl's excellent book on Master Scheduling. (Wallace & Stahl, 2003)

I worked with a company that made valves to go on the back of tankers and ships. Before I met them, they were working on a four- to six-week lead time because they wanted to avoid any commitment to the long lead time parts in inventory. But when the CEO understood how Planning Bills of Materials worked, he then implemented a two-week lead time, making a small investment in the unique components, and rapidly grew the business. He went on and bought another company and did the same again there, and so on!

A very useful idea. You can create flexibility through creating safety stock of those parts that make products unique (the red parts in the pen example. Over-planning the supply of these is the most cost-effective method.

Capacity-Based Forecasting

In a Make-to-Order environment, the critical constraint will be the amount of capacity that you have available. You can make whatever customers want, provided you can support the demand – and the customers will wait for the product.

In this case, you can convert the demand into the hours required to process them on a machine, and apply statistical formulae to the numbers worked on the history of hours.

Hence, the opportunity and how you deploy statistical forecasts will vary depending on the customer service strategy deployed.

I am not going to go into the detail of how statistical forecasting engines work – there are plenty of textbooks out there, and systems that support statistical forecasting.

I found Forecasting Methods and Applications (Makridakis, Wheelwright, & Hyndman, 1998) a useful text in this respect. It also covers neural networks and non-linear forecasting.

Statistical forecasting uses history to predict the future using various formulae or algorithms, and will provide the base, trend and seasonality for the underlying data. Hence, the quality of this data will depend critically on the quality of the history!

- **Capture Actual**

Where you are going to collect information to drive statistical forecasts, then you will need history. It is essential to collect the data based on actual <u>demand</u>, rather than actual sales (shipments).

This is because a customer may order 100 items for delivery on the 21st July, but there is none in stock. If the product is not available until 2nd August, the actual "sales" or "shipment" will be credited to August. The demand was for 100 in July. If we want the system to predict demand based on history, we want it to predict 100 for July and not August. This assumes monthly forecasting, and if you need to operate weekly, then you need to allocate the history to the correct week.

This means in turn that the systems must be capable of recording – for each order – the first <u>requested</u> date and quantity on order to feed the statistical forecasting engine, and provide information on true <u>demand</u>.

- **Filter Demand**

The customer demand recorded in this way may be exaggerated because of some event, which is not going to be repeated. Covid-19 was a classic example! Companies that provide disinfectant or loo rolls saw dramatic increases in demand in the early part of 2020. In 2021, they would need to review and adjust the history of demand.

Similarly, the 2019 World Cup cricket competition in the UK most likely increased the demand for beer across the country, particularly around Edgbaston, Lords in London, Durham, etc. The cricket World Cup only happens every four years, and India will host the 2023 competition.

Hence, if we are going to use history to predict demand, we need to "filter" the demand – thus we need to reduce the "historical demand" for items for which there is an extraordinary upward surge.

It would be right to use the historical trend demand predicted for the months or years as the basis for historical data if we see a significant increase in demand because of an unusual event.

Similarly, sometimes when companies look at their data, they find there are times when there are zero or small quantities, which happened when there were stock-outs. Hence, the company is recording invoiced sales, rather than orders requested by customers.

So, where there have been stock-outs, then the history should be adjusted (when using it for statistical purposes) to show the amount customers would have ordered if the product had been available. You should do this by interpolating the numbers that were originally forecast for the month/week.

I appreciate it seems crazy to try and forecast what you might have sold if you had been in stock – but it makes sense, if you want to make sure that the system provides a reasonable base forecast.

The key is that the purpose of the forecast is to provide a statement of customer volume requirements and the expected customer request date. Hence you must base the demand on real demand history.

- **Review Accuracy – Forecast Error and Bias**

The area of measurement of forecast accuracy and bias has probably occupied the most significant amount of discussion in the area of developing the IBP process than anywhere else. Finance directors want an accurate forecast to be able to predict cash flows. Supply chain/operations directors, sitting on assets which they need to use productively, are desperate for accurate forecasts to manage their plant and equipment.

Operations almost always defend failure to deliver to customers what they want and when they want with the excuse of, "If only we had a more accurate forecast." The whole subject can then disappear into arcane ways of measuring it, with arguments about the right way to measure it – Root Mean Square Error, Mean Absolute Error, etc. Before long, the eyes glaze over and everyone wishes someone else could take care of it. It is like the algebra moment at school, where those whose numeracy skills are not high give up with "numbers". Keep it simple is always a good motto!

There are two fundamental problems which we need to address as part of developing an effective IBP process in this context.

The first is to answer the question that relates to any measurement process: "How well have we done?"

Ask this question in most companies, and people will make an answer based on the latest financial report that compares actual to budget. Thus, we compare – usually – the actual vs the budget sales for the month, and the Actual Cumulative Sales for year to date vs the Budget for the year to date. If we are above, then the figures are highlighted in green, and if the numbers are below either figure, then the numbers are highlighted in red. At that point, someone reels out the appropriate excuse. Sometimes the excuse is as weak as, "we did not sell the budget because XYZ customer did not buy so much."

The second question is, "what is the true variability of demand?" – so we can know what to do about the inaccuracy of the forecast. Most of the financial numbers just look at the aggregate (in value terms), and providing the numbers are within some small percentage, then everything is okay.

However, the numbers at an aggregate level can conceal a considerable variation at a more detailed level, which is not made clear at the aggregate level. The analogy of the swan is appropriate; they are swimming along the river against the tide. On the surface, the swan looks remarkably calm and serene, but the legs are pedalling fast to keep reasonably still and make little progress.

The problem with the comparison with the budget is that if we are going to take the forecast and simultaneously drive financial projections against which to plan cash flow and drive material and capacity requirements (people and machines), then we should not deliberately make it wrong. It is okay for events outside of our control to make us wrong – but why shoot ourselves in the foot?

If we colour the difference between actual and budget in green and red (green is good, and red is wrong), then we are going to encourage the behavioural issue discussed before, which is driven by patting ourselves on the back if we beat the budget; human beings like to be patted on the back. So, when we ask someone to put the budget together, then they will under-call the numbers. If we are going to give people their marching orders if they sell below the budget, then they will understate the budget.

Then all we will do is end up suddenly having shocks to the operational side of the business when the extra sales come in. The more surprises we can provide, then the better we will look!

More subtly, actual invoiced sales – while true from the point of actual revenue recognition as part of accounting standards – does not show us how actual demand performed against forecast. Did we deliver what we said we would deliver from a business winning aspect?

So, saying we did well by comparing our performance to the budget is not a useful measure of how good we are at winning business, which should be about: did we deliver what we said we would deliver as demand?

The next important point is that companies usually prepare their budget once a year – let us say they finalise it in November for the next calendar-based Financial Year (Jan-Dec). That means we start the process around 15-18 months out from the year-end. Getting January right, should not be too hard. But making forecasts that far out for October, November and December is going to be extremely difficult, and in a fast-changing world, almost impossible.

Also, making the forecast once a year means we only have one occasion on which we create the forecast, and one instance of a process against which we can compare. But in practice, we should review our forecast frequently (i.e. each month), then seeing how good is our monthly process at providing a re-forecast. So when we ask the question of, "how well have you done?" the answer should be about how good we are at Demand Planning, and not how well have we done just against the one month. Panel 6 illustrates how one company managed forecast accuracy in practise and achieved stunning benefits.

Panel 6: Improving Forecast Accuracy

A major clothing company based in Europe found that they were struggling with too much inventory and poor delivery performance. Their clothing was made in the Far East, and being a fashion product, they had to plan around 18 months ahead to meet the autumn/winter and spring/summer fashion cycles.

One of the things they found was that a market could be finding it difficult to meet their sales targets selling trousers. So, they would sell T-shirts on a half-price promotion instead. While this met the numbers, it meant that this would cause enormous disruption across the supply chain.

So, they started to measure forecast accuracy – but to make sure this was taken seriously, they fined their countries based on the inventory they would create through inaccurate forecasting. Thus, if Germany and France both forecast 1,000 pairs of trousers but France sold 700, they would then get an invoice for the 300 jeans undersold.

This could be offset if Germany sold an extra 100 trousers – so countries could help each other out.

Forecast accuracy was improved by 35% and inventory was reduced by 30%.

That was a massive saving!

So, the first principle should be that if we are going to get away from deliberately biasing the forecast, then we should accept that the forecast is equally good either side of the demand plan; +/-2%, +/-5% or some number is acceptable.

The second principle is that in a fast-changing world, we need to move to at least a monthly forecasting cycle. In which case, we will have 12 instances of when we carry out the forecasting process. We should measure how accurate the forecast is <u>each time</u> we make the forecast – and therefore get a more regular review of how good our forecasting process is – 12 or 52 times per year.

The problem with the statement of "we have done well" at an aggregate level concealing the swan's paddling legs is essentially because the underlying changes in requirements will cause cost.

Either at the last moment, a sale will be made to reach the target and there will be disruption to the supply chain, or marketing will run a promotion (additional cost!) which will suddenly increase the pressure on the supply chain. Besides which, if you look at the evidence produced by Andrew Ehrenburg (Ehrenburg, 1975) you will see that he showed that promotions never actually increase real demand, they just reschedule the demand as people buy things during the promotion, and stop buying them after the advertisement.

So, while Sales make their targets, manufacturing misses theirs because of overtime, etc. Hardly fair – except in a silo-organised company!

Thus, the third principle is that we should have a way of measuring the "mix" error of the forecast.

Purpose of Measurement

1. The purpose of measuring the accuracy of forecasts is twofold: To get a handle on how much variation we should plan for in the supply chain, and to understand the risk we are going to take by holding inventory or spare capacity. Suppose we forecast 1,000 and plan to make 1,500 (because our forecast accuracy is +/50% to get 98% service level), then if we sell

up to 1,500, we will meet customer requirements (and be within limits). But if we end up selling 500, we could end up with 1,000 units in stock. That is okay, as it was a risk we took.

2. We need to see if we can improve the process in answer to the question: "How well have we done?" If we have a measure, then we can use the DMAIC process suggested above to improve the forecasting process. We need to answer the question, "What are the real causes of error?"

Process of Measurement

The standard way of being able to measure Forecast Accuracy – or whether we sold what we said we were going to sell – is to use the method called "Mean Absolute Percent Error". Mean is just a mathematical term for average. Absolute allows us to see the "mix error"; here we ignore the +/- of the error, treating an error as equally bad or good regardless. This motivates people away from the "it's good if I sell more than the forecast" problem.

We use per cent error so that a significant error over a small volume will balance a small error over a large volume. The following Table 13 illustrates the calculation.

Table 13 Illustration of MAPE Accuracy measure

Forecast Error Report
Date: Feb-20

	Forecast	Actual	Diff	Abs Diff	%
Family ABC					
Product 123	100	120	20	20	20%
Product 456	200	220	20	20	10%
Product 678	300	260	-40	40	13%
Total	600	600	0	80	13%
Family XYZ					
Product 587	400	500	100	100	25%
Product 649	300	200	-100	100	33%
Product 967	350	300	-50	50	14%
Product 834	200	220	20	20	10%
Total	1250	1220	-30	170	14%
Total	1850	1820	-30	250	14%

Thus, with family ABC, the overall error at the family level is 0%.
However, when we add up the errors in the "Abs Diff" (Absolute Difference) column, then the total error is 80 – which is 13% – 80/600 Forecast. This calculation is the "mix error".

If you do the same for family XYZ, then you will see that there is a relatively small error of 30 (1.6%) at the family level. But if you look again at the column "Abs Diff" you will see that the sum of all the errors is 170 – which works out at 14% error (170/1,250 forecast). Again, this is the "mix error" and indicates the disruption that the supply chain needs to absorb.

At the bottom, you can see the total error – which is 14% – which gives an overall average error calculation. Companies should use this as the measure in answer to, "how well did we do?"

Note that I have produced the report based on "error" – i.e. it states how wrong the numbers are. Many companies I have come across then go one step further to calculate accuracy by calculating the formula "1-error" – this would be 87% in the case of family ABC. This calculation works up to the point that the error is 100% or greater (and I have seen this!). At this point, the accuracy becomes 0%. If the error is 120%, then the forecast accuracy calculation becomes – 20%, which is odd. It was supposed to go on a scale from 0-100%, with 100% being the most accurate, but now we can get -20%. Hence, I prefer the calculation to show the error – which could go to 150% or more in exceptional circumstances.

Also note, that I have calculated the result as the Error/**Total Forecast**. Some companies calculate the error as Error/**Total Actual**. This is wrong. I prefer using the forecast because the above analysis of using forecast error is an input into the calculation of safety stock and capacity. If I am looking at a forecast in the future of 1,000, I want to know the error of that forecast – which is 13% in the case of family ABC above (i.e. will be +/-13%). Using actual as the "denominator" will give a different result, and it can be a significant difference depending on the difference in the totals.

Calculation aside, the question now is, "what do I with this information?"

The first thing is to answer the question of "how well did we do?" Here, we need to see if there is a problem with the process.

One client in the FMCG business did an analysis of the worst-performing items and found that these were mostly items which they promoted in the month, and they were over-forecast. Further discussion led to the realisation that they were over-forecast because sales wanted to make sure that the forecast that manufacturing would use was the forecast "<u>plus</u> some" so that if the promotion went well, there would be more in stock to meet the demand. However, this was in effect double-counting, because the planning system worked out the amount of safety stock needed based on the forecast.

They then got the Sales and Marketing departments to adjust their forecast so that they would aim for a realistic mid-point estimate.

In another company, they found that promotions were being agreed with customers too late. So, they then produced a policy which said sales needed to arrange promotions at least 13 weeks out. Simple but effective. This analysis leads to changing the process and ensuring we get a more reliable outcome.

One of the areas which I have not seen fully developed is the use of the "Six-Sigma" approach. This approach – very well described in a book called Six Sigma (Mikel Harry, 2000) – is well applied in Manufacturing and Design functions in the company, but not so much to the area of Sales and forecasting.

But the principles behind "Six Sigma" are the same everywhere. Take a problem, and then collect data about the situation. Analyse the problem to its root-cause. Often the first-level analysis does not reveal the root cause, and you need to dig much deeper into the issues behind the problem. To help this, you can carry out what is called a "fishbone diagram analysis". Figure 42 is an illustration of this concept related to forecasting.

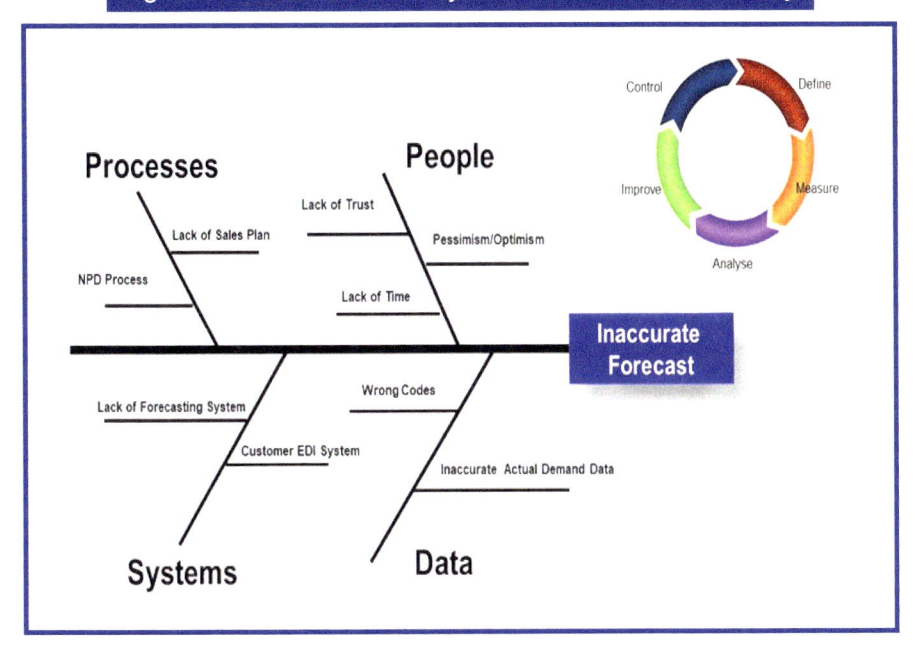

Figure 42: Fishbone analysis for Forecast Accuracy

Hence the first-level analysis is to break the causes of error down into the critical areas of processes, people, systems and data. You might also add another line for "Mother Nature" to cover issues like the weather, which are outside of the control of the organisation!

If we follow through the "people" bone, then we see there is the line of "lack of time".

I had one client who monitored how long their sales managers had spent on updating the forecast – they measured it in minutes! At the next senior leadership meeting the managing director – who was not satisfied with the quality of the information – made it clear to the sales and marketing director that he viewed putting together the forecast was one of the most important outcomes of the sales and marketing effort. Next time, the team spent much longer on forecasting!

The MD had been a manufacturing director in a previous company, and put a banner up in his office: "If you can't forecast it, then I can't make it." That helped form his view when he needed to exercise leadership as an MD! Education is a crucial result of understanding the problem with errors.

Targets and ownership

It is essential to establish targets, and ownership of those targets, to improve forecast accuracy. If you look at the chart in Table 13, then this analysis can be sorted by customer or sales manager or marketing manager, as required. With most other measures that companies use, then they are targeted based on a graph that heads to 100%. With forecast error, the objective is to reduce the error.

Many companies have tried to do this by measuring forecast accuracy going to 100% (=1-Error). But this is flawed by the calculation (as shown above). Importantly, we cannot expect forecasts to be 100% accurate, so aiming for 100% forecast accuracy is illusory; hence companies should base their targets on reducing the error.

Many people have asked what the "best in class" figure for forecast error is. It is impossible to answer!

Not only is difficult to get a standard definition across companies, but every company has different factors in play in its markets. I do not believe there is somehow a universal benchmark target that all can reach. I have seen numbers in some markets which are as low as +/- 10%, but this was more to do with the nature of the market being not very volatile. I have seen +/-50%. The literature tends to suggest that an error of +/-20% is acceptable.

What works better is to encourage a "continuous improvement" culture that drives people to look at how to improve the quality of the process. Ultimately, if you can eliminate all the errors in the processes and systems, you should come to "natural variation", which you can then buffer against with your supply chain.

As an extreme example, making bread is a simple activity; however, it is extremely weather dependent and if the summer is very hot (as in 2018 in the UK), then the demand for bread for barbecues etc. can explode. One company that is in this market has a complete

Demand

factory ready to be opened in the event of prolonged hot weather. That is useful in long hot summers!

So, carry out an analysis by area/specific responsibility for the forecast and set milestones and targets for the reduction of the error of the forecast. Figure 43 illustrates this.

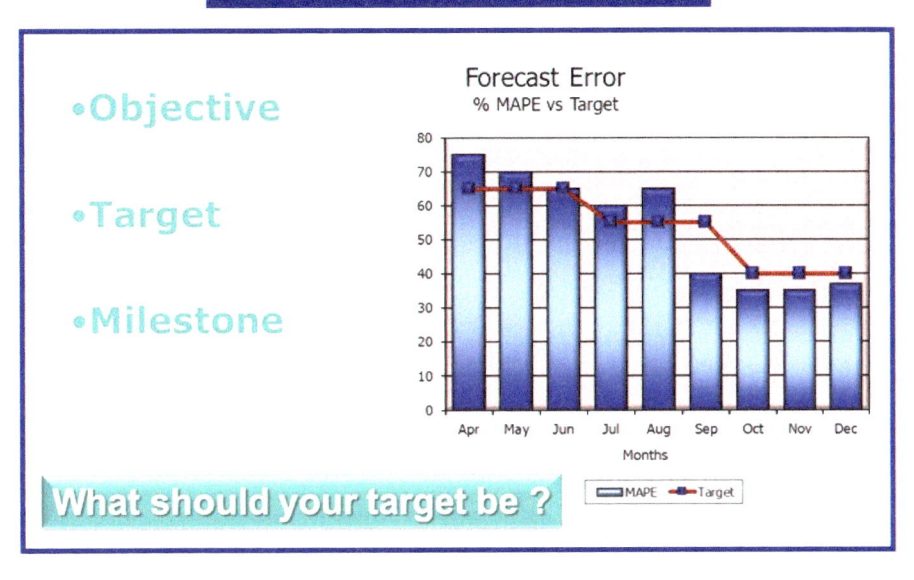

Figure 43: Forecast Accuracy Target

- Objective
- Target
- Milestone

Forecast Error
% MAPE vs Target

What should your target be ?

This chart shows how the target has been to reduce the error of the forecast over nine months. It is depicted over a relatively short period, to fit in the graph!

Rewards Drive Behaviour

Motivation in business is a vast topic. The measurement systems influence the way people behave in response either to what people do or say to them, or through the direct monetary payment process. If you want to achieve the objectives behind Integrated Business Planning, it is essential companies build a "reward culture" around the reduction of forecast error. This culture will promote the result of "one set of numbers working as one team."

In many companies I have come up against the "barrier" of sales bonuses – i.e. a reward to the salesman for exceeding the forecast or target. It is vital to eliminate this reward; instead, put in place a reward for achieving a reduction in error.

Thus, in one client, the sales manager created the "MAPE cup" and awarded this each month to the salesperson who showed the best MAPE score. MAPE stands for Mean Absolute Percentage Error. It contributed immensely to their improvements.

In another company, the regional VP asked the head of demand planning how he could help forecast accuracy. The head of demand planning suggested that he should ask questions of the country general managers at his meetings with them why they had not reduced error in their forecasts. He did, and they soon began to expect the question and prepare an answer.

Leadership is about determining the right behaviour, and then holding people accountable for doing the right things to get the correct behaviour!

Measurement of Forecast Bias

Forecast bias describes the situation in which people make forecasts, but we then observe that the actual result is either always above or always below the forecast. To have this same result time after time is progressively unlikely – assuming that the underlying data and process is based on truly random events.

As a simple example, if you take a coin and toss it to see if it comes up heads or tails, then the chances on the first occasion of the result being either heads or tails is 50%. This observation means that if you toss a coin 100 times, then 50 times it should come up as tails and 50 times it should come out as heads (this assumes the coin is not somehow weighted!).

The chances of tossing a coin twice in a row and finding that you throw heads twice is 25% (50% x 50%). Similarly, if you throw it three times, the probability is 12.5% (50% x 50% x 50%), and if you throw heads four times in a row, the chances of this occurring randomly is much lower – 6.25%. At this point, you might begin to suspect that the coin is weighted in favour of heads, somehow. You can do the same with dice, where throwing a six on a six-sided die is 1/6 = 16.6%, and throwing a die twice and throwing another six is 2.8% and so on.

The same principle applies to forecasting. We would suspect bias if each month the forecast is over or under the predicted figures, particularly four months in a row; it is unlikely to be a random process. The impact of bias in a manufacturing environment is that if someone constantly over-forecasts, then the result will be too much inventory, as the supply chain procures and makes, but the sales do not happen.

Similarly, if someone constantly under-forecasts, then the business will continually run short of product – leading to poor customer service. figure 44 summarises the issues – and shows that under-forecasting is as "bad" as over-forecasting.

Figure 44: Impact of Biased Forecasts

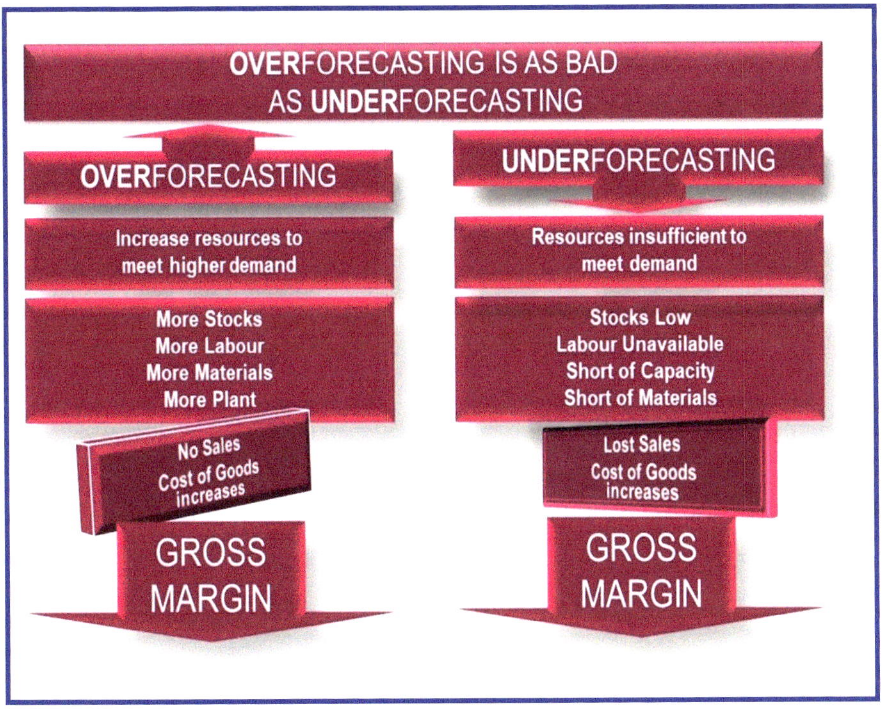

OVERFORECASTING IS AS BAD AS UNDERFORECASTING

OVERFORECASTING
- Increase resources to meet higher demand
- More Stocks
- More Labour
- More Materials
- More Plant
- No Sales
- Cost of Goods increases
- GROSS MARGIN

UNDERFORECASTING
- Resources insufficient to meet demand
- Stocks Low
- Labour Unavailable
- Short of Capacity
- Short of Materials
- Lost Sales
- Cost of Goods increases
- GROSS MARGIN

Experience suggests that bias is due mainly to the people making the forecast: in-built pessimism or optimism.

The same approach I suggested for forecast accuracy should be applied to bias – Define, Measure, Analyse, Improve, Control.

The **definition** of bias is based on an analysis of whether the forecasts are serially over or under the actual results. If we are to track this on a meaningful basis, then we should base the measurement on reviewing, at an item and a family level, actual vs forecast for four months, and then seeing if there is in-built pessimism or optimism. If the forecast is always over for the four months, then the forecast is optimistic; if less than actual it is pessimistic. This is illustrated in Table 14.

Thus, for the four months shown between Dec-19 and Mar-20, the forecast is always below the actual; the sum of the difference is 16.4%. The formula indicates it is "pessimistic" (or "pess"), by analysing the fact that the forecast has been below the "actual" for four months in a row. The same is true for the period Jan-18 through to April-18.

Table 14 Calculation of Bias

Juices Family	T-2	Dec-19	Jan-20	Feb-20	Mar-20	Apr-20
	Fcast	3450	3900	4200	7600	7900
	Actual	4500	4200	4700	8900	8200
	Difference	23%	7%	11%	15%	4%
	Bias				16.4%	10.2%
		+	+	+	Pess	Pess
				BIASSED		

Some companies and some systems measure bias based on the sum of the actuals vs the sum of the forecasts for a single month (taking into account the sign). While this does give an idea of the numbers for a single month, it fails to show if there is a serial trend – which is a correct way of looking for serial bias and indicates a problem with the forecasting process.

Someone is getting it wrong in the same way every month!

When do we "Freeze" the Forecast?

We can revise forecasts each month, which raises the question of: "at what point should we measure the forecast?" Thus, for every month, we will have forecast that month for possibly 42 months prior to that month.

The answer to this question depends on the answer to another one: "When are you 'committing' to the plan?"

If you look at changing the forecast, and the impact through the Bill of Material on assembled or purchased products, then any change within "cumulative lead time" will have an immediate effect on purchased raw materials, which will be challenging to fulfil. Hence, this cumulative lead time should determine your "time fences", and the point at which you commit to the forecast.

If you look at how an MRP system works, if you are planning to sell something in three months and the cumulative lead time is three months, then you will be placing the order this month for the long lead-time raw materials. This approach, however, looks at raw materials. You should also look at capacity. Thus, getting new equipment may take six months – if you add up the lead time for approval and installation and commission of the equipment.

Thus, in the IBP process, we also need to be looking at where are we committing to capacity when we are looking at forecast accuracy. This measure will be a feed into capacity expenditure decisions. If your forecast says you need two machines providing 12,000 hours of capacity, and your forecast accuracy is +/-50%, how are you going to plan for the extra 6,000 hours of capacity you might require? Another machine?

A feature of forecasting, generally, is that the further out you are trying to forecast, the more inaccurate the forecast becomes. So, if I am forecasting out three months, I might see a figure of +/20% error. But if I am looking out six months, I might see an error of +/-30%. It is, therefore, worth reviewing the error of the forecasts at different points in time, depending on whether we are looking at materials or capacity.

The way to review forecast accuracy, then, for material is to compare the forecast at the Cumulative Lead time (CLT). Figure 45 shows what I call a "waterfall chart", which illustrates the history of the forecasts made for a particular month, and then compares that with the actual for the month.

Figure 45: Forecast Waterfall chart

	Jul	Aug	Sep	Oct	Nov	Dec	Jan	Feb	Mar
Jul	100	100	100	110	110	120	120	120	120
Aug	90	110	110	110	110	130	130	130	120
Sep		105	110	115	115	115	115	115	120
Oct			115	120	120	115	115	115	115
Nov				130	125	125	125	120	120
Dec					120	125	125	125	130
Jan						115	105	105	130
Feb							90	105	130
Mar								110	130

☐ = Actual

Thus, if you look at the forecasts made for October, then in previous months the forecast had been 110,110,115,120, and the actual was 130. If the cumulative lead time is two months, then you will take (the beginning of) September's forecast (115) as the basis of the calculation.

The CLT can be different for different families or groups of products, depending on the lead times for the individual products within that family. In this case, the correct approach would be to calculate the CLT for each family, and calculate the right forecast to use for each family.

However, programming this in your computer would be complicated, and pragmatically it makes sense to select an average CLT across all products – e.g. month -3.

It is reasonable to analyse the accuracy of all the forecasts at two, three, four, five and six months before the month of actual demand.

Sometimes you can see that the forecasts six months before are always more accurate than Month 2, which can say that whoever is doing the forecast is "playing around" with the forecast too much as they approach the month of sale. This observation helps to get an appreciation that Sales should take a longer-term view.

- **Agree Commercial Plans**

Once we have got the base forecast in place, cleaned up, with reliable data, and forecast accuracy and bias measured, then we can add in the intelligence about what will be different about the future from what has happened in the past.

Most commercial people react to forecasting by saying, "How can I know what is going to happen? It is all very well trying to put together a forecast of what we are going to sell, but most times our customers don't know what they are going to sell!"

This statement is, of course, all true. But the discipline behind forecasting for IBP is that we need to be clear about the <u>assumptions</u> that are behind our forecasts. We should also recognise that forecasting is a multi-input process – we need to consult as many people about the forecast as possible, and in this way get away from the age-old complaint "how can you trust the forecast?"

But, mostly, this "reaction" is an initial resistance to the idea of putting together a forecast, and a feeling that life is hard enough selling, without an additional activity to do.

Education is a critical element of persuading people to undertake this activity. Part of the complex function of "selling" this idea to Sales is to make the process well thought through, and ensure that it will not be too difficult to do. "Segmentation" is a great way to facilitate this.

Segmentation

An excellent place to start is to ensure that you get the commercial team to focus on those products which are likely to cause most issues to the supply chain. In this respect, we should carry out an analysis of our products, examining the relative volatility of products, as compared to the value of products to the business. Volatility refers to the amount that the demand for an item varies relative to the forecast, which will cause issues in managing the supply chain, in particular.

We can categorise products simply as "high volatility" or "low volatility". We can also do this on a scale of X, Y, Z, where category X is low volatility, Y is medium volatility and Z is very high.

We can then also categorise products in terms of the value of usage (measured by Variable Product Cost), and then rank products on a scale of A = High Value, B= Medium Value and C = Low value. This analysis leads to the following (simplified) table, which enables you to categorise the importance of the requirement to review the forecasts.

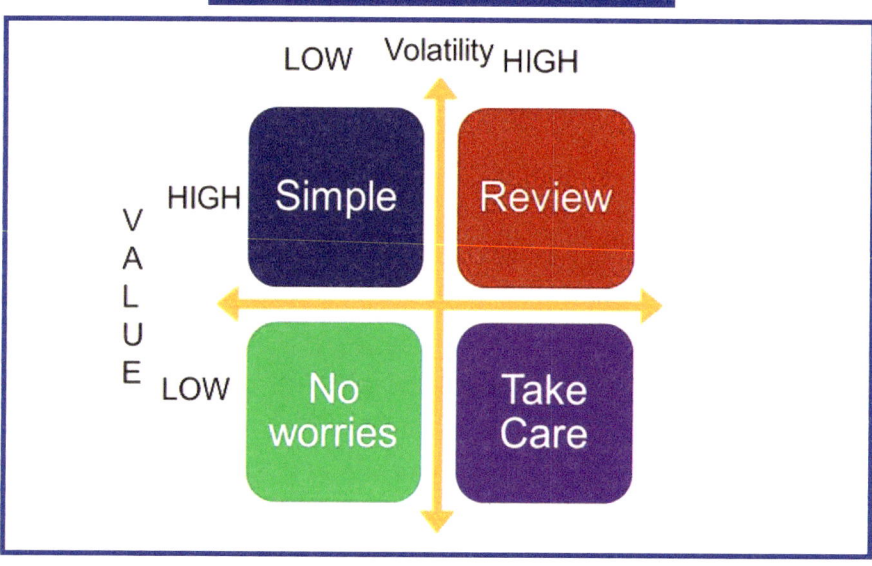

Figure 46: Product Segmentation

	LOW Volatility	HIGH Volatility
HIGH VALUE	Simple	Review
LOW VALUE	No worries	Take Care

Thus, Figure 46 illustrates that in the top left-hand corner of Low Volatility and High Value, you have your biggest sellers, which do not exhibit a lot of volatility. In the bottom right-hand corner you have the smallest of your product range, which show a lot of volatility.

You should measure volatility by calculating the "coefficient of variance". If you look at the history of the demand for a product – let us say over the last 12 or 24 months – then you will be able to get an average demand for the product.

Either from your forecasting system or through a spreadsheet, you should calculate the "standard deviation" of the error of the forecast for each item. If you then divide the standard deviation by the average of the demand, you get a measure of how volatile a product is.

Thus, if one product has an average demand of 100 units per month, and a standard deviation of 10 units, your calculation of volatility will be 10%. Around 98% of the time, the demand will be between the limits of +/-20 units.

Whereas if another product has an average demand of 100, but a standard deviation of 50 units, then the resultant volatility calculation will be 50%. There is the same level of demand, but this product is much more volatile. Ninety-eight per cent of the time it will be somewhere between 0 and 200 units. (You will need more safety stock for these items.)

Setting the analytical limits for your table will depend somewhat on your range of products but I typically would analyse into a coefficient of variation where Low = 0-100%; Medium, 100 % to 200 %; and High, 200 % and above.

Now, looking at Figure 46, the top right-hand corner indicates the critical set of products to **"Review"**. These are your most important products and are the most volatile. Getting the forecast wrong here will either consume a lot of inventory or cause problems with customer service.

"Take Care" are those products that are highly volatile, which you ought also to review. While they are the smaller products in your range, you could find you consume a large amount of stock by all of these products.

The products which we have labelled **"Simple"** in principle, are not very volatile and should be dealt with statistically. **"No Worries"** suggests that these products do not need much effort at all in the forecasting process. This analytical approach will enable you to filter out those products that require a salesperson's intervention.

To support all of this, you can create a code for your products, which goes from AX (top left-hand corner) to CZ (bottom right-hand corner), and can then sequence your list of items to be forecast from AZ (focus products) to CX (relax) when you present to the person who needs to forecast them.

This sorting will help cut the amount of time that needs to be devoted to forecasting.

Assumptions

One of the core elements of a good forecasting process is the quality of the assumptions. All forecasts will be wrong, but they will be wrong because of the quality of the assumptions that you make. At business school, I worked with models of the economy developed by the British economist Terry Burns – now Lord Burns – who went on to develop the models used by the UK Treasury to predict the economy. These were all built on a series of assumptions around how Gross Domestic Product would vary, dependent on several factors like assumptions on price and cost inflation, exchange rates, interest rates, wage rates, productivity, tax rates and so on. Change one "assumption" and the outcome on GDP would vary.

The accuracy of the result inevitably depended on the quality of the underlying assumptions. We would have a lot of fun varying our reaction to changes in GDP (spending more government money, for instance) and then finding the economy would go crazy a couple of rounds later. Just like real life!

The English genealogist and engraver Gregory King is credited to be the first great economic statistician, and he lived from 1648 to 1712. In 1695, he analysed past data and forecast that the England and Wales population would rise from 5.5m in 1695 to 6.42m in

1800, 7.35m in 1900 and 8.28m in 2000. He then forecasted that the population would hit a ceiling of 11m by 2300; the land would not be able to support any more! See page 55 of The Time Traveller's guide to Restoration Britain. London: Penguin Random House, (Mortimer, 2017).

The population rose to 11m in 1800, 32m by 1900 and 52m by 2000. So the forecast was wrong, even if Gregory King was forecasting back in 1695!

However, he did not foresee the improvements in agriculture and mechanisation; but he did make assumptions on the birth rate, death rate, illness, wars and the hazards of an occupation. So, he analysed and produced a good forecast, but it was wrong because the assumptions were wrong!

The fundamental principle behind this approach is that we should be able to update the forecast as time goes on. But when we move on, then our formal process should cover and understand both changes to the assumptions, and add any additional assumptions that we should include in our model.

An excellent principle is that a person can only change a forecast if they have supported that change by a **documented change in assumptions**.

Application of Assumptions

Let us now illustrate how to apply assumptions to the forecasts. You, of course, can work up your own set of assumptions that apply to your business.

Within the Make to Stock and Fast Moving Consumer Goods environment, companies frequently run promotions or do TV advertising campaigns. Thus, there is a need to make assumptions about the impact of promotions.

A good forecasting process would include analysing the planned and actual impact of promotions. Thus, we may arrange a 10% reduction in price for a certain period. We should then examine the actual impact on sales to the consumer, and see what the effect is – and see whether the effect of the promotion is positive.

There are good promotions management systems around, which enable you to record different types of promotions. Then they will store for you the effect of the different types of promotions so that the next time you run that type of promotion, it will work out for you the expected impact. That is a good example of the use of assumptions.

Within the Make to Order world, dealing with new contracts and new customers, there is uncertainty around whether you are going to win the business or not, and how long it will last. Hence, in this case, it makes sense to review the basis on which you might win the business. Thus, a matrix would be useful, which looks at:

- What is our competitive position with the customer?
- What is the strength of our technical offering?
- How strong are we on price?
- Has the client got budget approval?
- What is our connection like to the budget holder, technical expert, business contact/procurement person?

Within the pharmaceutical business, there is uncertainty about how many patients suffer from a particular disease and what governments will do or not do in funding their healthcare service, for example.

In the chemical business, there is uncertainty around the cyclicality of the industry, prices of commodities like oil, and so on.

Everyone has their own particular uncertainties. But the common factor should be that each business should derive their set of assumptions that have an impact on their business; they should then document these and the direction of travel for each of these assumptions.

There are three critical dimensions to pulling together forecast.

The first relates to facts about the market – i.e. the number of customers or consumers, the various sectors within the market, and trends. Market research and insights typically cover this activity. It tells you where the opportunity lies.

Demand

The second relates to factors which we can describe as external market drivers which cause changes to happen – like Christmas, Easter, the weather, changes in technology, changes in politics, to which we have to respond.

Finally, there are the internal "levers", which a company can manipulate within the sales and marketing areas to try and move demand towards it – the familiar aspects of pricing, promotion, packaging, advertising, distribution. Thus, if we change prices, we need to make assumptions about the impact of competitors and customers/consumers.

Hence, assumptions are core to a proper approach in IBP, as Figure 47 shows; it illustrates the link to the three key areas.

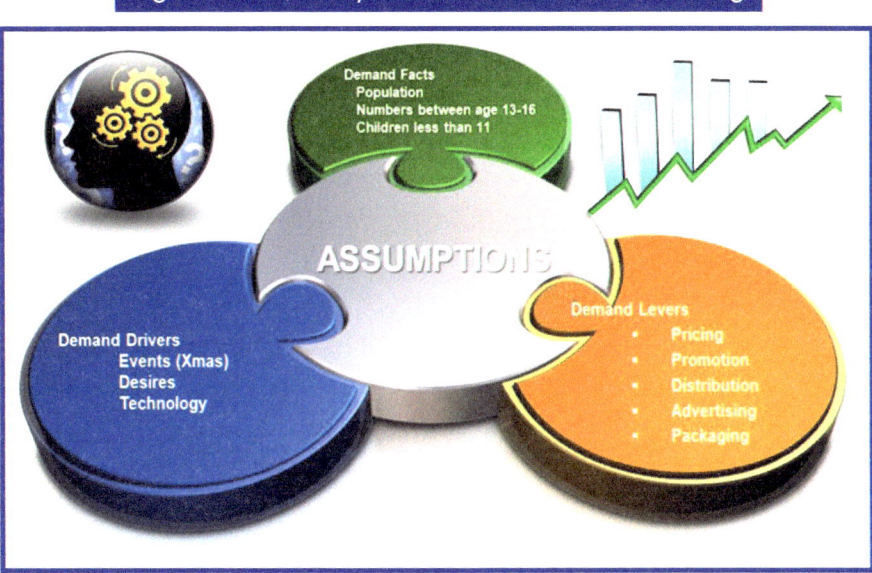

Figure 47: Assumptions are core to forecasting

Demand Facts
Population
Numbers between age 13-16
Children less than 11

ASSUMPTIONS

Demand Drivers
Events (Xmas)
Desires
Technology

Demand Levers
- Pricing
- Promotion
- Distribution
- Advertising
- Packaging

Demand Planning – Gathering the Assumptions

Gathering the inputs to these assumptions will require getting input from several functions – Sales, Marketing, Finance, Technical, etc. So, if you then look at the typical assumptions you can build up to support a forecast, they will include:

Sales	Number of customers
	Share of market/share of customers' purchases
	Price and cost (assumptions on margin)
	Distribution strategy – direct/indirect
Marketing	Promotions
	Advertising
	Product development
Technical	Product life cycle
	Effectiveness vs competition
	Patent protection/intellectual property
Finance	Exchange rates
	Interest rates
	Inflation rates

A good forecasting process will then support the creation of a database of assumptions. Then the challenge within the IBP process is to manage changes to these assumptions and to support the forecast changes with supply plan changes.

I show an example of how you might structure these assumptions in your process on the next page (which for convenience goes out 12 months).

Thus, a fundamental assumption might be that the market will grow by 3% per annum, which might relate to the market conditions. We might assume that our market share will increase from 10% to 15% (for various sectors).

From this, we can work out what our projected sales will be. Then, if our sales either exceed or fall short of this forecast, for whatever reason, we should be able to trace the problem back to either market growth or market share; this can then inform our forecasts for future periods.

You should gather the information for this as part of the monthly cycle through discussions with Sales, Marketing and Finance either through one-on-one meetings or one-to-many meetings – it is a collaborative process. That will then lead to a single number for each product (SKU) and family, which will then be fed into the ERP system to drive requirements.

It is for this reason that when companies have developed IBP, they have recognised the need for a particular role – the demand manager – who becomes a captain of the Demand Planning Process. This person needs to be commercially aware, have excellent communication skills, and have strong analytical skills.

It is a role which I have seen develop in the last few years, and it is slowly becoming recognised as the profession it ought to become. But there are still many companies who have not yet seen the need for a demand manager – or recognised the value it can bring to a company.

Table 15 Assumptions template

FAMILY:			Future Months			
			0-3	4-6	7-9	10-12
FUNCTIONAL AREA	Assumption					
MARKETING	Target End Users	Total #				
	Growth of Market	%				
	Number of Competitors	#				
	Market Price Movement	%				
	Promotional Activity					
	- Our Company	Hi/Med/Lo				
	- Competition	Hi/Med/Lo				
	Our Market Share	%				
SALES	Number of Customers - Large	#				
	Number of Customers - Small	#				
	Our Share of Customers - Large	%				
	Our Share of Customers - Small	%				
	Customer Price Movement	%				
	Price Movement to Customers	%				
	Competitive Activity	Hi/Med/Lo				
FINANCE	Exchange Rate	Rate				
	Product Cost Inflation	%				
	Currency Risk	Hi/Med/Lo				
	Credit Risks	Hi/Med/Lo				
DEVELOPMENT	Regulatory Constraints	Hi/Med/Lo				
	Time to Approval for New products	Months				
	Number of Types of Application approved	#				
	Competitive Activity	Hi/Med/Lo				
	Number of new products	# Launched				

- **Role of Demand Manager**

There are several times when companies have asked me to describe the job role, and I have summarised this in Figure 48.

Figure 48: Demand Manager job description

- Co-ordinates Forecasting process
- Review the numbers
- Challenge not changes the forecast
- Work with Master Scheduler
- Works with Sales and Marketing
- Manages Customer Service levels – 98 % to Req. Date
- Inputs on Safety Stock policies
- Participates in IBP Process
- Reviews Forecast Accuracy and Bias and gets to root cause
- Decide or facilitates decision on who gets what in allocation
- Manages the Customer Relationship Management system and process
- Enforces good behaviours

It is a complex role. Firstly as "captain" of the demand planning process, they need to pull together the numbers on a weekly or monthly basis. The responsibility for the forecast lies with Sales and Marketing. Hence, a demand manager is in a position where they can review the numbers and provide insights through a challenge process.

The production planner, planning manager or master scheduler is responsible for the supply side, and hence they are often a critical interface between the Supply side and the Demand side. The supply side is usually organised around products and factory capacity. Companies often manage the Sales and Marketing side around routes to market (geography, market sectors, and product categories), so the demand manager (or indeed demand managers) acts as a cross-over point between the supply chain and the market place.

They should assist in improving forecast accuracy and bias, using the analytical tools which we described earlier, and through helping to ensure that the right behaviours are in place.

Demand Control

Sometimes capacity has to be constrained for either internal or external reasons. When I was at ICI Agrochemicals, we had the unfortunate situation of a plant burning down one night, which meant a loss of approximately 75% of total available capacity for one product.

The demand manager then had to look into the system, remove all the planned safety stocks, look at how to reduce lead times, reduce order quantities to be as small as practicably possible, and work out what was the "true demand" across the network of subsidiaries and direct distribution. He then put together a proposal, based on a complex review of strategic priorities, profitability and so on, of the quantities that would be available for each country/market, which was then reviewed and implemented. This was all done in a week. Before having this system in place, it would have taken months to resolve the situation.

Since then, I have seen several occasions on which companies have faced similar situations. In fact, at one multinational company, they recognised that there was a critical difference between "demand planning" and "demand management". When they looked at the chart in Figure 49 they recognised that they needed to split the roles.

Figure 49: Demand Planning v Demand Management

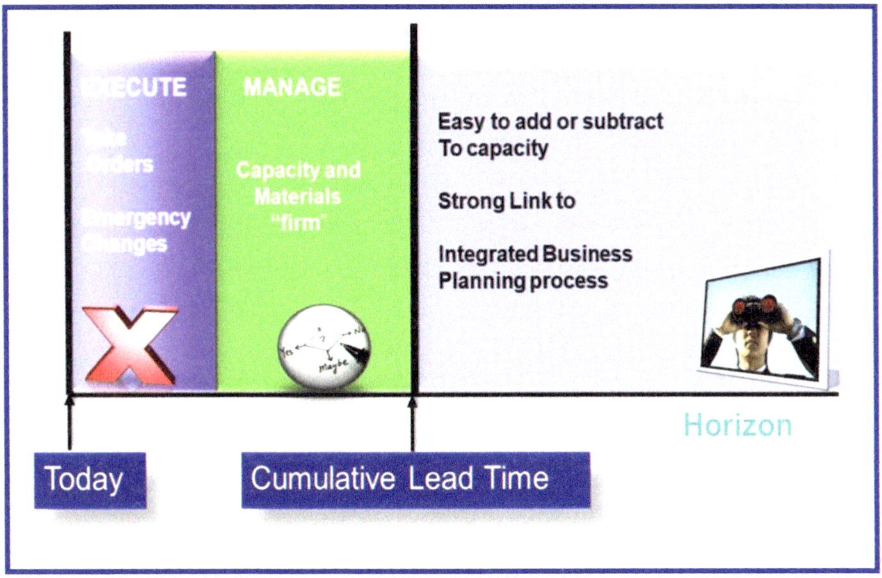

In the "manage" section, they needed demand controllers, who were located at the manufacturing plant to facilitate close communication with the supply side, and separately demand planners, who dealt with the right-hand side of the above diagram and who operated centrally, connecting with sales and marketing. This organisation encouraged a much better quality of process in both areas.

Demand control, therefore, is a crucial process to make sure you get a profitable use of scarce resources.

One of the problems that I have frequently seen, whether in multinational companies or companies within a country, is for some people not to bother to forecast, because when "push comes to shove", they know they can argue and get the product they want. The problem with this behaviour is that it means there is no incentive for those that do forecast to forecast correctly.

I came across one example of this in a company where they sold the primary chemical product as an ingredient to two market sectors – Pharmaceutical and Food. They had set up the forecasting process, and Peter (we have changed the names to protect his identity!) who sold to the Pharma sector had put in a forecast of 9,000 lbs (it was in the USA) of the product.

John, who sold to the biggest company in the food sector, never really forecast correctly. But when he went in to see his customer, they wanted 9,000 lbs of the same product. So, John said "yes", and the order was placed and delivered.

You can imagine how Peter felt when he went in to see the biggest customer in the Pharma industry, "sold" his 9,000 lbs, only to find there was no longer any in stock, and the lead time was going to be six weeks. Not only did the customer not get what they wanted, but he missed his sales target for the month. He was not particularly impressed with the process, and told me so! He was much happier when I explained to him the Demand Control process that they needed to put in place! In future, they treated a forecast like an order, and if there was not a forecast, one salesperson could not "steal" from another without checking first!

One of the most important activities they needed to achieve was enforcing good behaviours, and that required a radical culture change. I was pleased a few years later, when the planning manager got in contact to say how much easier it was to run the business with IBP.

- ## Risks and Opportunities

I have made a great emphasis on the fact that forecasts will be inaccurate.

I have also emphasised the fact that the forecast that drives the supply chain and financial plans should be a median estimate – i.e. bang in the middle of a range of a possible set of numbers.

That means, though, that we could have numbers both above and below the forecast, and that we often face opportunities and risks.

So let me first define what is meant by "risk" and "opportunity" in this case.

Opportunity is the potential business which we may get. Still, we do not want to put it in the forecast to drive materials and capacity requirements, as we are not confident that the business will materialise – (at least to the point we see it as a **signed request** for materials and capacity to be made available.)

Risk is business which we have forecast, and therefore have committed to making the materials and capacity, but which we might lose.

This approach should lead to a more formal way of recognising and managing opportunities and risks.

A good example of this is an agricultural chemical company which sells in several countries in Africa and the Middle East. They often quote in governmental tenders each year against several competitors.

They classify their "opportunities" as <60% probability, between >60% and <90%, and >90% probability of getting the tender. Their approach is that those tenders which they consider have a >90% chance of winning, go into the forecast. Those tenders which fall into the range of >60% but <90% are put into the forecast to drive capacity up to the cumulative lead time. After that point, they only include the tender in the forecast if the country manager signs an "Authority to Manufacture" – thus the commitment is clear. This process is a clear method for managing opportunities.

In another company, where they sold air-conditioning products, they would regularly be faced with the following situation concerning tenders from several potential customers, and were continually in the position of not being sure whether they would get the business. Table 16 illustrates a typical situation with a number of tenders at any point in time.

Table 16 Probabilities of winning tenders

Client	Quantity	Value	Probability of winning
Customer A	10	£200,000	60%
Customer B	6	£2,000,000	80%
Customer C	20	£500,000	30%
Customer D	4	£3,000,000	50%
Customer E	8	£2,000,000	70%

Before implementing Integrated Business Planning and clarifying what a forecast meant (i.e. a signed commitment to materials and capacity being made available), they would multiply the value of the tenders by the percentage and come up with a forecast.

Hence on these numbers, they would come up with a forecast of £4.65m and would plan for six of the items going to customer A, etc. They could not easily substitute the products across the five opportunities. Faced with the issue of how to make forecasts clear and transparent, the MD sat down with the sales and marketing director and explained it was essential to state which tender would go into the forecast.

The sales and marketing director then asked what would happen if he got the forecast wrong. The MD said he would fire him! So, they went through the list, and on the first pass – realising that if he got it wrong, he would get fired – the sales and marketing director put none of the opportunities in the forecast!

The MD then said, "In that case, I do not need a sales and marketing director!" This response encouraged the sales and marketing director to go back and look at the list. They then agreed that the business from customer B and customer E would go in the forecast, and the rest would remain as "opportunities".

This approach then helped the discussion, as they would work out what they needed to do in order to turn the 70% and 80% opportunities into 100%.

Their scoring was based on several criteria, as suggested above:
- Competitiveness in terms of price and technical solution
- Was a budget agreed?
- What was their position with the customer (did they have an inside salesman?)
- Terms and conditions. Tweaking one of these might help get the business.

It also meant that they would not spend any effort on customer C, whereas in the past they might well have done a lot of work, only to find they did not get the business. Focusing people's minds on the right priorities became key to expanding the business. But also, commitment to the forecast was vital for the rest of the company. It needed leadership to make this happen.

Strategic stocks

This company then recognised that they might need to hold strategic stocks to buffer against the products they did not expect to get.

The same or similar principle is true for many companies who have a critical raw material in their supply chain. Aluminium components need aluminium from big foundries and mills. Tea needs tea leaves, coffee needs coffee beans, crisps need potatoes, blackcurrant juice needs blackcurrants, and colds and flu need the active ingredient to prevent flu and colds.

These companies need to take a long-term view of the requirements for these ingredients, then look at risks and opportunities and decide how to hedge their bets.

This requirement, in turn, needs the ability to carry out simulations and understand the impact on their supply chain for the different scenarios, which will then potentially lead to a strategic purchase of the appropriate ingredient. The forecasting software needs to support this.

One client in the aerospace and defence sector used the IBP process to look at longer-term demand and then realised that there could be a shortage of titanium. By making a strategic purchase of titanium, they then managed to get a competitive edge by keeping their lead times down, while their competitors suffered.

Hence, we need to be clear – and list out – our opportunities and risks in a formal way, so we can see the median forecast, and where we might gain or lose business, and then make a plan as to how to secure the opportunities and mitigate against the risks. Commitment to the forecast is crucial.

So, once we have had our one-to-one meetings with the sales functions (or in multi-country global businesses held a local demand review), then we can pull together the information in the form of graphs as Figure 50 illustrates.

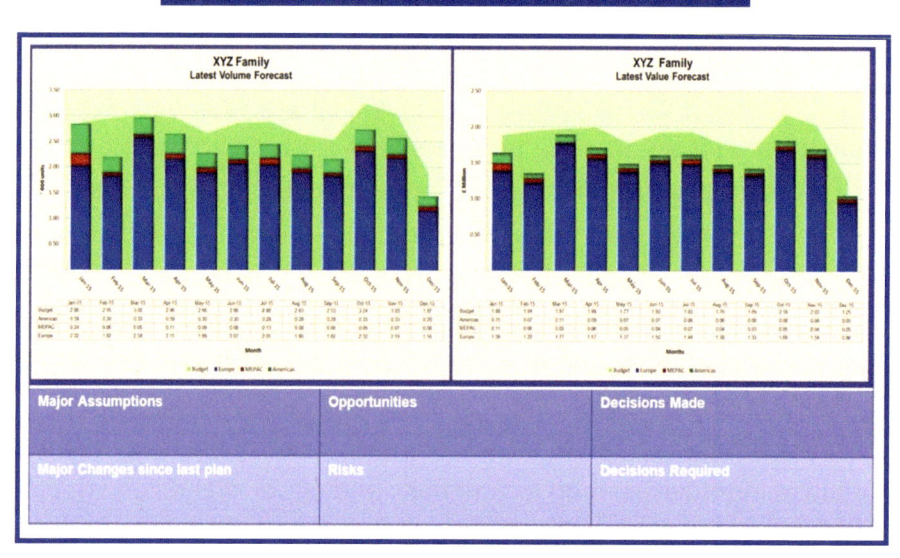

Figure 50: Demand review chart by Family

This chart summarises the volume and value projections, and compares against the budget in the background. Underneath is a summary table of the major assumptions, and changes to these since the previous meeting; the risks and opportunities; and then a box for decisions required and decisions made.

We might need to decide on whether we include an opportunity or to go ahead with a promotion, or change prices to respond to competition.

You should support these decisions with a paper and presentation on the costs and benefits of taking the appropriate action. The demand manager should collect the inputs and then circulate these to everyone involved 24-48 hours before the relevant meeting(s).

This meeting will happen either in a single Demand Review meeting or several – perhaps by business unit or sector or country. Typically, this would be structured as follows.

Figure 51: Demand Review Meeting template

Inputs
- Strategy
- Update on Assumptions
- New Product developments
- Major changes to Forecasts
- Competitive threats/opportunities
- Performance Measures

Behaviour
1. Realistic forecasts
2. Respond to accuracy measure
3. Its not supply chain's fault
4. Thinking beyond current year

Agenda
1. Revised Forecasts
2. New Products
3. Agree changes to Assumptions
4. Gaps to strategic plan and proposals for closing
5. Performance Measures
6. Agreed actions

Outputs
- Unconstrained Demand
- Agreement on risks and mitigation
- Actions to close gaps
- Financial projections
- Actions for improving process

Links
1. Bids/Quotes/CRM
2. Innovation/Supply reviews
3. Sales plans
4. Marketing plans
5. Financial plans

Do not forget that there may already be similar meetings which need upgrading to include some of the items in Figure 51. Do not impose another meeting on the business.

But this is the culmination of the Demand Planning process, which requires a combination of systems, processes, behaviour and organisation to function effectively.

Chapter 7

Demand Management

"Customer service should not be a department. It should be the entire company." – Tony Hsieh, CEO of Zappos

The customer service department in many companies is operated often as a standalone department, which merely processes orders (if not done electronically) and then deals with customer queries, and complaints. Some have cynically referred to their role as the "customer defence" department.

As part of the development of an IBP process, companies need to integrate this function into the process, which requires systems, behaviour, and processes all to be aligned.

Naturally, all I have said so far will do its best to ensure that we meet customer requirements 98% of the time on time and in full. Hence, when all is working well, then this section will only apply to problems for 2% of the orders received! Following the principles here will help achieve that goal.

The guiding principle here is that all customers should be able to receive what they want (required quantity) when they want it (required date and time) to the quality they want and with the required relevant paperwork. Hence the critical measure in this respect is the "Perfect Order" measure – DIFOTR = Delivery In Full on Time to Request.

If the product is not available when they request it, then the company should look into its ERP system, find out when the product will be available, and then give the customer a promise. Companies must keep their promises.

"A promise made is a debt unpaid," as Robert Service, the British-Canadian poet (often called "the bard of the Yukon"), said in his famous poem "The cremation of Sam McGee". The poem tells of the story of his friend who did not want to be buried, and his dying wish was to be cremated. He thought his friend had died in the frozen winter, and struggled to find somewhere to cremate him rather than bury him. When he did, he lit a fire; but Sam McGee thawed back to life!

Another critical measure is DIFOTP – Delivery In Full on Time to Promise.

While we might define a target for DIFOTR of 98% or 95% to relate to the risk we are prepared to take in being out of stock or unable to meet customer requirements, our target for DIFOTP should be 100%. The truth plays an integral part in IBP. Sales and Marketing should tell the truth when they are providing forecasts. Likewise, there is nothing more important than telling customers the truth when it comes to managing their expectations. I have seen companies display a customer service target of 95% to customer promise. This target is ridiculous. How are you going to choose those customers to whom to lie?

So, the first step must be to record for every order the requested quantities and dates and then be able to record the promised despatch date from source, and the promised delivery date to the customer at their premises, depending on the terms and conditions of the order.

When recording the requested date, we should record the requested date at the point when the order is _first_ received. Sometimes companies will adjust this first date simply because they do not have the product in stock. This process is not correct as it conceals the reality of the situation.

Sometimes companies – mainly Make to Order companies – will quote a lead time for customers in the form of "four weeks from receipt of order". In these cases, some adjust the requested delivery date to this date – even if it happens to be two or three weeks away from the date the order is received. The argument is that the customer has made an "unreasonable request" because they have ordered within the standard lead-time.

Again, this conceals the reality and is potentially dangerous.

One client operated based on lead times of six to eight weeks, making labels for the drinks industry. Their customer service performance looked good, at around 95%+. However, one day a competitor set up in business with a warehouse and offered 48-hour delivery ex-stock for the top-selling "runner items". The client quickly lost all their business. Customers wanted a 48-hour delivery service, and the client had not developed a way to be able to record what customers wanted. You need to know what response a customer requires.

You can deal with the problem of having customer required dates not aligning with standard lead-times separately in the system by setting up a "policy date" for standard lead times. The system can automatically calculate this date at point of entry. Thus, if the policy is to deliver within four weeks of the customer order date, then the system can add 28 days to the date of order receipt, to calculate the policy date. In summary, you should have available in your system:

- Customer Request Date
- Customer Promise Date
- Customer Policy Date

All of these dates need to be available and programmed in the system, and the reports on customer service should be available based on the dates in the system. Sometimes customers just write "ASAP" on their orders. In this case, your sales managers will need to educate customers on the value of dates.

System Features

There is also a need to make sure that the following system features are correctly calculated and operated within the systems. In many companies they are either misunderstood, wrongly programmed or not available:

1. Forecast Consumption
2. Forecast Roll
3. Abnormal demand
4. Available to Promise

Without this functionality being properly defined and working correctly, then you will not be able to have, or prove you have an effective IBP process, since the critical output of brilliant customer service will be impossible to understand and manage.

Forecast Consumption

Whether your products are Make to Stock, Assemble to Order, or Make to Order, you will need to have a forecast – it is just the level of detail required which changes. Before receiving orders, forecasts will drive the plan. When customer service takes the order, the system needs to replace the values of the forecast in the system. It is helpful to use the example in Figure 52 at this point.

Figure 52: Forecast Consumption table

Part Number: 123456 Lead Time 2 periods Safety Stock 0 Min Ord Qty 75 On Hand 100

Periods	1	2	3	4	5	6	7	8	9	10	11	12
Forecast	25	25	25	25	25	25	25	25	20	20	20	20
Actual Demand												
Proj Avail Balance	75	50	25	0	50	25	0	50	30	10	65	45
Available to Promise	100				75			75			75	
Cumulative ATP												
Master Schedule					75			75			75	

We have the necessary item Master information along the top. In the beginning, we have forecasts of 100 per month divided by the number of weeks in the month (4, 4, 5) along the top line.

We have 100 on hand, and we can project the available balance/stock as at the end of each week on the Projected Available Balance line – which is the amount that will be in stock, assuming the forecast comes in as projected.

The next line (Available to Promise) states how much of the current or projected inventory is uncommitted (free) to customers – thus does not take into account the forecasts. So, if a customer or customers want up to 100 in week one, they can have their orders. But the customer who wants the 101st item will (without changing the plan) only be able to get their product in week five.

The Master Schedule is the current production plan for this item, expressed by the date this will be available for sale in the Finished Goods warehouse or despatch area. The aim of the master production scheduler should be to keep the projected available balance above either zero or at the safety stock level. A sound ERP system will provide action messages to the master scheduler if not.

Let us now assume that a customer sends in an order, or makes an enquiry, and says they want ten units now. The process should typically be:

1. Check the Available to Promise – there is 100 there, so that looks fine
2. Confirm to the customer the order
3. Arrange shipment to the customer's premises
4. Send out invoice.

In an effective ERP system, the system enters the order in the system as "actual demand".

The demand that drives the Projected Available Balance line is the sum of forecasts plus orders.

Here is where forecast consumption kicks in. If the order was part of the forecast, then the system should net the 25 down to 15 in period 1. That keeps the Projected Available Balance the same, and – critically – the master production schedule the same – there is no need to get any more made.

But if the order was not forecast, what happens then? The order should be marked as such, and not allowed to "consume" the forecast. Many systems do not get this calculation correct.

Given it is crucial to know whether the order was forecast or not, and this impacts the calculation on the system, then the customer service agent needs to determine at the point of order entry whether the order was forecast. So many companies have customer service departments which just take orders, and never worry about this critical point. No wonder they get into a mess and deliver poor service, or have too much inventory!

It would be helpful in determining whether this order was forecast if we had the information shown in Figure 53 about each customer's demand pattern:

Figure 53: Customer order detail for consumption

Customer X   50 per month
Customer Y   10 per month
Customer Z   5 per month
Customers A... 35 per month

Total =   100 per month

Forecast at End Item Level

If it were customer Y, for example, then it would be easy to see that the order was forecast. But if it was customer Z, you might have to check.

This problem raises the question of whether you are going to forecast by customer, by product for all customers, or a mixture of both. You will need to address this issue as part of the establishment of the IBP process.

If you have one or two big customers, then it would make sense to forecast these separately, and then have another line for "all other customers". But if you do not have a big customer like customer X in the above example, then you might just want to forecast by product; in which case, you may well need to have a process that tracks the actuals vs the forecast over the month (if forecasting monthly) or over the week if forecasting weekly. The system will identify when the actual cumulative sales exceed or are lower than the cumulative forecast by a pre-determined percentage.

One client sold a product to both the UK market and to export markets. The problem they had was that the UK market was on a 24-hour delivery, but the export market was on a three-week delivery lead time. But customer services would only check if the product code was available, not from where the forecast came. So, on many occasions, the export market would order, and the customer would be promised and get an immediate shipment, even though there was no explicit export forecast in the system. In effect, they would be taking (some might say "stealing"!) the UK stock.

Their solution, which was the right solution, was to create an export forecast and then get the export order to consume the export forecast. That kept the UK forecast intact for supply to the UK.

They also programmed the system so there was a "UK" Available to Promise and an "export" Available to Promise line. This process in effect protected the stock for the two markets. They certainly understood how all of this worked.

So, that is forecast consumption, which has to be correctly programmed and managed in the system.

A secondary issue is how the settings for forecast consumption affect the calculations. Thus, let us assume that customer X wants 50 in week four in the above example. This 50 is in the forecast. Some computer systems are programmed by their users so that orders only consume forecasts if the order is in the next two weeks (they think that they never receive orders that far out). But if customer X orders, in this case, in week one, then this setting would give the wrong answer as it will add an extra 50 to the demand, causing an "action" message to alter the supply plan.

Similarly, some systems have a setting which says that the order will only consume the forecast in the week of the order if the company sets the system up to forecast weekly. In this example, this is a monthly forecast divided into 4/4/5 weeks. But the 50 in this one order is bigger than the average weekly forecast. This rule will add 25 to the total demand, which is an incorrect result. You would want the system to consume the forecast for the month.

If the ERP system is programmed to spread consumption of the forecast by the order, then it could apply it forwards or backwards from the week of the order. It could also extend it from the beginning of the month, or the end of the month. You have to be very careful to ensure that the system has programmed forecast consumption correctly.

Every ERP system appears to have created different rules, and few of them work correctly. The correct rule is that orders should reduce the forecast for the month where it is forecast, and reduce from the first week to the end of the month) if you are forecasting monthly. If you are forecasting weekly (each week is deliberately different), then the order should consume the forecast from the week of the forecast.

Thus, in the example above, the 50 needed for week three should reduce the forecast in week one and week two. We are forecasting monthly.

Forecast Roll

This functionality in the system relates to the fact that as each week rolls on, it is possible that we have a forecast left over at the end of the previous week. Thus, in the example above, if the order for week one were just for 10, then at the end of week one there would still be 15 left over. We then need to ask the question, "Do we roll the 15 forward to the next week, or do we drop it, or do we keep some and drop some?"

If we roll the quantity forward and add it to the following week's forecast, then the supply plan does not change and we will continue to make the product in line with the forecast. In this case, the forecast had not changed.

For some businesses, the answer depends on the product. Newspapers are an example. If you forecast 50,000 copies last week, but you sold 15,000 less than the forecast, this does not mean that you will sell another 15,000 (above the forecast) this week. Once the demand has passed it has gone! You should just drop the forecast. This is arguably true for breakfast cereals, foods and pharmaceuticals; because you sell less than the forecast one week, then you will not expect to sell more the following week. But in many businesses, the demand can be rolled forward.

You need to be careful as to how the system is programmed – is it set up to drop the forecast or will it automatically roll it forward?

More importantly, there is a need to review the forecast each week and compare this with the actual demand. The demand manager should get a report that identifies those products which are over- and under-consumed, and then have a discussion with Sales/Marketing on the right course of action to take.

One client called this their "subs and rockets" report. They made dairy products, and forecast every week. So, each Monday they printed out a report that identified those products where the actual demand was more or less than 10% of the forecast demand, and then took an active decision on whether they should change the forecast.

The same should happen every week with companies that forecast monthly. At the end of each week, they should take an active decision on whether they should change the monthly forecast.

Where companies are Make to Order or have to Make to Order products, then they may have a rule which says that they offer a lead time of four weeks; in which case, there should be no forecasts in the system within the next four-week horizon – which is a similar issue.

In this case, it is essential for the system to have a "Demand Time Fence" which detects any forecasts in the next four-week horizon, and either the system removes them or rolls them out into week five. Again, the demand manager should be reviewing what happens to these forecasts with the sales function/account managers.

Of course, some sales managers or account managers, asked as to whether they want the forecast to be dropped or retained, may well wish to keep "their" forecast in all circumstances – just in case they are going to get the order. All this will do is potentially increase stock, and use up capacity unnecessarily.

The process needs to be explained thoroughly to the sales teams, so that they learn not to do this, because of the adverse consequences of doing this on stock and cash flow.

Abnormal Demand

Many companies completely fail to manage un-forecast demand properly, even though everyone accepts that forecasts are going to be wrong. They have a customer services department that automatically accepts orders without reviewing the impact on demand. All companies must establish a formal "abnormal demand" process.

An Abnormal Demand process relates to the need to manage un-forecast demand effectively – significantly, when the demand exceeds forecast, but also where the demand is less than the forecast, which is arguably easier to manage.

Let us assume that we are in a situation where we have accepted an order from customer A for 10 units as shown in Figure 54, and the picture is as follows.

Figure 54: Order for 10 accepted from Y

Part Number: 123456 Lead Time: 2 periods Safety Stock: 0 Min Ord Qty: 75 On Hand: 100

Periods	1	2	3	4	5	6	7	8	9	10	11	12
Forecast	15	25	25	25	25	25	25	25	20	20	20	20
Actual Demand	10											
Proj Avail Balance	75	50	25	0	50	25	0	50	30	10	65	45
Available to Promise	90				75			75			75	
Cumulative ATP												
Master Schedule					75			75			75	

The forecast is for 25 a week. Customer Services have accepted the order from Y of 10 units, and so the forecast has been consumed down to 15. "Available to Promise" in week one is now 90.

Let us further assume that we have been talking to and cultivating customer Z for a while, who is potentially a big customer, but currently only buys five units per month from us.

Let us further imagine that our MD bumped into the MD of company Z at the golf club at the weekend!

After the usual pleasantries, our MD said, "we don't sell you much at present, only five per month. Do you buy a lot more than that?"

"Yes," says the MD of customer Z.

"What would it take to get your business?" says your MD, cutting to the chase.

"Just give us a promise you know you can keep. You have not been reliable in the past!"

"No worries," says your MD. "We have just implemented a new Integrated Business Planning process, and as part of that, we are determined to deliver 100% of all orders to their promise date. A promise made is a debt unpaid!"

The following Monday morning, the MD briefs everyone to make sure that everyone takes care of customer Z.

"We need the business, and if we can get this customer, the future will be much brighter, as they will probably take 100 per month – doubling our business for this vital product."

Sure enough, customer Z calls and says they would like 100 – now, if possible, but certainly by week five. Let us also assume that they want all 100 in one shipment.

A simple examination of the situation says we can offer the whole 100 in week five. We have 75 Available to Promise in week five and 90 in week one. So, we could say "yes".

Indeed, most companies without a proper Abnormal Demand process would say yes!

However, if you are to meet the requirement from the customer to give a promise you know you can keep, you should first check how much is forecast. The answer is five per month.

This observation should lead to a trigger to examine the fact that this is an un-forecast order. Indeed the system should be programmed to identify this.

But in this case, it is not necessarily that simple. The customer takes, on average, five units per month. So, the next question must be how much do we reduce the total forecast by, in order correctly to consume the forecast?

Do we take five just from this month, or five from this month and next month, etc.? It is going to be critical to know how much extra we might need.

We can only establish this through a conversation with the customer. The account manager should discuss this with the customer along the lines of: "if we deliver this, then will you still need the five a month you normally take?" Depending on the answer, then we will make the right decision on how to consume the forecast.

Let us assume they say that they will not need any more until month three. Let us also assume we want to try a promise of the 100 in week five. Then the situation will look as in Figure 55.

Demand Management

Figure 55: Example of Abnormal Demand

Periods	1	2	3	4	5	6	7	8	9	10	11	12
Forecast	10	25	25	25	20	25	25	25	20	20	20	20
Actual Demand	10				100							
Proj Avail Balance	80	55	30	5	-40	-65	-90	-40	-60	-80	-25	-45
Available to Promise	65				0			75			75	
Cumulative ATP												
Master Schedule					75			75			75	

Customer Z wants 100; week 5 can we supply it ?

Note that the system has consumed the five units forecast from week one and week five. The impact of this is that we will have a negative projected available balance from week five onwards. This calculation means we will not have enough to satisfy other forecast customers.

We now need to see if and when we can change the master schedule to include additional production. We know that we need at least another 90, and because the minimum order quantity is 75, this could either be two batches – which is 150 – or another production of 90. The question is, when can we add production?

This question illustrates where the concept of "Cumulative Lead Time" kicks in and why it is crucial. The lead time for this product may be two weeks (Lead time = 2 periods), but we should not just add production without checking that there is the availability of the raw materials for this product.

Let us assume that the cumulative lead time is eight weeks. This means it will take eight weeks to order and get delivered more raw material, process any sub-assemblies, and then pack the product and bring it into the warehouse ready to ship. In this case, the earliest we could make another 90 would be week nine.

The master scheduler now needs to consult with manufacturing and procurement, and check stocks and requirements from other products to come up with a potential solution. They should do this by looking through their ERP system and investigating the impact on the availability of sub-assemblies and raw materials. They should also review the availability of capacity.

They should also talk to the demand manager to find out about the forecasts and check if all customers are still likely to want their forecasts, and they may, in turn, check with account managers. This issue in itself requires great care. If you start to ask customers if they are likely to want their product, then the chances are that they are going to say "yes".

So, the first step of the process should be to investigate what is possible.

But let us assume for the moment that we cannot get any more made until week nine, to explore the implications of this situation. This means the "default position" would be that the earliest that the customer could get the order for 100 would be week nine. Any earlier will prejudice the ability to deliver to other customers, and we, of course, want to be able to make promises we can keep!

Many people might argue that we should just ignore the other forecasts. After all, "a bird in the hand is worth two in the bush". If we take this order, we will increase sales. We may have a future problem with other customers, but we can at least buy some time if we just promise this order to the customer for week five. This is the behavioural change core to Integrated Business Planning; if you are going to promise this customer 100 in week five, then how will you be able to respect the other forecasts? How will you manage those orders when they come in? What will your future customer service look like?

Companies must have a formal way of managing their demand.

The correct procedure is for customer services now to go back to customer Z and say that they can have the order in week nine. "It was an unexpectedly large order; we have other customers whom we do not want to let down. They would like us to be the sort of company that makes promises that a customer would know we can keep."

Now you may be thinking that this only applies and is an issue because this is an exceptionally great demand. But the same principles and problems arise if customer X wanted six units! It is simply the scale of the problem and the solution that changes.

In developing IBP, we need to have two policies in place:

1. An **Abnormal Demand Policy and process** to define what is "abnormal demand", and then have a strategy for how the company will deal with this issue. Having developed it, then everyone needs to follow that policy.

2. **An agreed policy for how to meet abnormal demand,** which can include safety stock and safety capacity; this can be of finished goods in the case of Make to Stock products, or raw materials in the case of Make to Order, as described before. The decision on this policy should only come from the executive team.

Of course, in the example above, when we go back to the customer and say to them that week nine is the earliest possible date, they may well say that is unacceptable and may even phone up the MD saying it is unacceptable, and "can you do better?" That might be the polite version of the conversation.

In many situations today, the MD may well go to the master scheduler and account manager and "force" them to promise delivery in week five. However, in this case, you would be putting at risk the other "loyal" customers, just for the sake of the immediate large order. If you do this, then the company is creating a risk to its service levels, as outlined above.

The crucial part of IBP is to recognise that the ownership of that risk belongs to the managing director and the sales director alone, and not the supply chain function. In many companies they frequently blame the supply chain director or manager for failing to deliver the product to the customer, even though sales had not forecasted it! IBP must create the environment for a change in behaviour based on clear responsibilities.

Hence the process for managing demand on receipt of order should be:

1. Check if the order is within the forecast
2. If not, check if some of the order is forecast, and consume the amount that is forecast
3. Check with the master scheduler when more could be available
4. Validate the forecasts
5. Promise the customer the un-forecast amount beyond the cumulative lead time
6. If the order is required earlier than the CLT allows, decide and record what to do about the potential impact on other customers.

Available to Promise

The example in the previous section shows the importance of having an Available to Promise calculation so that customer services can provide to customers the date on which they can rely. For this date to be valid, then the date for the Master Schedule due date must be reliable – which requires that the whole plan for capacity and raw materials is correct – which we will deal with in Chapter 9 under the Supply section.

But to emphasise the obvious, that also means that data which supports the planning process must be accurate, as well. Inventory, Bills of Materials, routings, and planning data all need to be >98% accurate for the ERP system to be reliable. Spreadsheets make the situation worse.

This explanation of the process should also illustrate why delivering good customer service is not just a function performed by the customer service department – although they often get the brunt of the issues caused. It requires that the company engages all functions within the business, and requires clarity on the individual roles and responsibilities for all functions.

Integrated Business Planning succeeds only if the foundations are solid.

It should also show that this whole area of detailed forecasting and planning should be reviewed and improved as part of developing an Integrated Business Planning process.

Effective leadership from the MD is essential to set the principles and policies by which the business will operate. It is also vital that sales and marketing are accountable for delivering against the performance measure of delivery to the customer request date. If the forecast is not accurate, then the company will not meet customer request dates.

Excellent customer service, which is at the heart of Integrated Business Leadership, is just as much about people's behaviours as it is about the processes and the systems.

Chapter 8
Collaboration with customers

"The biggest sources of opportunity are collaboration and partnership. And today, with digital communication, there is more of that everywhere. We need to expose ourselves to that as a matter of doing business."
— Mark Parker, CEO Nike Inc.

The discussion on demand planning above focused on the need to forecast at the boundary of our company and customers.

However, "forecasts" in this way are not necessary if we can work from our customers' forecasts. The aerospace material suppliers, who deliver to the major aircraft companies, can and do get visibility of customers' demands. FMCG companies supplying the major supermarkets on high streets across the USA and Europe can access the forecasts from their customers and use them in various ways.

My journey in this area started from the point that we were supplying 35 business units around the world. We had always received orders from them in the UK, which we translated into the production of formulated product in the UK and active ingredient across the UK and USA. Our original thought within the project was to forecast demand from the UK to subsidiaries and let them carry on ordering on the centre, which was the UK.

But then we came across the concept of "Distribution Resources Planning", explained in Andre Martin's book (Martin A. J., 1995). We changed our thinking when we met Andre. Fundamentally, he showed how we ought to get our business units (which belonged to ICI anyway) to forecast their demand. By using a software tool to work out net requirements (Distribution Requirements Planning), we could then provide what they needed, offset by the lead time from the business unit to the supply source, back to our central ERP/supply planning system.

So we then built the forecasting and DRP systems and ensured that each week a revised plan would be transmitted back to the plants, giving complete visibility of what was needed and when. It revolutionised our way of working, and facilitated the development of Global Integrated Business Planning.

Andre Martin was working on the principle, which he had picked up from a pioneer in this area – Joe Orlicky – who said: "Why forecast, when you can calculate?"

The next area we recognised was that, once you had a planning system, all you had to do was add in the prices and costs, and you could get a global financial picture. If you then made sure you had a horizon of 42 months, you could generate a rolling aggregate forecast of demand and supply to cover the financial planning requirements. This implementation was probably the first Global Integrated Business Planning process.

On the face of it, this looks remarkably sensible but in practice, there was a lot of work to be done. Most of the work related to persuading the heads of the local business units to accept this model of working! They did not trust centralised planning! When I worked with the general manager of the Italian subsidiary, I remember well him saying, "I don't like this, but if the CEO wants it, then I will implement it!" IBP does not work without the leadership from the CEO.

Fundamentally, this same process continues to operate in Syngenta today, (which was the result of an eventual merger with ICI Agrochemicals) which is a global business with a £10bn turnover, and the basics of the model of collaboration across all countries function well. The person who developed it over the last 30 years was the same person who became a master scheduler in ICI and progressed to being head of the global IBP process in Syngenta. The development also needs a standard-bearer.

We then developed this concept to link to some major customers in the major markets. This concept further transformed the business, both for customers and ourselves. The traditional model was, because it was a seasonal business, to sell large quantities to the customers at the beginning of the season, filling up warehouses, and hoping the weather would come right. But by using DRP with our customers, we enabled ourselves to be able to respond to customers as demand changed, reduce the cost of warehouse space, and still make sure that consumers got their product.

Since then, I have seen the idea of collaboration extend across many businesses and many countries. You can extend the basic principle of collaboration not only within your own company but also across the boundary with your customers. However, achieving true collaboration (sometimes called extended supply chain management) is never easy.

Collaboration progresses typically through several phases in the relationship with customers, which I summarise in Figure 56.

Figure 56: Collaboration progress

- Extended Business Leadership
- Trading Partnership
- Vendor Managed Inventory
- Data Exchange

Thus, initially, a customer might share information on forecasts through a portal which gives visibility of perhaps the next 12 months, with the next 13 weeks broken down by weeks. In the automotive industry, the schedule is broken down into hours!

The next step in the process might be one in which a company manages the inventory in the customer's premises – whether that is stores in the case of retail outlets, or factories. We refer to this concept as Vendor Managed Inventory (VMI). You work out a minimum inventory level, and work to keep the inventory above that level.

Thus, one client does a superb job of making sure that clients never run short of fastenings, by replenishing their clients' stock on a daily, weekly or monthly cycle, based on agreed demand and minimum stock patterns.

The next level is to develop a longer-term trading relationship between the companies, which usually involves a meeting between MDs, and this leads to sharing of the longer-term plans between the two companies.

I have then added another step to this process and called it "Extended Business Leadership". This development recognises that both your company and your customer have a formal Integrated Business Planning process in place, whereby the numbers are updated monthly, and innovation, demand and supply are jointly planned. With a shared vision, mission and strategy, it becomes Extended Business Leadership.

I have seen these concepts develop across several businesses, but it is clear that the success of this depends critically on the word "trust". If there is a fundamental trust between the companies it works; if not, it does not.

Trust only takes place where there is sufficient mutual interest to support such an approach, supported by a shared vision and goals.

- ## "Flowcasting" and the FMCG Business

Darryl Landvater has been a pioneer over the last thirty-five years in developing supply chain systems and processes. He was a founder of the ideas described in this book, with application to manufacturing companies. Andre Martin, the inventor of DRP, and Darryl Landvater recognised that the concepts behind "DRP" should apply to the supermarket retail sector to make sure that shoppers do not arrive at the shelf and find their favourite product is out of stock. It is so frustrating to find that little label saying, "we are sorry, but this product is temporarily out of stock". How much does "temporarily" cost? One client that provided toilet tissue found that "out of stocks" cost them £50m per annum!

Andre and Darryl decided to work with retail companies. They developed software that enables forecasting at the store level, working out net requirements at the distribution centres, and then working out net requirements on the supplier's factory. They called the concept "flowcasting", and Andre explains the ideas in the book "Flowcasting in the Supply Chain" (Martin A., 9 May 2006). He then went on to pilot the concept in a large food manufacturer with one of the major supermarket chains in the USA, which demonstrated a 10% reduction in inventory, and a significant reduction of the requirements for forecasting. They could reduce the number of people from eight to five in the forecasting department for the food supplier.

One afternoon, the VP of Sales of the food manufacturer and the VP of Supply Chain in the supermarket chain were sitting down discussing the results, and for interest looked at the numbers from a financial point of view. They now had complete visibility of both volume and value numbers. Suddenly they realised that their budgets were not going to be met based on the current forecast. This observation led to further discussion to enable a **joint** promotion to increase consumer demand (real demand only increases if consumers buy more!). The system then re-calculated what the food manufacturer was required to supply, and all worked out fine. But it was the joint focus on the sales to the consumer that prompted the discussion, and signalled the need for collaborative Integrated Business Planning.

Andre has always been a pioneer in this area, but as he said: "You can always tell you are a pioneer because the arrows hit your back!" Companies are taking a while to go down the collaboration route. Still, I am sure that this will be the way it will go, driven by artificial intelligence at the consumer end, and with a calculation rather than forecasting at the interface between companies.

While this example comes from the retail sector, the same principle should apply across all other businesses. The automotive industry has long worked this way. The key ingredient is trust – and leadership to drive down the right road of mutual advantage.

I worked with one major aeroplane manufacturer. They have approximately five suppliers, who each provided crucial components, based on machined aluminium. They, in turn, source their aluminium from major aluminium mills. Each of these five suppliers were relatively small companies.

The demand for planes in recent years had skyrocketed. The manufacture of the aluminium components required investment in expensive metal-cutting machinery.

The problem was that none of the individual component suppliers had any form of Integrated Business Planning. So, with guidance from the major aeroplane manufacturer, I worked with the component suppliers to deliver a standard IBP process, which had a significant impact on them being able to keep up with demand for the components for the aeroplanes.

In one company, we started the process around February (month two) of the current financial year. They now had a five-year planning horizon, whereas before they just had a one-year planning horizon (with a focus on the next three months). In that meeting, they realised that they needed to invest and install approximately £4m of machinery by November of the current year if they were going to meet the demands for the next five years.

With the visibility of demand, and the financial numbers now readily available, they went to their parent to ask for extra capital in March – and got it. The need for capital expenditure became apparent with the visibility of a five-year plan; the financial calculation was a by-product of the process. The need for customer collaboration was the driver.

Chapter 9
Supply

"No matter how great the talent or efforts, some things just take time. You can't produce a baby in one month by getting nine women pregnant." – *Warren Buffett, investor and CEO of Berkshire Hathaway.*

The next step in the IBP process is to ensure that we have the transportation, warehousing, materials and capacity in place to support the demand plan and the innovation plan developed so far. We also need to drive a culture of continuous improvement through the process. The real challenge in the supply chain is to design it in such a way that it can efficiently respond to the challenges of the new age of mass-customisation and flexibility, and to make sure we can support the long-term plans.

Henry Ford – as I stated in the beginning – managed to automate the automotive industry by making sure anyone could have a Model T Ford – providing it was black.

The major traditional issue for factories – and those in Europe and the USA who buy from factories in the Far East – is that operations professionals see efficiency as related to volume. The more efficient, the lower the cost.

This idea, in turn, comes from the costing model that many companies adopt.

This costing model comes from the fact that a factory consists of two parts – a building or buildings which contain machinery and equipment and people, which represents fixed (in the short-term) overheads, and variable resources which include people and materials. Sometimes labour is a fixed cost.

Typically changing from making one product to making another causes downtime. Downtime – or not producing – means not using the resources that sit within the factory.

The typical model, therefore, is based around a cost/volume model, described as "batch manufacturing", which needs companies to define and come up with an "Economic Batch Quantity" for each product made.

Indeed, we can calculate it using the following fearsome formula:

Equation 2 - EOQ

$$\text{Economic Batch quantity} = \frac{\sqrt{(2 \times \text{Annual Demand} \times \text{set-up cost})}}{(\text{Cost per unit} \times \% \text{ holding cost})}$$

Thus, we need to get a forecast for an item. Let us say that is 12,000 units for the next year. We then need to work out the cost of moving from one product to the following product (which is called set-up cost); from this, we can work out the top line. Let us suppose this is a fixed £200.

We then need the variable cost of the product – let us say that is £5, which adds up the material cost and the labour cost per unit. Let us then say that cost of storing items in a warehouse is approximately 10% of the material cost (interest cost for borrowing money plus pallets and warehouse space).

This formula is trying to address the fact that there is a fixed cost every time I move from one product to another. Therefore, the more I produce of each item, the lower the cost per unit becomes. The lower the cost, the more "efficient" the factory appears to be.

However, the more I produce – without a corresponding sale to the customer – the more I end up putting in the warehouse. This action costs more in storage cost and in the cost of money required to finance that stockholding – which can be very expensive, depending on the cost of capital the business has to pay to banks and shareholders, as well as the physical cost of storage.

There is a balance.

Thus, if the demand is 12,000 units per annum, and I make in one batch of 12,000, I make the product once and incur the set-up cost of £200 only once, but on average I will store 6,000 items over the year.

But if I make 12,000 units 12 times per annum because I make 1,000 units each time, I pay £2,400 for set-up costs, but now on average, I am stocking just 500 units.

The formula is a mathematical calculation which enables optimisation. The following table illustrates the trade-off for various batch sizes (from 12,000 to 1,000) and the resultant cost per unit.

Table 17 Calculation of Economic Batch Quantity

Economic manufacture

Annual Demand: 12,000
Set-up Cost: £200
Cost per unit: £5.00
Holding Cost: 10%

Batch Size	12,000	6,000	4,000	3,000	2,400	2,000	1,000
#of Batches	1	2	3	4	5	6	12
Average Inventory Holding	6,000	3,000	2,000	1,500	1,200	1,000	500
"Set-up Cost"	£200	£400	£600	£800	£1,000	£1,200	£2,400
Holding Cost	£3,000	£1,500	£1,000	£750	£600	£500	£250
TOTAL Cost	£3,200	£1,900	£1,600	£1,550	£1,600	£1,700	£2,650
Cost/Unit	£5.27	£5.16	£5.13	£5.13	£5.13	£5.14	£5.22

From this chart, you can see that as the batch size decreases from 12,000 each time to 1,000, then the total set-up cost increases from £200 to £2,400, while the "holding cost" decreases from £3,000 to £250.

Add the two together, and you see the "efficient batch size" is around four batches per annum of 3,000 units each time.

This calculation is entirely correct. The first problem with the formula is that all of the elements are a guess – apart from the number two! The second problem is that I have often found that companies rarely use this formula to judge the correct quantities. With one factory that made bottles, I used this calculation and demonstrated a 40% reduction in inventory, which excited the finance director. However, the CEO did not understand the concepts and believed that somehow an 85% efficiency factor was all that mattered, even though they had a big warehouse down the road storing empty bottles!

A core principle of the IBP process is to come up with a supply plan which balances – correctly – the need for "efficiency" with the need for a response to the customer and getting it right. It is not a simple mathematical formula; we need to understand the incremental costs and benefits of inventory versus the cost to the business.

While the optimisation formula is correct, it uses several assumptions. The first is that the set-up cost is a fixed number and occurs each time a change in production occurs. In the case of the bottle-making company, they employed a crew of people to change over the moulds along several lines, which took around eight hours, and hence that was a fixed cost. So, set-up costs were indeed not a trivial item, and they could calculate it.

The second is that the holding cost can be accurately determined. But it is a mixture of a guess on warehousing costs plus an estimate of the average cost of capital.

The square root of a guess/guess is still a guess.

The critical component in the formula is the set-up cost, and if you dramatically reduce this, then the economic batch quantity will tend to be one. Thus, you could make any product, any time, any day.

One key feature of the "Lean and Continuous Improvement" philosophy is to work on reducing the set-up time involved in changing from one product to another through the SMED (Single Minute Exchange of Die) concept, which drives changeovers to be less than 10 minutes. This idea drives a coach and horses through the need for batch sizes; it improves the flexibility of every company in responding to customers.

This idea also emphasises the notion that Lean principles and their understanding must be embedded into the Integrated Business Planning approach, to enable companies to get away from the idea that "more is good". Lean is not a different philosophy that replaces IBP.

Making what you need when you need it should be the driver, and your company should make the Supply plan on the understanding that there is a balance to be had between inventory and "efficiency". This balance needs a commercial decision-making process. If the volume forecast requires a third shift, then this will make the factory more efficient. However, we need to answer the questions of the incremental cost of the third shift. We also need to understand the benefit of any resources or inventory that may be required.

To get that balance right, then we will need to produce a balanced plan, which requires the master scheduler to come up with a plan based on the right materials and the suitable capacity.

Within the framework of Integrated Business Planning, we are also driving an emphasis on looking at the longer-term. In the longer-term, the question is more about how much capacity we need, and how much capacity we need from your suppliers.

Capacity Requirements

Working out capacity is, in principle, a relatively simple calculation. The basic principle is that the required capacity must be less than or equal to planned capacity. That means making the Production plan fit the available capacity.

To work how much capacity we need, then we need to multiply the quantity we are going to produce by the run time for each item (how long will it take to process that item on the machine or with the people that are going to make the item).

We also need to add in how much time we need, to be able to change over from one product to another.

Thus, if I want to make 200 units in a week, and it takes 15 minutes per item to process the unit, then I am going to need 50 hours. If I need 10 hours to set up the machine, then I am going to need 60 hours on that machine. That is my required capacity.

The next question to answer is: "Have I got enough capacity?"

In a week, I have 168 hours available – that is fixed, at 24/7!

But the answer to the question then depends on working patterns and the number of shifts that I am going to operate, and at this stage, it ceases to be simple.

If I have two machines which are going to be operating for 37.5 hours per week, then I have 75 hours available; it looks as though if I need 60 hours, and I have 75 hours available. I am going to be okay. Similarly, if I had one machine, and this was going to operate two shifts per day, then that would be fine.

But one of the principles that underlie Integrated Business Planning is that we need to have honest and **realistic** plans. If you look at most equipment running, then there are often times when it is not operating. So, the machinery may be available for 37.5 hours per week, but it may actually be running just 50% of the time. In which case, I can only plan on 37.5 hours in this example – and I am not going to have enough capacity. We need to have the right factor for this calculation.

I have seen some companies when calculating their available capacity using some standard factor, such as 80% of the available time. However, the issue here is that this is not a proven number.

The crucial input companies need is the **"demonstrated capacity"**, which will give the business a clear statement of the capacity against which it can plan. Panel 9 illustrates a real world example of the difficulties of getting to an agreed figure for demonstrated capacity.

To calculate demonstrated capacity, we need to know the actual number of hours worked and the standard times for the exact quantities produced during any given period.

> ## Panel 7: Demonstrated Capacity
>
> I was taken around a factory that was making landing gear for aircraft. These were large items, and went through a number of machining and assembly steps, finally going through a paint shop before final assembly. There was a flip-chart at the end of the line, which showed that the plan was to make one landing gear per day - five per week. It was late Friday afternoon, and the actual for this week was only four. I then looked at last week's plan. It said five, but the actual was four. I looked at the previous three weeks; the story was the same: plan five, actual four.
>
> I then turned round to my host, who was the planner, and asked: "How many are you planning to make next week?" I was a little surprised when he then told me "five". "But," I said, "you have only been making four per week. Why not four?" His answer amazed me. He said, "If I planned on four, then I would only get three!" We then had a discussion over the next couple of hours where I pointed out how he could not be creating a reliable plan for others to work on, and then he agreed that four was the right number to plan. But he also agreed that he had to get the whole factory to agree to and sign off to the plan, and make that plan.
>
> That is another key mantra of IBP: "plan the work, and work the plan." But the plan must be based on realistic and demonstrated numbers!

Typically, we should calculate it over a rolling four-week cycle – but sometimes it can be more than that. The following table illustrates the calculation of demonstrated capacity for a single week, based on a simple production of four items in the week on two machines.

Table 18 Demonstrated Capacity

Calculation of Demonstrated Capacity

Week Number				37
	Qty	Set-up (hours)	Run time/ Unit (mins)	Total Output (Hours)
Product A	100	1.0	5.0	9.3
Product B	200	1.5	5.0	18.2
Product C	150	1.0	5.0	13.5
Poduct D	150	1.0	4.0	11.0
Total Actual Output		4.5	47.5	52.0
# of machines				2.0
# of hours				37.5
# of shifts				1.0
Total available				75.0
Demonstrated Load Factor				69%

The top part of the table calculates the total actual output in hours, based on the standard times for the products. This calculation gives a total real production time of 52 hours.

The lower part of the table calculates the actual number of hours for which the machines were available (you can take either the physical shift time or make allowance for lunch and other breaks), which comes out at 75 hours.

Dividing actual output by available gives 69%. I describe this a "load factor", which is the way many systems describe the figure. You can then use this percentage figure for the forward plan, depending on the number of available hours you are planning.

Thus, if I am planning to work two hours' overtime per day (Monday to Friday) next week, then the available time for each machine will be 47.5 hours, and I can then plan on 65 hours for next week.

So now if I know that I need 50 hours, I will be okay.

The standard times need to be accurate, but I have seen these being so inaccurate that we must make it a rule to check these as part of the set-up of IBP.

- **Rough Cut v Detailed Capacity Planning**

In a sound ERP system, there should be two models for calculating capacity: Rough Cut Capacity Planning (RCCP) and detailed Capacity Requirements Planning (CRP). Panel 8 illustrates that it is useful to be roughly right, and that precision is sometimes an illusion.

Most computer systems today could have the computing power to be able to do a complete refresh of the Detailed Capacity plan in seconds, and technically there might be no need to have RCCP.

RCCP was "invented" in the 1970s and 1980s, when computer systems were not that powerful. However, RCCP still has a place, particularly in respect of supporting the long-term planning process that is at the heart of IBP. Panel 8 illustrates why it is simpler to be "Roughly Right.

Panel 8: Roughly Right

If you go to the Natural History Museum in London you will have a great time looking at all the creatures of the world many millions of years ago. I loved it as a child, looking at those great skeletons and exhibits.

Once, I went in there and saw this huge skeleton of a dinosaur, which roamed the earth many years ago. I wondered how many years ago they lived, and when that dinosaur was around.

So, I went up to the tourist guide by the side of the exhibit and asked him: "When did that dinosaur live on Earth?"

> He gave me a fascinating description of the Mesozoic era, and how this in turn was split into three separate times of the Triassic, Jurassic and Cretaceous eras. Amazingly, Earth was just one large single, land mass.
>
> I then reminded him that I wanted to know how old the dinosaur was, and he said 100 million and 32 years old.
>
> "Goodness," I said. "How do you know so precisely how old the dinosaur is?"
>
> "Well, son," he said, "when I first arrived at this museum I was told it was 100 million years old, and I have been here 32 years now."
>
> It is better to be roughly right, rather than precisely wrong.
>
> Rough Cut Capacity Planning. The point about RCCP is that it is a rough-and-ready calculation; after all, being roughly right is more manageable than being precisely wrong!

We are looking in the IBP process at the family level, and we have family volumes available to us.

Additionally, we do not need, in the IBP process to look at the details of capacity planning all the time. All businesses have some essential machines or resources which, if they did not have enough of them, would mean that they could not make anything.

These, we call "critical resources".

In Rough Cut Capacity Planning, we may have to look at both the capacity of machines and people (hours). We may also need to look at the requirements for critical materials, and other aspects like warehouse space.

The key raw material is different in different industries. In the pharmaceutical industry, it is "active ingredient". In the crisp business, it is potatoes. In the aerospace industry, it is aluminium.

Typically, critical resources are items of capacity that require expensive equipment, have long-lead times, or are difficult to source (there are only one or two sources of supply).

So, the first step in developing RCCP is for a company to create a list of "critical resources" in terms of machinery, materials and people.

The second problem to address is that we need to calculate the capacity requirement from the following:

Capacity Requirements = Volume x amount/unit

Thus, if we are looking at 100,000 units of production requirement which is going to go onto a filling machine, then we need to know how much time per unit we need on the filling machine.

Our units at the family level will be an aggregation of all the product types – thus one litre, two litres, etc. all add up to 100,000 litres of Lemonfresh product, to borrow the example we used in the discussion on families.

The information around how many lemons we need may be in the information about the detailed make-up of the individual product codes in their Bills of Materials and Routings. Hence, we may know that the one-litre product needs three lemons and may need five minutes per pack on the filling line.

But as part of developing RCCP, then we need to know, "how much does the **family** need?"

Since each item in the family may need a different amount, we will need to work out an overall number, based on the detail for each of the products within the family.

We can take an average: a one-litre bottle needs three lemons, and a two-litre bottle needs six lemons; therefore on average, we will need 4.5 lemons per bottle if our unit of measure is bottle. We could also use a typical unit – a one-litre bottle typically takes three lemons. Our unit of measure is one-litre bottle equivalents. We could also take a historical weighted average. The choice depends on your data requirements.

Naturally, RCCP is not going to be precise, but we will be accurate when we get to the detailed Capacity Planning and Material Planning process.

Equally, we may find that what we think are critical resources are not the only ones. One client made paint resins. They "cooked" these in a vessel for several hours, and saw the vessels as the most expensive items, and hence viewed these as "critical". However, when they got into the planning process, they discovered there was also a filtration process – which itself was expensive – which took a feed from several lines. This equipment turned out to be more of a bottleneck than the vessels. They then had to add this equipment to the list of critical resources.

Calculating the Quantities Required

The first step, then, is to look at our families and create a table of critical resources, with the amount needed per resource. Table 19 illustrates it.

Table 19 Critical resources and requirements per

Key Resources	Units	Families A	B	C	D	E	F
Supplier A	Lts	2.1	3.4		4.2	1.3	
Warehouse	Pallets	12		14	20	5	10
Quality Assurance	Hrs	3	5	3	10	7	2
Line ABC	Hrs		2	5	1	5.6	
Labeller	Hrs	4	7	2	5		
Filling m/c	Hrs	3	7	9	2	5	

So here we see six critical resources for six families on the left-hand side.

Family A takes 2.1 litres per 000 of the family unit from supplier A (this could be hours of capacity as well), 12 pallet spaces in the warehouse, three hours of Quality Assurance time (a resource that companies often forget), four hours of the labeller, and three hours of the filling machine. It does not go down line ABC but another line, which is not a critical resource.

Supply

In an ERP system, which manages RCCP appropriately, it will enable the creation of a "rough cut profile" and therefore will allow you to create a table which specifies the resources used for each family and how much of each resource that you need, as in the example. This could be called a "Bill of Resource".

The next step is to get the Aggregate Production plan.

These numbers should come directly from the aggregation of the detailed production plans from item to family going out over the full horizon – for instance, 42 months.

If we now look at a slice of this calculation (for month five ahead) then we will see the following information in the next table, which shows the required production volumes along the top, underneath each family.

Table 20 Production plans for Month 5

Key Resources	Required Production Volumes						Capacity		
	A	B	C	D	E	F	Req	Dem	Max
	220	200	35	40	150	15			
Supplier A									
Warehouse									
Quality Assurance									
Line ABC									
Labeller									
Filling m/c									

On the right-hand side, we now have additional columns, which is where we will calculate Required Capacity (Req), Demonstrated Capacity (Dem) and Maximum Capacity (Max).

Required capacity will be the sum of all the capacities needed for all of the six families. Demonstrated capacity will be as described above – the proven volume for that resource. The maximum capacity is not the total amount of capacity that we could have if the resources were working 24/7 and perfectly; that is a separate calculation (which might be useful to see how much extra could be available).

Maximum capacity should relate to the maximum based on demonstrated capacity, given the flexibility we have got. If the Demonstrated Planned Capacity for line ABC is based on two shifts for month five, and showed 1,000 hours available, but we could operate on three shifts, then the maximum capacity would be 1,500 hours.

If we could operate seven hours on Saturday, and the week was 37.5 hours, then the maximum would be 1,190 hours.

So, if we now multiply the volumes from the IBP plans by the resource requirements per unit, we come up with the following result.

Table 21 Result of calculation for RCCP

ROUGH CUT CAPACITY PLANNING
Result for Month 5

Production Volumes		220	200	35	40	150	15			
Key Resources	Units	Families						REQ CAP	DEM CAP	MAX CAP
		A	B	C	D	E	F			
Supplier A	Lts	462	680	-	168	195	-	1,505	1,500	2,500
Warehouse	Pallets	2,640	-	490	800	750	150	4,830	4,000	4,000
QA	Hrs	660	1,000	105	400	1,050	30	3,245	3,500	4,200
Line ABC	Hrs	-	400	175	40	840	-	1,455	1,500	2,500
Labeller	Hrs	880	1,400	70	200	-	-	2,550	1,500	2,500
Filling m/c	Hrs	660	1,400	315	80	750	-	3,205	3,000	4,500

From this, we can see that "supplier A" materials are okay, but we need some more warehouse space. QA is okay, line ABC is okay, but the labeller needs more capacity to be switched on in month five, and the filling machine is slightly over the top – do we need to be thinking about overtime?

If we look at the filling machine resource, we can see that there is a need for 205 extra hours. At this point, we should not just blithely go and set up extra overtime resource, but do some digging as to why the resource is required. If the 200 units in month five are being driven by a forecast of some low-margin business, it might not be sensible to put on potentially expensive overtime to make the product.

We also need to see the trends over time. I have only shown month five to support the illustration of the numbers. Figure 57 illustrates the principle.

Hence, there needs to be a discussion between the "captains" around what is causing the overload, and whether it will be worth putting on the extra capacity. If it is worth putting on the capacity, then fine.

If not, then we need to dig back to the product(s), creating the demand at the family level, and agree through the demand manager and the account manager to remove the forecast for that product (and then stop chasing after that business!).

This example illustrates that any decision will requires inputs from demand, finance and supply. The decision will require a careful analysis of the incremental costs of overtime compared with the incremental benefits of the production output. Making these decisions is at the core of the supply step, and (as we will see later), within the Prioritisation step of IBP.

If we then look at the labeller, it looks like we need to think about operating at least a third shift and overtime for month five. Setting up a third shift will be an expensive option, as we will need to recruit people (so we need the human resources function involved here) and check whether we can recruit the people and set up the equipment by month five. Also, doing all this just for month five would not make sense. We may well be able to build ahead in months three and four if we have spare capacity then. If we are going to build ahead, then we will take a risk on holding inventory, which we need to think through.

So, we need a chart that looks something like Figure 57 (which is the chart for the filling machine) for all of our resources.

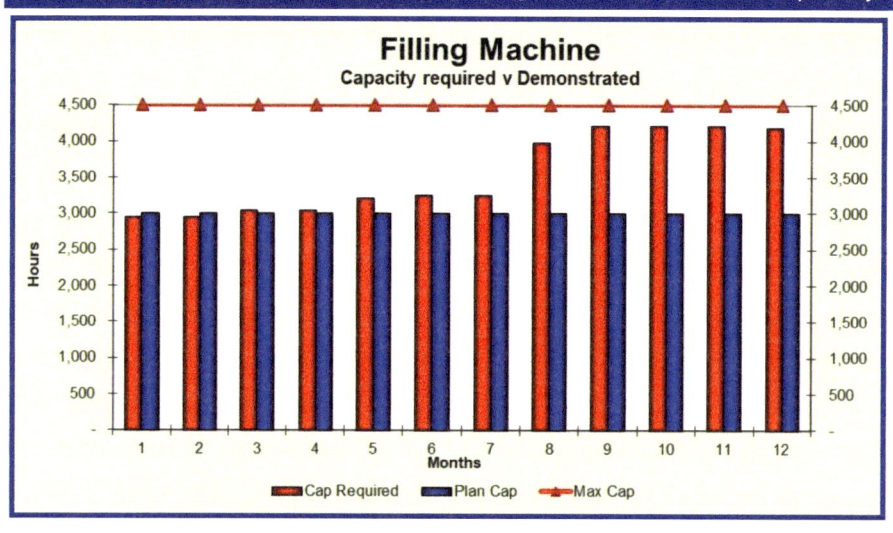

Figure 57: Graph of Required Capacity v Demonstrated Capacity

Filling Machine
Capacity required v Demonstrated

Thus, in month five we are okay on the filling machine – but when we get to months eight, nine and 10 then it looks like we need to be investing in additional capacity – either as another shift or another machine, or...

The purpose of this step in the process is to highlight the decisions that we need to make around the critical resources.

It also shows how we need to integrate all our functions to help make the decisions on the number of people/recruitment, additional costs and benefits, and so on. This argues for the involvement of finance and human resources, which sometimes companies have ignored in developing this process. I cannot see how you can leave them out when making decisions.

Often, I have seen people treat this step of the process purely as a review of whether capacity is required. It is about two factors:

1. Can we meet the plan? If we can, then we should commit to, and **sign off,** the plan.
2. If we cannot meet the plan, then we need to work out what options are open to us in the relevant timescale. We can take these forward to the priority review and the senior leadership team review for debate and final decision (if the level of the decision is such that we cannot take it in the meeting).

It also almost goes without saying, but it is essential to have unbiased and reasonably accurate numbers from the forecasting process to drive the Supply Planning process.

Scenarios

The fact that the numbers will be inaccurate requires that we must also look at various options and scenarios.

Looking at the requirement for 3,000 hours on the filling machine above for months one to seven, it looks like it is reasonably balanced. But if we looked at our forecast accuracy and saw, perhaps, that the demand could be (depending on the accuracy of the forecasts in hours) +/-10%, then we might have a problem.

So, looking at the fact that demand could be up to 3,300 hours, we should also be discussing whether we should be thinking about overtime, and when we need to be making decisions about this. Planning for the capacity available to be precisely equal to the capacity required is not sensible where forecasts are inaccurate (which is always!).

We need to discuss what are we going to do to ensure we have spare capacity to meet upsides in demand, or to operate very close to demonstrated capacity and potentially turn away business.

Sometimes the graphs and plans produced are done in a one-dimensional way – we either have enough capacity, or we do not. But the reality is that demand changes! We, therefore, need to understand "what would happen *if*?". We need a simulation capability. If we look at months eight to ten above on the filling machine, then another 10% would take us very close to the limit of an extra shift. It is arguable that forecasts further out are more inaccurate than shorter in, and so out there, the likelihood is that the numbers could be +/-15% – should we run so close to the wire? It is these kinds of discussions that are going to be the most important and valuable within the Supply step of the process.

One client recognised this, and when they produced their graphs would add 20% to the requirement six months out and plan to operate to this. When they looked at months three to six, they would add 10% to the plan. Then in the period zero to three months, they would operate directly to the requirements from the forecast which was driving the planning system. The resultant growth in their business was phenomenal.

IBP should be exploring the "what-ifs", and this is why RCCP is so key. If you can model changes in demand and impact on capacity at the push of the button, then that will be great.

If you had to wait 24 hours before you had an answer because you have to calculate through the system, then that is not good.

Planning is about thinking far ahead, understanding the potential outcomes, and being ready for all eventualities.

"Fortune favours the prepared mind," as Louis Pasteur famously said. Even better, "Luck is what happens when preparation meets opportunity," as the Roman historian Seneca said in the first century.

Planning should not be a once-a-year uni-dimensional process. It needs to engage all parts of our company by working out possible potential plans, and changing as circumstances change.

The critical advantage of Rough Cut Capacity planning is that it enables a high-level review of the critical resources by month or by week. However, it may well be that there are overloads on machines or resources that are not defined to be critical, by the week or by day. We need detailed Capacity Requirements Planning for this purpose.

Detailed Capacity Requirements Planning

We also need to have that <u>detailed</u> view of our capacity over the 30- or 42-month horizon. The total capacity for Lemonfresh (our family above) may look okay, but individual lines or areas of the factory may be issues.

The principle is the same:

> *Required capacity must be less than planned demonstrated capacity.*

But when we get into the detail, we need to have work centres clearly defined. A work centre is where you perform the work; you

Supply

can define a work centre as a machine or a group of machines, or people and groups of people. The units of measure usually are hours, but they can be tonnes or whatever is appropriate. Hours happens to be a useful common currency.

To work out how much time we need on each work centre, we need to have detailed routings, which provide us with information on how much time you require at each stage of the manufacturing process. We split the time into the following fixed and variable elements:

Queue   **Set-up**   **Run**   **Move**

You get the amount of time you need on any work centre, which occupies the capacity, from the set-up time (fixed) and the run time (variable).

The set-up time is the amount of time the machine is not available because someone is preparing the machine (or work centre) to go from making one product type to another. You measure it from the time you made the "last good piece" of the last product made, up to the time when you make the first good piece of the next product. The set-up time should be an average of the time between the finish of the last good piece and the start of the next good piece.

The queue and move times allow us to calculate "precisely" when you will require the capacity as the products go through the factory – so the result is precise in terms of timing and location. The queue provides a buffer in front of a work centre, typically to allow a balance between work centres that operate at different rates.

The "move" time enables a time after the work centre to allow for time for products to move from one work centre to the next. The process of making a product (achieving the schedule) is completed when you finish "running" the products in the batch.

Again, these times need to be accurate and updated.

I have heard so many times people tell me, "Oh, we put those numbers in when we first set up the system, and have not changed them since then!" There needs to be a transparent process for updating all the times. This action will also correctly update the costs for each of the products.

You have to be careful with queue, as it will create a self-fulfilling buffer, and of course, people always love to see a buffer of work around them – just in case. If the production lines are balanced, you will not need a queue. If the machinery is reliable, you will not need a queue. But if there is a problem and you build in a queue, you will not have the visibility to fix the problem when it arises – storing up trouble for later on.

The CRP system will then add up for each work centre the number of hours required by adding up the time needed for set up and the time required for running all the jobs through the work centre. The system should then offset the dates when the work is needed by the queue and move times to get to the right dates. You calculate the demonstrated capacity as shown above in Table 18.

This should then result in a chart along the lines of Figure 58.

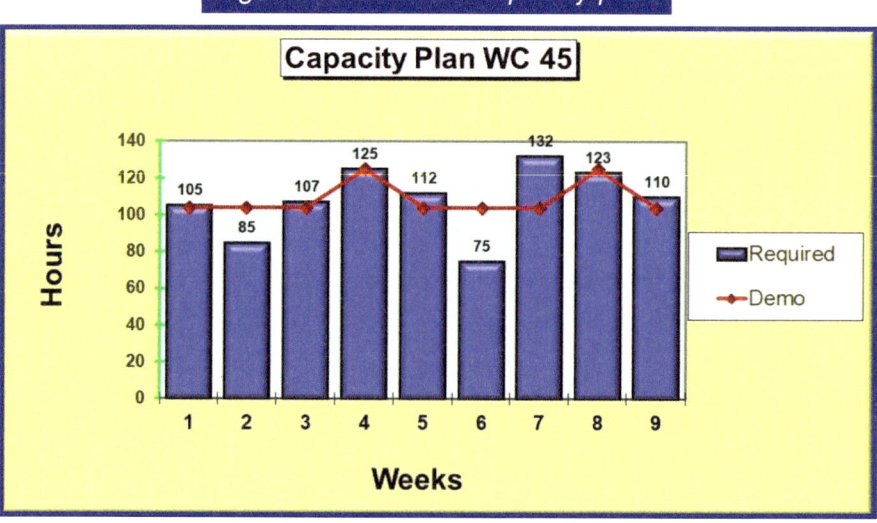

Figure 58: Detailed capacity plan

This chart shows that the plan is reasonably well balanced, apart from week seven, where this a requirement for 132 hours against a planned capacity of 105 hours.

The options open to us at this point are to:
1. Add capacity in the form of overtime.
2. Move the capacity from one machine to another.
3. Check if the capacity is required (is it a safety stock requirement driving the overload?).
4. Check the demand causing the overload – is it a "risk" item?
5. Reschedule the requirement from week seven to week six.

When most people look at this chart, I have found that they immediately go for "reschedule". They are being driven by an apparent need to fill the capacity, probably caused by an in-built desire to maximise productivity or utilisation – and they ignore the need to look at the other options.

It is essential that the master scheduler investigates the reasons for the overload. Let's look at some of the problems that rescheduling will create.

If we shift the production from week seven to week six, then this will bring forward the requirement on previous work centres and potentially imbalance those. So, we need to check the capacity of those work centres.

You will also need to check the impact on raw materials. If the cumulative lead time for items running through this work centre is six weeks, then the answer should be not to try to bring it forward.

It may also be that the lead time for getting additional capacity is longer than seven weeks. So, it is essential to be clear about Capacity Time Fences, and to manage and control changes in production taking this into account.

The constant searching for the consequences of bringing forward the production in search of illusory productivity may not be worth it! The master scheduler should do all of this detailed work daily. This activity will ensure that they have balanced the plan inside the time fence in readiness for the preparation of the monthly IBP supply planning meeting. This data will be a snap-shot of the current plan for the meeting.

Material Requirements Planning

We also need to use our detailed planning system to work out material requirements – through the Material Requirements Planning system – to make sure we have enough components.

I have heard so many times the cry that MRP does not work. It does! The logic is very simple and correct. It does not work in many companies either because the underlying data is inaccurate, or the planners do not understand how to use the system.

Previously we looked at a Bill Of Material for a pen, as Figure 59:

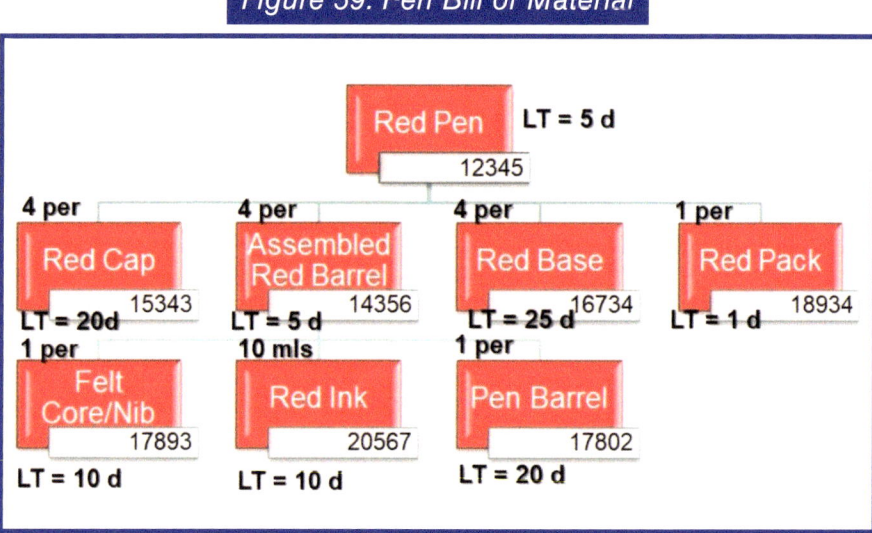

Figure 59: Pen Bill of Material

```
                        Red Pen    LT = 5 d
                         12345

4 per          4 per              4 per         1 per
Red Cap     Assembled            Red Base      Red Pack
              Red Barrel
       15343            14356           16734          18934
LT = 20d     LT = 5 d           LT = 25 d     LT = 1 d
1 per        10 mls             1 per
Felt         Red Ink            Pen Barrel
Core/Nib
       17893            20567           17802
LT = 10 d    LT = 10 d          LT = 20 d
```

Before IBM invented the first material planning computer systems in the 1960s, companies had to rely on "reorder point" to calculate the requirements for components like the red cap, assembled red barrel, red base and red pack. For each item, there was a need to calculate the average weekly or monthly usage. You then needed to know the lead time, and from this, you could calculate the reorder point – the level of inventory below which you needed to order some more.

Thus, if the average weekly usage were 100 red caps, and the lead time is four weeks, then the reorder point would be 400. When you got to 399, the system would recommend ordering some more. Every company had to calculate this "order-point" for each component.

The problems with "order-point" are well known. The system recommends the order whether it is immediately needed or not. The basis of the calculation is an average weekly usage, which is a forecast based on history. But if you will have a promotion in three weeks, it has no way of reacting in time. It also assumes the lead time is fixed – when in practice, it might be possible to make more or less of the same time to reduce the time it takes to make a batch.

MRP works in the following way. If you require 100 Red Pen packs, with four pens in each pack, then it uses the Bill of Material to order precisely the right number of components – 400. It will also net off any inventory, or work-in-process of manufactured items before calculating the requirements for each of the bought items. Simple!

Of course, the Bills of Materials need to be accurate, with correct quantities per parent. Stock and work in process data need to be accurate. But that does not mean that MRP does not work – no system does with inaccurate data. MRP is just a standard form of logic which works.

Key to effective use of the MRP system is the use of action messages. Thus, an effective planning system will provide alerts or messages to tell the planner where they have to adjust the plan.

As part of the detailed day-to-day process, planners should be working on resolving these messages by making sure there is a valid material plan. Every day a planner should clear their action messages.

The key issue to avoid is having past-due orders – i.e. orders with dates in the past. You cannot order anything yesterday. That sounds obvious, but practically every company, where I have initially had a look at their planning systems, believe that time-travel is possible!

Time Fence Policy

We came across the concept of the "time fence" above. If a planner makes changes to plans inside the cumulative lead time, then this will automatically cause the system to recommend the purchase of components inside their lead time. This activity leads to excessive expediting, which we do not want to happen.

A sound ERP system allows a planner to control their plans by "firm planning" them. That means the future planned orders will stay fixed. It is vital to "firm plan" the planned works or purchase orders for end items in the case of Make to Stock items, or "master scheduled" items in the case of Assemble to Order and Make to Order items (those items we want to manage and control). This activity will mean that the plan is under the control of the planner. This fact does not mean the planner cannot change the schedule; it is just that planner reviews the consequences of the changes with other departments in a controlled manner, by working through Capacity Planning and Material Planning processes.

Therefore, to support the preparation for the supply step of IBP we need to have a Time Fence policy, which recognises where there is scope for change in the plan, and where there is no scope for change in the schedule.

Typically, companies structure this around the Cumulative Lead Time. Beyond that point, it usually is easy to change the plan. When you get inside this period, freedom for movement becomes less and less. We may be able to move products from one line to another, or we may get suppliers to help; but we are into a period where the business knows that it needs to check before it makes a decision.

In the very short term, most factories benefit from having a period of strong stability. Thus, you want to avoid starting a product down the line today, and then in the afternoon have someone coming along and saying, "Stop that! Make this!", and then coming back first thing in the morning and saying, "No don't make that, make this instead, this is the higher priority!" In that world of chaos, we have an illusion of flexibility. Productivity tends to be incredibly low in this kind of environment.

This period could be just two to three days for some items, a week for others, and could be eight weeks when making a submarine. Figure 60 illustrates the concept of a time fence policy.

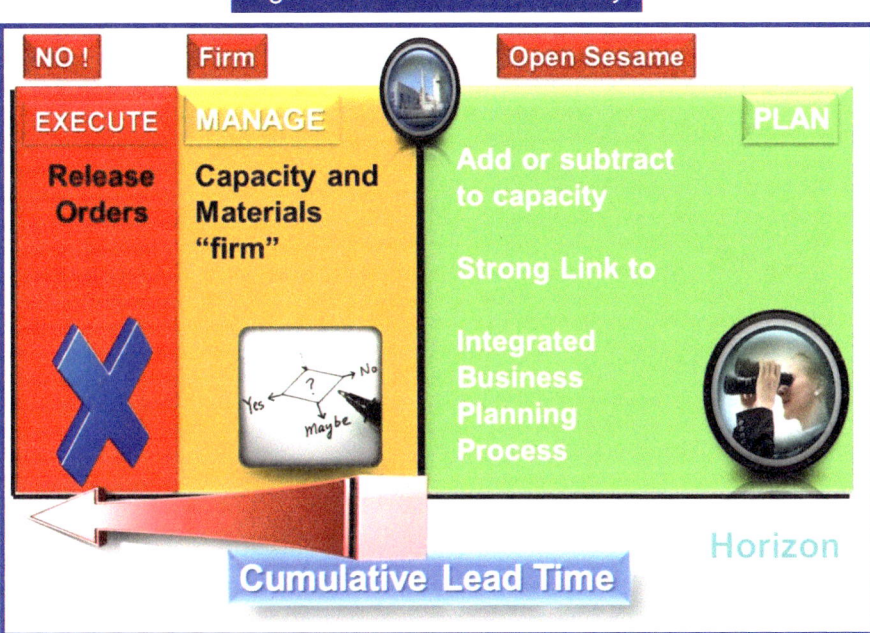

Figure 60: Time Fence Policy

NO! **Firm** **Open Sesame**

EXECUTE — Release Orders

MANAGE — Capacity and Materials "firm"

PLAN — Add or subtract to capacity

Strong Link to Integrated Business Planning Process

Cumulative Lead Time — Horizon

When we get to the short-term "execution" phase, when a planner releases orders to the factory, then change to the plan should be minimal.

To help establish discipline around this, there should be a formal request for change from the General Manager or the MD – which helps to make them even fewer!

One client at a pharmaceutical site was struggling with meeting requirements, and their customer service was around 50-60%. The general manager then introduced a rule that anyone changing the plan in the next seven days would need formal authorisation from him. On the first Monday, when he introduced this policy, there was a

queue of 15 people outside his door. The first one started out saying, "We need to change the plan because we are short of materials." The GM then said, "But why are we short of raw materials?"
The operator said, "The supplier failed to deliver some of the parts." The general manager countered with, "Why did the supplier fail to deliver the parts?" So it went on with each person in the queue.

Before long, the queue was down to one person each week. Meanwhile, the introduction of IBP helped increase their service level from 50-60% to 98%-99% each week.

The other exciting part of this project was that the general manager knew that if the plant did not improve its service, then the strategic plan was to close it. In fact, the VP of supply chain had told him to do so. He refused to accept closure as the only option, and the HQ eventually agreed to keep the site open, along with the jobs of around 800 people.

A fantastic vote for the principles and policies behind IBP.

The head of the supply chain at that site had started as a project leader for an ERP implementation. During the five days of the course he had initially attended, he realised that IBP was a crucial part of the program for making the ERP system work. He then arranged an in-house workshop for the senior leadership team, who then bought into the concepts associated with IBP. The result was that they led the implementation of the ERP system and all the processes that were needed.

Establishing the right policies needs leadership. IBP can also save jobs.

Performance Measures

Leadership is also about holding people accountable for delivery. Under the Demand Planning process, we showed how accountability for forecast accuracy lies with Sales and Marketing.

In the case of the supply-side, then the challenge is making sure we meet the plan. The mantra is, "plan the work: work the plan".

One of the frequent challenges in the supply side is that many companies still use traditional performance measures. Thus, companies continue to measure "productivity", and on the procurement side, they measure "purchase price variance".

Where companies measure factories financially (especially where sites are part of a multi-national organisation), they often measure "overhead recovery" as part of a standard costing system. This process requires a means for the allocation of overheads, based on the budgeted volume of work. This allocation becomes part of the standard cost of the product.

But in this process, when you put production into inventory, the overhead costs are stored in the inventory, which helps to hide the overhead costs.

The more you make (particularly as you get to the year-end) the better it is for profitability (but not for cash flow). So, the performance measure drives people to make more inventory, which is a potential financial disaster.

When I went in to see a new potential client, I interviewed the factory manager.

"What sort of week have you had?" I asked.

"Brilliant!" he said.

"Why was that?" I asked.

"We managed to make 400 tonnes output, which was amazing."

"How much did the plan call for?"

"300 tonnes," he said.

He could not understand why I then said, "But that was an appalling result!" They had not made the plan, just made as much as possible. It was the same way that the company had always run the plant!

When they implemented Integrated Business Planning, they implemented a measure of meeting the plan, and it transformed the effectiveness of the plant. At first, they were achieving around 30% of the schedule. This measure meant that they only made three out of the ten products in line with the schedule.

So, what is wrong with "productivity"? Companies usually measure productivity as the number of hours produced, compared with the number of hours available.

Thus, a machine is available for 50 weeks in a year, say, allowing for two weeks' holiday (for the people that operate it). On a one-shift basis, where a machine is available 37.5 hours per week, then the total available time is 1,875 hours. If we now record the amount of output (number of items x the time per unit) we might record output of 1,533 hours from that machine.

The productivity measure would then record a figure of 82%. If we then had a target of 85%, we would have performed poorly.

In this case, this measure drives the behaviour to make more — thus to achieve the 1,593 hours target. But if we make more, without corresponding sales, then this is going nowhere, apart from inventory, and adds cost rather than value.

If you were running a Model T factory where the only product is black, and the demand for your product is increasing all the time, then the business should be trying to maximise output. That was why Henry Ford chose black — because the drying time was quicker! Customers for cars now want all sorts of different options, and so companies have changed the whole manufacturing model — using Lean techniques.

In a client who made fine bone china, they measured the productivity of the workers. When the cups, saucers and plates came out of the kilns, they went into a holding area in a bare state. The people who then decorated the items would select which items they would paint. They got a bonus for the number of items they decorated. It was not surprising that the decorators knew exactly the shapes they could paint fastest, and they selected those! That meant the client ended up with a massive stock of painted items, which went nowhere. Everywhere I looked they had pots, cups and saucers idle on the factory floor. The measure drove the behaviour. They overcame the problem by forcing the shop floor to work to the schedule.

Hence, productivity drives making more of the same, even when we do not need it.

Back in 1990, the BBC ran a TV series called "The Troubleshooter", which featured Sir John Harvey-Jones, who had been chairman of Imperial Chemical Industries (ICI). He had turned the company around.

As part of the TV series, he visited a Polish glass factory. Everywhere he went, he could see masses of glasses stacked up. He said, "there must be a fantastic demand for your products." When they confessed to the fact there was little or no demand for their products, then his recommendation was simple: stop the factory now, and send everyone home on full pay!

We are not living in a typical 1990s Eastern European world of manufacturing factories, where keeping people busy is better than making what we need. We live in a world in which people want variety, and we respond to variety through marketing activities and product development for customers.

I have come across so many manufacturing managers and manufacturing directors who complain at the need to respond to the customer, with the result that the salespeople are left furiously believing they are "manufacturing-led".

Suppose we are going to focus on giving the customer what they want and when they want it. In that case, we need to change the behaviour by eliminating the Manufacturing measure of productivity. What is wrong with "Purchase Price Variance"?

Under this means of measuring the performance of Procurement, we determine a standard purchasing cost. Let us say that is £3.00 per unit.

Let us say the demand for the item over the year is 11,000 units. However, let us suppose that we get a discount for buying 5,000 units, which reduces the cost to £2.85 per unit.

The purchasing manager will then buy 15,000 units to get £2.85 per unit, which will then leave 4,000 units in stock. The total purchase bill at £3.00 per unit would be £33,000, whereas 15,000 units at £2.85 would mean we would spend £42,750 – bad for inventory, cash flow and risk.

The extra stock will, of course, be at a lower cost but would have to be stored, the cost of which will not be in the purchasing manager's budget or control. So, cash flow and inventory are adversely affected. Also, if we subsequently have to write off the extra raw material, the company will take a hit at that point in its P&L account; again, that cost will not usually be allocated to the purchasing manager.

Further, the specification may call for a certain quality of the material. But what if there is an alternative available which in theory looks the same, but causes a higher failure rate in manufacturing? This higher cost in manufacturing will not appear in the raw material cost of the product. Still, the procurement manager is "rewarded" for buying this product at a lower price, and so will buy the cheaper product without looking at the Total Purchase Cost.

The purchasing manager should be measured, and be accountable for the total purchase cost of raw materials, plus any inventory associated with the product. If there are quality costs related to the raw material, then we should allocate these back to the product, and to the purchasing manager who bought the material. That will generate the right behaviour; PPV will not.

Schedule Achievement

The central theme of the IBP process is to create a plan that meets customer requirements in a controlled manner. The plea is for planning to take centre stage, rather than the business being in a state of constant action and reaction, or just making what manufacturing think it should make to meet productivity targets. There is always a need to manage the balance between reacting instinctively to the customer and maintaining the required productivity along the supply chain. It is the planner – sometimes called master scheduler – who needs to decide within the framework of IBP. Once they have decided, then the plan is sacrosanct – not productivity for its own

Supply

sake. We then need to measure success as the execution of the plan, or schedule, which indicates the definitive statement of the plan.

So, the first essential measure on the supply side should be schedule achievement. The planner will release orders to the shop floor daily, with a quantity due, and a due date/time. In a "Lean environment" where works orders are not released, we can still measure plan attainment as the quantity due to be produced in a day (either by the hour or for the day). The principle is the same – do we make the plan?

The following table illustrates the plan based on a week of Works Orders, and the actual completion of those works orders in terms of quantity and due date.

Table 22 Schedule Achievement report

	WO #	Product Code	Date Due	Qty Due	Date complete	Qty complete	Hit/Miss
Monday	WO 1457	14378	02/03/2020	100	02/03/2020	100	Hit
	WO 1563	13567	02/03/2020	200	02/03/2020	198	Miss
Tuesday	WO 1675	19256	03/03/2020	400	03/03/2020	400	Hit
	WO 1745	19834	03/03/2020	300	03/03/2020	300	Hit
Wednesday	WO 1763	14378	04/03/2020	100	04/03/2020	100	Hit
	WO 1809	19635	04/03/2020	300	04/03/2020	310	Miss
Thursday	WO 1943	20436	05/03/2020	400	05/03/2020	400	Hit
	WO 1956	30896	05/03/2020	350	05/03/2020	350	Hit
Friday	WO 2012	20674	06/03/2020	400	06/03/2020	400	Hit
	WO 2016	19256	06/03/2020	500	06/03/2020	500	Hit

Week: 10   Mar-21

WO = Works Order   Schedule Achievement   **80%**

This report shows the works orders that were due to be completed each day, by the due date and due quantity. We can then record the actual quantity completed, and the date completed. If we hit the date and quantity perfectly, then the performance is good – if not, it is a miss.

Thus, the definition is:

Equation 3

$$\frac{\text{Number of works orders completed on time, in full}}{\text{Total number of works orders due to be completed in the week}} \%$$

The target should be 98% schedule achievement, minimum, per week.

Sometimes a small tolerance is allowed for quantity when the process is variable (e.g. a chemical manufacturing process, where the reaction can produce a variable output). But, generally, tolerance should not be allowed; this will drive continuous improvement.

The key objective of this measure is then to drive the business towards improving the manufacturing process. Hence, in the same way as with forecast accuracy, we should then carry out a root cause analysis of the problems, using a fishbone diagram, as illustrated in Figure 61.

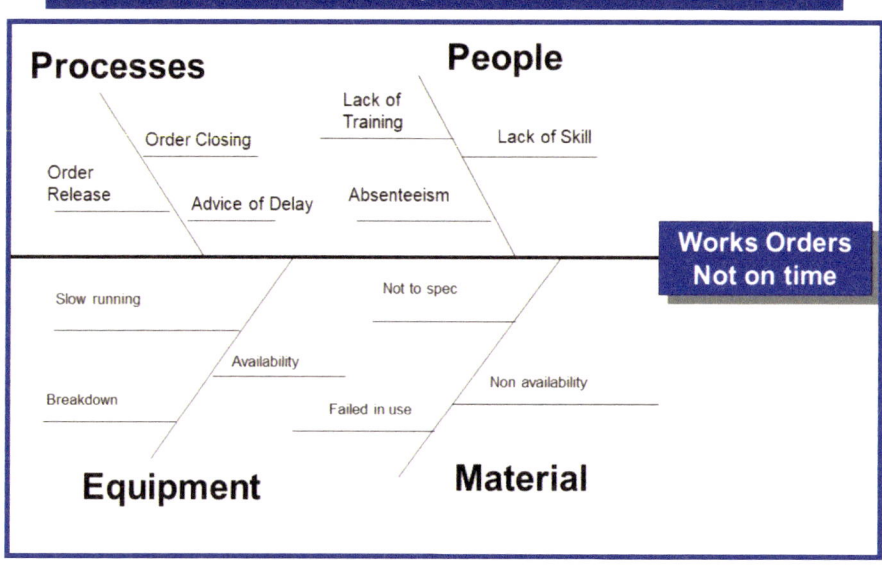

Figure 61: Root Cause Analysis for Schedule Achievement

Processes: Order Release, Order Closing, Advice of Delay
People: Lack of Training, Lack of Skill, Absenteeism
Equipment: Slow running, Breakdown, Availability
Material: Not to spec, Failed in use, Non availability

→ Works Orders Not on time

Thus, we should analyse the causes of failure into the sub-areas and then tackle them.

The accountability for achieving this measure belongs to the manufacturing director, and the responsibility for the measure belongs to each of the production line/area managers.

Right First Time

The second key measure is to ensure that the required quality of the product is delivered. It is possible to complete a product to specification, but to achieve that through reworking or reprocessing the product.

So, the measure of a quality manufacturing process is to measure the number of orders completed on time, in full: "Right First Time". That could be added as a column to the above report on schedule achievement or reported separately.

The definition of the measure is:

Equation 4

$$\frac{\text{Number of works orders completed "Right First Time"}}{\text{Number of orders due to be completed by day}} \%$$

Supplier Performance Measurement

Both of these measures should be applied to deliveries from suppliers as well. You should add "requested date" and contrast that with "promise date", in the same way as we looked at this under the heading of "customer service".

Customer Service (Delivery Performance)

On-time delivery performance to customers is a crucial measure for any organisation, but often it is not even measured – and indeed, few companies measure it properly, thinking of the impact on the customer.

As discussed above, we should measure against the request date and the promise date. The request date is a measure of whether the business has set out its stall well enough to be able to respond to customers when they want it, which implies the right amount of capacity and safety stock to take into account the forecast inaccuracies that the business experiences.

The delivery to promise is a measure of the robustness of the supply chain and the ability to be able to make a reliable promise. This is at the heart of the IBP process.

Customers place orders on companies and expect that the order is delivered correctly and in full. Hence, we should measure deliveries of orders based on the delivery of the whole order in full and as required. These measures are sometimes abbreviated to:

DOTIFR   Delivery On Time In Full to Request Date; and

DOTIFP   Delivery On Time in Full to Promise data

Sometimes, companies deliver multiple items on an order; in which case we would distinguish between "order fill rate", which measures how many orders were delivered with all items being delivered in full, as opposed to "line item" fill rate, which measures, in a given period, the number of items delivered to customers on time and in full.

It will typically be harder to deliver all orders fully, as opposed to all items.

I have seen this report completed in several ways – including just "In Full" deliveries, without reference to time. This type of report does not meet the requirements of today's supply chain, where customers want deliveries on the day – or indeed by the hour. It also has a dubious virtue of making the result look better than it should!

Some companies also measure customer service based on the total volume delivered as a percentage of total volume delivered (either in cases or in units). This weights the measure in favour of the total volume delivered, but conceals the number of orders which could be causing problems to customers. A business that wants to be genuinely customer-focused ought to use the measures as recommended above (thus DOTIFR and DOTIFP), to be able to pick up all instances of process failures.

The following table illustrates the calculation for "Request Date"; a similar one would be produced for "To Promise".

Table 23 Delivery performance

Customer Service - DOTIFR

Week 10

Order #	Item #	Qty due	Date Due	Actual Qty	Actual Date	Item Hit/Miss	Order Hit/Miss
17845	432496	100	02/03/2020	100	02/03/2020	Hit	
	438298	100	02/03/2020	100	03/03/2020	Miss	Miss
17945	438569	200	03/03/2020	200	03/03/2020	Hit	Hit
17467	449869	200	04/03/2020	200	03/03/2020	Miss	
	456399	300	04/03/2020	300	04/03/2020	Hit	Miss
17549	428657	300	05/03/2020	300	05/03/2020	Hit	
	427852	400	05/03/2020	400	05/03/2020	Hit	
	417843	300	05/03/2020	300	05/03/2020	Hit	Hit
17603	489456	300	06/03/2020	300	06/03/2020	Hit	
	436742	200	06/03/2020	200	06/03/2020	Hit	Hit

DOTIFR Order Fill 60%
Item Fill 80%

The target for "performance to promise date" should be 100% on time, in full delivery. Who wants to lie when they give a promise? The target for DOTIFR should be the service level agreed by the senior leadership team for all products/product groups, etc.

The responsibility for customer service – DOTIFP – should belong to the operations manager(s), and the accountability to the operations director. The accountability for delivery to customer request - "DOTIFR" - should be assigned to the CEO, GM, or MD. That is on the principle of the GM who recognised that "Customer Service is my job". The responsibility should be assigned to the person who heads up planning, for instance a "Head of Integrated Business Planning

Most of these measures are used and developed for IBP implementations.

The one area that I have rarely seen measured is "Planning" itself. Schedule achievement and customer service measures are output measures – do we make and deliver on time, in full? But if the plan was no good in the first place, then these measures are difficult to achieve.

There are, in principle two separate processes in the supply area, which are "Planning" and "Execution".

If you look at the correct procedure for Planning, then the planner should be managing the "master schedule" and ensuring that they keep the plan up to date, etc. Eventually, works orders (or Kanbans/signals in a Lean environment) execute the plan – i.e. make it happen.

The handover of responsibility to the factory and the suppliers can be characterised as a relay baton handover, as illustrated in Figure 62.

Figure 62: Responsibility for planning and execution

- **Master Schedule is the plan**
- **Factory have to execute the plan**

The handover is when the works order is released to the factory.

Hence, there is a need for a series of measures to judge the quality of the planning process, since the schedule achievement and Right-First-Time measures of quality and delivery depend on it.

- **Planning Performance Measurement**

The overall objective of the planner(s) should be to make sure that materials and capacity are in place to ensure the factory and procurement/suppliers can make/deliver to the plan.

Therefore, we should produce several measures to support this, as follows:

1. **Capacity availability.** If the planner manages the capacity planning process correctly, then we would find that capacity is available at all work centres. Hence, a measure should be produced, which calculates the number of work centres that are correctly balanced within the horizon for those work centres. In particular, there should be no overloads on any work centres. Thus, the measure is:

Equation 5

$$\frac{\text{Number of work centres with no overloads}}{\text{Total number of work centres}} \quad \%$$

2. **Past Due Orders.** A frequent error in ERP systems is the existence of Past Due Orders. These are either purchase orders or manufacturing orders where the release date or the due date are before today. The earliest you can do something which has not yet been done is now! This issue indicates that a planner has not updated the system to make sure it is valid. The measure should be the number of Past Due Orders. The target should be zero, as any number greater than that would lead to mistrust of the data in the planning system.

3. **Action messages.** Planners using ERP systems properly (which have the proper functionality) should be reacting to action messages. These action messages will typically be:

   - Reschedule in order
   - Reschedule out order
   - Add order
   - Cancel order
   - Firm plan order
   - Reduce order quantity
   - Increase order quantity

Each day, the planner(s) should review these messages and action them by the end of the day. Hence, there should be a measure produced of:

Equation 6

$$\frac{\text{The number of messages actioned}}{\text{The number of messages due to be actioned}} \%$$

The target should be >98% actioned.

6. **Plan stability**. In an ERP system with the right functionality, the system should recommend or automatically firm up works orders at the cumulative lead time. Once either the system or the planner has firmed the works orders as Firm Planned Orders, then they should be a minimal need for changes, provided the planner has set in place the right plan, with the right amount of flexibility with safety stocks.

Therefore, we should record all works orders when the system or planner first firms them, and then record whether the planner releases the orders on the due date. The measure of stability is then:

Equation 7

$$\frac{\text{Number of works orders released on the planned date}}{\text{The number of works orders due to be released in the week}} \%$$

The target should be 95%.

With these measures in place, we will then be in a position to make sure the planning process is working.

Planning Organisation – the right capabilities

I first came across the issue of the importance of having the right people in place during our project with ICI Agrochemicals. Once we understood what "master scheduling" was all about, and what it would be like to operate with an up-to-date ERP system, we set about recruiting five "master schedulers".

We realised that the current role would not work in the new environment where we drove the plan through forecasts and had a computer system that required active management of the master schedule.

One came from being a factory manager; another came from IT; another was a product manager/marketing; another was a sales manager; and one was already a production planner. Together, they were responsible for balancing the needs of the markets against the production sites' requirements. They were based in the headquarters and often travelled to the plants, as necessary. But that was the great thing about having a computer – everyone had access to correct live data, wherever they were.

In addition, we had four demand managers who liaised with our 35 overseas markets and dealt with direct sales to distributor territories.

But the critical challenge was to get everyone to realise the importance of the planning role, and to get everyone to understand the valuable role that they played in making sure there was a new world in which promises mattered. As the service improved (with less inventory), so the credibility went up, and the business improved. The master schedulers soon gained a great deal of respect, and the people within the company recognised the role as a critical one.

But it is still a surprise some 30 years on, across so many businesses, that this role is not recognised or trained up to be the role it should be – or given the recognition it deserves.

If you want to be an accountant, you have to go through a formal process of qualifying, and getting initials after your name. Being an accountant is doing a crucial role in a company. But so is a master scheduler; yet there is still no formal training required for this role, and no universal standard for people who call themselves "production planners" or "master schedulers".

The term "master scheduler" was introduced in the 1980s to create a distinction between the typical production controller/planning person, and someone who needed to take a much more pivotal role in the organisation, balancing supply and demand.

Figure 63 illustrates how the master scheduler plays a central role in the organisation, creating a balanced plan using practical tools. On the one hand, they feed the factory, and on the other hand, they deal with all the changes that hit the company in the form of forecasts and orders.

Figure 63: Master Scheduler is at the centre of a well-planned company

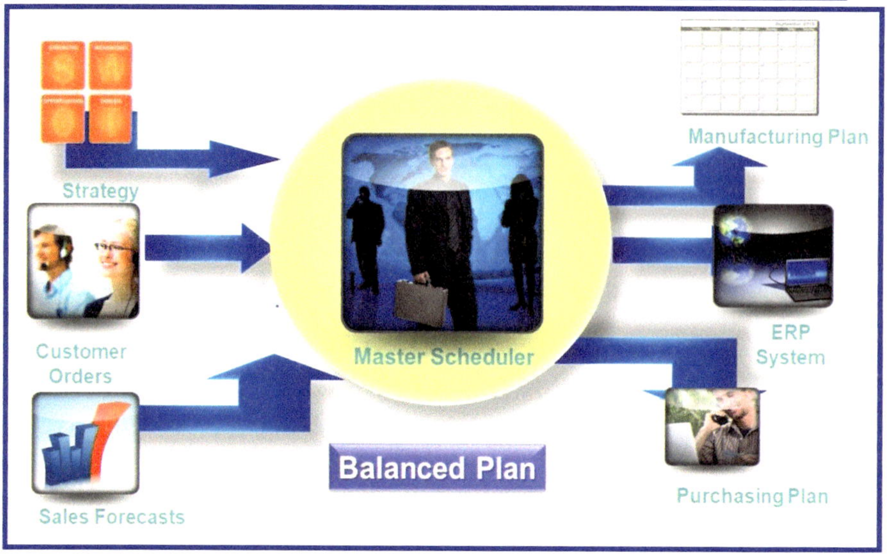

As we can see, on the one hand, you have customers wanting their product now.

Conversely, you have a factory that wants to have a productive facility. In the middle, you need a person who can control the changes needed to satisfy both "parties".

They have to have a particular skill set, which we can summarise as:

- Be commercially aware and understand the realities of the market place
- Understand the products
- Understand a P&L account and balance sheet
- Understand the factory and product base
- Have good negotiating skills
- Be unflappable in urgent situations
- Be assertive
- Have strong numeracy skills
- Be driven to deliver good customer service.

An excellent master scheduler, or master schedulers, are at the heart of the whole IBP process, and often this requires a good, hard look at the skills needed in this area. They also need to represent an independent position between Sales, Marketing, Finance and the Supply Chain.

I have also worked with clients who recognise this requirement for independence, and they have created a "head of Integrated Business Planning", who manages the whole Planning process. In this case, they took responsibility for the master scheduler (who managed the supply plans at four factories) and the demand planner (who managed the Demand Planning process across two business units). This person should ideally report to the CEO or MD of the organisation, but could equally report to the finance director, sales and marketing director, or the operations director.

Any of these functional reporting lines could inevitably attract criticism of a lack of independence of the head of IBP. Finance: "too cost-driven"; sales: "too customer-driven"; operations: "too factory-driven". It will be down to the individual involved and their character to ensure that managers respect the person concerned to act independently. They need to be conscious of the requirement for independence at all times. They need the wisdom of King Solomon.

We will see in the chapter on strategy how a company needs to make a clear choice between being driven by the customer (customer intimacy), driven by cost (operational excellence) or driven by innovation (product leadership). The chosen strategy might drive the logic of where to locate this role. Thus, it will help customer intimacy if the "head of Integrated Business Planning" reports in to Sales and Marketing.

But the right way to address this would be to elevate the planning process to the point of having a planning director in the senior leadership team who has accountability for the Planning process.

This approach is a rare feature of most organisations, mainly because planning does not have the organisational prominence it deserves.

Companies (before implementing IBP) seem to focus too much on the "doing" phase of activities. Thus, in making things happen, there are two phases: thinking and doing.

Suppose you look at the psychological side of human behaviour. In that case, you can categorise the people in an organisation into several behaviour types, which reflect a mixture of essential behavioural natures – sometimes characterised in the colour wheel of blue, yellow, green and red.

Red and yellow tend to be more extrovert and dominant. Green and blue tend to be more introverted. Blues tend to be more analytical, and so on. Red and Blue act more on their own, not really acting as team players. Whereas Green and Yellow are more socially oriented. (The science gets a lot more complicated here!)

But the interesting observation in this area is that a person who is a good master scheduler needs to deploy the right combination of analytical behavioural characteristics, together with an ability to reach sound decisions quickly; they also need to be sociable in order to influence people but be direct and individualistic to get to the right decisions effectively. It is a challenging mixture of elements to find! Figure 64 illustrates that they need to be able to operate in the middle, balancing thinking and planning, with doing and execution, while keeping an eye on the long-term vision of the organisation.

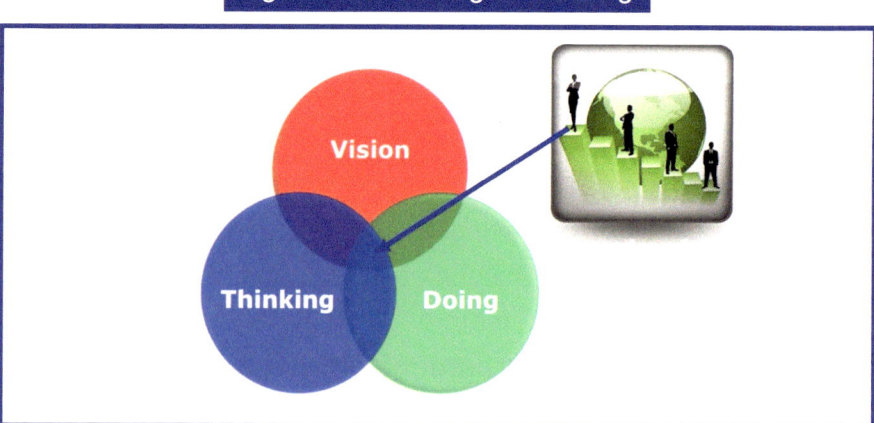

Figure 64: Thinking and Doing

Also, they need to understand your business and be familiar with the products and issues your business faces. It is therefore probably better to choose the right person and then train them into the role, rather than recruit a master scheduler who does not know the company.

Getting the right balance of behaviours is more important than the organisational structure, but core to the Integrated Business Planning process is to encourage a culture of planning. It is getting the right balance, as the following diagram shows, in support of effective leadership.

- **The Supply Review Meeting**

We have described the activities that need to go on in a company on a day-to-day basis to manage the Supply process. Once a month, we need to gather together the data to work out the key issues, look at the scenarios, pull together the performance measures and make the required decisions.

So, this now will lead to a Supply Review meeting, the objective of which is to determine whether the business can support the demand and innovation plans included in the previous steps of this process. Traditionally, this step (because of the SOP/operational planning flavour of the model in those companies) has focused on factories and procurement activities – making and buying.

However, this step should look at the supply of any resources which are required to satisfy the demands.

For instance, one client had a business where they provided vehicles and equipment to the ministries of defence around the world. A vital aspect of this was to provide training to customers to support the use of the equipment. Providing the people to do the training was a separate, but linked, part of the organisation. Initially, they did not see this activity as part of the IBP process, but when it did become part of the Supply Review process, it meant they were joined-up.

Sometimes quality control and quality assurance are set up as a separate function; in this case, we need to plan the resources for this area, as part of the supply review.

I once worked with a subsidiary of a major pharmaceutical company, which had a significant increase in workload in their quality department, which resulted from the introduction of several new products, and substantial changes to existing products.

They usually allowed for a four-day lead time to test product, but the increased load meant that the time through Quality rapidly increased to approximately 15 to 20 days. As a result, they were running short of critical components, which they needed to test as they came into the factory. The quality department was holding them up.

It was not long before service levels dipped to 65% OTIF, and the factory was under real pressure. We quickly resolved the situation by working out the resource requirements for the quality department and treating them like any resource. We rescheduled the requirements on the factory and managed demand.

It took a couple of weeks to fix the problem, and the service levels quickly climbed back up again. Quality needed to be a regular part of their IBP process.

Multi-site Factory Organisation

In an organisation which is multi-site with multiple factories, there will be a need to have a supply review at each of the sites, during which they look at their capabilities and sign off their ability to meet the Supply plan.

Where an organisation has multiple sites but shares capacity across several locations, then it will need to have a central supply organisation which looks at the planning of resources over the long-term horizon, and which should determine the most cost-effective configuration of factories and business units.

It will then be essential to have standard ways of working, and definitions of capacity in these situations, to make sure you are adding up apples and pears across several different sites.

Supply

One organisation migrated from having factories in every country to having a "hub and spoke arrangement". Because they then had proper visibility of accurate requirements of capacity, they reduced their capital expenditure budget by a phenomenal amount!

Figure 65 is a generic example of the Supply Review meeting:

Figure 65: Supply Review meeting template

Inputs
- Update on new Products/Projects
- Latest Forecast of unconstrained demand
- Rough Cut and Demonstrated Capacity
- Detailed capacity issues
- Material constraints
- Performance Measures

Behaviour
1. Demo capacity
2. Trusting the forecast
3. Responding to changes
4. Thinking beyond current year

Agenda
1. Required Supply plans [factories and external suppliers]
2. Issues in meeting plan
3. Proposals for resolving issues
4. Capex projects
5. Performance Measures

Outputs
- Issues
- Recommendations for resolving issues
- Actions to meet plan
- Agreed signed-off Supply Plan
- Actions based on measures

Links
1. Engineering Plans
2. Innovation/Demand reviews
3. Quality plans
4. Supplier strategic review

The key output of this meeting will be an agreement that the Supply plan is achievable based on the realistic plans available, and if not, what needs to go forward to the following steps of the process for review and decision.

It is essential that this meeting can make properly costed decisions, so finance will need to be involved. If there are decisions that include people, then there may well be recruitment, training or downsizing implications, and hence it is vital to get Human Resources involved. Integrated Business Planning is about making decisions in an integrated way across the business.

The final point is that this meeting must review the new performance measures and drive towards the effective, continuous improvement of planning and execution of the supply resources within the company.

Chapter 10
Lean

"A relentless barrage of "whys" is the best way to prepare your mind to pierce the clouded veil of thinking caused by the status quo. Use it often." – Shigeo Shingo

Back in the 1990s, when I was part of the team that arguably created the very first global IBP implementation, I read a book on Just-in-Time. We were fixed on what was called MRP II at the time – Manufacturing Resource Planning. JIT was "invented" by Shigeo Shingo and others as part of the Toyota Production System, and gathered speed in the 1980s.

Wound up by the power of the JIT thinking, I then went to a colleague and said: "Should we not be implementing JIT?" He looked at me patiently and said, "I think we have enough on our plate implementing MRP II at the moment. Let us do that later." That has now been rebadged as "Lean".

Around the same time, I had the pleasure of listening to Eliyahu Goldratt, who was the author of "The Goal" (Goldratt, 2004) – an excellent read; I finished it in a night! His presentation was brilliant. He explained the links between "throughput", "inventory" and "operating expense" on an overhead projector (a pre-cursor to laptop and projector!), and meanwhile challenged operations directors in the audience on how much inventory they had. "Three months," said one poor unfortunate. Fifteen minutes later, Goldratt went over to the same person and said, "and how long does it take to make your product?" "Around 15 minutes," said the operations director.

"So why do you have your product sitting around for three months?"

One of his main themes was: *"If we reduce batch sizes by half, we also reduce by half the time it will take to process a batch. That means we reduce queue and wait by half as well. Reduce those by half, and we reduce by about half the total time parts spend in the plant. Reduce the time parts spend in the plant and our total lead time condenses. And with faster turn-around on orders, customers get their orders faster."*

I then went on to learn that there were three strands of thinking that contributed to what was called "Business Excellence": MRP II (Planning), JIT (Waste elimination) and TQM (Total Quality Management). You can find an excellent description of this integration in Phil Robinson's book "Business Excellence" (Robinson, 2006).

The problem has always seemed to be that these are seen, somehow, as competing philosophies and that somehow all others are entirely wrong. Thus, many people who adopt Lean thinking have said: "MRP II is wrong; it forces companies to make in large batches. Large batches are waste. Lean is about eliminating waste. Use JIT/Lean, and then you do not need MRP II." Not true! MRP systems recommend making what the user tells it to recommend to make. It is the humans that make a mistake, not the system.

There is a current "movement" which goes under the heading of "DDMRP", or Demand Driven MRP. It started on the basis that if you just reacted to orders and have inventory buffers in the right place, you will respond quickly to customers, get rid of the infamous "bullwhip" effect, and reduce inventory created by batch quantities.

Initially, the idea was that you did not need forecasts to drive what you make. Now it is recognised that you might need forecasts where you cannot rely on historical weekly rates of use. This school of thinking is now adopting "Adaptive SOP" – with help from Dick Ling – which recognises the need for the longer-term thinking to provide long-term capacity planning. Again, it is supported by a strong theme that it is the only way to manage the supply chain, but it is very similar to Goldratt's Theory of Constraints and uses Lean as a pillar of its approach. The replenishment process is a sophisticated variant of order-point used in the early 1900s, which was replaced in the 1960s by MRP. It seems that there is not anything new under the sun – and there cannot be, in the world of inventory management! DDMRP afficionados claim it to be an improvement over standard ERP systems.

"Lean" and indeed "Six Sigma" – as the modern-day version of Total Quality Management as developed by Deming and Crosby in the 1960s – should not be seen as competitors to planning.

Lean is fundamentally about eliminating waste, and leads to the ability to manage operations based on "flow" – setting up a constant, reproducible rate of production. Problems will occur, but the people at the shop floor level solve problems – the experts within their own three square-feet. Fujio Cho, president of Toyota, summarised this view:

"Many good companies have respect for individuals and practise Kaizen (continuous improvement) and other TPS {Toyota Production System} tools. But what is important is having all of the elements together as a system. It must be practised every day in a very consistent manner – not in spurts – in a concrete way on the shop floor."

The quality system must use performance measures to get to the root causes of issues to identify where to make improvements.

This thought-process is consistent with much of what I have been saying thus far concerning Integrated Business Planning. We cannot do IBP without using all the standard tools to improve the way we operate. They are not separate schools of thought.

If you want to get to the pragmatic details of how "Lean" works, then Chris Gray wrote an excellent book – "Lean Standard System" (Gray, Lean Standard System, 2008). In Chapter 1, he shows how a Lean system is driven by "Sales and Operations planning", which is his term for Integrated Business Planning.

He also shows in his book on Sales and Operations Planning (Gray, Sales and Operations Planning Standard System, 2007) how to convert the Demand plan into "Takt Time". Takt time is the rate per hour or minute at which we will sell, which in turn we should balance with the Product Takt time, which is the rate at which the company needs to produce.

A Lean environment will facilitate making "what you sell" and "what you make" equivalent. But the plan is vital in setting up the right capacity, which is where Integrated Business Planning becomes essential.

As part of the Lean environment, we also need to develop visible performance measures at shop floor level to support this. These measures will include quality and rate of production, together with root cause analysis. I have seen these built around at least the common areas of Cost, Quality, Delivery, and Safety, and Training, with boards summarising performance in each area.

There are a few other measures that are important, and which need clear understanding.

- **Operating Equipment Effectiveness**

The first is Operating Equipment Effectiveness (OEE), which examines the amount of waste seen when operating machines. You can develop a similar measure for people. This measure requires the separation out of three elements:

- Availability of equipment
- Performance as related to the speed of production
- Quality (amount of right product produced)

Time has always been important in managing operations. It is crucial within the "Lean" philosophy, as the elimination of waste needs the identification of all of the activities that take up unnecessary time, and for companies to eliminate these activities.

It was the Babylonians who "invented" the basis of structuring the day into 60 seconds in a minute and 60 minutes into an hour, and then 24 hours in a day with seven days a week, in around 1500 BC. That much is constant.

To measure OEE, we start with the fact that there are 168 hours available per week. If we could operate our equipment (as Henry Ford was trying to do) all the time, then we should be able to achieve 168 hours of output. Thus, if we are making widgets, and each widget had an identical time of five minutes per piece, and we produced 2,016 items, we could, in theory, have achieved 100% effectiveness. But in making those 2,016 units, we need to understand if there were any opportunities for improvement.

Producing 2,016 units might be fine – but if the demand were for only 200 units, we would end up with 1,816 items just going into inventory. That would not make sense. We should not aim to make what is unnecessary. We can measure against the total time available. We call this a measure of Total Effective Equipment Performance [TEEP], which is a wider measure than OEE.

Hence – as we have described through the Integrated Business Planning process – we need to understand our plan. We may plan to run our equipment for five days a week, and if the shift arrangements are for all people to clock on and clock off for 8½ hours a day, Monday to Friday (start work at 8am and finish at 4.30pm, allowing for 30 minutes for lunch), we then have 40 hours per week available. If we can operate machines while people are at lunch, then we would have 42.5 hours available. Here we will assume 40 hours, for ease of calculation.

In 40 hours, therefore, we should be able to produce 480 units, assuming we have a cycle time of five minutes. Let us look at the detail behind OEE.

Availability

Our first source of waste is going to be availability – time lost through the machine(s) breaking down, or the line stopping for whatever reason. We need to record this time and the reasons so that we can get to the root causes of the problems. Thus, the line may break down because a gear in the machine breaks. However, we then need to find out what was the cause of the breakage. Was it checked when you last did routine maintenance of the machine? Was there regular maintenance of the machine? How long should the gear last – what is the mean time between failure? Have we allowed a proper time to make sure we replace equipment in a timely fashion, and so on? The five-minute cycle time used as an illustration is the total time taken between making one piece and the next. But we might find that we lose time because we produce in batches when we set up. Hence, also excluded from this calculation should be any time lost for setting up the line in between batches. This is a loss of time.

Note that, above, in Chapter 6 when we were calculating the amount of capacity required, and the capacity achieved (demonstrated capacity) then we specifically allowed time for set up times, because we need to make an allowance for this when we are planning how much capacity we need. But in a Lean environment, we are aiming to focus on pure value-adding time, which is the run time per piece, when the item is being processed through a machine or an assembly area. Calculation of Demonstrated Capacity and Operating Equipment Effectiveness are different calculations in this respect.

Let us assume, then, that the line is down for five hours in the week. You calculate availability as 87.5%.

Speed of Production

So far, we have used a run time of five minutes per unit. This figure is the standard time for the production of the product going down the line.

If multiple products are going down the line, we will use the standard time for each of these items. Again, we need to validate these as being correct.

However, not every piece will likely take the same time (or indeed some operators may be more experienced than other operators and time will vary for this reason). For planning purposes, we may well rightly use an average, or standard, time of five minutes per piece.

But if you could make improvements to the process (operating the equipment faster, changing the process so you could make each unit faster), which results in a faster run time, you should use that in the calculation of OEE. Let us say that we have reviewed the process through industrial engineering, and that time could be four minutes.

This figure is then the "ideal run time" or "minimum theoretical time" per unit; we could be more effective if we could get to that.

Hence, the current performance relating to the speed at which we produce is 80% (4/5).

We would need to calculate "fastest run time"/ "standard run time" for the number of products made in the week where multiple products are involved.

Again, when we are planning capacity requirements and demonstrated capacity, it should be based on a standard time, which would be the average time it takes to produce an item (for both the set-up time and the run-time). We plan on the basis of what we do, and not what we might be able to do.

Quality of Output

Finally, suppose we made 420 units in 35 hours at five minutes per piece. We might find that we had reworked 50 units, leaving you making only 370 "good units" Right First Time. This is also not adding value.

So while the machine has been operating, it has not produced "good output". This is why we base this element of the measure on the "Right First Time" concept". If the 50 parts are not scrapped, but we reprocess them down the line, we should ignore this production in the calculation of OEE.

In which case, our quality performance element is 88% (370/420).

So, we can calculate our Operating Equipment Effectiveness for the line for the week as:

$$87.5\% \times 80\% \times 88\% = 61.6\%$$

We should also identify "schedule losses"; for instance, we might only plan to make 400 units for the week – because that is what we need. To try to make 480 units and put another 80 units into inventory would not make sense. So there are other losses. This factor would require us to distinguish between planned production, and planned available time. The concept as described is designed to get us to the point where we can identify our losses, and work to eliminate these. It is crucial to include this measure to see what we can do to improve capacity availability, where we need it. But it is not the same as the calculation of capacity for planning purposes.

World-Class Standard

While there is a theoretical "World-Class Standard" of 85% documented across the literature, the fact remains that this depends on so many factors that it is best focusing on the losses, and what can be done to reduce them. We should make these improvements using the standard Lean toolbox.

OEE is, therefore, a critical performance measure, designed to support continuous improvement.

- **Velocity**

The other key measure which supports the Lean philosophy is Velocity. I have not found many companies which use this measure. The Lean philosophy focuses on the elimination of waste, and we view "non-waste" as the time where we spend adding value to the product – carrying out an activity for which the customer would pay. As a simple example, if I am taking a flight from London Heathrow to Paris, I am paying for being in the air getting from London to Paris. Standing in a queue to get on the plane is not value-adding. Waiting for the flight to leave or get to its stand at the airport is not adding value.

You can see how the pursuit of the elimination of waste forces people to act in line with the aims of the business! Adding value is, therefore, where the customer would be happy for you to spend time on doing something in the supply chain that adds value to them – i.e. converts raw materials into the finished product.

A typical flow diagram – actually more of a "stop" diagram – is described in Figure 66, which shows the usual steps of a production process, and the steps that many companies follow.

Figure 66: Flow diagram

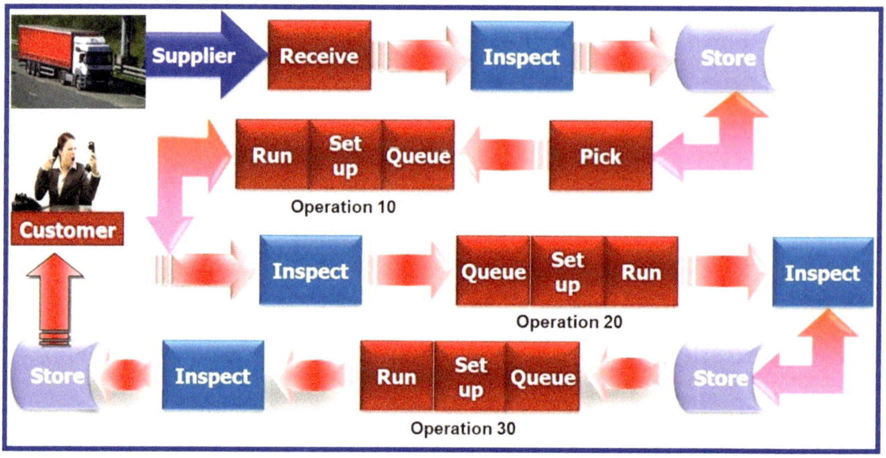

Set-up Times

All the set-up times in the diagram are waste – we could get rid of them through a Single Minute Exchange of Die (SMED) programme. We would look at the elements of the set-up process and see how we could eliminate all or some of them.

Queues

Queues of work at each work centre are a waste. They are typically there because of a lack of balance of capacity between work centres. These would be removed by creating a balanced flow of production through the process, and only making when needed.

Inspection

Inspection as a separate process is a waste, as in-line process control would eliminate samples going to the laboratory (which themselves go through a similar "flow" process). Understanding where the operating process causes defects and fixing the process, rather than looking at a product in microscopic detail, would be more effective.

Storage

Storage is a waste. Having an in-bound goods receipt area is also a waste. You can replace this with Direct Line Feed – delivery to the point-of-use stores. You can eliminate incoming inspection by ensuring the supplier carries out a proper review before the goods leave, and then provide a certificate of conformance or similar.

A Lean Workplace

When we have completed all this, we can probably find that we can link two manufacturing processes together, and so the diagram ends up looking like the example in Figure 67.

Figure 67: A Lean process

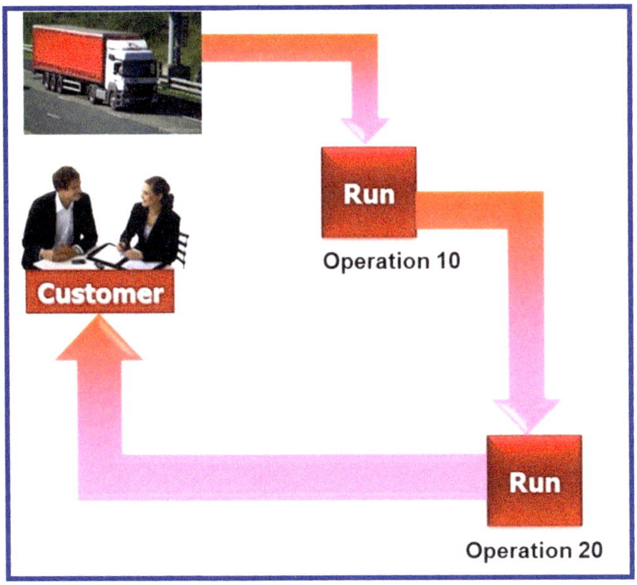

So we should now measure the time our current manufacturing process for a typical product within our IBP family adds value as a proportion of the average time that the product takes through the plant. This observation is what Eli Goldratt was doing in the presentation that I was describing; if it usually takes something like three months to get through a factory, but it only takes 15 minutes to make the product, then there is a considerable amount of waste.

Value Stream Analysis

You need to carry out a Value Stream analysis to get to the detail. When you do this, you can calculate the sum of the run-times through the manufacturing process. You calculate velocity as the following:

Equation 8 - Velocity

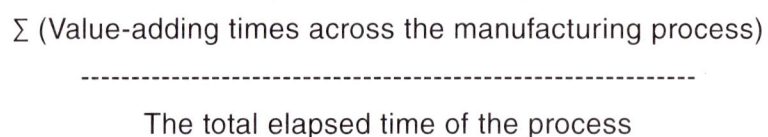

$$\frac{\sum (\text{Value-adding times across the manufacturing process})}{\text{The total elapsed time of the process}}$$

I illustrate a typical value stream map in Figure 68. This is an example from a company that makes lights which are used in offices. They process aluminium sheet, which is delivered in rolls, through stamping, pressing, welding, test and assembly into ceiling lights.

The total elapsed production time is 60 days – including time spent sitting in inventory.

The Value Added time is eight minutes and eight seconds = 488 seconds.

Hence the velocity ratio is a tiny 0.009%! But in most companies, the velocity ratio is minimal, at around 1 or 2%, which represents an enormous opportunity to reduce cost, reduce waste and improve flexibility to customers.

The measurement of velocity and the adoption of Lean principles is a vital part of the planning process, which is core to Integrated Business Planning. It will identify opportunities to create more capacity.

You should use Lean principles to make sure that they create the space and time in which to be able to be flexible to customers and increase your throughput in the time available.

Figure 68: Value Stream Map

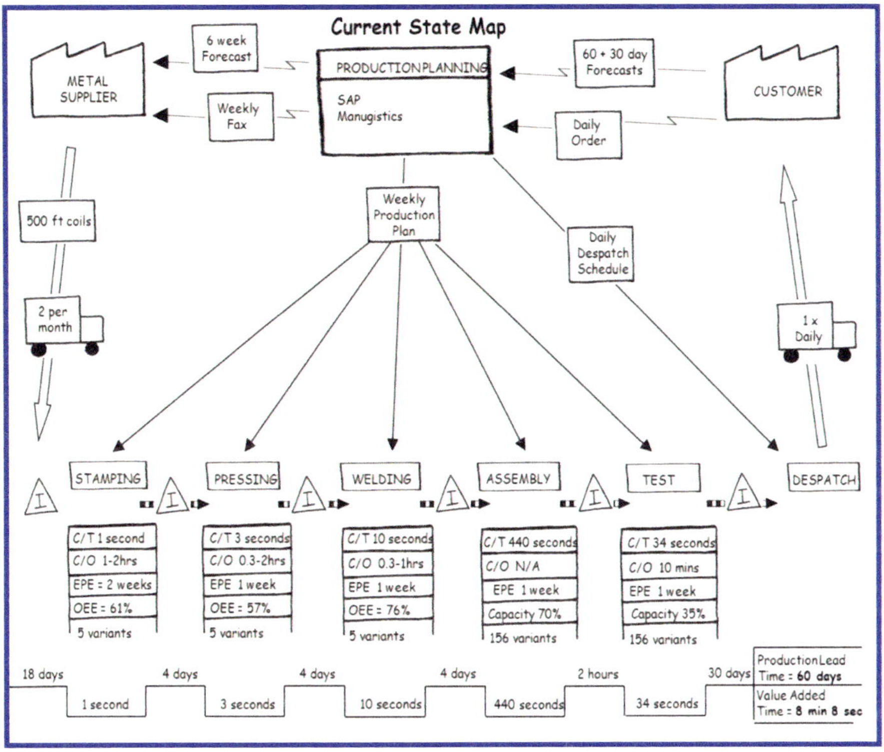

Current State Map

[Value Stream Map showing flow from Metal Supplier through Production Planning (SAP Manugistics) to Customer, with 6 week Forecast, Weekly Fax, 60 + 30 day Forecasts, Daily Order, Weekly Production Plan, and Daily Despatch Schedule.

500 ft coils, 2 per month delivery; 1 x Daily despatch.

Process steps: STAMPING, PRESSING, WELDING, ASSEMBLY, TEST, DESPATCH

	STAMPING	PRESSING	WELDING	ASSEMBLY	TEST
C/T	1 second	3 seconds	10 seconds	440 seconds	34 seconds
C/O	1-2hrs	0.3-2hrs	0.3-1hrs	N/A	10 mins
EPE	2 weeks	1 week	1 week	1 week	1 week
OEE	61%	57%	76%	Capacity 70%	Capacity 35%
	5 variants	5 variants	5 variants	156 variants	156 variants

Timeline: 18 days — 4 days — 4 days — 4 days — 2 hours — 30 days
Value added: 1 second, 3 seconds, 10 seconds, 440 seconds, 34 seconds

Production Lead Time = 60 days
Value Added Time = 8 min 8 sec]

The I in a triangle represents inventory. C/T = Cycle Time; C/O is Change Over Time; EPE (Every Piece Every) is the frequency you can cycle through the product range, and the OEE number is the Operating Equipment Effectiveness figure, as calculated above.

- **Additional Lean Measures**

There are additional supporting measures which can be adopted to test the extent to which the company has adopted Lean principles. These should include the number of "Kanbans" and "Point of Use" stores.

Number/% of Kanbans

A kanban is a signal to make or move an item. In principle, where it is to make an item, then it will replace a part number. We should be aiming to increase the number of kanbans in use to support the simplification of Planning and Execution. Hence the measure is:

Equation 9 - Kanban usage

$$\frac{\text{Total number of kanbans}}{\text{(Total number of kanbans + total number of parts)}} \%$$

Number/% of Point of Use Stores

A "traditional" factory will have a goods-in warehouse, and a finished goods-out warehouse, with locations for each. Where companies implement point-of-use stores, then there will be multiple line-side locations where components are stored. They can be delivered there by suppliers via direct-line-feed where they are bought-out components, or by the central stores (which we could also eliminate). Hence the measure would be:

Equation 10 - Point of Use Stores

$$\frac{\text{Total number of Point of Use stores}}{\text{Total number of storage areas}} \%$$

- **Application to Other Areas of the Business**

These ideas can all be applied to the other parts of the business as well. It sometimes takes six weeks to recruit a new person, but some people decide within two minutes after a candidate has walked into the interview! The velocity ratio of the recruitment process is 0.003%! Looking at how the whole recruitment process works will enable the company to become more responsive and more flexible. Elimination of waste associated with checking purchase and customer invoices is another source of value.

Hence, the purpose of this section is to make a case for the fact that Lean is not another philosophy competing for space with Planning, but must be seen as an integral part of Integrated Business Planning. It will reduce capacity required as a company reduces cycle times and set-up times, which frees up available capacity. The company should fill this with additional work which it wins through the speed of response and improved quality of deliveries.

However, many companies implement Lean projects as "cost reduction projects". Companies introduce them when a business is struggling.

The core of the Lean philosophy is that you need to harness the expertise of the people on the shop floor to gain the improvements available.

But if a company introduces Lean as a "headcount reduction" exercise, this will destroy the confidence of the workforce in the motives of management. This lack of trust will then stop the flow of ideas that you rely on to get continuous improvement.

It thus requires a long-term commitment to the workforce and effective "Lean leadership" to make the changes necessary.

Leadership is about taking a longer-term view of the business and not reacting to short-term changes.

Integrated Business Leadership should embrace all of the continuous improvement tools – like Lean, Six Sigma, Total Preventive Maintenance – as part of an integrated approach to transforming the way a business runs.

Success depends on displaying the right attitude to the people within the company. There is no longer a place for Victorian values of "bosses versus workers" for companies of the future.

Chapter 11
Finance

"People are accustomed to thinking of accounting as dry and boring, a necessary evil used primarily to prepare financial reports and survive audits, but that is because accounting is something that has become taken for granted." – Eric Ries, author and entrepreneur.

One of the significant deficiencies in the development of Integrated Business Planning has been the failure fully to integrate the finance function into the process. In many companies, people have developed "Sales and Operations Planning" as if it were purely a supply chain tool.

This probably is because everyone has blamed the supply chain director for poor customer service and too much inventory. He or she has then valiantly attempted to implement "SOP".

He or she has then struggled to get the full buy-in implied by "Integrated Business Planning", but says at least they have implemented "SOP". Sadly, many have then come to think of IBP as a separate step in an evolutionary process.

SOP and IBP have always been about making decisions, and you cannot make decisions without understanding the potential financial outcomes of various plans – whether at an aggregate or detailed level. Finance is not the only area that is crucial to the process. We also need to plan and manage the talent – Human Resources – and the data – Information Resources – within the business.

It is for this reason that I have developed a separate discrete step within the process, which I have called "Support" – which covers finance, human resources and information resources. These can be three different steps or one, depending on the organisational structure.

Thus, if there is a HR director in place, there would be a separate step for HR.

In this section, I am going to concentrate on the financial aspects of the IBP process.

As part of the ICI project, we understood very clearly the need to have an integrated approach to finance. Hence, we put into the Distribution Requirements Planning (DRP) planning system for our overseas units the prices and costs of all the products. In our manufacturing systems, we had the detailed plans for our components and raw materials, bills of materials and routings so that we could work out our manufacturing costs.

We then created a financial reporting tool which enabled us to take the operational numbers and convert them into global revenues, costs, gross margins and net profit.

One afternoon, the group finance director came into my office. It was September, and the board were going through the annual planning process. He asked me if I could look into the financial model for him, and come up with the numbers based on the operational forecasts. That afternoon, I went back to him with the answers for the budget for the following year, and he was happy. I had worked out the revenue at something like £1,232,450,000. He looked at the numbers and said, "£1.2 billion? That's about right!" *He* appreciated roughly right rather than precisely wrong, based on one set of numbers.

Before we got to that point, the Finance function had operated with a whole series of complex spreadsheets, which they used to create the annual business plan and monthly reports, taking into account transfer prices, local costs, central costs, etc. But when we initially compared the numbers from the operational system, and values generated, there were some wild deviations.

Volumes were different; costs differed, and so on. We had a discussion about which numbers to use and finally concluded that the operational numbers had to be the basis of the financial projections. If we were planning to make it, then we should plan to stock and invoice it. Fortunately, as part of our project team we had someone who knew the accountancy systems inside out; he and I had designed the forecasting and DRP systems.

Before long, we could also work out the stocks we had in transit from the plant to overseas territories. We knew the inventory projections for the next three years. We could work out projected stocks from the manufacturing planning system at the manufacturing sites – it did not take much to then work out projected cash flow.

One set of numbers seemed to be so obvious then, as a concept. Yet people in many companies appear still to argue about the need for it, and whether it is the right thing to do. If nothing else, how else can you make decisions that will integrate all parts of the business, unless the company operates with one set of numbers?

So the objective of the Finance step in the Integrated Business Planning model is fourfold:

1. To create an up-to-date projection of the cash flow and P&L position each month to support the effective management of finances. But in principle, that should be automated, as should the required financial reports.

2. To support the business in making the right decisions based on the financial numbers throughout the IBP process. Thus Finance is involved in each step of the process, enabling and assisting managers and directors in choosing the right long-term solutions.

3. To help make the IBP process so robust that the Annual Budget process becomes a direct by-product of the process and capable of being completed within one monthly cycle. This activity will also enable the CFO/FD and the CEO to present to shareholders each year/quarter the numbers based on the current projections direct from the IBP process. Shareholders have a portfolio of shares and invest in them for a desired return and risk balance. They need to know the truth, as well; they dislike surprises.

4. To ensure that the business has an integrated set of performance measures in addition to the traditional financial measures of gross margin percentages, net margin percentages, debtor days, creditor days and Return on Capital Employed.

The objective of a business organisation should be to increase the Net Present Value (NPV) of the company, which will then lead to an increase in the share price/value of company. The management should do this subject to good corporate and social governance.

Shareholders are willing to invest in a company and pay for shares because of the anticipated future returns from the shares. The difference between the current and future price of shares represents the return on investment that the shareholder makes. This change, in turn, will be reflecting the expected dividend yield and growth in the price of the shares.

Hence, all projects should be calculated based on the NPV of the project – taking into account real incremental revenues, costs and cash flows.

NPV is the sum of the cash flows over the required horizon, discounted at an appropriate rate, which each company needs to work out for each project.

This calculation requires a current up-to-date forecast over at least three years – if not longer – of volumes, sales revenue, gross margins, incremental overheads, and incremental fixed and current assets.

If those forecasts are biased, or inaccurate because of "behavioural" issues described elsewhere in this book, then the investment decisions will themselves be flawed.

I often put together commercial cases for investment and put together spreadsheets. We would calculate these in precisely this way, and present them to the Executive for their approval – whether it was for acquisition, investment in new plant and equipment, or launch of a new product.

However, these were often prepared "ad hoc" with crude assumptions like a 10% per annum growth in the market. Before implementing MRP II, there was no simple basis for establishing a forecast based on the commitment from all overseas subsidiaries. There were occasions when we put together numbers to support an argument, rather than basing the argument on realistic assumptions!

Integrated Business Planning and its principles made a difference in getting us to the point where an agreed, realistic set of numbers supported the financial case, which in turn validated and supported realistic decisions. I have seen this happen many times since in clients, who have embraced IBP.

The other key aspect that a company needs to manage is the source of its finances, where it needs external financing, with a mixture of debt from banks and additional funds from shareholders, and make sure that its rate of return meets their requirements.

A company can get debt from banks and similar institutions. Bank debt is risky because failure to repay will ultimately lead to the closure of the company. Interest rates are possibly fixed for the time of the loan.

The company can also raise money from shareholders, who will require a rate of return that covers their risks, which ultimately could lead to them losing their money in the event of failure of the company. Let us suppose that a company finances bank debt at an interest rate of 7% per annum.

Let us assume that the shareholder-required rate of return is 12% per annum. Suppose that the company finances itself with 30% of debt and 70% from shareholder funds. Then the rate of return the business should be earning should be 10.5% per annum (weighted average cost of capital), as its required rate of return must be able to cover the rates of return required by debtholders and shareholders. A good background book is Principles of Corporate Finance by Brealey, Myers and Allen (Brealey, Myers, & Allen, 2010).

The aim should then be to generate a return which exceeds the rates of return required by shareholders and debtholders (sometimes called "Economic Value Add"). In this way, the company will continue to survive and grow.

IBP will facilitate a forward-looking view of all of this, and enable the executive team to make decisions, which will increase shareholder value.

Hence the decisions that a business needs to make is critically supported by the Finance step of the process. In particular, when a company needs to make a decision, then the executive team needs to look at whether that decision increases the projected "value-added cash flow" for the business.

We need to understand the base case – i.e. continuing status quo, and the incremental value of the proposed investment, or decision.

I looked around for a book that tackles the financial area for modern companies, and came across the term "Lean Accounting".

I had not seen "Lean" applied to accounting areas, but then I met up with Brian Maskell – who wrote a book called Practical Lean Accounting (Maskell, 2004). It is a great read and creates a significant link between the concepts of "Lean thinking" and the financial area. Some of his principles are:

- **Plain English Accounting**

One of the first areas he covers is the fact that many CEOs and boards of directors receive sets of management accounts which are incredibly difficult to understand. A considerable part of this is to do with the costing system, which many companies adopt: "standard costing". His plea is to get rid of standard costing and create reports that are in "plain English", which centre around the idea of understanding accounts built more around cash flow, rather than some of the arcane areas of profitability.

Companies can still meet institutional and legal requirements separately.

- **Value Streams**

The second area he addresses is the idea of value streams – which sometimes maps onto "Business Units". Thus, the Lemonfresh product group described earlier could be part of several drinks products that the company sells to major supermarkets; supermarkets could be a value stream. By focussing on this area, and the consumers who visit those supermarkets, a company can focus on adding value through that value stream. In principle, though, it is a little more complicated than that. A value stream aims to bring together all the revenue and costs associated with a value stream, separating the overheads out which cannot be directly attributable to a value stream.

That way, a business can have a "value stream manager", who is responsible for the revenue, costs, and assets that are directly attributable to a value stream. Thus, if you have production lines which are directly related to a particular product group, then you would allocate those to that value stream.

"Adding value" carries with it the idea that we should also be focusing on how to increase the speed of response, reduce lead times, and reducing inventory. Where companies adopt "standard costing", then overheads will be allocated to the product cost, based on some formula. A programme to reduce inventory will, therefore, reduce profit, and prevents many finance directors from writing off or reducing inventory.

The Value Stream approach welcomes inventory reduction.

So, it is not just about managing the profitability of the "business unit".

- **The Failure of Standard Costing**

One of the fundamental problems that some companies face in trying to get a handle on their profitability is the way that they calculate costs. With accurate Bills of Materials and proper Routings, we can get exact variable costs direct from the system, which will cover material costs and labour conversion costs.

However, this is only part of the cost; if there are internal factories, then there will be overheads in the form of lighting, heat, electricity, factory buildings, etc.

Where companies have inventory and want to value inventory, then companies will typically allocate these manufacturing overhead costs to the cost of the product to come up with a "standard cost".

You can do this on some formula like 3 x the material cost, based on the ratio of overheads to labour costs. This calculation would require a review of the overhead costs across the business, and then an analysis taking into account the budget volume taken from the budgeting process.

For a simple example, let us take a factory where the total overheads for the year for a product area = £1.2m; let us say that the budgeted volume is 100,000 units. Let us assume that the budgeted material cost for those 100,000 units is £0.4m; hence you would base the overhead allocation on 3 x material cost. In this case, the product cost will be made up as follows for each product:

Product 183567	Description:	Widget ABC
	Cost per unit	
	Labour	£ 5.00
	Material	£ 4.00
	Overhead Cost	£ 12.00
	Total Cost	£ 21.00

If we then plan to produce 100,000 units, then the cost of production will be £2.1m (simplified to be based on just this product), which we charge out to the Profit and Loss (P&L) account. But of course, the budgeted volume of 100,000 units is just a forecast!

If we subsequently by the end of the year actually produce and sell only 90,000 units, we have a problem. We will have accounted for only £1.08m of the overheads. Assuming the £1.2m of overheads still happens, then the accountants will create an "Overhead Recovery

Variance" of £0.12m – because the overhead costs are fixed and have happened; only the standard costing system did not reflect this in the P&L account. Confusion now starts to reign in some managers' minds. This year's profit is made worse, because we did not produce enough.

Even worse, I have seen this encourage operations directors to make more, to avoid the adverse variance – which of course adds inventory and additional cost. Suppose in the above example, we had only sold 90,000 units. When the factory makes 100,000, then the overheads will be "recovered", with the £0.12m of overhead then being "concealed" in inventory, making this year's figures, on the surface, look better. Since the company is just focused on the P&L account, because that is the headline figure for shareholders, and we are short-term focussed, then this will "look good". But from the perspective of cash flow, it will not.

Hence, the Lean approach is quite clear – companies should not use standard costing. The principal reason for standard costing is to support the costing of inventory. If a lean approach creates minimal or zero inventory, then this need for standard costing will disappear. The right way to tackle this is to identify the overheads attributable to each value stream, display these, and separate these from the non-attributable overhead costs, which are a "central" overhead.

Note also – in the light of the above – it is a positive event if the company reduces inventory. One of the odd features about inventory (correctly from a double-entry book-keeping view) is that companies treat it as an asset. There are countless numbers of companies sitting on obsolete inventory, unwilling to write them off simply because of the impact on that month or quarter's profit.

Being able to sell more in a period by reducing inventory is a good thing, and we should treat this as a positive addition to the value of the business. The finance director can deal with the financial impact on the published P&L account and balance sheet separately.

With proper management of obsolescence, then this will become a non-issue.

The following illustrates a suggested way of reporting "value-add" by value stream, as described by Brian Maskell and Bruce Baggaley.

Table 24 Report of Value added by Value stream

£ Million	Value Stream A	Value Stream B	Non-allocated expenses	Overall P&L/Value Add
Item	Mar-20	Mar-20	Mar-20	Mar-20
Revenue	10.2	15.3		25.5
Material Costs	3.7	5.2		8.9
Variable Conversion Costs	3.2	6.3		9.5
Value Stream Overheads	1.2	1.9		3.1
Value Stream Profit	2.1	1.9		4.0
General Overheads			1.5	1.5
Company Profit				2.5
Inventory Δ (+ve if reduced)	0.2 -	0.1		0.1
Value Added	2.3	1.8 -	1.5	2.6

This calculation, then, makes it clear how much each part of the business has achieved in the way of real value-add.

Once we have a clear understanding of the variable and fixed costs in the business, then we can also make better decisions.

If the volume in value stream A is going to increase over the next 24 months, we can see the impact on direct material costs (which also means that if there are future cost changes, then these need to be reflected in the future costs).

Suppose we need to recruit more team leaders or factory managers (who would typically appear in the overhead calculation); in that case, we can be explicit about these costs in the financial case.

The impact on cash flow from changes in fixed and current assets can be accurately calculated, and hence the future cash flow properly calculated.

As stated above, you should base the business case for any investment decision on the real incremental costs associated with that decision.

Within the monthly Integrated Business Planning process, therefore, you can take the status quo directly from last month's plan. You can then base the revised proposed plan on the revised forecasts generated through the current month's Innovation and Demand cycle. You can then include any changes to Fixed Assets for Capital Expenditure and Current Assets because of inventory and fixed asset changes, through the Supply cycle.

We can then express the resultant business case in terms of NPV. If this number is positive concerning the "difference case", then, in principle, the decision should be taken to go ahead.

Further, you can analyse the risks and opportunities involved, and whether the decision supports the strategy of the business in terms of area of operation, growth and profitability. Hence it is essential to create scenarios which explore the upsides and downsides concerning the decision.

Table 25 illustrates a simplified analysis based on a three-year projection of cash flow, and simple assumptions concerning current and fixed assets, concerning a new product.

The analysis should also include impacts on the cannibalisation of sales of existing products into the new product proposal.

Thus, the NPV of this project is positive, at £2.2m, and the decision should be to go ahead.

In terms of the specifics of the IBP process, the Innovation meeting would review the new product and agree to the resources required, and the requirements for development. The Demand Review process would provide revised forecasts. The Supply review would then work out the additional resources necessary for increases in variable, fixed and operational overheads, and the financial stage can confirm the impact on cash flow and calculate the above.

Finance

The investment is for £2m and therefore requires sign-off by the senior team. So this would go forward to the senior leadership team for review, with a recommendation that the project is accepted.

Table 25 Example of Capital Equipment Expenditure Case

Capital Expenditure Proposal

£ million	Months 1-12	Months 13-24	Months 25-36
Incremental Revenue	5.0	10.0	40.0
Incremental Margin	3.0	6.0	25.0
Incremental Overheads	5.0	4.0	7.0
Incremental Operational Cash Flow	- 2.0	2.0	18.0
Δ in Current Assets – exclude cash	- 1.0	- 2.0	- 8.0
Increase in Fixed Assets	- 2.0	-	-
Net Cash Flow	- 5.0	-	10.0

Discount Factor (% per annum)   15%

Net Present Value   £ 2.2 m

All things being equal, this should occur within a one-month cycle, thus potentially speeding up the whole normal decision-making processes, which plague capital expenditure (capex) planning processes. I have seen so many companies taking ages to make these decisions – losing a lot of the opportunity at the same time! The decision-making process is probably the most expensive part!

- **Annual Budgets**

Brian Maskell and Bruce Baggaley's book, in chapter 13, covers Sales, Operational and Financial Planning (SOFP), which describes perfectly the issues concerning annual budgets and the opportunity that SOFP provides. Their comments on the Annual Budget are:

- An annual budget quickly becomes out of date
- The budget process is highly wasteful. Most companies spend significant time developing budgets. Managers play political games
- People focus on the financial outcomes of the budget and, not enough on the quality of the operational inputs.

As mentioned previously, there is an organisation called the Beyond Budgeting Institute which states on its website:

'Beyond Budgeting' means beyond command-and-control toward a management model that is more empowered and adaptive. Beyond Budgeting is about rethinking how we manage organisations in a post-industrial world where innovative management models represent the only sustainable competitive advantage. It is also about releasing people from the burdens of stifling bureaucracy and suffocating control systems, trusting them with information and giving them time to think, reflect, share, learn and improve.

See: https://bbrt.org/what-is-beyond-budgeting.

This objective seems remarkably sensible, and Integrated Business Planning provides the process with which to achieve this. There is also an excellent book called Implementing Beyond Budgeting, by Bjarte Bogsnes (Bogsnes, 2008), which explains how the principles apply, and the benefits gained. It is more than just about how you replace budgets; it is also just as much about the need to get away from the detailed command and control environment which plagues so many companies – it is better to be roughly right rather than precisely wrong.

Not many companies have got to the point yet where they have eliminated the budget, and it is very much work in process. Most argue strongly in favour of keeping the annual budgeting process as sacrosanct (a bit like the finance director that I met while watching cricket!).

Many companies argue that they need to go through the process because they report to shareholders: the New York or London Stock Exchange, etc.

This requirement may well be correct, but this is not an argument against using the IBP process to produce the annual budget. The aim should be to make it so simple that you can complete it in one monthly cycle.

The impact of something like COVID–19 probably made an even stronger case to be able to operate a continuing Financial Planning process, rather than a single, annual process.

Some argue that you need to keep the budget as a single measure of performance. Thus, if executives in some major companies do not hit the Budget, they will soon enough get fired, or promoted sidewards to another opportunity, or find themselves in charge of "special projects". If you meet or beat your budget, you get promoted. This creates the wrong behaviour, since all executives who know this will under-budget, which leads to inadequate operational resources, etc., as described above.

I also came across an inspirational book by Aubrey Daniels called "Bringing About the Best in People" (Daniels, 2016). At the risk of summarising his thoughts too much, he suggests that you best manage performance by ensuring you present feedback positively, rather than in a way which feels like negative criticism. You should also provide feedback close to the event which prompts the feedback. Finally, individuals will want both positive and negative feedback. (There was a psychological study which showed that rats reacted to both negative and positive feedback, but the situation that caused the most distress was when they got no feedback!) The individual should be sure that they will get feedback.

A client gave me a perfect example of where a bad outcome in terms of behaviour will result. They compared this approach to what happens when a camera catches you speeding, and you receive a fine. This "feedback" process fails on the Aubrey Daniels criteria because:

1. The feedback is not immediate – you have to wait (in the UK at least) up to 14 days before you get the letter in the post.
2. When you get it, it is a shock and unpleasant, and you are required to pay a fine of around £60.00 (although it can be a lot worse), which is not "positive feedback".
3. Finally, while you may see the camera flash as you go by, or you speed

by without a flash, then there is no certainty that you will get the "feedback".

Hence, this "performance measure" will not work to create the right response and behaviour. Far better are the electronic signs which, as you approach them, light up in green and red, and advise you of the speed. These types of speed control devices work better because:

1. The feedback is immediate, as you approach the sign.
2. The feedback is not unpleasant – it is factual and straightforward (either red or green, and turns green if you reduce your speed, which is the desired objective).
3. Is certain, as long as the light is on – and if it is not, you get no feedback.

I thought this approach made a lot of common sense.

The Budget as a measure of performance acts similarly to the speed camera analogy.

1. You only get the feedback once a year, at the end of the year. Sometimes, of course, there is a quarterly review in some companies; but that suffers from a similar problem.
2. The feedback may not be positive – if you fail, then you get fired.
3. It is not always sure what will happen.
4. So the Budgetary Performance Measurement process fails to act as a proper way of providing positive reinforcement, bringing about an improvement in the way the managers run the business.

Integrated Business Planning, with its monthly and weekly cadence, provides the opportunity of providing a practical Performance Measurement framework.

1. There are 52 or 12 opportunities to provide feedback.
2. If we use our Performance Measurement process to get to the root-cause of problems with procedures, then the result will not be "unpleasant". As someone once said to me: "To err is human, but we

should seek to get rid of the errors, and not get rid of the humans." The problem often lies in a lack of robust processes to ensure that the error cannot happen.

3. If we build performance measurement into our monthly IBP process, then the feedback becomes certain.

- **Improving the Quality of the Budget and Shareholder Information**

Most companies spend a period of three to four months, creating the budget. This process is flawed by the fact that it continually changes, and is subject to all of the political behavioural issues illustrated elsewhere in this book.

However, a monthly IBP process, with a rolling 42-month horizon, provides the opportunity to create a plan for the current and next budget year. This fact means that the senior team will review the following financial year at least 12 times – which gives the company 12 opportunities to refine the plan.

Combined with a universal commitment to telling the "truth as we know it", and realism, the budget at the point you need to prepare it will be the best available information at that time, with a considered detailed process to support it.

This information is what shareholders surely want, as they want to have a projection based on truth as we know it? After all, the reason they hold shares is to have a balanced portfolio, which will enable them to diversify away from the risks that they hold. Why add to that risk by presenting a view that does not tell the truth of what lies ahead?

Exact documented changes in assumptions will support changes in circumstances in the external or internal world. The board can then inform the shareholders of reasons for changes in outlook.

One company, when it developed this process, went to the local bank to explain why it needed to borrow money to finance capital expenditure. The MD and FD took with them their model. When the bank manager saw this, he started to ask questions like, "what if the sales do not happen? What if the costs increase?", etc. The bank manager was much more relaxed about the loan when he could see the company had thought about the risks through the process. The banks will likewise be more impressed if they can see the basis of the numbers.

So, the IBP process must lead to the simplification or elimination of the Budget process.

Much of this improvement will also relate to getting the right set of performance measures in place across the business – as previously outlined.

- **The Right Measures**

As part of the development of the MRP II project in ICI Agrochemicals, I faced the task of presenting to the board a 30-minute session on Performance Measures. When I went through the presentation first time and talked about customer service, schedule achievement and forecast accuracy, my finance director said he really could not understand what this was all about. In particular, he could not see how these measures related to the essential issues of improving the company profitability.

I then realised that I needed to correlate the underlying connection between these measures and "Return on Capital Employed" (ROCE). I recalled an MD once explaining how he was responsible for improving ROCE, and how these worked through a standard "tree" of financial ratios.

Based on this, I then developed the concept that these "operational measures" are the foundation of ROCE.

I illustrate this in the chart in Figure 69, which shows how/where the "Perfect Order" measure contributes to the improvement to Return on Capital Employed.

Thus, the Perfect Order will reduce Material Costs; it will also increase sales as more customers buy from you, and products are delivered right first time. Stocks will decrease as you reject less product. You will improve debtors as there will be fewer claims, and so on. All of these outcomes, in turn, affect profitability, which impacts ROCE.

If you take each of the measures, you can quickly see how each of those will impact on ROCE. In a book I wrote with Rod Clarke (a founder partner of Delos Partnership) called CEO's Guide to Performance Measurement, we showed how each of these measures provides the foundation of ROCE (Watkins & Clarke, 2003).

It is essential that in our measurement framework, we differentiate between the results and those measures which give rise to the results.

The financial results – sales, profit, etc. – are just that: results. When we show the calculations and calculate sales, gross margin, and so on, we are displaying the results.

The operational measures report on the **processes** which give rise to these results, and we should review these to get to the root cause of the problems to improve the business processes, as illustrated in Figure 70.

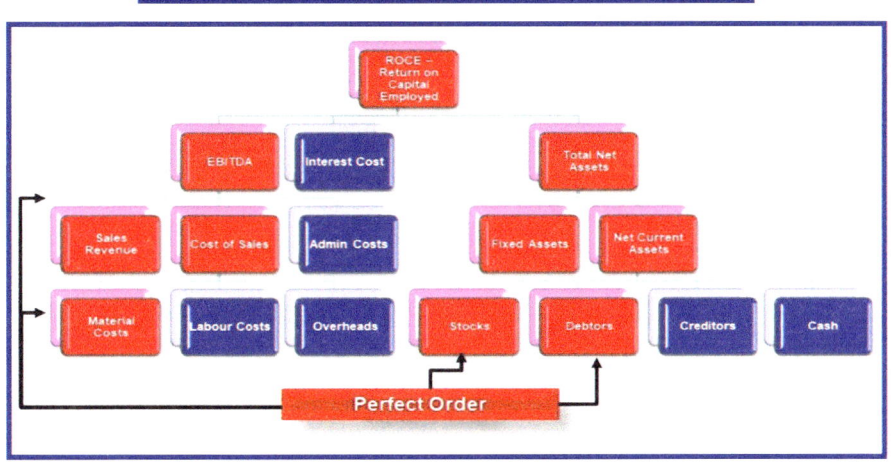

Figure 69: Impact of Perfect Order on ROCE

Take this analogy: if you want to lose weight, then you can stand on the scales, which will tell you if you are too heavy. Actually, you need to know your Body Mass Index (BMI), which tells you the right weight for your height. BMI is a measure of a result.

But you only lose weight if you eat less and exercise more. So, the processes involved are eating and exercising. Hence the "operational performance measures" should be based on the number of minutes exercising and the number of calories input. Measures of health on mobile phones recognise this and support them.

Just knowing your BMI index is too high might incorrectly lead you to believe that you can improve your situation by growing taller! You need to understand and measure the connection between food and exercise and your BMI!

The table in Figure 70, illustrates the seven key measures that we outline in the book, and their impact on the results of sales revenue, profit and the balance sheet.

The "results" are equivalent to the weigh scales. The "measures" are the figures on calorie count, and time and distance exercised.

Figure 70: Effect of core measures on Profit

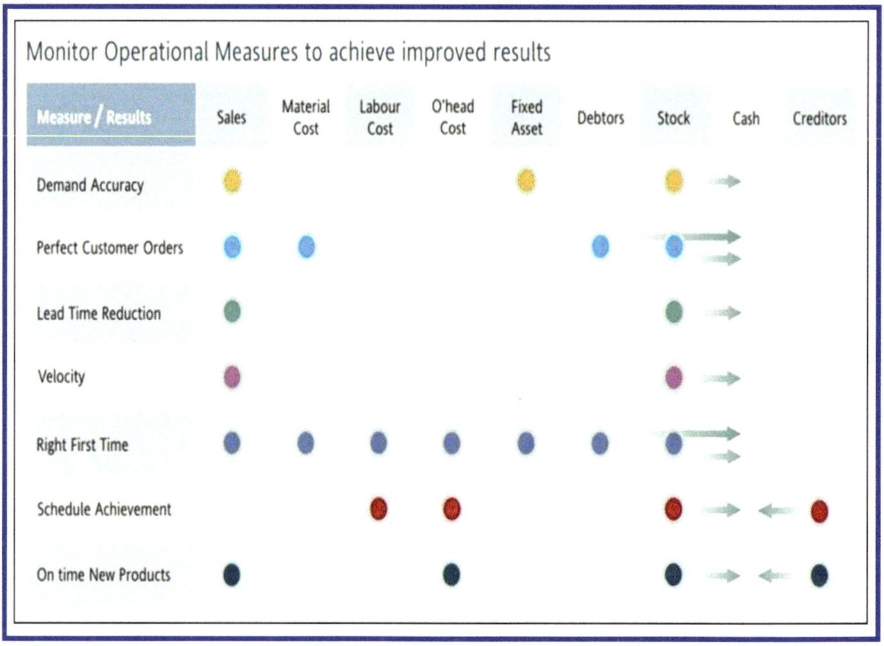

Monitor Operational Measures to achieve improved results

Measure / Results	Sales	Material Cost	Labour Cost	O'head Cost	Fixed Asset	Debtors	Stock	Cash	Creditors
Demand Accuracy	●				●		●	→	
Perfect Customer Orders	●	●				●	●	⇒	
Lead Time Reduction	●						●	→	
Velocity	●						●	→	
Right First Time	●	●	●	●	●	●	●	⇒	
Schedule Achievement		●	●				●	→ ←	●
On time New Products	●			●			●	→ ←	●

Measuring the right things will change the behaviour and get the right financial results!

- **Throughput Ratio**

I worked with one client who made air-conditioning units. They developed the concepts put forward by Goldratt, and came up with an overall financial measure, which they called "Throughput Ratio". They defined this as:

Equation 11 - Throughput ratio

$$\frac{\text{Revenue} - \text{Variable Costs}}{\text{Inventory plus Fixed Operating Expense}}$$

This ratio points the business in the right direction. If the ratio improves, it is because the company has done the right things. It also gets away from the use of "Profit" as a measure.

They applied this to the whole site and then took it down to the critical business areas in the factory.

- **Box Score**

Brian Maskell and Bruce Baggaley's book (Maskell, 2004) introduces the concept of the Box Score for reviewing the performance of "value streams". This idea, in effect, proposes that companies should report the performance of value streams through a mixture of Financial and Operational measures.

It would be excellent to introduce this approach through the IBP process, and link it to the various stages. Leadership is then about setting the right targets, and ensuring the right achievement of the objectives in line with the Vision and the Strategy.

Their book looks at operational, capacity and financial dimensions, and the measures that go with these. I believe it would be useful to extend this to all of the areas covered within the scope of Integrated Business Planning and Leadership, as illustrated in the following table.

Table 26 Box Score concept applied to IBP

		Month -3	Month -2	Month -1	Plan mnths 1-12
Innovation	Cost Index	1.1	1	0.95	1
	Schedule Index	1.2	0.9	0.95	1
	NPD Revenue (£m)	1	1.1	1.2	3
	NPD Value Add (£m)	0.2	0.22	0.3	1.6
Sales and Marketing	MAPE Forecast Error	23%	25%	21%	15%
	Forecast Bias	2%	3%	2%	0%
	Revenue (£m)	5	5.2	6.3	60
	Aggregate Error	-2%	2%	-2%	0%
	Perfect Order (Request)	94%	92%	93%	98%
	Margin	2.5	2.6	3.2	6
	AR Days	93	92	90	80
Operations	Perfect Order (Prom)	95%	97%	96%	98%
	Sched Ach. (Factory)	98%	99%	98%	98%
	Sched Ach. (Suppliers)	98%	97%	98%	98%
	Right First Time	99%	99%	97%	100%
	Dem Capacity	63%	65%	69%	75%
	Free Capacity	5%	10%	7%	15%
	Velocity	23%	25%	23%	40%
	Material Cost (£m)	2	2.1	2.5	24
	Conversion cost (£m)	1	1.1	1	12
	AP Days	61	60	59	60
Finance	Value Stream Profit (£m)	2	2	2.8	24
	Δ In inventory	0.2	0.1	0.1	2
	Value Add (£m)	2.2	2.1	2.9	26
	Central Overheads	1	1	1	12
	Company Value Add	1.2	1.1	1.9	34
	Current Assets				5
	Fixed Assets				60
	ROCE %				52%

This table is designed to be an illustration, which companies can adapt to their circumstances. Management reports should cover both operational performance and financial measures and results, within the scope of the Finance step of the IBP process.

These procedures should all then lead to the Finance Review process step or meeting.

Sometimes, I have found that it is not essential to have a Finance Review meeting, as it is largely a process of collecting the numbers and reports together. However, as the chart in Figure 71 illustrates – as with the other sections – the process step for finance:

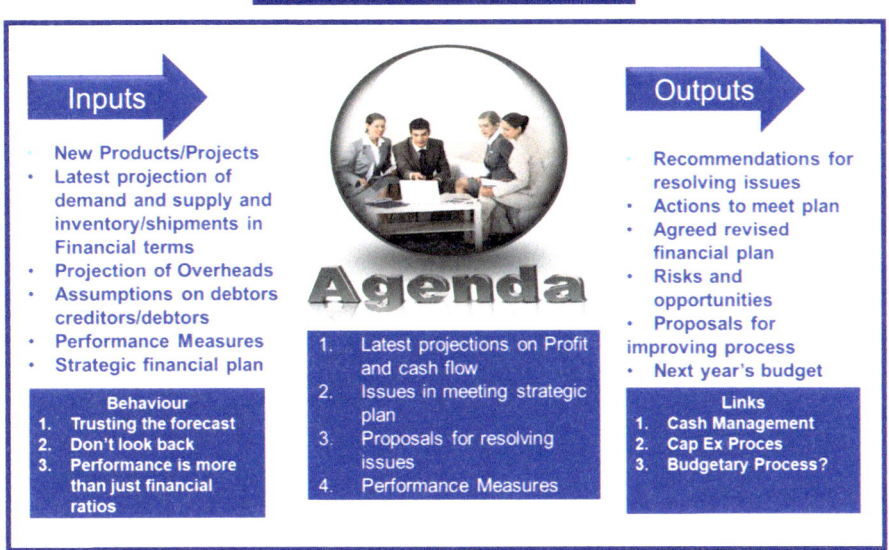

Figure 71: Finance Review

Inputs
- New Products/Projects
- Latest projection of demand and supply and inventory/shipments in Financial terms
- Projection of Overheads
- Assumptions on debtors creditors/debtors
- Performance Measures
- Strategic financial plan

Behaviour
1. Trusting the forecast
2. Don't look back
3. Performance is more than just financial ratios

Agenda
1. Latest projections on Profit and cash flow
2. Issues in meeting strategic plan
3. Proposals for resolving issues
4. Performance Measures

Outputs
- Recommendations for resolving issues
- Actions to meet plan
- Agreed revised financial plan
- Risks and opportunities
- Proposals for improving process
- Next year's budget

Links
1. Cash Management
2. Cap Ex Proces
3. Budgetary Process?

In most companies, there is a financial manager or financial controller, who reports into the finance director. They will be the "captain" of this step of the process. They will have the usual requirements for that role in terms of their capability. They will also need to lead on the development of the KPIs.

The vital part of this step in the process is that it underpins the decision-making aspects of the IBP process. With improved forecasts and realistic plans, together with more accurate data, the quality of the decision-making process will improve.

The Finance step is a crucial part of the Integrated Business Leadership process to help with making those right decisions, and partnering with the business to make sure it achieves the proper objectives of increasing real shareholder value.

Chapter 12

People

"Teamwork makes the dream work, but a vision becomes a nightmare when the leader has a big dream and a bad team." – John C. Maxwell, American author and speaker.

One of the areas I have found strange about SOP, or Integrated Business Planning, is the lack of engagement from those that are involved in the Human Resource (HR) or people side of the business. This outcome has much to do with the fact that companies have perceived that the original SOP was purely about Sales and Operations Planning, which – on the face of it – looks like it has nothing to do with "people". Yet there is much in this area that requires the engagement of people.

IBP must include planning the number of people that the company requires. It must cover motivation and improvement of the skill base within the business through education and training. Recruiting people can be a hugely expensive business (estimated at around £5,000 per hire). Once people have joined, it can be an even more expensive business to lose talent – particularly if they go to the competition.

Overall, the application and implementation of Integrated Business Leadership often requires a massive change of culture across the business, in developing teamwork, communication and education. The argument for the involvement of HR is clear.

The reasons for the inclusion of HR in the IBP process are:

1. Any company planning for the longer-term must make sure that it has the right mix of skills to support the long-term aims of the business. One client, as a result of their IBP process, started to plan

for the 120 engineers in the business. They looked at the road-map that supported their innovation plan, and the need to migrate from one set of products to another set of products. They then realised that the skill-set they had today was not appropriate for the skill-set they needed for tomorrow. The VP for human resources rapidly got involved with their IBP process to develop a plan for long-term skill development, and management.

2. Any company looking at the shorter-term needs to be looking at the short to medium planning of people, whether it is how many people we need on a production line, or creating new shifts, through to ensuring that they recruit the managers to support the growth of the business.

3. All companies need to ensure that they enhance the skills within the business. Hence, there should be detailed training plans in place to support personal development. World-class performance for a business is supported by allowing people approximately 25 days per annum in education and training events, to support personal development. On average, companies allow for a maximum of two to three days per person (or even less in some companies).

4. The constant theme with the IBL model is that people respond to the reward structure in the business. People will always work out how they can benefit the most from the reward system; that is human nature. If you reward people on actual vs budget, then guess what? They will try and make the budget as small as possible. If you reward the senior team on short-term targets like Earnings per Share, then they will focus on how to increase short-term earnings per share. Many of the issues that lie within a business hide within the company bonus scheme. Contradictory measures cause contrary behaviour. If customer service is the overriding objective, then a bonus based on customer service would make real sense. If forecast accuracy is a critical objective, then a bonus based on forecast accuracy makes sense. The HR function should address the reward structure of the company.

5. Every business and organisation knows that it will work better as a team. However, I have sat in many embarrassing senior team meetings

where there is a fractious, electric atmosphere, which occasionally erupts into violent battles between members of the "team". There is a call for an external coach to come in and somehow magically make the people work better together. But to get those sorts of coaches in place requires the "team" to admit they are not a team in the first place! I have walked about the business and seen the pictures of eight people rowing a boat, with the word "teamwork" across it. I have soon found out that the intent is there, but the reality does not support the goal. "When the elephants fight, it is the grass that suffers," as the Kenyan proverb puts it. The people part of the IBP process should address how to get people to work as a team. This area involves a complex mix of human psychology, motivation and behavioural interaction, and needs experts in this area to get involved.

So, the Human Resources (HR) part of the IBP process should address all of these elements.

- **Resource Plans**

The Rough-Cut and Detailed Capacity Planning process of the Supply Review should and will provide a profile of the number of people required to support the medium- to longer-term plans for the business. There should be a review, therefore, carried out within the HR function of the skills profile requirement, and how to go about recruiting them.

In practical terms, it makes sense for HR to be involved in the Supply Review whenever there is a need to change the level of resources within the business.

- **Training Plans**

Every business needs to put together an education and training plan for its people. It is a sad fact that when budgets and costs come under pressure, then the probability is that the training budget is the first one to suffer. This action is a short-term, knee-jerk response which leads to demotivation and de-skilling in the longer-term. The evidence is that "Millennials" who are joining companies today are going to be more inspired by those companies which support long-term personal development.

Typically, companies put training plans together once a year and then they manage them through the remainder of the year. Including HR in the IBP process will encourage a more regular review of training plans as part of the monthly cycle.

Training plans are no different to Supply and Demand plans, and so companies should put in place performance measures on the completion of training plans.

- **Bonus Structure**

Tackling the bonus structure in any business often appears to be a step too far, when people talk about SOP/IBP implementation. After all, we are just talking about improving customer service and reducing inventory, aren't we? Why should we even think about reward structures?

One client saw that improving customer service was a key objective of what they wanted to do. When you walked into reception, as I often did, then you would always see their measure of performance of customer service prominently displayed. Not surprisingly, they saw their customer service increase, inventory reduce, and business revenue, profitability and cash flow improve. They were a class "A" company, driven by their CEO.

In another client, they saw that customer service, lead time reduction and total site profit were the three key desired outcomes. They displayed those measures everywhere around the site.

"What gets measured, gets done."

I mentioned earlier how the MD of a garden products company had said: "Customer service is my job." He then changed the performance measures structure. He ensured the company built the rewards into the job descriptions for each of the people in the company. This policy brought about a radical shift in the way the business operated.

Bonus and reward can sometimes be about money; it is also about how managers praise or otherwise encourage subordinates in doing their work. It is about how you set the objectives for their roles and monitor their performance against those objectives.

If you look at the bonus structure and this does not support the aims of SOP/IBP of telling the truth as we know it, looking at the long term, and operating through genuine teamwork, then change the bonus structure.

- **Teamwork**

Teamwork is an essential requirement for IBP to work. Sometimes I have found that the structure and make-up of the team and the people is such that genuine collaboration is unlikely to occur.

In this situation, the companies need to undertake a review of the different behavioural types within the business – like a Myers-Briggs assessment.

They then need to work on how to ensure that there is a balance between the different members of the senior team, and throughout the organisation.

The Myers-Briggs model is based on a classic psychological study of different personality types. It works on the principle of characterising people's personality around four different "dimensions", and "binary choices", as follows:

People and Ideas	**I**ntroverted	or	**E**xtrovert
Facts and Possibilities	**S**ensing	or	i**N**tuitive
Logic and Values	**T**hinking	or	**F**eeling
Lifestyle structure	**J**udgement	or	**P**erception

Your personality is then – on balance – a mixture of the four dimensions.

Thus, you could be described as INTJ, which suggests that your character is Introverted, Intuitive, Logical/Thinking, and broadly that you want a structured lifestyle based around what you judge is the right thing to do.

Having a team of everyone with the same personality is unlikely to work, and unlikely to happen! It is essential to get together a team of different "personalities" who behave with each other to make the right decisions for the business. Personality is a complex mixture of nature and nurture. It is difficult to change.

But we can train behaviour into people, and where people do not work well as teams, then the company will need to address the behaviour.

Along the same lines of the interaction between personality and behaviour, I have seen an excellent model from an organisation called Emergenetics International. This model will help people work together, taking into account their in-built personality. It is based around the structure shown in Figure 72.

Figure 72: Emergenetics Wheel of Behaviour and Thinking

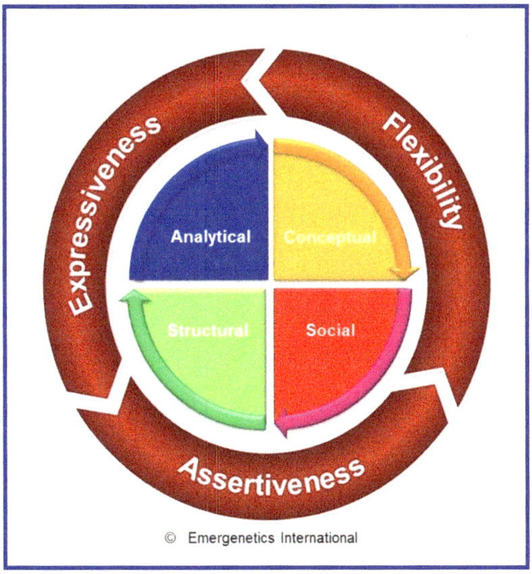

It explores how different behavioural types can learn to work with other behavioural types to ensure that effective teamwork results. You can find out more at: https://www.emergenetics.com/emergenetics-explained/.

Thus, for instance, you will have in your business "Analytical" types of personality (e.g. finance directors and managers, and technical scientists); you will also have those who are conceptual in their approach (e.g. marketing). There will be those who are structural (e.g. operations), and some are social in their approach (e.g. sales). The difficulty in any organisation is how to get these various "functions", who are often wrapped up in different personality types, to work together.

That is where effective leadership concentrates on harnessing the multiple talents in one direction.

This factor is why it is essential to address this *people* dimension in establishing the IBP process in the business.

Where teamwork is not present, the first step is for the leader to recognise the issues, and want to deal with them. A resolution will follow from people recognising their personalities and how they need to behave between themselves to make the most of the different characters. This behaviour will be more effective than the action of people who set about destroying each other, as sometimes happens in a "political" environment.

Organisations flourish where people work as genuine teams, rather than as individual self-centred political animals, which sometimes happens.

Getting the right measures and reward structure in place will also help. Defining clear roles and responsibilities, and an organised way of working will help, as these will take away some of the enormous stresses that can create barriers to teamwork.

Ultimately, teamwork requires a shared vision and purpose. If the goal of the individuals who "work as a team" is to play politics with each other and cause each other damage, then each may have a common goal – which is to play politics.

However, this will not produce the desired outcome of delivering the vision and the strategy of the business, which, of course, is to satisfy customers and to give to shareholders what they want in return for the funds that they invest in the company.

Integrated Business Leadership must address how to get the executive, managers and the people in the business to work as one team, which requires a company to address the values they display towards people.

- **People Values**

The values which a company adopts and displays towards people underpin all of this. They define the attitudes in the minds of the people whom it employs.

Figure 73 summarises a generic view of the traditional, current and future state of companies, concerning the values they express in the way they manage people.

Figure 73: People Values

	Traditional	Now	Future
Process problems	Not my job	Ownership	Accountability
Management Style	Supervise	Facilitator	Coach
Working Style	Individual	Team	Empowered Teams
Training and Education	Non-existent	Luxury	Necessity
Knowledge	Ignorant	Understands	Expert
Attitude to People	Liability	Cost	Asset
Measurement	Personal reward	Team recognition	Team Reward

The style of the traditional company – which relates to the 1920s and earlier types of manufacturing management – is one in which, where there is a problem, people will say, "it's not my job" or, "it's more than my job's worth to deal with this". The management and supervision style is 1:1 and built around direct control of the individuals through constant supervision. We do not trust individuals to operate on their own. Development of the individual is non-existent. Early industrial companies designed their production line so that people could come to work, do their job based on repetitive tasks, and go home; they hung up their brains with their hats at the factory gate.

Training and education are non-existent, as there is no commitment to personal development. People in their role need to refer back to their bosses to find out what to do, as they will not understand what they need or are allowed to do.

The attitude to people is that they are just part of the cost base, and if costs are getting tight, then cost reduction means getting rid of people. They appear as a liability in the profit and loss account. Lastly, the measurement process focuses on the individual and their performance, and they are rewarded (through promotion or financial reward) through their performance.

In one organisation, the company assumed they could get 1,400 hours per annum of output from each person – that was the target. They were in a vehicle repair business. When they looked at their order book for the following year, they determined they could reduce their workforce by 10% – which itself was an expensive exercise. So they got rid of 10% of their workforce.

However, their demonstrated output was closer to 1,200 hours per annum. So the following year they discovered the business was "under-performing", and failing to deliver to the customers what they wanted. They had to recruit the same workforce back into the organisation, which was an even more expensive solution!

In this case, the leadership was responsible for the underlying failure because of the values they adopted. They took an unrealistic view of the output of the workforce, and treated people just as a cost, which led to a failure to perform.

The company of the future is aspiring to a completely different set of values; one in which roles and responsibilities are clear, and there is a clear RACI structure built around processes. The management style should operate around managers being coaches, and effective empowerment of the people.

People are assets; in fact, many companies now view employees as a fixed salaried cost like the management team.

The reward structure should be built around rewarding teams and less about the performance of the individual.

Once, I was going through a description of the performance measures structure in a workshop, and showing how (as I showed above) performance measures support the ROCE tree.

One of the people in the group – who was part of the pioneering team for one of these projects – came up to me in a break and said that the tree of measures looked remarkably like an organisation chart.

My point related to the tree was that the measures at the bottom of the tree were the basis of the performance of the company. ROCE is a result; the measures are the foundation.

He said it was similar to the concept that the success of the MD/CEO is the result of the people in the business.

They had tackled this issue and rewritten their organisation chart to get away from the typical organisation chart, built with the CEO at the top; thus, their original chart looked as shown in Figure 74.

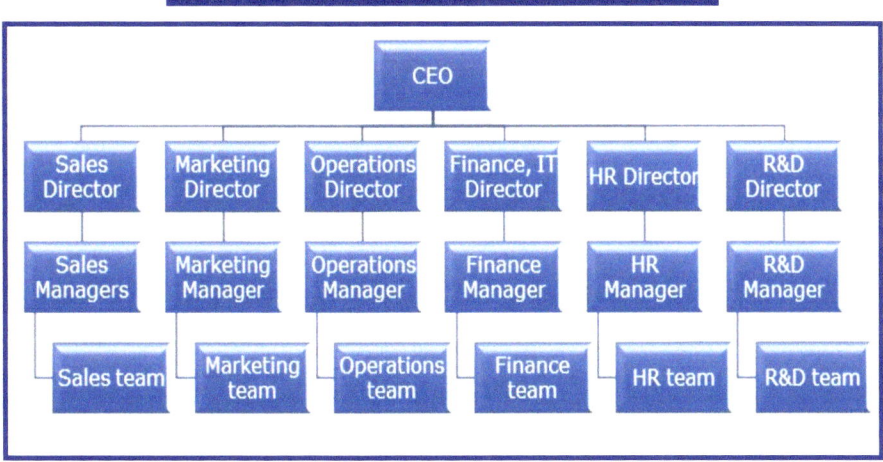

Figure 74: Typical organisation structure

Their revised chart showed this chart upside down with the CEO appearing at the bottom; the "people" were at the top. A simple thought, but powerful in communicating the leadership style of the business.

A vital part of the philosophy of Integrated Business Planning, is that a company requires a considerable degree of "democracy" in coming up with an agreed set of plans. That democracy builds ownership.

But once the business has agreed to the plan, then autocracy is key to making plans happen: "plan the work" and then "work the plan". Likewise, "plan the sale", and then "sell the plan".

That democratic structure, where people are free to contribute their thoughts for the plan, and take ownership because they believe it is realistic and achievable, is crucial. If this style is in place, then the execution of the plan is likely to happen.

Getting this right structure in place is a crucial feature of getting the people side to work as part of Integrated Business Leadership.

One client ran their monthly IBP process. The forecasts for the business showed it was going to increase over the next six months. The planning manager put forward the proposal to increase the workforce by eight people. The manufacturing director, however, did not believe the forecasts and argued against the recruitment. The MD decided that recruitment should happen.

However, the manufacturing director did not recruit eight people. In three to four months, they were struggling to meet the increase in business and customer service suffered.

The problem lay in the failure for all to agree to and execute the plan. It was not the failure of the people to deliver the output.

- **People Performance Measures**

The key performance measures which will address the success of the Human Resource process will be:

1. **People** turnover – This is defined (for a given period) as:

Equation 12 - People Turnover

$$\frac{\text{Number of people leaving the business}}{\text{The average number of people employed}} \times 100\%$$

2. **The Bradford Factor**, which measures absenteeism, and provides a figure weighted by the number of times people are off sick. The measure is:

Equation 13 Bradford Factor

$$B = S^2 \times D$$

Where B = the factor, S = the number of occasions off sick and D is the total number of days off sick

3. **Training plans achieved**. This measure will judge if a company achieves its training plans. The definition for a given period is:

Equation 14 Training plan performance

$$\frac{\text{Number of training plans completed in full}}{\text{Total number of training plans due to be completed}} \times 100\%$$

- **IBP Meeting**

The organisational requirement for a separate meeting is going to depend in part on the basic organisational structure of the business. Sometimes HR is part of a general "support" function, which combines HR, finance and IT. Sometimes HR is separate from finance and IT. I have also seen an organisation where they combined HR and IT into the responsibilities of one director. All things are possible. So, this will need to be considered when structuring the process.

Assuming that there is a separate HR director or head of HR, then it would make sense to formalise a HR meeting as part of the IBP process. The HR director would chair this, and their direct reports would attend it, with attendance from other parts of the business as required (e.g. if there were a need to run a third shift, the planning manager might attend).

Figure 75: Human Resources Meeting

Inputs
- New Products/Projects
- Latest projection of demand and supply and inventory/shipments in Financial terms
- Projection of Overheads
- Assumptions on debtors creditors/debtors
- Performance Measures
- Strategic financial plan

Behaviour
1. Trusting the forecast
2. Don't look back
3. Performance is more than just financial ratios

Agenda
1. Latest projections on Profit and cash flow
2. Issues in meeting strategic plan
3. Proposals for resolving issues
4. Performance Measures

Outputs
- Recommendations for resolving issues
- Actions to meet plan
- Agreed revised financial plan
- Risks and opportunities
- Proposals for improving process
- Next year's budget

Links
1. Cash Management
2. Cap Ex Proces
3. Budgetary Process?

Figure 75 then describes the inputs and outputs of the HR process. The owner of the process should be the HR director, and the HR manager will act as the "captain" of the process.

• IBP and Unionisation

As I said above, it is curious how the HR function is not an explicit part of the IBP process.

In many companies, they manage the workforce with many of the people being members of a union.

It has been interesting to see the impact of IBL in the interface with the union structure.

In one client, they had identified a long-term capacity issue. They had large machines in operation, which required one person per machine under the operating rules. However, the operators could leave the machines for periods while they were carrying out their functions.

As part of their IBP process, they recognised that demand was exceeding supply, and they needed to find a way to increase output. Getting hold of trained people within the timeframe in their area of the UK was going to be impossible, and so they concluded that they needed people to double up on machines.

As a result, they had to approach the union to address the issue of working practices and got into negotiations with the unions to enable individual operators to work on multiple machines.

Initially, the unions thought that this was a "plot" to downsize the workforce. The management shared with them the information that they derived from the IBP plans and proved that this was the only way that the business could manage the long-term capacity problem. The unions accepted the arrangement as soon as they could see the facts in the case, and that there was no downsizing planned. It illustrated the value of the process and the value of sharing the inputs and outputs of the process. It was also critical to the continuing success of the site.

With another client, I was running a two-day workshop in a pleasant hostel by a lake near Eskdale in the Lake District. It was a great training venue.

When the delegates were introducing themselves, one said: "I am John, and I am the union rep for the site." I asked him why he was there, and he explained that the IBP project leader had persuaded him to attend; he had thought it might be interesting for the union rep. Halfway through the second day, while on a break overlooking the lake, I talked to John and asked him what he thought about the course. He said he thought the ideas were brilliant. The only issue that he could see was persuading the senior management team to take on board the ideas.

They did, and IBP became, in the words of the site manager, "the way they ran the business". The unions were behind it too.

Both of these examples reinforce the philosophy behind IBP – it only works if the company properly engages people through the Implementation process.

Chapter 13
Information Resources

"Information technology is at the core of how you do your business and how your business model itself evolves."
Satya Nadella, CEO of Microsoft

Most companies are involved in developing IT systems of one sort or another, at some time in their development. Many companies that I have seen have implemented ERP systems.

One operations director characterised this kind of project as being "2:2:½", which was an interesting statement. He explained, "They take twice as long to implement as planned, cost twice as much to implement as planned, and deliver half the benefit that they are supposed to deliver when originally sold." How true that can be!

Ironically, a few years later, another division of that business implemented an ERP system, and it went seriously wrong. They had successfully implemented an SOP/IBP process – but separated this from the ERP implementation. Data was inaccurate. They had not trained the people adequately. They had not discovered and tested systems issues through proper business pilots (the individual system modules work, but it is different when you run them as an integrated business pilot).

The result was catastrophic. The local senior leadership team spent the next six weeks after go-live trying to work out who had received what, what they had actually made, and so on. Customers cancelled orders, and the total cost rose to around £25m. They fired the local project leader, the local general manager, and eventually, the shareholders fired the chairman of the whole group; he had concealed the scale of the disaster from the shareholders.

It is entirely possible to implement an IBP process as a standalone project designed to put in the meeting structure, disciplines, and culture and behaviours described in this book, with the foundation of a properly functioning ERP/business system. In this case, it is mostly about developing reports fed directly from the ERP system.

SOP was invented in the 1980s as a model or process which a company should implement as part of an "MRP II" implementation. Thus, when a company decided to buy and implement a business system, which covered everything from forecasting, sales order entry through to purchasing, then it made sense to implement the concepts of SOP/IBP as outlined in this book.

The simple analogy was that you were buying a car complete with all of the elements of a gearbox, engine, wheels, etc.; SOP enabled you to drive it in the right direction, and have a good idea of when you will get there!

Only in this way would the system be positively contributing to the way that the business ran.

Thus, implementing ERP systems without implementing IBP is not sensible, even now, for the same reason. The system may well operate at the transaction level; if you do not have the disciplines around accurate data, accurate forecasts, and control over the Planning process, you will not get the system to work. The old GIGO maxim applies: "Garbage in, Garbage Out!"

Similarly, implementing IBP without tackling the system infrastructure in the business could be of value, but does not make sense. I strongly recommend addressing people, processes and systems simultaneously. Apart from implementing ERP systems, many companies implement various other computer systems – like customer relationship management, web portals, warehouse management, forecasting systems, and so on.

The common issue is that companies seem to implement all of these systems as a separate stream of activity. They do not think through the resource implications well enough. The timelines lengthen. Costs escalate.

Companies should integrate IT projects into the IBP process.

Much in the Innovation section above applies to the subject of IT project management. Many large-scale projects suffer because the business fails to co-ordinate the resources across the whole business. The IT director/manager is left perpetually trying to persuade the company to free up resource, while the firm assumes that the IT project is working all right.

One large client had a reasonably sizeable IT department. They had several systems and infrastructure projects to manage and implement. They also had a support function with a helpdesk to sort out the problems that occurred from time to time.

They looked very much like a mini-business, with a mixture of Innovation (new projects), Demand (for people wanting help), and Supply (resources to support the projects). They also needed to report back to the board their progress every month. The IT director had been involved with the business setting up an SOP process, so understood the principles very well.

He organised a workshop, within which we could design and develop a "mini-SOP" process within their IT department!

He thought it was brilliant, and he got the required visibility and control of his IT projects in a way that many companies achieve when implementing SOP/IBP. He could then present to his MD each month the progress against projects based on facts.

I see very few companies explicitly integrate their IT processes into their IBP/SOP process.

The elements required for IT are the same as anywhere else in the company. There should be an IT strategy determining the longer-term direction, with strategic actions which support that strategy. There is a need for supply and demand balancing across all projects.

Performance measures of schedule index and cost index apply, as they do in any projects.

So it would make sense to do so, and I expect to see more doing so in the future. It will enable the business to gain control of their project costs.

Chapter 14

Priorities

> *"The bottom line is when people are crystal clear about the most important priorities of the organisation and team they work with and prioritise their work around those top priorities, not only are they many times more productive, they discover they have the time they need to have a whole life."* – Stephen Covey

The original model of SOP had a step before the central senior leadership meeting called the "Pre-SOP" or "Pre-Meeting" step. The diagram shown in Figure 76 illustrates the Wallace and Stahl model, used by many companies.

Figure 76: Stahl and Wallace 5-step diagram

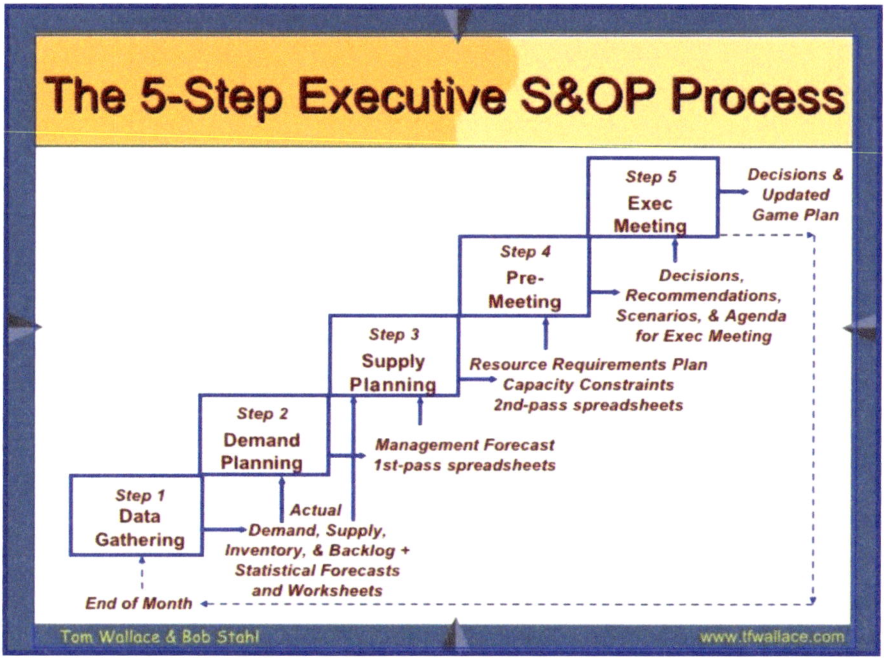

The 5-Step Executive S&OP Process

- **Step 1** Data Gathering — End of Month → Actual Demand, Supply, Inventory, & Backlog + Statistical Forecasts and Worksheets
- **Step 2** Demand Planning → Management Forecast 1st-pass spreadsheets
- **Step 3** Supply Planning → Resource Requirements Plan, Capacity Constraints, 2nd-pass spreadsheets
- **Step 4** Pre-Meeting → Decisions, Recommendations, Scenarios, & Agenda for Exec Meeting
- **Step 5** Exec Meeting → Decisions & Updated Game Plan

Tom Wallace & Bob Stahl — www.tfwallace.com

The problem of having a "Pre-Meeting" is that while this may happen, it is often a process, rather than a meeting where the issues from the previous steps of the process are collated and analysed before they go forward to the executive meeting.

The Oliver Wight company – founders and thought leaders in this area – later turned this step into "Integration and Reconciliation". Figure 77 shows "Integrated Reconciliation" and "Reconciliation Review" as a step before the Management Business Review.

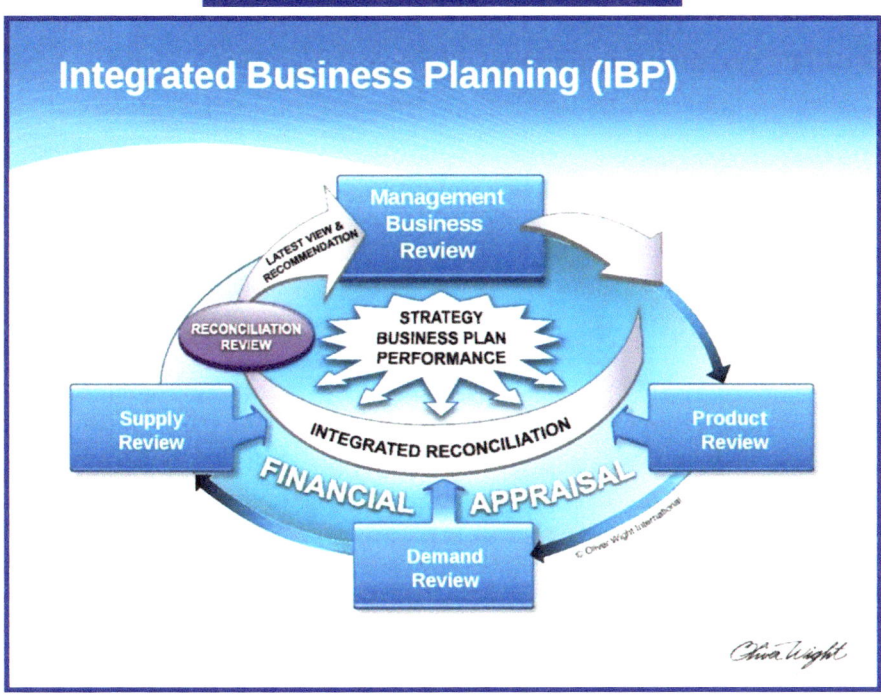

Figure 77: Oliver Wight IBP model

This term, although lengthy, is fine as it describes what needs to go on at this stage of the process. However, there is no step for "Finance, HR and IT", which appears to miss out these important functions.

When I reviewed these models, I looked for something that was different as a title. I wanted a title that communicated the idea that this was a step which was going to sort out the agenda for the senior leadership team meeting. This approach suggested reviewing the **priorities** for the business.

It is like a place where the different streams of the river come together before they go to the final stage of going out to sea. But we need a controlled process, rather than just to let the water flow freely and chaotically into the senior team review. Hence, my term for this step is "Prioritisation", which can be a meeting or a process – or both!

- **Fortune Favours the Prepared Mind**

The essential purpose of this step is to make the senior team review a productive meeting. I have sat in many senior team reviews. Most meetings are either information-sharing meetings or decision-making meetings; in many cases, they quickly become "random discussion meetings".

The world over, people like to get together to have discussions. In India, for instance, they have the Rachabanda, where the elders of the village sit under a Banyan tree, which sounds a delightful setting.

A person makes a presentation (without a slide in sight), and then they make decisions.

The same goes on in companies (except they often use too many slides!). But without preparation, they can be chaotic meetings, wasting people's time.

There are many books and articles about how to have quality meetings; I am not about to add much to that here. However, 90% of the early sessions which I have seen, fail to be proper decision-making meetings entirely because of lack of preparation going into the discussion. "Prioritisation" provides that preparation.

The fundamental rule that the IBP process mandates is that the material for the senior team review should be available 48-24 hours before the meeting, to enable the members of the board to review the information and prepare themselves for the meeting. There is nothing worse than turning up to a meeting where someone hands out the agenda at the start of the meeting.

I sat in one of those meetings in Paris, and before you knew what was happening, the operations director had already hijacked the meeting, gone to page 63, and started to talk about that. It was not on the agenda!

- **Input into the Process**

The issues identified at previous steps, which require senior leadership team review, are the input to this step. As an example of topics that I have seen:

- There is a need to constrain demand for a particular product group. The Demand and Supply reviews have identified a short- to medium-term capacity constraint. The company needs decisions on who gets what, and when.
- There is a long-term capacity shortage of a particular product area, and a capital expenditure proposal is required.
- A new product has come forward for approval as part of the Gate 3 decision-making step. The Demand review needs now to incorporate the Sales plan; the Supply plan needs to be signed off; and the capital expenditure required needs to be signed off.
- The company needed to arrange an additional shift for a particular line in three months.
- Overtime is needed for the next four to six weeks, to meet the demand resulting from a promotion.

There first needs to be clarity around what the senior team wants to discuss. Thus, for instance, if there is a request for capital >£100,000, then that has to go to the senior team. If there is a need to arrange overtime, then does the operations director need to get authorisation from the senior leadership team, or this is entirely within the scope of the operations director?

The company needs an exact RACI process for making these decisions.

- **Who Manages the Priority Process?**

We have identified "captains" of each step of the process, who are typically the managers reporting in to the directors of each step of the process.

The Priority step of the process should bring these captains together to review the issues identified, and then either make the decision there and then or initiate further discussion with the people involved in previous steps of the process.

If they cannot resolve the issues in this way, then they should arrange to put together a presentation on the issue to the next or later senior team review.

I have seen this meeting chaired by the finance director, as that person takes a vital role in the business, providing a view across all functions, and also providing a critical understanding of the financial numbers and the value that the decisions will add to the company.

They also act as a critical resource to the MD, who relies on the FD to provide an overall business perspective.

Within the ICI Agrochemicals project, we created the role of "planning manager", and the person filling that role was brilliant at pulling together the facts and recommendations. He played a central part in reviewing Demand, Supply and New Product plans, and presenting them to the board.

I have also seen companies develop a role (which I outlined above) which is called "head of Integrated Business Planning".

This role balances the requirements of all parts of the business.

For instance, Sales and Marketing could want to beat the competition by offering competitive prices to win the business, provide short lead times, or run short-term promotions. We are not going to – and nor should we – stamp out these approaches.

However, the company needs to balance these strategies against the requirements for the other parts of the business; it needs to judge the impact on resources, profitability, the time it takes to recruit people, etc. IBP facilitates managing this in a controlled manner through the business.

Thus, we need to establish the issues that any approach to the market may create, evaluate the impact, and come up with a formal decision on the outcome.

It is here that you would use the STP chart described earlier in Figure 20. For convenience, the chart is repeated in Figure 78:

Figure 78: STP document

Situation:	Target
There is insufficient capacity to meet requirements in Jun-Dec 2019	To build temporary capacity from Jun-Dec 2019 in the xyz factory
Proposal	
Run a third shift from Jun-Dec 2019	
Risks	Mitigation Actions required
Business may not materialise as expected	Only confirm recruitment in May 2019 IBP cycle
Benefits	Costs
Decision made :	Date : __/__/____

Putting it on one page at this point like this helps in getting brevity and clarity in place. The addition of a box called "Risks" and another for "Mitigation" helps understand the downsides to the decision. Add in Benefits and Costs (which would be an input to the Prioritisation process), and you have a one-page summary for the decision.

Requirements for "Head of IBP"

As described earlier, this prioritisation process emphasises the observation that a head of IBP has to have the qualities of understanding the business, being empathetic to Sales and Marketing, and simultaneously sympathetic to Production and Operations.

They need to understand the business and organisation, and understand the ins and outs of business (thus have an MBA-type qualification). They would then be ideal for managing the whole process and chairing this Prioritisation meeting, supported by the captains of the other steps of the process.

- **Prioritisation for Multi-National Business/Multi-Site Business**

In multi-national businesses, there would possibly be several priority reviews.

If you look at Figure 79 based on Figure 21 earlier in the book you will see and additional prioritisation step prior to the global Senior Team review (shown in green). That step helps the Senior Team Review be more focused.

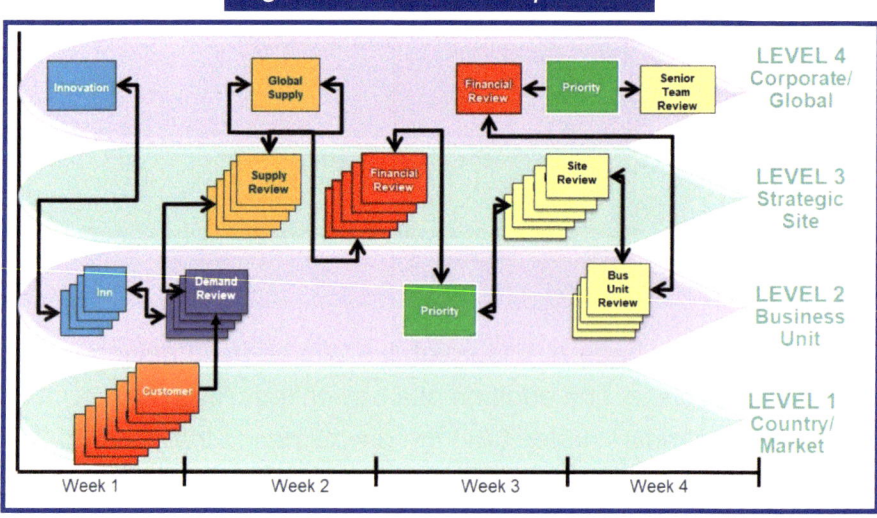

Figure 79: Global IBP process

In other words, you may well need to define where you take critical decisions within the business and design a preparation step before that meeting.

Prioritisation in a Multi-Business Unit Structure

Many companies have multiple business units, which are pretty much self-contained. They have heads of those business units, who are accountable for the P&L of that business unit. Sometimes manufacturing assets align with those business units, sometimes not.

In this case, there needs to be a decision-making process for the individual business unit. There may well be certain decisions which they cannot make within the scope of the business unit (particularly where there are shared assets), which require escalation, but otherwise they make the decisions.

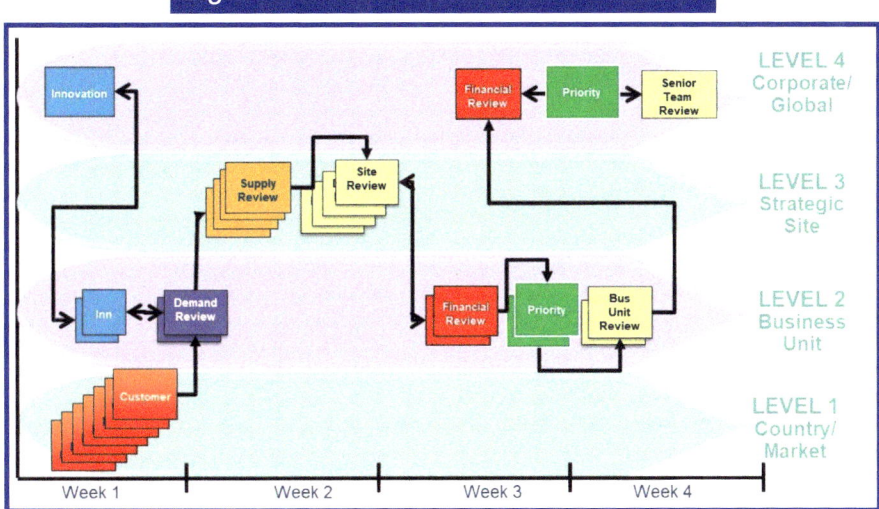

Figure 80: Multi business unit structure

In this situation, it is vital to have a preparation/prioritisation process for the business unit decision-making process, and similarly as an input into the overall decision-making process. Figure 80 illustrates an IBP process for a company which had two separate business units (level 2 in the diagram).

There are two green prioritisation boxes, which are inputs into the Business Unit Review meeting.

There is also another green box which goes between the Global Financial Review and the Senior Team Review.

Thus, prioritisation is a term to describe the process by which we prepare for making decisions, wherever these decision points occur.

Part of the design process must determine the decision-making points through the business wherever they occur in single-site or multi-site companies.

Figure 80 illustrates that there is not a single solution which operates for every company, but some basic principles which must be adapted to the structure of the organisation.

Summary report

One of the critical parts, therefore, of this stage in the process is to pull together a co-ordinated summary pack of material to go to the Senior Team review.

This pack should consist of slides containing information about each family.

The pack should summarise the information on the areas of:
- Innovation
- Demand
- Supply
- Finance
- HR, IT

Companies usually structure the pack for the Senior Team review around each family (which aligns with each of the meetings).

It should also focus on delivering the critical issues for decisions, and hence, should use the STP format shown earlier.

From a presentation point of view, many companies develop slides with countless tiny numbers on the sheet, which are impossible to read. It is much better to display graphs which tell the story rather than take people through the painful exercise of reading lots of numbers.

It is also essential to try and keep the number of families down to as small a number as possible; if not, the report produced could be massive!

Figure 81 illustrates the kind of report to use. I summarise it on one page for convenience.

The critical point is that it is useful to break this section into the six summary areas in the boxes below the graphs. This structure provides the key focus of discussion for the meeting:

- **Major Assumptions**: what are the major assumptions behind the numbers for Demand and Supply?
- **Decisions made**: what decisions have been made since the last meeting?
- **Decisions Required**? What are the decisions required of the meeting, with input from the STP form?
- **Costs/Benefits**? What are the summary costs and benefits of the decisions?
- **Risk and Opportunities**: what are the risks and opportunities that affect this family?

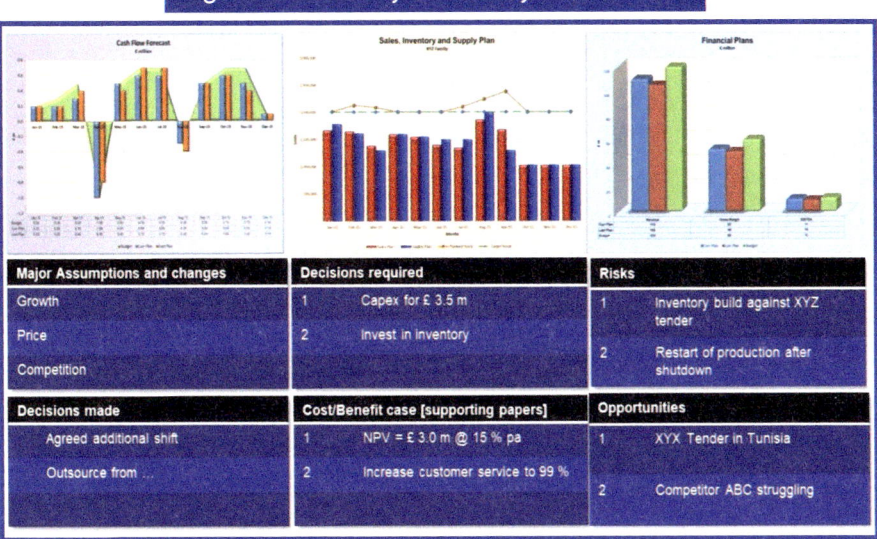

Figure 81: Family summary information

Major Assumptions and changes	Decisions required	Risks
Growth	1 Capex for £ 3.5 m	1 Inventory build against XYZ tender
Price	2 Invest in inventory	
Competition		2 Restart of production after shutdown
Decisions made	**Cost/Benefit case [supporting papers]**	**Opportunities**
Agreed additional shift	1 NPV = £ 3.0 m @ 15 % pa	1 XYX Tender in Tunisia
Outsource from ...	2 Increase customer service to 99 %	2 Competitor ABC struggling

Thus, this summary page will build on the information from the previous steps of the process, including significant assumptions (and changes in those), highlights the decisions required, and summarises the risks and opportunities faced.

This format summarises a "Plan on a Page", which is a great idea. In practice, every company will produce its own style of document, and there may be several pages for each family. This document illustrates a standard approach to the information, which the team should prepare at this stage.

You may also need to pull together simulations of outcomes at this stage, to look at alternative demand plans or alternative supply plans. Hence, the ability to have a simulation facility within the IT infrastructure is essential.

The decision-making process is going to be more robust if you look at multiple scenarios – but based on a single database. We know the future is uncertain, but we can make it more understandable if we look at the various outcomes.

Planning is clearly about thinking about various results and putting in place your resources to meet the potential outcomes.

Naturally, any company cannot control forces outside of its span of control; it can collaborate with its customers and suppliers as much as possible.

But ultimately it must cost-effectively marshal its resources to meet potential outcomes, and that must be the output of this step of the process: recommendations to the board as to what to do to meet the future risks and opportunities, and close gaps to long-term strategic plans.

Sir John Harvey-Jones was a charismatic chairman of ICI. He was initially turned down for the job because he did not follow the typical career path for this high-profile role – he had been a submariner. He presented the "Troubleshooter" TV series mentioned earlier.

He made the insightful statement in respect of people's reluctance to plan:

"Planning is an unnatural process; it is much more fun to do something. The nicest thing about not planning is that failure comes as a complete surprise, rather than being preceded by a period of worry and depression."

So at this point, we should have a pack of information with decisions and recommendations to go to the Senior Leadership Team meeting. Some companies think that "SOP" should be an item on the agenda for the Board meeting. Hopefully at this stage we can see that this notion dangerously signals that the company is giving a much lower sense of importance to this process. It should be unnecessary to talk about "IBP".

It also fails to recognise the importance of the integration of the business into "one plan". Hence this step should lead to the creation of the Board Agenda each month.

It is the prime difference between a supply chain focused SOP process and an "Integrated Business Leadership" approach. IBL is about managing a business, not just a few departments within that business.

But before we review the inputs and outputs of the Senior Team review, we need to ensure the business has a vision and strategy.

Chapter 15

Vision and Mission

Alice: "Would you tell me, please, which way I ought to go from here?"
The Cheshire Cat: "That depends a good deal on where you want to get to."
Alice: "I don't much care where. So long as I get somewhere."
The Cheshire Cat: "Then it doesn't much matter which way you go." – Lewis Carroll

Lewis Carroll was, in fact, the pen name for the famous Dean of Christ Church in Oxford – Charles Lutwidge Dodgson. He translated his first two names "Charles Lutwidge" into Latin as "Carolus Lodovicus", then Anglicised them and reversed their order into Lewis Carroll. He was an excellent mathematician.

You might be wondering now why we should be talking about "Vision" and "Mission"; surely, IBP does not cover that as well? Is it not just about the balancing of supply and demand?

In fact, they are critical inputs into the process.

This area often gets put into the category of "let's think about this once a year", or even worse: "Let's think about this every five years." As a result, many companies do not revisit this area often enough or ensure that they align the decisions that they take with the Vision and Mission of the business. It all becomes too remote.

However, competitors and the economic situation are not going to align themselves directly with your internal timetable for establishing a Vision and Strategy. Sadly, Covid-19 was an extreme example of this fact. How many companies had to realign their strategy because of the global impact of this pandemic?

Hence, there should be an ongoing process for developing and managing the Vision and Mission, which should be subject to review as part of the Integrated Business Planning process.

There has been a lot written on "Vision", and there is no need to repeat this in detail here.

I summarise this as being the creation of the direction for the business, which neatly covers the "Unique Selling Proposition" of the company. It closely aligns with the Mission – which describes for a company or organisation **why** it does what it does.

These two elements should answer the question: "What is the problem that your company is trying to solve for its customers?"

If I can use the analogy of the tanker delivering cargo, there has to be a view of the where the tanker is going and then the rest of the activities follow. If the captain – being asked, "where are you going?" – said "somewhere", then they would be acting like Alice in Wonderland.

Simon Sinek is a great speaker, and explores how successful leaders in business are clear about the "why" they are in business. He has a book which expands on this. (Sinek, 2011). In summary, he distinguishes between three aspects: what, how, and why? "What?" is the product that a company makes. "How?" is the way they work. "Why?" is the core reason for the company doing what they do. He uses the example of computers.

Some companies will make computers. That is the "what".

Computers are great at storing, manipulating and processing information. That is "how". These are features of the product.

But computers that revolutionise your life and make it all the more comfortable to live provides the compelling, "why?".

He illustrates with the example of Apple Inc. and how they have become highly successful in helping people to organise their lives with an **integrated** set of products – everything from communication, to entertainment, to keep fit. That is why they are successful. That vision helps Apple to continue to persuade people to buy Apple products, rather than competitive copying products.

Steve Jobs went through many stages in developing Apple and helping to build the global company that it now is. His vision covered revolutionising the way we communicate. This is captured in this quotation:

"I think Henry Ford once said, 'If I'd asked customers what they wanted, they would have told me, "A faster horse!"' People don't know what they want until you show it to them. That's why I never rely on market research. Our task is to read things that are not yet on the page."

- ## Vision/Mission Statements

It is usual for a company's Vision and Mission to be summarised into short statements to help clarify a company's purpose in life.

There are some excellent Vision/Mission statements which companies have developed, and I include some of these here to illustrate what other companies could imitate:

Walt Disney: "To make people happy."

Nike Inc.'s corporate mission is "to bring inspiration and innovation to every athlete in the world."

Wal-Mart: "To give ordinary folk the chance to buy the same thing as rich people."

Bell Telephone: "A phone in every home."

McDonald's: its vision is to be the UK's best quick-service restaurant experience. This will be achieved through five strategies: Development, Our People, Restaurant Excellence, Operating Structure, and the Brand.

- *Development:* lead the Quick Service Restaurant market by a programme of site development and profitable restaurant openings.
- *Our People:* achieve competitive advantage through people who are high calibre, effective, well motivated and feel part of the McDonald's team in delivering the company's goals.

- *Restaurant Excellence:* focus on consistent delivery of quality, service and cleanliness through excellence in our restaurants.
- *Operating Structure:* optimise restaurant performance through the selection of the most appropriate operating, management and ownership structures.
- *The Brand:* continue to build the relationship between McDonald's and our customers to be a genuine part of the fabric of British society.

Note that the McDonald's vision is then supported by its strategy, which carefully relates to some of the critical elements of Integrated Business Planning:

- Innovation
- People
- Operations
- Finance
- Marketing

So, every company should create its Vision which makes clear why it is in business – what is the unique proposition that will drive people to its door? If your company does not have a recognisable vision, expressed simply, then start developing one straight away.

It is not something that should be revisited in full every year, as the intent is for it to be an overarching statement of the purpose of the business. It should be made clear to employees and should be a guiding input into the IBP senior leadership team process.

If McDonald's started buying and operating good-value hotels, then that would not be directly in line with the "best service restaurant" experience. However, if they served Big Macs in the restaurants, accommodation might add value to the restaurant business!

"Leadership is the capacity to translate vision into reality" is a great summary statement from Warren Bennis, a professor of business administration at the university of California, widely regarded as a pioneer of the contemporary field of leadership studies.

Without a vision, it is difficult for a leader to guide their people.

If a company does not have a vision, then the leader must create the process, through which all share the vision of the company.

Integrated Business Leadership thus requires having a clear vision to guide the decisions made through the Senior Team review. When conditions change, then it may well be necessary to change the long-term vision and the consequent strategy.

As observed above, Nokia was a company that moved from being a company which made paper in Finland to making mobile phones. To support this they acquired a telecoms company. The logic for the acquisition came from the fact that they defined their vision as being in communication. Paper made newspapers. Telecoms would be the new news.

They then developed into mobile phones with technology from the communications business. Between 1996 and 2001, revenue increased from €6.5 billion to €31 billion. It sold off much of the rest of their business.

Companies change; technology changes. Economic environments change. But within that turmoil, a clear vision helps to give clarity and constancy of purpose.

Vision is about being clear about the area that a company occupies, and sticking to the mission that it has adopted.

Chapter 16
Strategy

> *"Strategy is about making choices, trade-offs; it's about deliberately choosing to be different."* – Michael Porter, professor at Harvard University

A further key input into Integrated Business Leadership is the business strategy. As outlined before, we should not see the strategy as a once-a-year exercise. In the fast-changing environment of today, it is essential to be able to think about the business strategy regularly. Time should be devoted in the IBP process to dealing with strategic choices. It must inform and be informed by the IBP process. In an article on establishing strategy, Michael Porter in the May 1979 edition of the Harvard Business Review (Porter, 1979) outlined the "Five Forces Model". This model helped to explain how companies exist in their market place. It showed how they are always subject to the threats from competitors, pressure from customers, the increasing power of suppliers, the substitution of new products from developing technologies, and the threat of new entrants into your market. All of these forces can render a company obsolete. Many businesses have failed to survive. It is the job of the Leadership team to create a strategy which prevents their company becoming obsolete over the medium- to long-term. They need to have a plan to deal with the threats from competitors, customers, suppliers, new technology and new entrants.

In the book, Strategy focused Organisation (Kaplan & Norton, 2001), Kaplan and Norton introduced the related Balanced Scorecard model. This book described a comprehensive measurement framework, which showed how companies should measure performance as they juggle between the competing demands of shareholders (and debtholders), customers, suppliers, and learning and growth. Companies need performance measures to judge success in each dimension.

Both of these books point to the importance of having a strategy and a way of measuring success, which is core to the Integrated Business Leadership approach.

It probably needs some further additions to this model to cover developments in the 21st century.

- **Governments/Political Change**

A perpetual threat to companies' positions in the modern world, is the dimension of governments, who are creating legislation, fighting wars, raising tariff barriers, reorganising alliances in Europe, Asia, Middle East and the Americas, all of which can fire off at any time. The current high-profile threat to sue Google for abuse of a monopolistic position is a clear example.

With the rise of the use of social media as a means of communicating government policy, and the rise of tyrannies and dictators, the impacts of governments can rest on the whim of one or two individuals. As at 2019, some 2.6 billion people (34% of the world's population) across 51 nations live in countries ruled by dictatorship. Arguably countries like the USA, while a democracy, can also be highly dependent on the whim of one president who imposes tariffs at a moment's notice in trade wars through executive orders.

Companies need to be able to adapt their business strategies to respond and react to the sudden changes brought about by governments.

- **Freedom of Movement of People**

The freedom (or lack) of movement of people can cause enormous strains on economies and business. Migration, doctrines on the freedom of movement, and changes in the population across significant economies in China and India make for substantial changes in the expectations of people concerning working conditions. People will move to earn money for their families.

Back in the 1990s, a client which was a sock manufacturer in the UK was looking to become more profitable. Eventually, it succumbed to the pressures of international competitiveness, and moved its manufacturing to other countries. Around ten years later, I saw a supervisor in Sri Lanka who was tearful because their factory was about to be closed down and moved to Vietnam. Companies have to adapt to the costs of people across the globe all the time.

Thus we need to be looking at companies in the competitive maelstrom as having to struggle, simultaneously, to deal with more than just the four or five forces of competition.

In the modern world, there are six key areas which companies need to address, as illustrated in Figure 82.

Figure 82: Strategic Dimensions

Finance
Shareholders and Banks increasing costs of finance

Customer Power
Customers dominate driving down prices and increasing speed of response

People
Freedom of movement across the globe

Innovation
New products and services threaten our position

Supplier Power
Increasing cost and lead time

Government
Legislation, rivalry, trade alliances

Competitive Threats to us

STRENGTHS | WEAKNESSES
OPPORTUNITIES | THREATS

You could also add the impacts of environmental issues, and the vast need to ensure that we respond to social pressure. For the moment, I will include that in the "Government" area, as the impact will depend on the action – or inaction – of governments in seeking to meet global targets like becoming carbon-neutral by 2030 or 2050.

It is clear that the move towards becoming carbon neutral will have a significant impact on the operations of all companies, and will need a substantial behaviour change. Everything from changing products, stopping international air travel, to encouraging people to go vegan is within scope.

Within this framework, companies must create their unique position to ensure their continuity. This strategy, in turn, will provide value to all of those associated with your company.

Customers will buy the product/service for which they have a need. Suppliers earn revenue and employ people by providing products and services. People gain employment and a way of living that manages a trade-off between leisure and work. Shareholders and banks make money from their investments, which facilitates the financial support of the organisation.

Governments maximise their returns from the tax systems, as best they can, to support the citizens within their borders.

Innovation allows the human creative mind to continue to introduce new ideas, and technology into the mix to create novel products and services.

The strategic process needs, then, to scan the competitive landscape and get the company to review its **Strengths, Weaknesses, Opportunities and Threats** from each of these dimensions, and create its position – which will ensure survival.

It needs to have a strategy/plan for each of these dimensions to create long-term survival for the company. Thus, it needs to work out strategic actions to build on its strengths and counteract weaknesses. It needs to maximise the value of its opportunities and work out steps to neutralise threats.

But these threats and opportunities do not appear once a year. Hence, within the Integrated Business Leadership process, companies need to review their strategy to respond to changes as they occur.

If we take the obvious example of the car market, then back in the 1920s with Henry Ford's Model T, it was all straightforward. The strategy was one car for the mass market. Ford had the technology, could convert the car from steel to automobile quickly, and through mass-production make it affordable. People were happy to get away from horses.

But now consumers want more and more choice in colours, etc.

The climate crisis is forcing governments to create new regulations on diesel and petrol to favour electric. This development is challenging businesses to provide the electric points where people can charge up their cars.

Tesla has entered the market to create electric cars.

Traditional motor companies are developing electric or hybrid cars. Competition occurs in Korea, Japan, USA, China.

BYD was a battery maker and moved up the value chain to make electric cars as an output for its batteries. They got US tycoon Warren Buffett to finance them, with a $250 million shareholding.

Contemporary Amperex Technology Ltd, or CATL, also sells batteries, and it is now planning a $1.3 billion factory to make electric cars from 2020 in China. The Chinese government is seeking to support them. All other companies need to work out their response to this and determine how they are going to survive. From this will follow a series of actions (which I call strategic actions) which they need to execute to enable the survival of their company. You cannot separate this activity from the IBP process.

- **Market Disciplines**

One of the fascinating areas that I have seen over the years concerning the understanding of what is unique about organisations, is the confusion at Senior Executive level around the strategic focus that companies must show concerning their particular competency. In their 1997 book Discipline of Market Leaders, Michael Treacey and Fred Wiersema (Treacey & Wiersema, 1997) came out with a brilliant book on "strategic differentiation".

Their basic premise is that several companies can exist in the same market place; but market leaders are those who are clear about their market position, based around three fundamental choices. Your company can either compete on "customer intimacy", "operational excellence" or "technology excellence".

Several times, I have asked executives about where their focus lies today, and they are often confused. Different directors of the same company are not clear about whether they are "customer-intimate" or "operationally excellent", for instance. There is even more confusion when you ask the question of where the plan is to be in five years.

Customer Intimacy is the desire to appear and be very close to customers, giving them exactly what they want and when they want it.

Operational Excellence is the strategy of creating a business that is a low-cost organisation, offering few frills for customers, attracting consumers who do not want to pay much for what they need.

Technical Excellence is for those companies who want to sell to, and attract, consumers, who search for the latest technology.

For instance in the travel market, there is Virgin Airways, which will pick you up from home, take you to the airport, and make their customers feel second to none. That is Customer Intimacy.

In the travel market in Europe, there are Ryanair and EasyJet, which are aiming at the low-cost market, enabling flights at extraordinarily low prices, providing basic seats, and charging for food, luggage and newspapers as an incremental value-add. I would describe that as "Operational Excellence".

Virgin Galactica and Tesla are lining up to fly people into space using the new technology of spacecraft. A 90-minute flight will cost $250,000 – around $2,800 per minute.

That compares with approximately $5.70 per minute for an Upper-Class flight from Heathrow to New York for a 495-minute journey! That is "Technology Excellence". People will pay for it because it is new.

In the Hotel market, there are hotels like the Savoy in London which thrive on customer intimacy. You can pay £1,500 and more per night for the experience. Others attract the business market by including iPads in rooms, with free Wi-Fi. At the lower end of the market, there are budget hotels, providing straightforward accommodation, at a price that occupancy rates ensure the rooms maximise revenue and profit.

The different companies survive by creating their particular customer value proposition.

Tracy and Wiersema's theme is that the companies which are successful understand their position in the market place, and that customers also buy from them because of that clarity. Each member of each market place will be successful as long as it focusses on their area of differentiation.

- **Impact on Measures**

This approach, in turn, drives Integrated Business Leadership to make sure that the internal focus aligns the strategic choice with all functions in the business. It must also address the performance measures for the company, and make sure these are aligned.

Kaplan and Norton addressed the issue of creation of the strategy, and aligning the measures with the strategy. So we must make sure that we adopt this approach within the development of Integrated Business Leadership.

One client I saw was in the business of making CDs, DVDs and similar media for music and TV. They had a factory in the UK in London, which produced smaller-volume titles. It needed flexibility and speed of response. The same company had a factory in Spain, which handled the blockbuster films and music CDs. They were producing high volumes.

They measured, however, both factories on the utilisation of factory output. This measure caused a lot of frustration and confusion.

Spain performed well because it had the volume to make it efficient. London could not compete on "efficiency", and so the measure threatened the London business. But the purpose of the London site was to provide flexibility for providing the less popular titles. Eventually, they closed the site.

You can have different strategies for different business sectors, but do not measure them in the same way. The company could have measured the Spanish factory on Operating Equipment Effectiveness (OEE), but they should have measured the London factory on the speed of response, and delivery to request date. Measurement purely based on efficiency promotes the wrong behaviour, as explained in the supply section.

It is for this reason that the measure of factory performance, should be driven by schedule achievement, rather than merely "widgets per minute" or "tons per hour", particularly if you want to respond to the customer with "customer intimacy".

If you are operating an Operational Excellence strategy, then Operating Equipment Effectiveness will be a crucial measure, alongside schedule achievement. This measure will drive improvement in operational methods.

- **Impact on Functions**

This choice of strategic direction leads to the observation that the different functions will also play different roles, depending on the choice of the value proposition. Figure 83 illustrates.

Figure 83: Functional activities aligned with market discipline

	Sales	Marketing	Finance	Manufacturing	Design
Customer Intimacy	Frequent contact. CRM a key tool. Quick response. Customer is king.	Intense understanding of customer needs. Tailored approach.	Focus on total long-term value of customer, and not profit per unit.	Flexible strategy. Mass customisation.	Custom configuration; focus on customer.
Operational Excellence	Focus on key customers; product focus and not customer focus	Standard product for all customers. limited range. Simple brand	Utilisation key, and manage carefully to minimum cost	Limited product range; efficiency is the watchword.	Limited range of core products. Design not a key element of the proposition
Product Leadership	Persuades to take new products, rather than old.	Focus on the new products, and constant brand development around technology	Project costing and management key, with focus on Product Lifecycle management.	Capable of managing disruption of new products, first of kind etc.	Key element of the strategy, and constant need to develop new ideas.

Thus, in the **customer intimacy** "stream", sales and marketing are crucial and will develop a range of products that will suit a diverse range of customers and markets. The Operational strategy will support flexibility.

With an **operational excellence** value proposition, then sales and marketing should focus on product rationalisation, and the factory should be built and used to achieve maximum effectiveness.

Where IBL will begin to add value is where it supports an intelligent debate within the company about how to align the supply, commercial and innovation strategies in the same direction, and to measure accordingly.

Because companies reward and motivate people without thinking through the value proposition, then you get competition between the functions.

Therefore, I have seen companies that are trying to compete on customer intimacy (Sales and Marketing lead), but have operations continually calling for a smaller product range and complaining at changes in production plans all the time. One function is pursuing a customer-intimate strategy and the other an operational-excellence strategy. The back-biting across the senior leadership team table becomes intense. It is not the personalities that are at issue – it is the lack of a proper strategy.

So once there is a clear view of the strategic focus, and alignment across the functions, then a company can develop strategic objectives and actions for the company.

Thus, if the strategy is to innovate, based on a technical excellence value proposition, the company will need to translate that into an objective to develop an XYZ product range by 20xy [date], to create a competitive edge. They will need to invest in XYZ capacity to give more flexibility in responding to customers.

This strategic process will provide the company with the building blocks for IBP for the next two to three years.

This set of strategic actions will then give the framework for the input into all the steps of the process, as described in previous chapters. The IBP process will then measure the success of achieving the strategy.

Success in developing the strategy should lead to the ability to capture the Vision, Mission and Strategy onto one page, which has the merit of keeping it as simple as possible, and the ability to review it quickly as part of the IBP process.

the chart in Figure 84 shows a generic statement of how this would look.

Thus, in the top triangle, you can capture the critical statement around Vision.

Under that, you can articulate the Mission. Then down each of the columns you can populate the strategic principles (e.g. to increase market share or customer base), and then outline the key strategic activities (gain customer ABC, promote XYZ product range).

Figure 84: One-page strategy

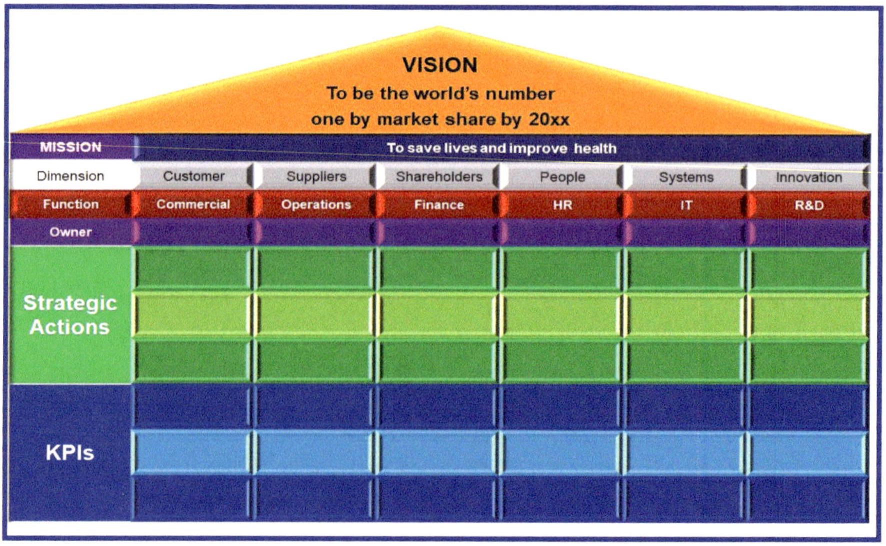

	Customer	Suppliers	Shareholders	People	Systems	Innovation
MISSION			To save lives and improve health			
Dimension	Customer	Suppliers	Shareholders	People	Systems	Innovation
Function	Commercial	Operations	Finance	HR	IT	R&D
Owner						

VISION
To be the world's number one by market share by 20xx

Strategic Actions

KPIs

At the bottom is a space for the key KPIs for that pillar, and the targets. Each of the pillars then links to the steps in the IBP process.

In this way, we can develop a coherent Vision, Strategy and Objectives that provide a framework and input into the Senior Team review.

The Senior Team meeting should then allocate time at least once/quarter if not once/month to review progress against the strategic actions against this framework.

One client adopted this approach. The MD used to carry the vision document around with her wherever she went. In fact, the first time I met her was in a hotel in the USA. She was standing there talking to her colleague about the form, which is how I knew she was the person I was due to meet at the hotel!

When I asked her what she thought about the "one-page strategy", she said it was brilliant. She said, "Having it all on one page avoids having the myriads of documents that we used to have to describe all of the things we were going to do."

Chapter 17
Senior Team Review

"I can't change the direction of the wind, but I can adjust my sails to always reach my destination." – James Dean, actor

Every company and every subsidiary of every company that I have come across has a Senior Leadership Team Review meeting, which generally happens once a month. Many times, there are weekly meetings of one sort or another, and then there are lots of ad-hoc meetings which keep on filling up the diary and making up for a horrendous schedule. Most people complain about the fact that they never have enough time in the day.

The truth, of course, is not that people do not have enough time. Twenty-four hours and seven days per week (plus an extra day each Leap year every four years (except for years which are not divisible by 400)) is a construct invented by the Babylonians. The Western world has adopted this structure, with a few variations over the years until our Gregorian calendar, established in 1582. The amount of time available is fixed.

The issue is more to do with how you prioritise your time within that day, and how you make use of the time more effectively. Part of the objective of the IBP process is to ensure that the senior team have more time to focus on what matters. What matters is the longer-term view and strategic actions to close the gap between "truth as we know it", and the direction we want to take so we reach our destination. This objective will require constant adjustment through keeping a hand on the tiller, to use the sailing boat analogy.

The Senior Team review is made more effective through preparation before the meeting and a proper focus on the critical issues. Hence the importance of the Prioritisation, as outlined above.

It should be a decision-making meeting, as emphasised in the prioritisation section above.

- **Preparation**

The Senior Team review should last between a half to a whole day, depending on the complexity of the business and issues.

The "head of IBP" should prepare the agenda in conjunction with the CEO, and members of the SLT, or the local general manager in local business units, and sites in a multi-site business.

It should cover a review of the business, its performance and outlook – based on the outputs from the previous steps of the process, with a precise input of the decisions required at the meeting (based on the STP format).

- **Focus on the Far-Term**

One of the frequent issues I have found is that businesses spend an excessive amount of time looking backwards at what has happened, which frequently leads to excuse-finding and defensive behaviour.

Indeed, we can learn some things from the past (history is not entirely bunk), but there is no point in wishing the past had not happened, which is what most people want to do.

Equally, many senior teams spend a considerable amount of time just focussing on the short-term – usually the next three months. Of course, if the senior team responds to the "old behaviour" of meeting or beating the budget, the short-term becomes shorter and shorter as you approach the year-end. It is like approaching a speed camera and slamming on the brakes just as you enter the camera zone. Dangerous!

I attended a (virtual) meeting of the European division of a major international FMCG branded goods business with a turnover in Europe of $3bn, sales in every country across Europe, and half a dozen factories. The whole three-hour meeting just focused on the next three months. The UK MD appeared for approximately 15 minutes to complain vociferously about the availability of a product and then disappeared again.

The next VP of Europe changed the whole process to become more long-term and threatened to fire anyone who dared to talk about any event that was going to happen in the next three months. That had the desired effect.

Another client suffered too much from three-month short-termism syndrome and took the extreme step of producing the monthly reports for the next 24 months, and then greyed out the next three months. It helped.

So one of the main behaviours to encourage in developing this process is to get away from too much navel-gazing and spend time looking at the longer-term future. The example set by the leader of the organisation will make a difference.

The fundamental model is that the senior team looks out beyond the cumulative lead time to make the enabling decisions for the managers of the business to execute the plan. This needs effective chairmanship and leadership.

This fact does not mean that the short-term should be completely absent from the meeting. It is a senior team, and stuff happens in the short term requiring their decision. It is just that this is not where the focus should be. Eighty per cent of the time spent on the long-term is a good rule of thumb.

- **How Does the Multinational Business Work?**

In a multinational business, then the factories will execute the plans that have been developed (within their cumulative material and capacity time horizons) through the IBP process.

The business units will execute their local sales and marketing plans to deliver the sales that consumers and customers will give to the company.

The delivery process (lorries and warehouses) will make sure that the product gets to the right place at the right time, with the proper paperwork (= perfect order).

The IBP process steps will measure the quality of all these processes. The plans need to be communicated from the centre and back through the decision-making process. So there will be a cascade of Senior Leadership Team meetings through the business.

Figure 85 (produced by a colleague – David Christian) is a great illustration of how this should look and work.

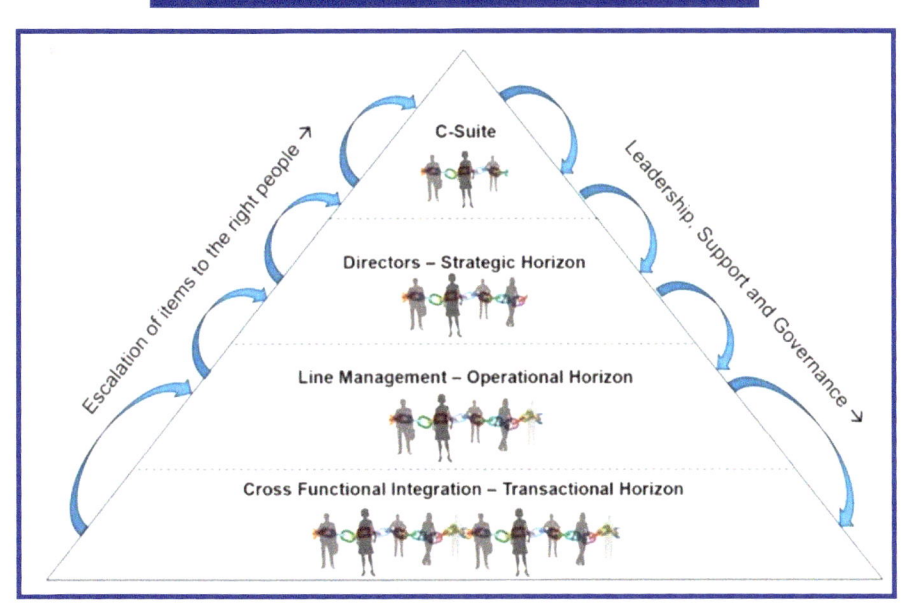

Figure 85: Link from leadership to execution

- **Structure of Senior Management Review meeting**

Who Attends the Senior Team Review?

Looking at the design of the Senior Management review, I would assume that there are (usually) the following members:

    CEO/GM/Leader

    Head of Innovation/R&D

    Head of Sales

    Head of Marketing/Product Development

    Head of Operations/Supply Chain

    Head of Finance

Head of HR

Head of IT

Depending on the organisation, one person can carry out more than one of these roles. It is also essential that each of these people will have chaired and led the previous steps of the local or global IBP process, as appropriate.

Hence, they come to this meeting fully prepared to address the issues that the previous steps will have identified. The senior leadership team thus deals only with those items/subjects that fall within the prescribed limits which govern what this meeting discusses – depending on the limits of authority.

- **The Agenda for the Meeting**

The key focus of an effective IBP process – as we have said – should be to identify what has changed from the previous plan, the impact of those changes and the decision(s) that is/(are) required. So let us take four examples to follow these through, and how these might work in a typical IBP meeting:

1. A new product has reached the point where it needs to move on to full development. The business case has been prepared and shows the need to spend £4m in capital expenditure over the next two years with a net present value of £10m @ 15% per annum.

2. Marketing has reduced the growth projections for the market over the next three years because of changes in the global and local economies, which impacts next year's and the following years' projections.

3. The latest market demands show that we need to put on a third shift in our factory from six months onwards. There is a need to recruit specialist skills to support this.

4. A competitor is up for sale; it is struggling because of rising costs. Their manufacturing process is a bit old-fashioned, and we have unique cost advantages in our manufacturing process, which would enable us to take them over, be more profitable and increase our market share.

New Product
The Head of Innovation would make a brief presentation concerning the current status of projects. They would then present the business case for the new product, supported by the head of Sales and head of Marketing on the business case. The head of Finance would comment on the financial projections, and then the CEO would get a collective agreement (or not) to go ahead with the implementation of the next phase for the new product.

The Head of Innovation would review performance on the Cost and Schedule Index for each of their projects, and there would be an agreement on actions required to improve the Innovation processes.

Change in Outlook
The head of sales and would present the current business situation, comparison against the current financial year, and Years 2 and 3 (if they have changed).

The head of marketing would then present on the impact of the changes to the current business plans for Years 2 and 3 of the horizon, with a comparison against the Strategic plan (which the team would last have reviewed at the quarterly Strategic Review session).

They will present their recommendations on proposed actions to get back on track – principally through product development (agreed with the head of innovation). The team will agree with any expenditure required. The head of sales will comment on the impact on the sales channels, and the need to develop these.

Again, the CEO will get agreement on the proposals.

Supply
The head of supply will outline the current demand for products, with commentary from sales and marketing of the reasons for the changes. The head of HR will comment on the impact on recruitment. The planning manager will then present the costs/benefits of various alternatives (outsourcing to a third party, purchasing new equipment, cutting back on demand).

The planning manager/head of IBP will present the basis for the recommendation for going to a third shift for approval, and the CEO will look for consensus on the way forward.

Finance

The head of finance would then present the current picture for Value Add, P&L and Cash Flow for the current financial year and next two/three years, and show the impact of previous discussions on these numbers.

There would then be a review of the performance measures. The team will then discuss and agree on the financial impact of the actions that have been proposed by the heads of the Functions/Processes.

This statement would be the agreed business plan with which the company is going forward, now.

Acquisition

Lastly, the business would turn to the proposal for acquisition of the competitor. The FD might present the strengths that the investment would bring, and how this fits into the strategy.

They would complete this with a review of the NPV of the acquisition, based on the forecasts from the Demand Review meeting.

The CEO would then seek a decision from the group, and the team would agree on the required actions.

The head of IBP would attend the meeting throughout, to provide background information where necessary based on their discussions with the "captains' council" and knowledge of what is going on. They can sometimes act also as the "secretary" to the meeting, ensuring that they record the actions, minutes made, and then circulate the inputs and outputs after the meeting.

At the end of the meeting, the "secretary" will circulate the actions and decisions to all managers within 24 hours. I had the good fortune to work with someone who was a chartered secretary. They were brilliant at summarising all the actions during the meeting, and then sending the minutes and actions out immediately after the meeting.

Each of the heads of the function will then debrief their team on the discussions, and the agreed actions.

In one client, they made sure that all mobile phones were placed on a table at the end of the room (on a chart with people's initials on them) and had a rule that people could only use them at the official breaks! They also did not allow laptops to be open unless they were making a presentation or consulting something relating to the topic under discussion.

These little housekeeping rules also help the discipline of the meeting.

- **Organised Common-Sense**

Of course, as you read this, then I can imagine you think, 'Surely the above is what happens at all of these Senior Team meetings?"

True, it should do. It is not rocket science. However, it does not always operate this way.

But even if it does operate in this way, there is a real difference between this meeting and the ones that happen in many companies. The significant difference is this meeting directly connects to the previous steps of the process. There are clear accountabilities for the procedures/meetings in place, and agreement on the issues which should go to the senior team.

They also happen on a regular cycle, which ensures the right people attend the right meetings.

The right measures will also generate the proper discussions about where real improvements to the way the business works (via root-cause analysis) will also make a huge difference.

The other key aspect that I have observed is that many companies fail to make this senior-level meeting **the** decision-making meeting. Thus, they come to this meeting, try to tackle an issue and someone will then say, "We do not have enough information to make the decision now; let us have a meeting off-line to discuss this."

This comment is often "code" for: "We would like to make the decision elsewhere." It is sometimes an indication of poor preparation. It is also sometimes an indication that the business does not really believe in this IBP process, and hence it never takes hold.

When you hear these words, someone should stop the meeting and say: "No! We should make the decision here and now. We have as much information as we are likely to get."

I also saw one client formalise this whole process and the Senior Management Review into a one-hour meeting, which was called the IBP meeting.

This meeting was then immediately followed by another management meeting, which lasted the rest of the morning. The only difference was that the planning manager left after the first meeting.

This is not the way the process should run. There just needs to be one decision-making meeting as a culmination of the IBP process. Where this happens, it indicates that the CEO/MD does not understand the real purpose of the IBP process – it should be how we run the company.

It also sometimes signals the difference between Sales and Operations Planning and Integrated Business Planning, and why SOP fails in many companies and gets stuck as a short-term mechanism for sorting out supply and demand issues. The leadership team have been unable to develop an Integrated Business Planning process, and provide the direction to turn it into "Integrated Business Leadership".

Description of the Senior Leadership Team review brings an end to the process and can be characterised with the following inputs and outputs shown in Figure 86.

So, we have now covered all the elements of the process and the meetings. I hope I have given you some inspiration to want to implement IBP within your business.

Most of it – hopefully – will appear common-sense at this stage. It has often been called "organised common-sense". But in summary, the model has always been about the integration of the business, and the vital impact of leadership.

Figure 86: Senior Team Review template

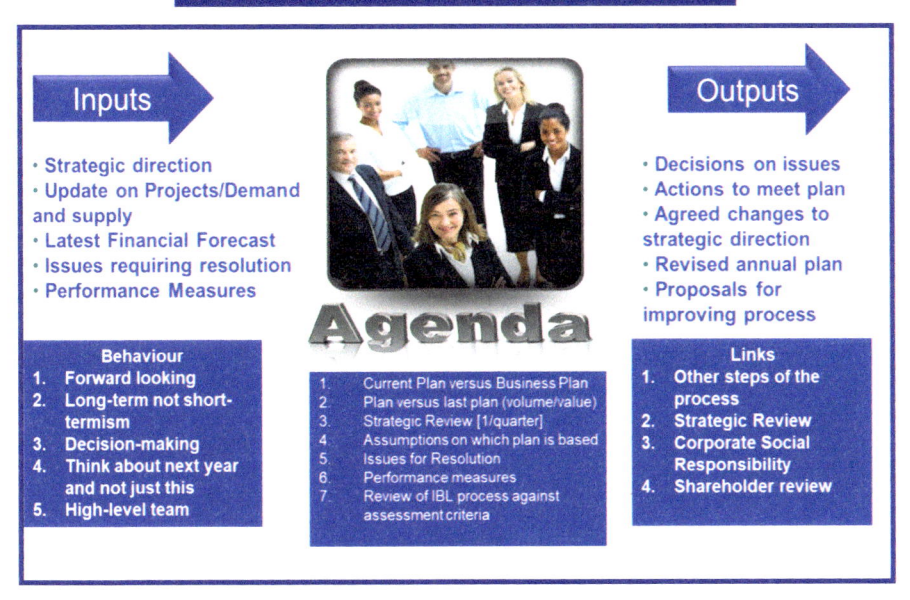

Inputs
- Strategic direction
- Update on Projects/Demand and supply
- Latest Financial Forecast
- Issues requiring resolution
- Performance Measures

Behaviour
1. Forward looking
2. Long-term not short-termism
3. Decision-making
4. Think about next year and not just this
5. High-level team

Agenda
1. Current Plan versus Business Plan
2. Plan versus last plan (volume/value)
3. Strategic Review [1/quarter]
4. Assumptions on which plan is based
5. Issues for Resolution
6. Performance measures
7. Review of IBL process against assessment criteria

Outputs
- Decisions on issues
- Actions to meet plan
- Agreed changes to strategic direction
- Revised annual plan
- Proposals for improving process

Links
1. Other steps of the process
2. Strategic Review
3. Corporate Social Responsibility
4. Shareholder review

The concepts started as SOP and covered much of what I have outlined in this book. The scope has been expanded to make sure that companies get the most from their implementation, and so it is called "Integrated Business Planning" – but at heart, it is the same concept.

Implementation of IBP is a challenge to systems, processes and above all, the behaviour of the organisation. There is a difference between Integrated Business Planning and leadership. Leadership requires making decisions in an organised way and holding people accountable for the decisions and actions identified. It needs a clear vision and strategy in the background to make it operate. It requires clear shared goals.

This is the reason why the process needs the knowledge and enthusiasm of the leader, without which it is impossible to make these concepts work.

You can try to chase after changes in any one of people, processes and systems, but you will not achieve superlative results unless you change all of these simultaneously.

Figure 87 brings together a summary of the whole process.

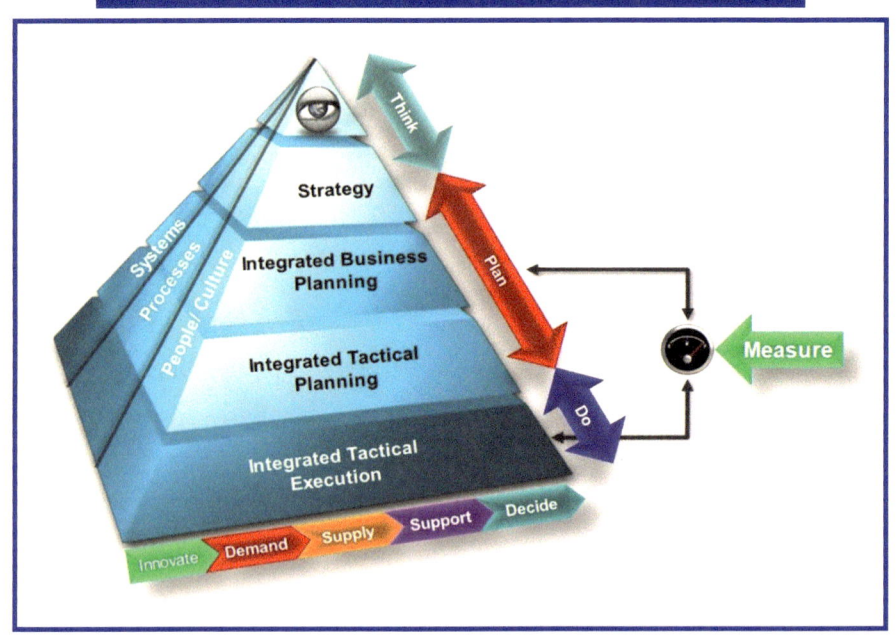

Figure 87: Three-dimensional view of the IBL model

At the top is the vision and strategy for the business. The Integrated Business Planning process is the next layer, which we have described in this book.

This process links in to the more detailed layer of "Integrated Tactical Planning" for the key processes – Innovation, Demand Planning, Supply Chain Management, Support (Finance, IT, and HR). This level is the place where companies create detailed plans for each week and each day.

This layer then leads to Integrated Tactical Execution level, which is where the plans turn into action. Our progress is measured by KPIs, which provide feedback back up the layers, to provide continuous improvement.

Down the left-hand side of the pyramid, we support the planning and execution with integrated systems, processes, and culture.

Thus, the business translates vision and strategy down to operations and tactics, and the results are fed back through the company.

The objective of the implementation of these ideas is so that the CEO will recognise that this is now the way we run our business.

IBL is about how companies run their business. The choice is between on the one hand of short-termism, chaos, firefighting and silo management, and on the other hand of an environment where the leadership provides a clear vision and strategy, concentrates on the future, and empowers its people to execute the plan. There is no blame; there is clear feedback, and an organised feel about the way people work.

It is the leader who provides the framework within which the people enjoy working, and loyalty is a mutual attitude. Success for customers, employees and shareholders is the result.

In the next section we will show how to make this change happen.

Chapter 18

Making it Happen

"Vision without action is merely a dream. Action without vision just passes the time. Vision with action can change the world." – Joel A. Barker, author

Back in the 1980s, SOP was a new "thing". Companies were implementing MRP systems, which are now called ERP systems. The basic premise was that implementing a complex transactional system is all very well, but if you do not ensure that the quality of the numbers going into the system is right, you will get rubbish. Hence, SOP thrived on the concept of "one set of numbers", "truth", "honesty", and so on. You had to implement "SOP" alongside implementing your MRP II system, or it would all be a big failure.

If you did not, then you would get all of the new system operated with the old behaviours. It is the biblical parable of "new wine in old bottles" all over again. The wine disappeared as the bottles leaked. Since then, many companies have implemented MRP II or ERP systems, and then decided that they needed to implement SOP. Then the industry decided to call this "thing" IBP, and so some of those companies that had already implemented SOP said, "We have done SOP, but now we need to implement IBP." The confusion started to reign.

Indeed, I have worked with clients who have ancient ERP systems, which do not work well. I have then helped them run a project which became the implementation of IBP across several countries of the world while keeping the old system in place.

We got IBP to work, but it soon showed up the inadequacy of the old systems, and that then spawned further work on getting the systems to work. In some cases, it has meant getting new systems. But this just makes the whole project longer and more complicated.

Of course, implementing good behaviours, getting the right responsibilities in place, and so on, can be done without an ERP system. Using spreadsheets does not necessarily mean it is impossible to implement the right behaviours – it just makes the whole process more unreliable, and a struggle when you start to try to use the spreadsheets. That structure can quickly lead to failure because the spreadsheets are so disintegrated, slow, and cannot provide universal visibility of the information.

When you are approaching the issue of implementing IBP, it helps to be clear upfront on what you are trying to tackle in this project. This book also emphasises the importance of aligning the leadership.

Is the objective to implement a whole new business system, and at the same time to transform the entire organisation as well?

Or are you trying to leave alone the existing system, which technically works well, but you see that the right behaviours, responsibilities and processes are not in place, which is at heart the reason why the system does not perform as expected?

Fortunately, whatever you do, the process of change management and transformation is the same and has the same barriers to success.

But you will need to be clear about the scope of what you are trying to do.

If you are going to implement a new business system with the aims of improving customer service and reducing costs, then you need to implement all the elements described throughout this book.

If you have a system already, then you will need to transform processes, the organisation and the people.

A transformation programme of this sort at the high level has to address the following elements:

Policies	- e.g. Abnormal Demand policy, Time Fence policy
Processes	- How things get done in the business
Roles	- Who does what
Responsibilities	- What are people responsible and accountable for
Measures	- How do you know people are managing properly?
Data	- The quality of the data that populates the system
Software	- The systems.

The theme of this book is that many people try to implement software, but do not tackle the culture and organisation, and then are surprised when the people blame the software for a failure to deliver the promised benefits. So do not tackle just one area on its own. Ensure you address software, processes and people.

Hence, the critical challenge in the implementation of IBP is to put in place different policies, processes, roles, responsibilities and measures. It requires the commitment of the Leadership to make changes happen.

There is, also, software out there which will help aggregate the data from the ERP system and will support IBP. This software will be very useful in avoiding the need for spreadsheets. Research these to see if they will be helpful.

Few of the transactional ERP systems in place today provide the necessary tools to enable aggregation of data by a family in the way suggested, which is a shame.

But this could be all that is needed if you already have a "transactional" ERP system in place which takes customer orders and process them into works orders and purchase orders.

In this section, I will focus on the change process, which will either require a new or existing system, and I will look at the typical requirements for bringing about change to implement IBP.

- **Change Management**

In most of the projects where a change in people and processes is needed, the difficult part of the implementation lies in changing people.

For some reason, the natural preference of people is to stay with the status quo. Despite all the frustrations of the way we work, we are happy to continue working and behaving that way. "Comfortably numb" (Pink Floyd's lyrics) might well describe the state of mind.

An excellent book on Change Management, which does not take a long time to read, is by John Kotter and Holger Rathberger: Our Iceberg is Melting (Kotter & Ratherberger, 2006). It describes how a penguin discovers their iceberg is melting, but no-one initially believes him. It is a fun book, but very serious too.

Dr Spencer Johnson wrote the foreword to the book. He also wrote a book called Who moved my Cheese? (Johnson, 1999), which is another easy-to-read book on why people struggle to accept change. Do read both. They are inspirational and informative.

- **What Encourages Change?**

Change happens in principle when three things take place:

1. There is genuine discontent with the present set of circumstances.
2. You have a vision of where you want to get to.
3. There a proven pathway to get there, so that people will be comfortable with trying to get there.

Companies start to travel down the road of a change project but it falters because, fundamentally, people are happy to carry on working with the way they do. There needs to be a *real* discontent.

The most significant barrier is the one which follows the theme of, "we are very successful today. Why would IBP (and indeed how will IBP) be able to improve what we achieve today?"

The need for the vision is that human beings will work towards an end state, providing they can be clear about what they will see when they get to the end of their journey. This fact is true across many aspects of life.

Finally, people are reluctant to be pioneers. The astronauts who landed on the moon made a great "leap for mankind". Since then, astronauts have made many journeys, and now Nokia has a contract to develop a mobile phone system for the moon. Travel to the moon is not an alien concept.

This chapter will focus on how to structure this change process.

However, before we go down this route, I was given a fascinating description of the framework for the problems experienced. I owe Ian Small big thanks for this idea, from the time when he was HR director at Sanofi Aventis Dagenham.

When bringing about a change of the sort that IBP implies, the two elements that need we need to bring together are "Enthusiasm" and "Knowledge".

A simple lack of enthusiasm for a change project provides a clear symptom of resistance. Thus, when faced with change, people will challenge IBP and say things like, "It will never work for us; show us a company like us where it has worked."

When I started down the road of helping a submarine company in the UK, someone asked me to find another submarine company who had implemented SOP. I said I believed a boat-building company in the USA had implemented it. That was not enough; boat-building was a very different industry. Submarines were a lot more complicated, as they involved building cramped spaces that would survive underwater.

Besides, the USA was far away, and they would like to see it operate in a company nearby. When I explained that submarine manufacture was not something that operated in every town because of the nature of the product, and the demand for it, they were convinced it would not work.

Fortunately, when they discovered it was just common-sense, they went ahead and implemented it. But the first step is always the same – "show me somewhere where it works."

The Knowledge dimension covers how well people within the company understand the need for change and understand what people need to do to make the change.

Some people, particularly those that have been in the company for twenty or more years, are well aware of the changes that need to happen. When you start to talk about getting rid of chaos and firefighting, they know that the processes within the business will have to change. It is just that: "that is the way we have always worked here."

So, when you look around the company, there will be a mixture of those who are highly enthusiastic, and those who are positively unenthusiastic about change.

There will be those who are highly knowledgeable about what is required, and those who do not know.

When you combine these elements, illustrated in Figure 88, you find the following "characters" and attitudes amongst the people in the company.

Figure 88: Who resists change and its impact

		ENTHUSIASM	
		Low	High
KNOWLEDGE	Low	WEAK LINKS	LOOSE CANONS
	High	BLOCKERS	AGENTS OF CHANGE

Thus, those who are not very enthusiastic about change, and also do not understand the need for change, we describe as **"weak links"**. It will be very difficult to persuade them to change.

There will be some who are very keen to change but who do not have a knowledgeable grasp of what needs to change. These people are **"loose canons"**. Explain to them what the change means, and they go, "Yes, that would be great." But nothing progresses.

I once did a workshop with one senior team, which was great fun. When I got to this part of the workshop, one of the directors stopped me and said: "Before you say anything, I think you are referring to us!" We laughed that laugh that recognises the truth.

The most challenging group to change are those who, when they understand what needs to change, understand perfectly well what is involved. But they prefer the "games" they play currently, and do not want to make changes which might threaten themselves and their careers. They are the **"blockers"**.

Sadly, blockers come in two varieties. Some are open about the fact they want to block progress, and then there are those who are not open – and work "underground" to make the project not happen. Sometimes these are senior, and that is where the CEO needs to lead this project.

Lastly, there are those (usually few) people who not only understand the need for change and what is involved but also end up being passionate about making the change happen. I was one of those. Since then, I have met many more who have ended up as **"agents of change"** and suffered the same problems which I saw in overcoming the barriers of the minds that put "walls" in the way of progress.

The task in making IBP happen is to increase the numbers of "agents of change". You achieve this by persuading some of the "loose cannons" (sometimes the senior executive team) to change. The more people you change, the easier it becomes to change the minds of the "blockers".

The key to the change is to increase knowledge, which often increases enthusiasm. However, to get the change to happen,

I have used a framework which is a proven methodology for making IBP happen.

The proven steps for change are as follows:

1. Executive Briefing

The first step is to get the senior leadership team up to speed with the basic concepts.

An introductory presentation on this will help them either to decide it is not for them, or to decide it is the thing to do. It always takes a while to get what John Kotter calls the "guiding coalition" together, so the quicker this happens, the better. This presentation takes a half day, and must be to the whole senior team. If the CEO says he or she is too busy, then definitely don't go ahead.

The presentation will cover an outline of the main features and benefits of IBP, covering a summary of what you find in this book. The second half will cover the approach to implementation, so the team knows to what they are signing up.

The outcome will either be a decision to stop there or a commitment to go the next step.

2. Assessment of Current State

If the Executive Briefing persuaded the senior team (or sometimes as a prelude to persuading them), then it is always useful to carry out an assessment. This activity will complete a review of the current processes, systems and culture, which cover what I have described as Integrated Business Planning. It will identify the scope of what you need to do.

It will also set out a draft timescale, and probable costs and benefits of the implementation of IBP for your organisation. This analysis is a vital part of the process.

The project needs to rank high on the list of projects for the company. I have developed an assessment document which supports this process explicitly; it covers all the areas covered in this book. It grades the company on a scale of "Bronze" to "Platinum". The assessment will involve detailed interviews of the people involved in the current ways of working, and it usually takes between two to five days per site, depending on the size and complexity of the business.

The Oliver Wight company also has a very useful "Class A checklist", which they have developed over the last fifty years into a very comprehensive book. It describes all aspects of a company, and how you can determine best-in-class performance (Oliver Wight, 8 May 2017). Their partners will carry out an in-depth review, based on years of experience in this area. "Class A" is a stage in the development of an organisation towards true world-class business excellence.

This assessment will provide your company with an open and honest critique of your performance, with a clear road-map of how you can build on what is good today, and make tomorrow excellent.

3. Senior Team Education

The next step is to carry out an in-house education workshop with the senior team and senior managers. Many managers are reluctant to engage in education; it sounds like going back to school. There is also a determination to keep on running the business.

It is vital at this stage that all of the senior managers hear the same message, and debate and discuss the relevance to their company at the same time.

Therefore the workshop has two objectives.

Firstly, the instructor will explain all the parts that this book contains and covers, which enables the team to understand the changes they will need to make in the systems, processes and behaviours. The intent is to ensure that managers see that they need to make a significant culture change happen to implement the principles of IBP.

It is not just the system: people need to change.

Secondly, more importantly, it allows the people involved to begin to design the process that will work for them. All companies are uniquely different. There is no "one-size-fits-all" approach. All humans need clothes to wear. To make clothes fit, you have to put together the right sizes, colours, and shapes to work for you. A good tailor will help you look much better.

During the workshop, you will put together a template of how it all works.

I remember organising a two-day workshop for a company. It was due to happen at the beginning of the year. I was away on holiday for the New Year period and got an email from the project leader to say that the managing director and the sales director could not attend day two.

Although I was on holiday, I quickly sent back an email saying it was essential that they attend, because their presence was crucial. During the second day, they were always discussing the process, how it would work, and saying how essential it all was. It is this design step that gets the right people on board.

As people see what it covers and why it will work, they always develop a massive enthusiasm for the concepts, and so it enables the "Enthusiasm" dimension of the change program. The "knowledge" of education leads to the "enthusiasm" to propel action.

4. Cost/Benefit Analysis

Nobody ever wants to go down any route like this without understanding the costs and benefits of doing this project. There can be a significant investment in systems, as well as the time of people in the project.

So the next step needs to look at the total costs, which will include costs of systems, project team and education and training, and indeed the benefits of implementation of IBP.

There is a fair amount of published information on the specific benefits that people gain from the implementation of IBP.

In particular, Chris Gray and John Dougherty put together a great book which documents the real benefits companies got from their implementations (Gray & Dougherty, Sales and Operations Planning - Best practices, 2006). It builds on a series of case studies of specific clients, using actual figures to support their review of benefits. It also includes invaluable anecdotal statements from the companies involved.

I have analysed the results across these case studies and other companies, and found benefits come from a revenue increase of between 2% to 5%, raw material cost decreases of around 3% to 5%, overhead reductions of between 2% to 5%, and inventory reductions of 40%.

The benefits apply to several parts of the Profit and Loss Account and Balance Sheet.

The interesting observation is that when you apply this to a typical company, the benefits work out at around 2% to 3% of total revenue. Thus if your sales revenue is £100m, the benefit in terms of profit will be around £2m to £3m per year. So if your net profit is about £10m, then this means a 20% to 30% increase at the bottom line. Naturally, I have seen many companies with a profit margin of less than 10%, who have benefitted even more.

Also, there will be an important freeing up of cash, from inventory reduction, enabling investment in other projects without having to go to shareholders or banks.

It is also essential to work out the cost of delay, as many companies often take a lot longer than they should with these projects.

Companies delay projects because of several "urgent" issues. These issues are always to do with the fires that are burning today, which IBP will extinguish in the future. But while we enjoy chaos and firefighting, it is tough to give up the "fun" of today for the organisation of the future.

The monthly "opportunity cost" of delay is the annual benefit of the IBP project divided by 12. So if the benefit will be £2.4m per annum, then the cost of delay is £200,000 per month.

This analysis means that every month you delay the project for whatever reason, then the company is throwing away that amount of money. A dramatic gesture would be to put 20,000 £10 notes on a fire and burn them! It is sad how many companies do not fully understand the time-value of money. It is often the simple lack of education, which leads to knowledge and enthusiasm, that causes the delay.

The outcome of this step will be a formal document which is like any other capital expenditure proposal for investment in the project. Of course, it will require proper assumptions to support the document, and the outcomes will not be sure.

But it will ensure that the company gives the right level of attention and urgency to the project.

5. Establish the Project Team Structure

The next step is to establish a Project Team structure, which is lead by the CEO and the senior team.

The typical structure which I have seen companies use, and which works is illustrated in Figure 89.

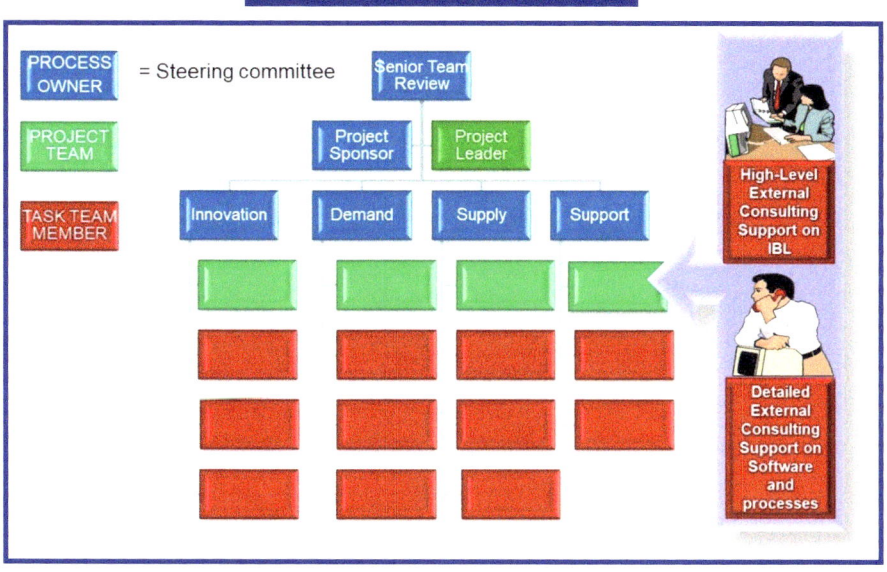

Figure 89: Project Structure

The "Blue team" is the leadership team, which includes the "process step owners" leading the development of each the process steps. These process step owners should come from the senior team.

The CEO should guide the development of the Senior Team review. There is then a need for a **project leader**, who should be an "Agent for Change" and who has the universal respect of the rest of the senior team to "get things done".

They should understand the business, want the company to change, and have the guts and determination to get the change to happen. The best description of the right person is a "bulldozer with tact"!

I have worked with many project leaders over time, and have come to recognise that the choice of the project leader is unbelievably critical. Often CEOs want to allocate the role to someone relatively junior.

The company wants its key managers to carry on running the business. A good test of the right person is that if people are not prepared to free a person up, then it is likely that this person is the one to lead the project.

Sometimes, I have seen companies want to recruit someone from outside the organisation. I have indeed worked in situations where the CEO has recruited someone from outside. It usually does not work well, as the outsider has to understand the products, and more importantly, the people. Where resistance to change is rife, then the words "you do not understand our business" quickly come to the doubter's lips, and change does not happen.

Sometimes CEOs attempt to put this type of project into the hands of the people responsible for the IT and business systems. They think it is a systems project. However, it is not a systems project. It needs someone who fully understands the way the business runs, and the interpersonal issues that are behind the problems that IBP resolves. Giving the project to the IT manager does not convey the right message, even if the IT person is well aware of the issues; they will continually state that the people in the business needs to change, and not the systems.

You also need a **project sponsor** from the leadership team, who ideally is the CEO, or someone very close to the CEO. One client had a CEO who was very frustrated with the way things worked in his company. He had two manufacturing sites.

The current supply chain director had been the finance director, who had been involved in the implementation of "SOP" around five years previously (he had been a bit of a blocker then, but got converted!). The CEO turned to him to be the sponsor, and he was fantastic at facilitating the development of the project, and if he had any problems, could always talk to the CEO to help make things happen, which he needed to do on several occasions.

The best projects I have seen have always been the ones in which the CEO provides clear, unequivocal support for the project, and will do whatever it takes to get the project to work.

One of the first projects I helped with was with a company where the CEO was one of those characters who was impatient to make things happen and was continually pushing people. He was a very dynamic character. He had seen the business lose some critical contracts, and when he understood what "business excellence" and IBP meant, became desperate to make it happen. He was also operating on wafer-thin margins.

One day he learnt that his manufacturing director had been saying to people that he did not think this project would work. He was a typical "blocker". When the CEO heard about this, it was not long before the manufacturing director was looking for a new career opportunity. This outcome was an extreme solution. But sometimes it is needed.

The "Green team" are the **project team,** who are senior managers and very experienced in the business.

One client invited me in one day to discuss with the CEO how IBP worked. They were implementing an ERP system and were going through the required developments to change the system.

However, during the initial discussion, it was clear that they were not addressing the issues that I have addressed in this book, under the heading of "Integrated Business Leadership".

They were not dealing with performance measurement and critical business processes.

They had the classic "divergence of views" between the factories and sales and marketing. Manufacturing blamed forecasts for being inaccurate.

In parallel, they had a board member developing the business strategy, which was a new event for them. They were putting together the long-term plan. The CEO knew they needed to transform the business. The CEO then appointed them to be the sponsor of the project, which was perfect as they could then develop IBP as the means for executing the strategy. They were also clear on the need for a proper communications strategy.

They then decided to appoint the factory manager of their biggest factory in the group to lead the project. It was a risk to take him out of that role for a while, but they chose him because he is a great project manager.

They then appointed two product managers to represent the two different business units, the purchasing manager to represent supply, and a finance manager to represent the finance team.

This group quickly formed into a brilliant team, and together they came up with a great model of how the business would operate IBP. It would not have worked if the CEO had not seen the value of the project, and was 100% behind the project sponsor and project leader. With that level of enthusiasm, they completed the IBP element of the project within five to six months, which became an excellent platform for ERP development.

6. Future Blueprint

The task for the project team is to develop the "blueprint" for the operation of IBP in the company. This document will describe how to deploy the concepts contained within this book.

It should have sections which describe the Vision and Strategy, and then the roles and responsibilities, policies, procedures and measures for each of the steps of the process, leading up to the

Senior Team review. Thus it makes sense to have a section for Innovation, Demand, Supply, Finance, Human Resources, IT and the Senior Team review.

It will describe today's operating practices, and then provide an outline of the future desired ways of working. The purpose of the document is to be able to take it to the senior team so they can sign off that this will be the way the company will work in the future.

Within this step, it is essential to develop a software solution to support the process.

This solution should include an ERP system for day-to-day business transactions, a forecasting system (either specialised or integrated with the ERP system), a project management system, and perhaps a Customer Relationship Management (CRM) system for management of sales opportunities, prospects and current relationships.

This software solution, as indicated earlier, could be based on the current ERP system, or you may require some additional software solutions to support the new ways of working. While much of what I have discussed in the context of IBP can operate within spreadsheets, it is best if you replace these with more robust systems.

There will likely be a need for a reporting system to provide financial reports, and then all of this will feed the monthly reporting process (using PowerPoint or similar slides as little or as much as possible). It is still the case that most ERP systems do not have reports as a standard which support the IBP process.

Fortunately, there are several business information systems which you can acquire, which will report in the ways described in this book. Thus, you will be able to compare last month's plan with this month's plan, sliced and diced by family, region, and business unit as required.

Over the years, I have seen several ways that companies have approached this stage, and there is a standard generic blueprint for it. You will not be able to cut and paste your name into the document and then claim it as your own; every company is different.

It covers an outline description of the process, the responsibilities, the meeting steps and who attends etc., and represents a great start down the road.

7. Education

A critical input into this stage of the process will be detailed education on the principles that underly each step. This education will help the project team and the members of the process development teams (the Green and Red teams), to flesh out the detail of the operating practices.

Thus, for example, sales forecasting and demand management need the development of assumptions, a formal weekly or monthly process, and then demand control to make it all work effectively.

A workshop on sales forecasting and demand management will ensure the team all develop a comprehensive, robust process to support this area.

The output of this step will be a comprehensive document that will enable you to implement new ways of working. Before you build a house or a kitchen, then the architect's drawings and the specification of the materials provide the basis for the next step. This "blueprint" stage fulfils a similar function.

8. Initial Pilot

Once you have completed this document, it is time to carry out a pilot of the process. Thus, it is excellent to get the senior team, senior managers and the project team together into a room and run the cycle through a couple of times using representative data.

With one client, they had an HQ in the UK. They had factories in China, France and the USA. Their sales regions are in the Far East, Middle East and Africa, and the Americas.

So the process involved product development globally and within the regions. Each of the sales regions would develop their forecasts. Those forecasts then fed the Supply plans in each of the plants, which had their local ERP systems. The challenge was to bring this all together into one way of operating.

So they brought their managers together from China, USA, France and UK to a hotel in Manchester Airport.

We set up tables for the factories – China, France and the USA. We had tables for the markets – Asia, Europe Middle East, and Americas.

We started the session off with a description of the whole process.

There was a central table for the head of IBP. There were tables for each of the sales regions, and each of the factories.

Using representative data for existing and new products, we then simulated the new process.

So, we ran through a cycle of Innovation, Demand Review, Supply Review and Finance before having a Senior Team review. Everyone could then see how each step of the process fed the next step.

They could see the need for realistic numbers, and along the way, the project team and the senior management team reinforced the need for new behaviours.

Everyone went away more knowledgeable and enthusiastic about the process they were about to adopt. The teams could see that they were going to do what the business needed to do, in a common-sense, organised way.

They then got sign-off for full development of the process.

9. Developing the Detail

So far, we have got the overall blueprint of the process. We then need to get the details of the process worked out. The extent of the work required here depends on the current quality of the ERP transactional systems, the processes and the measures. It depends on the extent to which the company needs to change these.

Assuming that the current situation is imperfect, then it is essential to set up cross-functional process teams to work out and document the detail required to support the processes.

This is the stage where the "red teams" come in. These task teams will take the blueprint and work out the details required, which will cover, for instance:

- Definition of families
- Horizons
- Time fences
- Detailed responsibilities
- Performance measures
- Definitions of abnormal demand, etc.

This activity will then lead to a description of all of the business processes.

There are several software solutions which will support the formal documentation of business processes, to align with the IBP process. The International Standards Organisation (ISO) has created several standard documents which provide excellent guidance in support of companies developing their quality systems. Within this, there is a standard for companies to adopt in the area of Business Process Management and quality – ISO 9001:2015.

The structure of the business standard relates very well to the concepts behind Integrated Business Leadership, and both complement each other. Business process ownership and measurement are core to the ISO approach and Integrated Business Leadership.

If your organisation has not adopted ISO 9001:2015, then you should seriously consider doing it.

I had a client who did an excellent job of this. They bought some software which you could use to create a description of business processes, describing responsibilities, procedures and measures.

You can access an overall process model on the screen, and then click through to the underlying detail, as you want. The lowest level of detail comprised the detailed operating instructions for that part of the business.

As they were implementing IBP, the highest level of their model represented the model described in the book. So it showed Vision and Strategy, Innovation, Demand Planning, Supply Planning, and so on.

The system allowed them to click on Demand Planning and that in turn allowed them to access a process map which described customer relationship management, bid management, and forecasting. From there, you could click into the detailed policies and processes that supported each of these areas.

This solution not only enabled them to qualify for ISO 9001:2015 but also allowed them to run the company. Approximately three years later, they restructured the organisation into a different type of structure, which they built around several business units.

They managed to replicate the new structure within their quality system quickly, and hence succeeded in adapting their business procedures very quickly, to suit the new organisation.

10. Training

All of this could involve brand new ways of working, and hence there is a need to develop educational and training material.

These teams will also prepare this material. This step is a critical area, as often companies have informal ways of working and informal training methods. They assume that the people there today will always be there.

So when new people do join, there is a complete lack of a formal way of training people in how the Integrated Business Planning process works. Even worse, there is no explicit training material to explain to the joiner how to do their job.

Pilots who fly planes go through a rigorous training process on how to use aeroplanes. When people first get into a car, there is a standard requirement for receiving training in how to drive a car. This training includes learning the Highway Code in the UK (which you could describe as the policies and procedures).

You then learn, with a driving instructor, how to accelerate, brake, reverse, and so on. Eventually, you have to pass a driving test. That allows you to get a driving license.

Sadly, I have seen so many companies where they have not adopted this kind of approach to training such vital roles.

It seems to me that companies think anyone can plan and manage the demand and supply chains, without any proper education and training, or detailed training in the business processes.

11. Roll-out the Process – Education and Training

The next step, therefore, should be to roll out the process across the business.

The critical element is to change the behaviour of the business. Hence, this step requires the company to roll out the education and training program to the whole company, to help people see how the process works and then perform their functions effectively.

Thus, when the person in Customer Services receives an order, they will know to check whether the order is forecast. They will then know to call the master scheduler and account manager to discuss what to do if it is un-forecast.

There are two parts to this step: the first is "Education" and the second is "Training".

I have talked about the fact that salespeople, for instance, must get away from under-forecasting. Their psyche incorporates this today; it is key to how they behave. To get away from this behaviour, they will need what I call "Education". Their mindset will change.

Separately, they may need to learn how to use a new forecasting system and the process that goes with this. Learning to use the new system will require "training". It is a subtle but essential difference.

Education is about getting people to have an answer to the question "why?"

Thus (and it starts in childhood!) when you face people with a change, they will want to know why they should change.

When you are trying to persuade anyone of doing anything, you will need to convince them that it will do something positive for them. Simon Sinek's approach to "start with 'why'" is a brilliant explanation of this approach (Sinek, 2011). You have to get to the inner workings of the mind to persuade someone to do something different.

Education is much like selling. Selling is always about outlining the benefits of a product or a service, and not the features.

A new car may have lots of features in it like Sat Nav, electrically heated seats, rain-sensitive windscreen wipers; but if the customer does not feel that they need or want these, then they will not buy the car with the features.

People also look to their superiors for guidance on what they should do and when. External consultants cannot and should not provide this training.

The members of the green team should therefore carry out the education, supported by the members of the blue team (directors), in a series of sessions to stretch over the whole company.

Figure 90 describes the specific structure of these sessions.

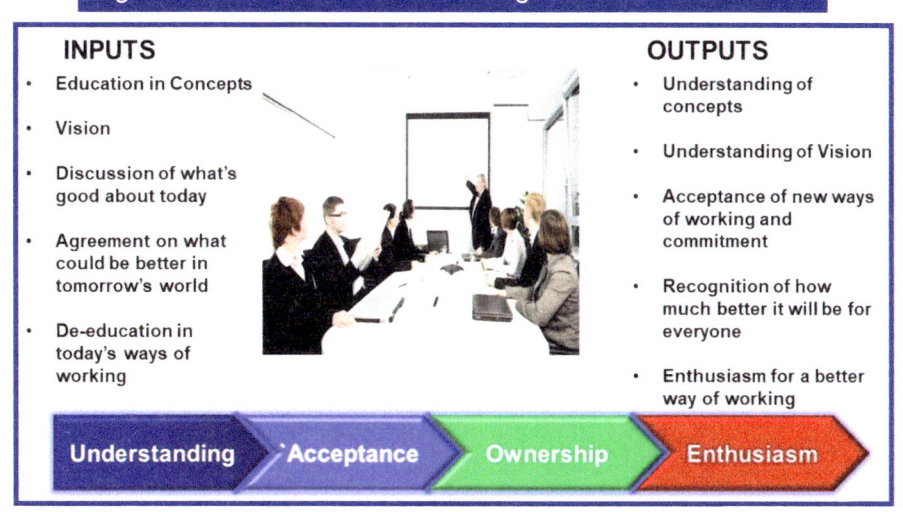

Figure 90: Education and training in conference rooms

INPUTS
- Education in Concepts
- Vision
- Discussion of what's good about today
- Agreement on what could be better in tomorrow's world
- De-education in today's ways of working

OUTPUTS
- Understanding of concepts
- Understanding of Vision
- Acceptance of new ways of working and commitment
- Recognition of how much better it will be for everyone
- Enthusiasm for a better way of working

Understanding → Acceptance → Ownership → Enthusiasm

You will take people through a "journey" within these education sessions, where they will first understand the principles.

Let us say that one principle within sales forecasting is that the concept will be that Sales will be accountable for the forecast. The salespeople will then see how the sales forecast will drive the Sales plan, and ensure that the supply side will respond to what they want to sell. This step will lead to the acceptance of the principle.

Once the salespeople have accepted the principle, then they can recognise that the new ways of working will enable them to achieve the business objective of delivering to the customer what they want and when they want it. That will lead to ownership.

In the session, they may well recognise situations where they have been under challenging conditions with customers when the company has failed to deliver.

They will learn that the Performance Measurement process is not about finding fault, but about improving the process.

At the end of the meeting(s) they will appreciate that it will make their job fundamentally easier, and more personally fulfilling, and at that point, they will become enthusiastic about the new ways of working. The education may not work exactly like that, but hopefully this illustrates the stages that people go through when on a journey of change.

The diagram above shows how education must demonstrate the vision of the future, leading to an agreement about what will be better in tomorrow's world, leading to that enthusiasm.

Structure of the Training

This should be structured around a program which reflects the chapters of this book:

Vision and Strategy

Innovation

Demand

Supply

Finance/IT

Human Resources

Senior Team Review

The trainers will deliver to each of the people in each department the education and training which is specific to their area, in appropriate detail.

But everyone will need training in all areas of the business so they can appreciate how the whole process will work.

Thus, the people in the Product Development department will need training, for instance, in the detail of how the development process, project management, and performance measurement will work. You will need to train them, if appropriate, in the mechanics of using a project management system. This activity is detailed training.

They will interact with the Sales Forecasting and the Supply Planning process. Thus, you will need to ensure that they understand at an appropriate level, the differences that will occur in these areas.

The content of the education and training will cover:

Roles/responsibilities

Policies/procedures

Software

Behaviour

Performance Measures

This whole area is core to the success of the process, and you will require a clear education plan to make sure the project is a success. This is how we take people from a position of not understanding what the process is about, to becoming enthusiastic about the new ways of working. As people begin to see the process operate, and understand what difference it can make to their daily lives, they will buy into the process.

People only buy into something when they see and understand "what is in it for them". It is human nature.

- **Changing the Rules Needs Leadership**

Hopefully, you can now see the prerequisite for the success of implementing IBP is leadership, and why throughout this book, I have emphasised the use of the word "leadership".

This is because, in all of the clients where I have seen the process work, it has been the CEO or general manager who has made the difference.

Shortly after I left ICI Agrochemicals and entered into a brave new world of helping people implement SOP/IBP, I got a call from a friend to visit the site of a company in south Wales.

They also were implementing a new ERP system, so the project was about changing the whole site. But without the CEO's burning enthusiasm for the project, it would have been tough to make things happen. Their logistics manager was a very persistent and patient project manager.

Shortly after they went live, a customer phoned the sales director, saying he had asked for delivery of a product within two days. The customer services person had stated that they could only do it in four weeks from receipt of order.

The air had gone blue!

The sales director flew down to the logistics manager's office and asked why was the product not instantly available?

The logistics manager walked over to a screen and asked: "Is the product Make to Order or Make to Stock?"

When they both looked at the screen, there was an "O" against the field labelled "Service Policy". That was a field that the project team had set up, although it was not standard; it meant it was Make to Order.

The logistics manager then asked the sales director, "What is the quoted lead time on the product?" He said, "four weeks." (You could also see that on the screen.)

"Is there a way we could have been able to deliver quicker?" asked the logistics manager.

"Yes," said the sales director, "if there had been a forecast for it."

"Was there a forecast for it?" asked the logistics manager.

"No," said the sales director.

It was then that the sales director said, somewhat unusually in my experience, "I am sorry to have bothered you. I will go back and explain the situation to the customer."

"Sorry" was not a word understood by the previous sales director. In this company, the finance director had taken over the sales director's role, and he understood the processes well. He had been a key part of the IBP/ERP implementation.

They saw significant benefits from their project.

Commitment from the top meant that the business got the benefits that they wanted. Without the original vision and leadership from the CEO, none of it would have been possible.

In the ACE project, of which I was a part, we had a consultant who came in regularly, who was well known for "telling it as it is".

The senior team had a "SOP" meeting one afternoon.

At the end of the meeting, the chairman turned to our consultant and said, "What did you think of the meeting?"

Without a moment's hesitation, the consultant replied: "I thought you were a lousy chairman".

You can imagine the reaction to that. The meeting stopped. The chairman asked the consultant to come to his room and explain.

The consultant explained: "Somewhere during the meeting, the marketing director turned round to the operations director and said, 'We have a great opportunity to sell a large amount in the Far East; will operations be able to support that?' Then the operations director said, 'Yes!'"

"What was wrong with that?" said the chairman.

Our consultant said, "It would have been more useful if the marketing director had given details on what was needed, when, and how much – i.e. a forecast," said the consultant.

"Oh!" said the chairman. "I did not think we needed detail, as we were being strategic! You had better go and explain all this to the marketing director".

Somewhat relieved that it was the marketing director's fault, the chairman escorted the consultant to the marketing director's huge office and explained all of the above.

All was well, after an hour or so!

Three months later, the consultant came back and sat in at the same SOP meeting. The marketing director went through each of the markets, stating the key volumes, values, profitability, etc. etc.

It was a fantastic display of all the facts for each of the markets he covered.

He was a director who was brilliant with numbers. His negotiating ability was astounding.

At the end of the meeting, the consultant said to the marketing director: "That was fantastic! I have never seen anyone provide such a detailed presentation; it must have taken you ages to get that together."

"Nonsense," said the marketing director. "I always know this stuff. It is how I do my job."

"What has changed, then?" said the consultant.

"The only thing that has changed is you got the CEO to change the rules of the game."

In many ways, IBP is about changing the rules of the game and making sure people follow the new rules. If today's rules mean you do not behave correctly, then you need to change the rules.

But in doing so, we know that humans respond to the way that their superiors guide them, treat them and measure them. That is why the implementation must focus on human behaviour and not just the systems and processes.

If you do not change behaviour, then you may have new systems and new ways of working, but you are likely to get the same old results.

Ultimately, the success of SOP or IBP rests entirely on the quality of the leadership, and hence I have called it "Integrated Business Leadership".

Leadership is about creating the vision and strategy, and taking a business in the direction that it needs to go. The company will only execute the vision and strategy effectively if the people in the company work with one set of numbers, with standard ways of working, with one system. Leadership, Planning and Execution are the elements that go together to make the successful company.

Getting to that state from your current environment, which you might describe as chaos, firefighting and confusion, requires education – changing people's mindsets.

All of this approach will help you compete better, improve profitability, and deliver to your customers and shareholders what they want. It is what I saw ICI Agrochemicals do, read about in countless books and articles, and have helped many companies do.

I hope this gives you some of the knowledge and enthusiasm to implement these ideas in your business and make a fantastic success for you, your people, and your shareholders.

Bibliography

Adams, D. (1994). *The Hitchhiker's Guide to the Galaxy.* London: Weidenfeld & Nicolson.

Bogsnes, B. (2008). *Implementing Beyond Budgeting.* New York: John Wiley & Sons.

Brealey, R., Myers, S., & Allen, F. (2010). *Principles of Corporate Finance.* Asia: McGraw Hill.

Cotter, J. (1996). *Leading Change.* Boston: Harvard Business School Press.

Daniels, A. (2016). *Bringing Out the Best in People.* McGraw-Hill Education.

Ehrenburg, A. (1975). *Data Reduction.* London: John Wiley and Son.

Goddard, W., & Ling, R. (1988). *Orchestrating Success.* Essex Junction: Oliver Wight Publications Ltd.

Goldratt, E. M. (2004). *The Goal: A Process of Ongoing Improvement.* Routledge.

Gray, C. (2007). *Sales and Operations Planning Standard System.* Victoria, BC: Trafford Publishing.

Gray, C. (2008). *Lean Standard System.* Victoria: Trafford Publishing.

Gray, C., & Dougherty, J. (2006). *Sales and Operations Planning - Best practises.* Virginia BC: Trafford Publishing.

Harvey, J. B. (1974: Volume 3, Issue 1. Pages 63-80). *The Abilene paradox: Management of Agreement.* Elsevier: Organisational Dynamics.

Johnson, D. S. (1999). *Who Moved My Cheese?* Vermilion.

Kaplan, R., & Norton, D. (2001). *The Strategy-Focused Organisation.* Boston: Harvard Business School.

Kotter, J., & Ratherberger, H. (2006). *Our Iceberg is Melting.* Macmillan: London.

Makridakis, S., Wheelwright, S., & Hyndman, R. (1998). *Forecasting Methods and Applications.* Hoboken: John Wiley and Sons.

Bibliography

Martin, A. (9 May 2006). *Flowcasting the Retail Supply Chain.* New York: John Wiley and Sons Inc.

Martin, A. J. (1995). *DRP: Distribution Resource Planning : The Gateway to True Quick Response and Continuous Replenishment.* New York: John Wiley & Sons Inc.

Maskell, B. (2004). *Practical Lean Accounting.* New York: Productivity Press.

Mikel Harry, P. a. (2000). *Six Sigma - the Breakthrough Management Strategy.* New York: Doubleday.

Mortimer, I. (2017). *The Time Traveller's Guide to Restoration Britain.* London: Penguin Random House.

Oliver Wight. (8 May 2017). *Class A Standard for Business Excellence.* Wiley.

Peters, S. (2012). *The Chimp Paradox: The Mind Management Programme to Help You Achieve Success, Confidence and Happiness.* Vermilion.

Porter, M. (1979). How Competitive Forces Shape Strategy. *Harvard Business Review*, 8.

Robinson, P. (2006). *Business Excellence.* Hove: BPIC Business Performance Improvement Consultancy.

Sinek, S. (2011). *Start With Why: How Great Leaders Inspire Everyone To Take Action.* London: Penguin.

Slack, N., Chambers, S., & Johnson, R. (1995). *Operations Management.* Harlow: Pearson Education Limited.

Slack, N., Chambers, S., & Johnston, R. (2004). *Operations Management.* Harlow: Pearson Education Limited.

Treacey, M., & Wiersema, F. (1997). *Discipline of Market Leaders.* Basic Books.

Watkins, R., & Clarke, R. (2003). *The Chief Executive's Guide to Performance Measurement.* Ipswich: The Delos Partnership Ltd.

Author biography

Richard Watkins

Richard was part of a team in ICI Agrochemicals (now Syngenta) which implemented 'MRP II' and achieved Class 'A' across the world. The team improved customer service to >98% and reduced inventory by 27%. They implemented the first Global Sales and Operations Planning process. Syngenta, was a merger that absorbed the original ICI Agrochemicals still operates the same process today.

Since 1991, Richard has worked with Mike Salmon's MRP Ltd (1991-1998) and then Oliver Wight (1998-2002), providing external courses and internal workshops in best-in-class planning, performance measurement, and ERP implementation. He founded Delos in 2002 to provide a tailored and customer-focused approach.

He has worked with many companies, in diverse industries from engineering, through chemicals to Fast Moving Consumer Goods, and from very large to very small. He is passionate about helping people to get away from the frustration of firefighting to a more ordered world of integrated business systems, processes and, above all, people. This experience and approach results in much more competitive and profitable organisations.

He has worked with boards of companies, down to the shop floor, helping them develop Business Excellence. The approach is practical, and the education is direct and easily understood.

He educates in Integrated Business Leadership, Sales Forecasting, Supply Chain Management, Performance Measurement, Data Accuracy and ERP Implementation; all critical parts of the Integrated Business Leadership model.

Author biography

He has an MBA from London Business School, where he specialised in Operations, Marketing and Finance, and a BA and MA from Christ Church Oxford in Philosophy, Politics and Economics. Before that, he studied Latin, Greek, Ancient History and Russian. He has also learnt Swahili and French. He appreciates the value of having a common language. All contributed to an understanding of the logic and illogicality of human behaviour.

Integrated Business Leadership

INDEX

A

A-class items	78
ABCD analysis	77
Abilene Paradox	126, 382
Absolute Difference	163
Adams	55, 382
Adams, Douglas	xii, 55
Adaptive SOP	261
Additional Lean Measures	271
Africa	93, 185, 370
Agent for Change	366
Aggregate Production plan	227
Agrochemicals	xi, 33, 38, 44, 91, 182, 209, 252, 377, 381, 384
Alice	326-7
Amazon	64, 140
Amazon Prime	ix, 64
Analytical types	302
Annual Business Planning processes	43
Annual Operating Plan	106
Apple Inc	327
Application and implementation of Integrated Business Leadership	296
Application of Assumptions	177
Applying measures	105
Aquapure	58
Assemble-to-Order	84
Assemble to Order and Make to Order	238
ATO	67
Aubrey Daniels criteria	287
Availability of equipment	263
Available to Promise calculation	206
Available to Promise line	197
average CLT	172

B

Babylonians	263, 342
Baggaley, Bruce	283
Baker, Brian	55
Bank debt	278
company finances	278
Banyan tree	316
Barker, Joel A.	354
Behaviour and Thinking	301
Bell Telephone	328
benefits of implementation of IBP	363
Bennis, Warren	329
Berkshire Hathaway	215
Biased Forecasts	169
Big Hairy Audacious Goals	36
Bill	151, 153, 171, 237, 244, 275
accurate	280
Bill Of Material	236
Bjarte Bogsnes	286
Blue Pens	153
BMI (Body Mass Index)	292
BMW	64
Board Agenda	325
Bohr, Nils	133
Boston	382
Box Score	293-4
BPIC Business Performance Improvement Consultancy	383
Bradford Factor	307
Breakthrough Management Strategy	383
Brealey	278, 382
British-Canadian poet	192
British economist Terry Burns	176
Bronze	361
Bruce Baggaley's book	285, 293
Buckingham, Marcus	100
Buckminster Fuller	46
Budget Example	27
Budgetary Performance Measurement process	288
Budgeting	286, 382
beyond	286
Budgeting Institute	286
Buffett, Warren	215
Business Excellence	261, 367, 383-4
true world-class business planning	362
collaborative Integrated	213
implemented Integrated	241
implementing Integrated	186
Business Process Management	13
Business process ownership and measurement	372
Business Unit Review meeting	321

C

Calculation of Bias	170
Calculation of Economic Batch Quantity	217

Capacity and Operating Equipment Effectiveness	265	Cost and Schedule Index	347
Capacity-Based Forecasting	155	Cost/Benefit Analysis	363
Capacity Requirements Planning (CRP)	49, 223	Cost Schedule Control	128
Capital Employed	28, 277, 290	Cotter, John	56
Capital Equipment Expenditure Case	285	Covey, Stephen	314
Capture Actual	156	Covid-19	156, 326
Carroll, Lewis	326	the cremation of Sam McGee	192
Cars, Morgan	64	Cretaceous eras	224
Cash Flow Forecast	53	Critical resources and requirements	226
CDs, making	337	CRM (Customer Relationship Management)	148, 312, 369, 373
CEO	ix, xi, 12, 25-8, 30-1, 61, 78, 106, 209, 305-6, 347-8, 360-1, 365-8, 377, 379-80	CRM Pipeline	148
CEO and Coach	100	CRM system	148-9
CEO manages performance	30	Crosby	262
CEO Nike Inc	208	CRP (Capacity Requirements Planning)	49, 223
CEO of Microsoft	311	CRP system	234
CEO of Mobil	55	Cumulative Lead Time (CLT)	49-50, 65-6, 70, 84, 134, 136, 171-2, 203, 206, 235, 238
CEO of Zappos	191	customer ABC	340
CEOs and boards of directors	279	Customer Policy Date	193
CEO's burning enthusiasm	378	Customer Promise Date	193
CEO's Guide	291	Customer Relationship Management (CRM)	148, 312, 369, 373
CEOs hate variance	100	Customer Service Factor Table	75
CEOs love processes	100	Cyhalothrin	62-3
Chambers	77, 383		
Changing behaviour	24	**D**	
Charles Lutwidge Dodgson	326		
Cheese	357, 382	Dancers	132
Chemical companies	93	Daniels, Aubrey	287
Cheshire Cat	326	Darwin, Charles	57
Chief Executive's Guide	383	Data Accuracy	384
Chimp Paradox	24, 383	data for IBP	84
China	93, 332, 335, 370-1	Data Reduction	85, 382
Chinese government	335	DDMRP	261
Chris Gray's book Sales	80	DDMRP concept	134
Christian, David	345	Dean	326
Clarke, Rod	291	Dean, James	342
CLT see Cumulative Lead Time		Deciding Targets	77
Cold War	4	Decisions Required	323
Coldrick, Andy	46	Defensive functional behaviour	20
Commercial Plans	173	Definition of forecast	145
Common Measures	97	Definitions of abnormal demand	372
Competitive Forces Shape Strategy	383	Delivering/shipping	69
Competitiveness	187	Delos Model	33, 103
Conflicting Objectives	3	Demand Execution	34
Consistent performance measures	39	Demand in forecasting	141
Contemporary Amperex Technology Ltd	335	Demand Management	135, 183, 190-207, 370
Continuous Replenishment	383	formal	95
Corporate Finance	278, 382	Demand Plan Error	138
Correct data	17	Demand Planning and management	136

INDEX

Demand Planning process 138, 143, 181-2, 190, 240, 255
Demand review chart by Family 188
Demand Time Fence 200
Deming 262
design Bills 124
Detailed Capacity plan 223, 234
Detailed Capacity Planning process 298
Detailed Capacity Requirements Planning 223, 232
Detailed responsibilities 372
DIFOTP 192
DIFOTR 191-2
Digital Equipment Corporation 118
Direct Line Feed 269
Distribution of Demand 74
Distribution of height 72-3
Distribution Requirements Planning *see* DRP
Distribution Resources Planning 208, 383
DMAIC process 162
document RACI 143
DOTIFP 248-9
DOTIFR 248-9
Dougherty 382
Dougherty, John 363
Dried raspberries 58
DRP (Distribution Requirements Planning) 209-10, 212, 275, 383
DRP systems 209, 276
DVDs 337

E

Early industrial companies 304
earned Value 128-9
Earnings 28, 278, 297
Easter 30, 179
Eastern European world of manufacturing factories 243
EasyJet 336
Economic Value Add 279
Education and training in conference rooms 375
Effect of core measures on Profit 292
effective IBP process xii, 109, 158, 194, 346
Effective performance measures 132
Ehrenburg 85, 161, 382
Electronics sector 114
Eliyahu Goldratt 260
Elsevier 382

Emergenetics International 301
Emergenetics Wheel of Behaviour and Thinking 301
Engineer to Order 67
Engineering Management 101
English genealogist 176
engraver Gregory King 176
Entrepreneurial model 12
EOQ 216
EPE 271
ERP/business system 312
ERP development 368
ERP Implementation 240, 311, 384
ERP planning system 154
ERP system-type projects 130
ERP system work 240
ERP systems 16-17, 23, 59, 63, 191, 198, 204, 206, 251-2, 311-12, 354-6, 367, 369
  current 369
  effective 195
  implemented 311
  implementing 312
  local 370
  new x, 378
  sound 195, 223, 238
  standard 262
  transactional 356
ERP transactional systems 371
Eskdale 309
ETO 67
Exact documented changes in assumptions 289
Example of Abnormal Demand 203
Example of calculation of Earned Value 129
Excellent customer service 207
Executive Briefing 361
Executive Leadership 56
Executive Sales and Operations Planning xi
Extended Business Leadership 211
Extraordinary Project Management Ltd 115

F

Failure of Standard Costing 280
family ABC 163
family XYZ 163
Fast-Moving Consumer Goods 135
Fast Moving Consumer Goods (FMCG) 5, 66, 177, 384
featured Sir John Harvey-Jones 243
features and benefits of IBP 361
Fence Policy 238-9, 356
Fiedler, Edgar 135

Filter Demand	156
Finance Review	295
Finance Review meeting	295
Finance Review process step	294
Finance to attend	131
Financial Management	101
Firm Planned Orders	252
Fishbone analysis for Forecast Accuracy	165
Five Forces Model	331
Fixed Operating Expense	293
FMCG (Fast Moving Consumer Goods)	5, 66, 177, 384
FMCG, major international	343
FMCG Business	212
FMCG businesses	146, 164
FMCG companies	208
Food Processing	33
Football	39
Ford	2-3, 215, 335
Ford, Henry	2, 215, 242, 264, 328
Forecast Accuracy Target	167
Forecast/Demand Plan	144
Forecast Error and Bias	157
Forecast Roll	194, 198
Forecast Waterfall	172
Forecasting/Demand Planning	140
forecasting for IBP	173
Forecasting Methods	156, 382
framework of IBP	244
France	95, 160, 370-1
Frankfurt	ix
Frankfurt exhibition	113
Freedom of Movement of People	332
Freeze	171
Fujio Cho	262
Functional activities	338
Functional Organisation	6

G

Galaxy	55, 382
Garbage in	312
Gate process	116
Gateway activities	116
General Manager	239
George Bernard Shaw	1
Germany	95, 160
GIGO maxim, old	312
Global Financial Review	321
Global IBP process	210, 320, 346
Global Integrated Business Planning process	209
Global Sales and Operations Planning process	384
global VP	97
Goddard	382
Goddard & Ling	ix
Goddard, Walter E.	ix
Goldratt	260, 293, 382
Goldratt, Eli	269
Goldratt's Theory	261
Granada TV area	37
Graph of Required Capacity	230
Gray	80, 262-3, 382
Gray & Dougherty	363
Gray, Chris	262, 363
Great Leaders Inspire	383
Gregorian calendar	342

H

Happiness	383
Harlow	383
Harry, Mikel	164, 383
Harvard Business Review	331, 383
Harvard Business School	382
Harvard Business School Press	382
Harvard University	331
Harvey	126, 382
Harvey, Jerry B.	126
Harvey-Jones, John	324
Head of IBP	255, 319, 343, 348, 371
Head of Innovation/R&D	345
Henry Ford's Model T	334
Highway Code	373
Hitchhiker's Guide	55, 382
Hoboken	382
Holger Rathberger	357
Hospital	33
Human interface	85
Human remains department	9
Human Resource process	306
Human Resources Meeting	308
Hyndman	156, 382

I

IBL	xiii, 36, 143, 308, 325, 339, 353
IBL model	297, 352
IBM	110, 117-18, 132, 236
IBP (Integrated Business Planning)	x-xiv, 12-13, 32-3, 37-42, 54-7, 83-5, 94-6, 106-10, 204-7, 219-21, 240, 255, 262-3, 274, 278-9, 318-19, 350-1, 354-8, 361-4, 366-9

INDEX

IBP
  developed 181
  developing 87, 205
  establishing 11
  implemented 39, 51, 103
  implementing 256, 312, 355, 372, 377
  knit 46
  IBP element 368
  IBP/ERP implementation 378
  IBP family 269
  IBP implementations 249
  IBP Innovation process 125
  IBP Meeting 307, 346, 350
  IBP model 112
  IBP philosophy 84
  IBP plans 228, 309
  IBP process 37-8, 40-1, 80-1, 92, 99, 103-4, 107-8, 110, 125-6, 130-1, 135-8, 140, 257-8, 275-6, 293-9, 308-9, 312-13, 331, 340, 350
  good 91, 139
  IBP process development chart 108
  IBP process steps 345
  IBP project 23, 364
  IBP project leader 13, 309
  IBP project team 78
  IBP senior leadership
  team process 329
  IBP/SOP 25
  IBP/SOP process 313
  IBP team 77
Ideation 118
Impact of Perfect Order on ROCE 291
Impact on Functions 338
Impact on Measures 337
impact on ROCE 291
Imperial Chemical Industries 243
implementation, global IBP 260
implementing JIT 260
implementing MRP II 260, 278
implementing MRP systems 354
implementing SOP/IBP 313
Inadequate formal control 32
India 157, 316, 332
Information Resources 274, 310-13
Initial Pilot 370
Innovation/R&D 345
Innovation step 112, 114-15
Inspection 268
Integrated Business 23
Integrated Business Leadership x-386
Integrated Business Leadership approach 325, 332

Integrated Business Leadership process 295, 334
Integrated Business Model 34
Integrated Business Planning *see IBP*
Integrated Business Planning and leadership 351
Integrated Business Planning approach 219
Integrated Business Planning Most 249
Integrated Business Planning process 56-7, 77, 207, 257, 264, 327, 350, 352
Integrated Reconciliation 46, 315
Integrated Sales and Operations Planning xi
Integrated Tactical Execution level 352
Integrated Tactical Planning 352
international FMCG company, major 95
International Standard ISO 13
International Standards Organisation *see ISO*
INTJ 300
Inventories 44
Inventory and Operations Planning xi
investor and CEO 215
Ipswich 383
Iraq war 92
Ireland 97
ISO (International Standards Organisation) 13, 39, 100, 372-3
ISO
  adopted 372
  developed 100
ISO approach and Integrated Business Leadership 372
Italy 95
item Master information 194

J

Japan 335
Japanese company 8
JIT 260-1
JIT thinking 260
Johnson, Spencer 357
Johnston 77, 383
Judgement 300
Jurassic 224
Just-in-Time 260
Justification 124

K

Kaizen 262
Kaplan 55-6, 331, 337, 382
Kaplan & Norton 55, 331
Kenyan proverb 298

key KPIs	340
King, Gregory	177
Kissinger, Henry	44
Kotter	382
Kotter & Ratherberger	357
Kotter, John	357, 361
KPIs	295, 352

L

Landvater, Darryl	212
leadership, clear CEO	xiv
Leading Change	382
Lean	34, 219, 260-73, 279
Lean Accounting	279, 383
Lean and Continuous Improvement philosophy	218
Lean environment	245, 250, 263, 265
Lean leadership	273
Lean philosophy	267, 273
Lean principles	219, 270
Lean process	269
Lean projects	273
Lean Standard System	262, 382
Lean system	262
Lean techniques	242
Lean thinking	261, 279
Lean Workplace	269
Leap year	342
Leicester City	40
Lemonfresh	58, 60-1, 232
Lemonfresh brand	59
Lemonfresh fizzy products	60
Lemonfresh product	225
Lemonfresh product group	280
Lever Style	80
Lexus	18
Lifestyle structure	300
line ABC	228
down	226
Ling	382
Dick	x, 261
local CEO	29
London	ix, 19, 157, 177, 223, 267, 336-7, 382-3
London business	337
London Stock Exchange	286
Long-term planning	25
Lord Burns	176
Low value	174
Lucas, George	33
Luck	232

M

Macmillan	382
Make	55-6, 66-70, 79-84, 134, 139, 149, 177-8, 192, 194, 200, 205, 238, 378
Make-to-Order	82-4
Make-to-Order and Make-to-Stock	83
Make-To-Order and Make-to-Stock	84
Make-To-Order basis	4
Make to Order companies	192
Make-to-Order companies	83, 135
Make to Order environment	149
Make-to-Order environment	83, 155
Make-to-Order format	83
Make to Order items	238
Make to Order mechanics/maths	79
Make to Order products	83, 200
Make-to-Order products	84
Make-to-order strategy	148
Make to Order strategy	79
Make to Order world	178
Make-To-Order world	134
Make to Stock	66, 68, 80-1, 84, 134, 194, 378
Make-to-Stock	80, 83-4
Make to Stock and Fast Moving Consumer Goods	177
Make to Stock companies	69
Make-to-Stock environment	78
Make to Stock items	238
Make to Stock products	83, 205
Make-to-Stock products	84
Make to Stock strategy	70
Make-to-Stock world of Fast-Moving Consumer Goods	135
Makridakis	156, 382
Management Business Review	315
Management of risk	70
Managing Resources/Priorities	112
Manchester Airport	371
Manufacturing measure of productivity	243
Manufacturing Resource Planning	260
MAPE	168
MAPE Accuracy measure	162
MAPE cup	168
Mark Parker	208
Market Disciplines	335, 338
Marketing/Product Development Head	345
Marketing's function	6
Martin	208-9, 212, 383
Martin's book	208

INDEX

Maskell	279, 293, 383
Maskell, Brian	279, 283, 285, 293
Master Scheduling	49, 155, 252
Material Requirements Planning	49, 236
Maxwell, John C.	296
McDonald	328-9
McDonald's team	328
McDonald's vision	329
McGee, Sam	192
McGraw-Hill Education	382
MDs	211
Mean Absolute	168
Mean Absolute Error	158
measure Forecast Accuracy	160, 162
measure OEE	264
measure of Total Effective Equipment Performance	264
measure R&D	9
Measures and Prioritisation	33
Medium Value	174
Meetings	
central Supply Planning	89
monthly IBP supply planning	235
multiple Demand Review	89
Microsoft	118, 311
Microsoft Project	128
Middle East	93, 185, 332, 370
Migration	332
Millennials	299
Mind Management Programme	383
mini-SOP process	313
Mitigation	319
Mixture of Make-To-Order and Make-to-Stock	84
mixture of Make-to-Stock products	84
mixture of Make-to-Stock products and Make-to-Order products	84
Mobil	55
Monday	199, 223, 239, 264
monthly IBP process	122, 289, 306
Mortimer	177, 383
Mother Nature	165
MPS	152
MRP	134, 236-7, 261-2
MRP II	260-1, 312, 384
implemented	354
MRP II project	290
MRP II system	354
MRP system works	171
MRP systems	237, 261
MTO	67
MTO format	82
MTO items	83
MTS	66
MTS Format	81
MTS items	83
Multi	91
Multi business unit structure	321
Multi-National Business/Multi-Site Business	320
Multi-site Factory Organisation	258
Multiple spreadsheets	16
Myers	278, 382
Myers-Briggs assessment	300
Myopia	36

N

Natural History Museum	223
Net Present Value *see* NPV	
Newport	36
Nike Inc	328
Nissan	66
Nokia	119, 330, 358
Norton	55, 331, 337, 382
Norton's book	56
NPD	38
NPD and supply-side projects	132
NPD Performance report	128
NPV (Net Present Value)	53, 120, 124-5, 277, 284, 348
Nuclear Fuel re-processing industry	38
Nuclear Processing	33

O

Objectives for Integrated Business Leadership	35
OEE (Operating Equipment Effectiveness)	263-7, 338
OEE, calculation of	266
OEE number	271
Oliver Wight 5-step process	47
Oliver Wight IBP model	315
Oliver Wight process	90
Oliver Wight Publications Ltd	382
Olsen, Ken	118-19
On-time delivery performance	247
Operating Equipment Effectiveness *see* OEE	
Operating Equipment Effectiveness figure	271
Operations Management	77, 383
Operations Planning process	384
Operations Planning Standard System	263, 382

Operations/Supply Chain Head 345
Opportunities and Threats 35, 334
Orangefresh 61
Orchestrating Success ix, 382
Organisational Dynamics 382
Orlicky, Joe 209
OTIF 258
OTIF performance 97
Over-planning 155

P

Palmatier, George x
Panel 15, 77, 91-2, 97, 126, 160, 220-1, 223
Paris 18-19, 267, 317
Pasteur, Louis 232
Patent protection/intellectual property 180
PC (personal computer) 117-18
Pearson Education Limited 383
Pen Bill 236
Penguin Random House 177, 383
People and Ideas 300
People Performance Measures 306
People Turnover 307
People Values 303
Perfect Order 290, 344
Perfect Order on ROCE 291
Perot, Ross 44
personal computer see PC
Peters 24, 184, 383
Pharma industry 184
Pharmaceutical companies 3, 93
Picture of Pen 152
Pink Floyd 357
P&L 281, 321, 348
P&L account 244, 254, 282
P&L forecasts 14
P&L position 276
Plain English Accounting 279
Planning Bill 154-5
Planning Bill structure 154
planning manager/head of IBP 348
Planning Organisation 252
Planning Performance Measurement 250
  effective Business 39
  formal Integrated Business 211
  monthly Integrated Business 284
  new Integrated Business 201
Point of Use stores 271
Policies/procedures Software 377
Polish glass factory 243

Porter 331, 383
Portfolio Resource Management 115
PPV 244
Practical Lean Accounting 279
Pre-Meeting 315
Pre-Meeting step 314
Pre-SOP 314
Pre-SOP process 46
Premier League 40
Prime Minister xii
Priorities 88-9, 125, 314-25
  higher 238
  important 314
  right 187
  strategic 55, 183
Prioritisation 33, 316, 320-1, 343
Prioritisation and Senior Team review 94
Prioritisation for Multi-National Business/Multi-Site Business 320
Priority Process 318
Process Map 103-4, 373
Process Mapping 106
Process Performance Checklist 99
Process Steps 87, 100-9, 295, 365
Product Group/Brand 26
Product Segmentation 174
Product Takt 263
Production and Operations 319
Production Plan for Pens 152
Production plans for Month 227
Productivity Press 383
Profit and Loss Account and Balance Sheet 364
Project Management processes, detailed 131
Project Management Reviews 131
Project Structure 365
Promise 192, 194-5, 197, 202, 206
Promise calculation 206
Promise data 248
Promise line 197
Pseudo Bill 155
Purchase/Make to Order 134
Purchasing forecast 15
Pyramid of Families 59

Q

Quality Improvement 104
Quality of Output 266
Quantities Required 226
Queues of work 268
Quick Service Restaurant 328

R

INDEX

Rachabanda 316
RACI process, exact 317
Ratherberger 382
RCCP (Rough Cut Capacity Planning) 223-5, 228, 232
RCCP, developing 225
R&D 9, 26, 31, 117
Reconciliation Review 315
Red Pen 150-1, 153, 237
Report of Value 283
Reschedule in order 251
Responsibility and Accountability for Demand Planning 141
Responsibility for planning and execution 250
Restaurant Excellence 328-9
Restoration Britain 177, 383
Result of calculation for RCCP 228
Retail Supply Chain 383
Review Accuracy 157
Rewards Drive Behaviour 167
Ries, Eric 274
Right First Time 247
good units 266
Right First Time concept 266
Right-First-Time measures 250
Robert Service 192
ROCE 290-1, 305
foundation of 290-1
improving 290
ROCE tree 305
Role of Demand Manager 181
Roles/responsibilities 377
rolling Business Plan 84
Roman historian Seneca 232
Root Cause Analysis for Schedule Achievement 246
Root Mean Square Error 158
Rosalynn Carter 44
Rough Cut Capacity Planning see RCCP
Rough Cut v Detailed Capacity Planning 223
Roughly Right 223
Routledge 382
Rumours 21
Ryanair 336

S

Safety 263
Sales, Operational and Financial Planning (SOFP) 285
Sales and Marketing and Operations 107
Sales and Marketing departments 164
Sales and Operations Planning and Integrated Business Planning 350
Sales and Operations Planning Standard System 263, 382
Sales' failure 10
Sales/Marketing 143
Sales/Marketing director 30, 144
Sales Region 370-1
Sales Region of Revenue and Gross Margin 26
Salmon, Mike x
Sanofi Aventis Dagenham 358
Satya Nadella 311
Savoy 336
Schedule achievement and customer service measures 249
schedule achievement and Right-First-Time measures 250
SCOR model 101, 103
score, best MAPE 168
Segmentation 173
Senior Leadership 91
Senior Management Review 345, 350
Senior Management Review meeting 345
Senior Team Education 362
Senior Team meeting 298, 341, 349
Senior Team Review 94, 316, 318, 320-2, 325, 330, 341-53, 366, 369, 371, 376
Service Factor 76
Service Policy 378
Shareholders in Hong Kong ix
Shigeo Shingo 260
Sigma 34, 104, 164, 273, 383
six 164, 262
Sigma/DMAIC approach 106
Sigma DMAIC chart 105
simple Planning Bill example structure 154
Sinek 327, 374, 383
Single Minute Exchange of Die (SMED) 218, 268
Six-Sigma approach 164
SKU forecast 63
SKUs 57, 59, 61, 63, 181
Small, Ian 358
SOFP (Sales, Operational and Financial Planning) 285
Solomon, King 255
Sony 120
S&OP ix-xi
SOP (Standard Operating Procedure) ix, xi, xiii, 15, 274, 296, 312, 314, 350-1, 354, 379-80
SOP
 implemented xi, 354, 358

ran	xi
S&OP and IBP	xi
SOP and IBP	274
SOP/IBP	xiv, 22, 50-1, 109, 139, 300, 312, 377
SOP/IBP implementation	97, 299
SOP/IBP process	36-7, 48, 87, 311
SOP meeting	379
S&OP process, global	x
SOP process, new monthly	95
Source Make	101
Southampton airport	18
Southampton area	19
Spain	95, 337
Spanish factory on Operating Equipment Effectiveness	338
Sri Lanka	333
Stage 1/Idea	117
Stage and Gate process	116
Stage/Gate process	116
Stahl	314
Stahl, Bob	46, 155
Stahl 5-step process	47
Stahl model	314
standard IBP process	213
standard Lean toolbox	267
Standard Operating Procedure see SOP	
Standard System	17, 80
Statistical/Computer-Based Forecast	147
Statisticians	73
Steve Jobs	110, 328
Stock and work in process data	237
Stoke-on-Trent	21
STP	90
STP chart	319
STP form	323
STP Format	90, 322, 343
Strangers	77
Strategic and Annual Business Planning processes	43
Strategic Dimensions	333
Strategic Review	57
Strategy and Objectives	341
Strategy-Focused Organisation	382
Strategy for Innovation	131
Strategy Innovation	376
Strategy Map	55
Strategy to Operational Terms	55
structure, clear RACI	304
structure of IBP	64
Structure of Innovation meeting	131
Structure of Senior Management Review meeting	345
structured IBP process	87

success of IBP	xi
Summary Table for Integrated Business Planning	85
Supplier Performance Measurement	247
Supply and Inventory plans	81
Supply and New Product plans	318
Supply Chain Management	101, 352, 384
Supply Chain/Operations function	143
Supply Chain Planning Process	107
Supply Execution	34
Supply of capacity	248
Supply of flexibility	239
support IBP	67, 103, 109, 356
Support Review	88
Switzerland	140
Syngenta	44, 209-10, 384

T

T-shirts	160
Takt Time	263
target for DIFOTP	192
target for DIFOTR	192
target for DOTIFR	249
Targets and ownership	166
Technical Excellence	336
Technical function	7
Technology Development	101
Technology Fit	122
TEEP	264
Telecoms	330
Television	118
Tesla	335-6
Tony Hsieh	191
Top-Down planning	43
Total Effective Equipment Performance	264
Total number of kanbans	272
Total number of Point of Use stores	272
Total number of storage areas	272
Total number of training plans	307
Total number of work centres	251
Total Preventive Maintenance	273
Total Quality Management	261-2
Toyota Production System	260, 262
TPS	262
Traditional motor companies	335
Trafford Publishing	382
Training and education	304
Transformational change	56
Traveller's Guide	177, 383
Treacey	383
Treacey & Wiersema	335
Triassic	224
Trident	62

INDEX

Troubleshooter	243
Troubleshooter TV	324
Trudeau, Justin	xii
TV	119, 142, 177, 243, 337

U

UK	72-3, 157, 166, 197, 208, 328, 333, 337, 344, 370-1, 373
UK forecast	197
UK market	197
UK Ministry	4
UK subsidiary	41
UK Treasury	176
Underlying Process Steps	100, 102, 104, 106, 108
Unionisation	308
Upfront education	48
US Defence department	128
US tycoon Warren Buffett	335

V

Value Add	348
Vanguard class	62
Variable Costs	216, 293
Variable Product Cost	174
Variance in customer service	100
Vendor Managed Inventory (VMI)	211
Victoria	382
Victorian values	273
Vietnam	333
Virgin Airways	336
Virginia BC	382
Vision and Mission	326-9
Vision and Mission to entertainment	328
Vision and Strategy Innovation	376
Vision/Mission Statements	328
VMI (Vendor Managed Inventory)	211
VP of production and demands	96
VP of Sales	212
VP of supply chain	212, 240

W

Wal-Mart	328
Walkman	120
Wallace	47, 314
Wallace & Stahl	155
Wallace, Tom	46, 88, 155
Wallace 5-step diagram	314
Walmart objectives set	36
Walt Disney	328

Walton, Sam	36
Watkins & Clarke	291
Weaknesses	35, 334
Weidenfeld & Nicolson	382
Widget ABC	281
Wiersema	383
Wiersema, Fred	335
Wight, Oliver	x, 46, 88, 315, 362, 383-4
Wikipedia	12
Wiley, John	382-3
Wimbledon	39
Wonderland	327
World-class performance	297
World-Class Standard	267
World Cup	157
Worries	176
Wound	260

X

Y

year-end Business Plan expectation	92
Yukon	192

Z

Zanuck, Darryl	118
Zappos	191

Integrated Business Leadership